大变局下的全球安全

Global Security under Great Changes

——第二届万寿国际安全研讨会论文集

——Anthology of the Second Wanshou Dialogue on Global Security

王亚军/主编

安月军 陶涛/执行主编

Wang Yajun：Chief Editor

An Yuejun，**Tao Tao**：Executive Editors

当代世界出版社
THE CONTEMPORARY WORLD PRESS

图书在版编目（CIP）数据

大变局下的全球安全：第二届万寿国际安全研讨会
论文集 = Global Security under Great Changes:
Anthology of the Second Wanshou Diologue on Global
Security / 王亚军主编 . -- 北京：当代世界出版社，
2019.12
　　ISBN 978-7-5090-1546-9

　　Ⅰ.①大… Ⅱ.①王… Ⅲ.①国家安全－世界－学术
会议－文集 Ⅳ.① D815.5-53

中国版本图书馆 CIP 数据核字 (2019) 第 282140 号

书　　　名：大变局下的全球安全——第二届万寿国际安全研讨会论文集
出版发行：当代世界出版社
地　　　址：北京市复兴路4号（100860）
邮　　　箱：ddsjchubanshe@163.com
网　　　址：http://www.worldpress.org.cn
编务电话：(010) 83907332
发行电话：(010) 83908410（传真）
　　　　　　13601274970
　　　　　　18611107149
　　　　　　13521909533
经　　　销：新华书店
印　　　刷：北京中科印刷有限公司
开　　　本：710毫米×1000毫米　　1/16
印　　　张：26.5
字　　　数：383千字
版　　　次：2020年1月第1版
印　　　次：2020年1月第1版
书　　　号：ISBN 978-7-5090-1546-9
定　　　价：98.00元

代　序

全国政协副主席、中国人民争取和平与裁军协会会长马飚在第二届万寿国际安全研讨会开幕式上的致辞

（代序一）

很高兴同朋友们相聚在北京，我谨代表中国人民争取和平与裁军协会，向出席第二届万寿国际安全研讨会的各位嘉宾和代表表示热烈欢迎！

习近平主席指出，当今世界正面临百年未有之大变局。当前，和平发展大势不可逆转，但大国竞争博弈明显加剧，地区安全秩序深刻调整，新兴科技对全球安全的影响日益凸显，安全观念相互激荡交锋，传统安全与非传统安全问题相互交织，全球动荡源和风险点增多，人类仍然面临许多共同挑战。我们要坚守和平初心、担负时代责任，为维护国际及地区的和平、安全与稳定贡献智慧和力量。在此，我愿提出几点看法：

第一，我们要做大国安全合作的助推器。当今世界大国关系总体稳定，对话、交流、合作在继续，但大国之间防范、对立、甚至对抗日渐突出，讹诈、施压、制裁等错误做法频现，国际安全格局仍处于深刻调整过程中。

大国对世界和平肩负特殊责任，我们希望大国加强协调，管控分歧，增进互信，构建总体稳定、均衡发展的大国关系框架，建设更富包容性和建设性的伙伴关系，推动大国合作共同应对国际安全威胁。

第二，我们要做地区热点问题的冷却剂。当今世界，战乱、冲突和动荡仍困扰许多地区，恐怖活动猖獗，不少国家民众特别是儿童饱受战火摧残。朝核、伊朗核、叙利亚、巴勒斯坦、阿富汗等热点问题亟待妥善解决。

地区热点问题已成为人类文明的伤痛，我们希望以和平方式解决矛盾争端，反对为一己之私挑起事端、激化矛盾，反对以邻为壑、损人利己。我们要努力探索符合地区实际、满足各方需要的安全架构，推动实现地区热点降

温趋缓。

第三，我们要做应对安全挑战的智囊团。全球新一轮科技和产业革命蓬勃发展，既带来发展机遇，也产生安全挑战。非传统安全挑战增多，新兴科技军事化应用给全球安全带来巨大的负面影响，网络、外空、人工智能等领域的竞争博弈正在重塑安全秩序和安全治理模式。

安全挑战是人类面临的难题，我们要坚持与时俱进，紧跟新兴科技的发展前沿，研判大势，把握方向，趋利避害。在网络、外空等新兴领域，我们要积极推动各国共同建立新机制、制定新规则，打造合作共赢的新平台。

第四，我们要做践行安全新理念的引领者。当前，各种安全理念碰撞激烈，民粹主义、保护主义、孤立主义等思潮不断泛起，一些国家仍坚持你输我赢、零和博弈的冷战思维，推行单边主义和强权政治，全球安全治理困难重重。

新时代呼唤新的安全观，我们要广泛传播和平理念，践行共同、综合、合作、可持续的新安全观，旗帜鲜明反对单边主义和保护主义，奉行双赢、多赢、共赢理念，加强文明沟通和交流互鉴，坚持共商共建共享的全球治理观，以合作谋和平、促安全，为充满不确定性的世界注入稳定性和正能量。

全球化时代我们安危与共，"滴水不成海，独木难成林"。期待各位嘉宾和代表在研讨会期间深入交流、集思广益、凝聚共识、汇集力量，为构建持久和平、普遍安全的世界作出积极贡献！

俄罗斯联邦公众院副主席谢尔盖·奥尔忠尼启则在第二届万寿国际安全研讨会开幕式上的致辞

（代序二）

感谢中方组织举办此次重要国际研讨会，这让我们能够共同思考、交流看法。我们要将共识告诉各国政府和世界人民。

当前，国际形势处于关键时期，全球安全、战略稳定面临诸多严峻挑战。各国博弈情况决定着国际关系的发展，多极世界正在形成。但个别国家奉行单边主义，有些国家竭力搞排他性的小圈子，加强军事同盟，削弱国际机制，无视国际法和国际准则，企图动用各种手段，向其他国家施压，企图实现自私自利的目的。这种行径导致大国互信缺失，国家间正常关系受到影响，贸易冲突加剧，经济不稳定性增加，全球安全挑战增多。同时，移民难民增多，恐怖主义、气候变化等非传统安全挑战依然严峻。

近来，普京总统和特朗普总统都反复强调，希望俄美能在一系列国际议题上达成共识，但美国政府却迟迟不采取行动，导致俄美关系充满变数，双方很难在国际事务上有所作为。俄美总统虽一直表示愿意合作减少军备竞赛，但并未建立对话机制。美国宣布退出《中导条约》，俄罗斯也退约。国际核裁军体系逐一瓦解会给世界带来更大的不确定性。美俄《新削减战略武器条约》将于2021年到期，但美国至今仍未作出延长与否的明确承诺，俄对此极为关切。美国要建设太空部队，一些北约欧洲成员国决定加入太空部队建设。现在迫切需要控制太空军备竞赛，要对在外空使用武器制定具有法律约束力的行为准则。美国如在太空部署武器，太空军备竞赛将难以阻止，将会影响到全球战略稳定。

应对复杂挑战，维护绝大多数国家利益，需要坚持基于规则的多边主义，支持联合国等国际组织发挥更大作用，推动国际关系民主化。世界上没有什么"天选之民"，无论是在联合国还是在全世界，各国人民的权利都是平等的。各种文明要平等相待，相互包容。《联合国宪章》虽是 1945 年通过的，但对当今世界仍具有指导意义，仍需遵循和维护。

老挝国会副主席、老挝和平与团结委员会主席宋潘·平坎米在第二届万寿国际安全研讨会开幕式上的致辞

（代序三）

我谨代表老挝和平与团结委员会感谢中国人民争取和平与裁军协会邀请我出席在北京举办的第二届万寿国际安全研讨会。不久前，二十国集团领导人峰会刚刚闭幕，人类和平与发展等重大问题成为世界各国领导人聚焦的议题，中国人民争取和平与裁军协会此时举办这一重要会议可谓恰逢其时，我对此表示高度赞赏。此次会议为各国及国际地区和平组织准确研判国际形势、提出合作举措提供了宝贵平台。

我高度评价在中国共产党领导下，中国在各个历史时期为维护国际安全稳定作出的积极贡献。特别是进入新时代，在中共中央总书记、国家主席习近平领导下，中国在推动国际社会解决和平发展、气候变化、饥荒灾害等问题上发挥了重要作用。

当前国际形势深刻复杂演变，我们的世界仍遭受着武力威胁，政治矛盾、战争冲突、恐怖主义、领土争端以及民族、宗教、人权等问题依然存在，自然灾害和传染性疾病也对发展构成重大阻碍。这些问题仅凭一国之力无法解决，加强国际合作成为当前形势下的不二选择。各国要加强沟通、共享信息、交流看法、共建机制，将我们的世界建设成为持久和平、普遍安全的世界，为各国共同发展创造良好条件。

老挝曾遭受几百年战争的蹂躏，是世界上被炸弹轰炸数量最多的国家。没有和平就没有发展。老挝人民经历过战争，深知和平的珍贵。老挝愿在力所能及的范围内，同国际社会一道，促进世界和平稳定、繁荣发展，让世界各国人民生活在远离恐惧、共同发展的环境中。

老挝和平与团结委员会与中国人民争取和平与裁军协会长期保持良好合作关系，每年都相互交流工作经验和对国际形势的看法，达成了诸多重要共识，为维护世界和平稳定贡献了力量。希望在此次会议期间，与会代表能够积极坦诚地就维护世界和平与稳定的机制化合作交换意见、分享智慧。

上海合作组织秘书长弗拉基米尔·诺罗夫在第二届万寿国际安全研讨会开幕式上的致辞

（代序四）

在当前国际形势复杂动荡的背景下，中国人民争取和平与裁军协会举办第二届万寿国际安全研讨会，十分重要且正合时宜。当今世界，不稳定因素正在增加，新一轮军备竞赛的危险上升，局部地区冲突持续升级，恐怖主义和极端主义组织给欧亚大陆的和平与稳定带来的威胁仍在增加，恐怖组织与跨国犯罪组织还有同流合污的趋势。通过贩毒、非法贩卖武器和贪腐等为恐怖组织筹款的新方式正在出现。从中东热点地区回流的叛乱分子已准备好针对上海合作组织成员国继续实施恐怖和极端的行动。在这种情况下，上海合作组织协调国际社会采取集体和有效的方式应对地区和全球安全挑战的作用日益增加。

上海合作组织成员国重申，支持联合国作为国际多边组织所付出的努力，主张加强联合国安理会的关键作用。根据《联合国宪章》，安理会被赋予了维护国际和平与安全的基本职责。上海合作组织成员国认为，有的国家或国家集团单边地、无限制地建设弹道导弹防御系统使国际安全受到损害，使世界局势产生动荡。这些国家意图以牺牲他人的安全为代价来保证自身安全，让人难以接受。

上海合作组织作为现代国际关系体系中有影响力和负责任的参与者，将提升参与度，努力维护和平与安全，坚定拥护在相互平等、互相尊重主权和领土完整、互不干涉内政、不使用武力或威胁使用武力等原则基础上，通过和平、政治和外交方式形成解决有关地区和国际冲突的决议。为落实《打击恐怖主义、分离主义和极端主义合作纲要》，上海合作组织积极努力防控恐怖主义和宗教极端主义性质的犯罪，清除恐怖分子的秘密据点。

上海合作组织各成员国定期共同参与和举办"和平使命"联合反恐军事演习。所有成员国呼吁国际社会充分发挥联合国的核心作用，加强全球反恐合作，按照《联合国宪章》和国际法的要求，不搞政治化和双重标准，尊重所有国家的主权和独立，全面执行联合国安理会有关决议和联合国《全球反恐战略》，同时努力推动《关于国际恐怖主义的全面公约》有关谈判尽快达成共识。

稳定阿富汗局势是保证上海合作组织所在地区和全球整体安全的重要条件之一。所有成员国高度评价 2019 年 4 月 19 日在比什凯克召开的"上海合作组织——阿富汗联络组"第三次会议所取得的成果，以及 6 月 14 日上海合作组织比什凯克峰会批准的《"上海合作组织——阿富汗联络组"下一步行动路线图》。上海合作组织成员国强调，通过由阿富汗人民开展并主导政治对话、执行包容性的和平进程来解决阿富汗冲突是唯一选择，呼吁充分发挥联合国的核心协调作用，有关各国和国际组织加强合作，以此稳定和建设阿富汗。

上海合作组织成员国还特别关注网络安全。打击网络信息攻击，打击利用互联网宣传恐怖主义、分离主义和极端主义，防止通过网络破坏政治、经济和公共安全是上海合作组织在本地区的重要任务。我们认为，有必要为各国在网络空间的负责任行为制定通用的规则、原则和准则，同时在这一领域采取若干举措来保证上海合作组织成员国的信息安全。

过去的十八年，上海合作组织经受了国际安全形势新发展的考验，开展了卓有成效的务实合作，获得了国际社会的普遍赞誉。特别是印度和巴基斯坦成为正式成员后，上海合作组织的国际影响力和汇聚力进一步提升，各成员国的国家间关系也成为国际关系中的典范。上海合作组织得以发展壮大的关键就是"上海精神"，即"互信、互利、平等、协商、尊重多样文明、谋求共同发展"。

为促进共同安全，上海合作组织将继续坚持不与任何国家集团结盟的原则，也不针对第三方，不与第三方搞对抗。我相信，上海合作组织内部合作的进一步发展将更加促进彼此互信，也将使该组织更有能力应对成员国所面临的挑战和威胁。

美国前总统里根特别助理、
卡托研究所高级研究员道格拉斯·班多
在第二届万寿国际安全研讨会开幕式上的致辞

（代序五）

　　当今世界既有好的一面，又充满危险。世界比以往更繁荣，但在一些国家内部和国家之间存在很多问题。新技术的两面性更加突出，既可改善人类生活，又会带来安全风险。这个世界充满政治变数，民粹主义领导人在很多国家上台执政。叙利亚、利比亚、也门等国战火仍在继续，一些国家领导人在作出战争决定时并未深思熟虑。

　　我们应更加关注大国关系。大国无论在经济、军事还是拥有核武器的数量上都具有其他国家无可比拟的影响力，大国关系决定着世界走向和平还是战争，大国可以把小国拖入战争，处理好大国关系有助于创建和平与安全的世界。世界正向多极转变，充满不稳定性和不确定性。这需要大国发挥领导力，调整地区安全架构，加强国家间交流。

　　新兴技术影响着各国之间的关系和互动形式，需关注新兴技术带来的新挑战，特别是太空、网络安全方面的新挑战。新兴技术改善了人们的生活，但也带来风险。我们要趋利避害，学会驾驭新兴技术。

　　当前联合国主导的国际体系自身存在一些问题。国际和地区面临的安全挑战更加复杂多元，如中东安全、亚太安全、核不扩散、能源安全、移民难民等问题。解决人类面临的共同挑战，需要完善现有机制，还是创建新的多边机制，都值得大家深入研讨。

目 录
CONTENTS

● **代序**

● **第一编：大国安全关系新变化**

● 第三编：新兴科技与全球安全

● **第四编：安全观念演变与全球安全治理**

Contents

● **Acting Prefaces**

● Session I. New Changes within Security Relations among Major Countries

● Session II. New Adjustments in the Regional Security Order

● **Session III. New and Emerging Technologies and Global Security**

● **Session IV. Evolution of Security Concepts and Global Security Governance**

● **Acting Postscript**

第一编

大国安全关系新变化

当前大国安全关系的新变化及前景

中国人民争取和平与裁军协会常务理事
国防大学国家安全学院教授

孟祥青

大国关系是世界格局的骨架，在相当程度上决定着世界格局的走向。大国安全关系又是大国关系中最核心和最敏感的重要组成部分，某种意义上也是大国关系的"晴雨表"。冷战结束已将近 30 年，同前 20 多年相比，一个有目共睹、毋庸讳言的基本事实是：今天的大国安全关系进入到不稳定性和不确定性激增、竞争和对抗明显加剧的新阶段。大国安全关系的新变化及其未来走势，不仅关系到世界格局走向，更关系到世界和平与发展。

一、当前大国安全关系中竞争和对抗的一面凸显是主要特征

冷战结束后相当长一段时间，大国关系较为稳定。大国之间有合作也有竞争，总体以合作为主。共同安全威胁增加和共同安全利益的扩大，使得大国间广泛、密切的安全协调与合作成为常态。冷战结束后，大国安全关系大致经历了三个阶段。第一阶段是 20 世纪 90 年代的相对稳定和协调期。冷战结束和两极格局瓦解给大国安全关系既带来机遇也带来挑战。尽管在 90 年代发生了一些影响大国安全关系的重大消极事件，如 90 年代初美西方国家对华经济制裁，90 年代中期发生台海危机，90 年代末美国轰炸中国驻南联盟大使馆，90 年代北约东扩对俄进行战略空间挤压以及伊拉克战争和科索沃战争爆发等等，大国安全关系一波三折，甚至时常伴随危

机，但总体上看，大国关系改善的大趋势没有改变，在安全领域的对话、交流、管控危机升级是主流，合作与对抗并存，但以合作为主。第二阶段是从 2001 年"9·11"事件到 2016 年特朗普当选美国总统。某种意义上，这一阶段可谓是大国安全关系的"蜜月期"。"9·11"事件是个重大转折点，大国之间安全合作的需求不断增多，合作的制度化日益增强。大国在反恐、防扩散、应对气候变化、打击海盗等非传统安全领域的合作达到了新高度，经历了安全合作十分难得的"蜜月期"。第三阶段是从 2017 年至今，大国安全关系发生新的重大变化，由过去以合作为主转向竞争和对抗加剧。这期间发生的几件大事直接影响着大国安全关系的走势。一是特朗普上台后相继"退群"并大力推行单边主义和保护主义政策；二是乌克兰事件；三是美国出台"印太战略"。特朗普政府的单边主义和保护主义政策几乎搞坏了与所有大国的安全关系，甚至包括与其盟友的关系。乌克兰事件使美俄关系恶化、欧俄关系紧张。"印太战略"加剧了这一地区的安全对抗。总体上看，当前大国安全关系仍然是合作与竞争并存，对话与对抗同在，但一个不争的事实是：战略竞争与对抗的一面明显增强。近年来，大国安全关系中，值得关注的变化有以下四个方面：

一是大国地缘政治博弈加剧。在欧洲，美俄、欧俄围绕北约"东扩"较量不断，美俄在乌克兰、叙利亚、伊朗等问题上斗争尖锐，冲突升级的危险加大。同时，被民粹主义和非自由化浪潮席卷的欧洲各国分歧严重，因英国"脱欧"带来的地缘政治风险愈演愈烈。在亚太，美国在政治、外交、经济、科技、军事、文化等领域持续强化对中国的全方位打压和遏制，使中美关系严重倒退，增加了两国发生军事摩擦或因卷入地区危机而升级为冲突的危险。

二是大国军事竞争加强。近年来，世界主要军事强国持续加大军费投入。据瑞典斯德哥尔摩国际和平研究所（SIPRI）发布的《2018 年全球军费开支分析报告》显示，2018 年世界军费开支达到冷战结束以来的最高值，约为 1.822 万亿美元。2019 年，各主要国家军费预算均大幅上涨。其中，美国达到了 7163 亿美元，增幅达 11.9%，超过全球排名前九个国家的总和。世界主要军事强国在人工智能、定向能武器、高级无人武器系统、太空武器、网络空间战、高超音速武器等领域展开激烈的军事技术竞争。2019 年年初，美国公布了升级版《导弹防御评估报告》，宣布全面更新导弹防御系统，宣称要"确保能发现并摧毁任何时间、任何地点发射的针对美国任何地方的任何导弹"。这份展示冷战姿态的新版"星球大战计划"加重了大国间的战略防范，给国家间的安全互信造成严重破坏。

三是大国在新兴领域的争夺激烈。在太空、网络、深海、极地等新兴领域，从价值观的争论到技术的发展再到国际规则制定及话语权的争夺，主要大国纷纷展开全面竞争，并呈现出日趋激烈的态势。新兴领域中的大国关系折射出了现实空间的力量格局变化，对国际安全秩序的调整以及新型安全关系的构建都将产生重要影响。

四是大国在多领域的安全合作不进反退。美国出台的《国家安全战略报告》《国防战略报告》《印太战略报告》等系列报告表明，美国不再把恐怖主义作为国家安全的主要威胁，而把大国竞争看作主要威胁。和以前相比，近年来大国在反恐、维护地区安全、军控与裁军、应对气候变化、打击海盗和走私等重要领域的安全合作动力明显不足，有的出现弱化，有的不进反退。

造成大国安全关系竞争与对抗一面增强的主要原因有三：一是大国力量对比发生变化，这是根本的一条。特别是中美两国在国民生产总值、国际影响力等一些领域的差距在逐步缩小，引起美方严重关切和焦虑。这里的核心问题仍然是：如何看待中国，如何看待中国的崛起。美国如果不能正确、公平、公正地对待中国崛起，仍然抱有强烈的冷战思维，从霸权逻辑出发，立足于打压中国、遏制中国，那么对抗就难以避免。二是主要大国国家安全战略尤其是美国国家安全战略的重大调整。近年来，世界主要国家相继出台一系列新的战略报告，重新定位传统大国关系，突出了大国竞争在国际安全中的地位和作用。尤其是美国强调以"美国优先"重塑国际安全秩序和大国格局。近年来，美国频繁退出多边协议，挑起同世界主要国家的摩擦，加剧了地区紧张局势，导致大国间矛盾冲突全面升级。可以说，美国安全战略的一系列重大调整是导致国际安全不稳定不确定因素增多的根源。三是去全球化思潮与民粹主义合流恶化了大国安全合作的氛围。去全球化思潮是全球化负面因素的产物。近年来，国际政治也出现了民粹主义和民族主义同时上升的趋势，三者合流严重冲击着国际安全和大国关系的稳定。特朗普上台以来，主动迎合民粹主义，大搞单边主义、贸易保护主义，以贸易摩擦为借口，推行"逆全球化"行为，对中国、欧盟、日本、印度等多国频繁进行关税施压。美国的错误做法进一步加剧了大国竞争的风险和国际局势的动荡。

在上述形势下，世界主要大国之间虽有对话交流与合作，但防范和摩擦此伏彼起，冲突的危险增大，且呈现出长期化的趋势。因此，今后一段时间，如何管控好风险，如何防止危机升级为冲突，将是大国安全关系的主题。

二、重构、重建以良性竞争为基础的新型大国安全竞合关系是大势所趋、人心所向

在可预见的未来，大国安全关系将主要有三种发展前景。一是大国间的分歧、摩擦持续上升，形成全面恶性竞争、甚至走向"新冷战"；二是因误判或擦枪走火、或激烈的地缘政治博弈导致军事冲突甚至战争；三是重构、重建以良性竞争为基础的新型大国安全竞合关系。目前看，前两种前景可能性比较小，但却在上升，令人十分担忧，必须高度警惕。可能性较大的是第三种前景，即大国之间经过一段时间的摩擦碰撞，在博弈中竭力避免大的冲突并逐步找到良性竞争的方法与途径，形成新的相互适应，从而构建起新的安全竞合关系。之所以这种前景的可能性比较大，主要是因为：

一是全球化和科技发展的大趋势使然。随着全球化和科技不断进步，一些新作用要素相继出现。国家间界限在网络、太空、金融等越来越多的新兴领域变得难以区分。同时，跨国性和全球性安全挑战也随之不断增

多，而霸权国家当前能够提供的公共产品已很难有效应对。这使得一国为了维护自身利益，必须兼顾战略对手利益，并与别国展开合作。

二是随着非国家行为体继续大量涌现和网络信息技术飞速发展所带来的权力扩散，大国关系的性质与以往相比已发生根本改变。国家间利益关系多维交织、错综复杂，"非合作即对抗"的零和思维越来越不合时宜，仅靠传统权力政治或武力冲突已越来越难以有效维护本国利益。非零和博弈在国际关系中的成分继续上升是大势所趋。

三是核恐怖平衡以及防扩散的共同需求从根本上是难以削弱的，仍在强化的跨国、跨区域联系等一些基础性要素在综合发挥作用，使得包括中美在内的大国间战略平衡得以继续维持。

四是通过伙伴关系、对话协商和共同发展的方式来解决全球安全问题，构建新的全球安全治理模式的呼声日益高涨，并越来越多地得到国际社会的认同，国际安全协调和国际安全治理需求不断扩大，许多国家已经开始行动。

五是面对中美战略竞争的加剧，中国政府及战略研究界认为，战略竞争并不是中美关系的全部内容，决不应将中美关系简单地定位为战略竞争关系。中国领导人和中国政府已多次明确表示，中方决心为推进以协调、合作、稳定为基调的中美关系做出长期不懈的努力。中国的政策将对未来中美战略竞争以及大国关系的走向发挥重要影响。

六是世界主要国家都不希望大国走向对抗与冲突。合作共赢的新型大国关系和新型国际关系符合绝大多数国家和人民的利益。

三、管控好风险、防止危机升级是当务之急

一是在当前，各主要大国间应尽最大努力保持对话和交流，特别是在非传统安全领域保持合作，这将有助于大国间管控竞争、减少误解误判、防止危机升级。

二是大国间要坚决避免走向全球军备竞赛和恶性竞争。应充分认识到

大国关系中日益上升的军事安全风险，当务之急是进一步完善并强化大国间的危机管控机制，把防范危机升级放在第一位，并把现有对话和沟通、交流机制落实到位。

三是世界主要大国应共同维护、加强和完善多边合作机制，维护全球化，积极推动建设开放型世界经济，构建人类命运共同体，促进全球治理体系变革，同时努力管控其消极面。

四是中美两国的经贸和科技不应脱钩、也不可能脱钩，更不能对抗。双方要努力将经济与科技竞争建立在国际法律法规和市场经济的基础上，争取形成良性循环，从而保持双方的经济、科技合作，对世界和平与发展起到稳定器的作用。

大国历来对世界的和平与发展负有更大的责任，理应承担更多的义务。大国之间的安全关系在相当程度上决定着世界的稳定与繁荣。当前，大国安全合作充满挑战，但也面临新的机遇，和平、合作、共赢是大势所趋、人心所向，重构、重建以良性竞争为基础的新型大国安全竞合关系是时代赋予大国的历史使命。

美中安全关系新变化：特朗普时期的美中博弈

美国丹佛大学科贝尔国际关系学院教授、美中合作中心主任

赵穗生

自从特朗普执政以来，美国的对华政策正在发生由接触到全面博弈的巨变。特朗普政府不再将中国视为与美国价值观和利益趋同的转型国家，而将中国宣布为战略竞争对手和挑战美国的"修正主义国家"，发动贸易战并且将其升级为一场与中国的全面冲突。

一、特朗普当选总统后美中纷争加剧

尽管美中关系在此之前已经麻烦不断，特朗普上任后美中纷争日益加剧。激烈的竞争主要集中在经济领域。2016 年总统竞选期间，特朗普指责中国用不公平的货币政策与压低出口价格来促进中国经济增长。他承诺采取更加强势的政策，包括对中国出口美国的产品加征 45% 的关税。特朗普的言论在美国引发极大共鸣。正如前任商务部长普利茨克所说，多年来美国人被告知中国是一个发展中国家，因而不应该将发达国家的标准强加到中国身上。但中国的成功严重削弱了这一逻辑论点，靠廉价制造业起家的中国迅速发展成为全球的技术中心。美国人认为中国的成功至少有一部分是建立在他们的牺牲之上，中国没有遵守游戏规则，不断违背自己许下的国际承诺，利用不公平竞争使其有利于中国公司。"无论有没有特朗普，美中关系都在迅速地走向一个十字路口。"

曾经是特朗普首席战略师的斯蒂芬·班农处在这场"圣战"的最前线。班农将美国工人阶层和中产阶级的损失归咎于中国，宣称向中国发起

一场经济战。尽管班农是一个共和党的鹰派，但很多分属不同政治派别的人都认为班农是对的："中国在经济上打击美国，但美国政府和企业多年来无动于衷。"甚至一些突出的全球主义者，如奥尔布赖特、托马斯·弗里德曼、法里德·扎卡利亚都表现出深深的担忧，批评中国成了一个出口大国，但却收紧外国商品的市场准入限制。

以支持接触政策立场著称的戴维·兰普顿抱怨中国在美中双边贸易中获得了贸易盈余，借"入世"抓住了对外开放经济的机会，却没有为美国及其他国家提供对等的国内准入。结果，"对等"和"公平"问题成为美中关系中最突出的问题。美国国际集团的前任首席执行官莫里斯·格林伯格曾是中国"入世"的大力支持者，但他也认为"中国若不愿意对等，便不能期望继续在外国市场中获得优惠的贸易和投资条件"。潘文（John Pomfret）发现"美国国内在酝酿一场对中国的强烈抵制运动，且远超特朗普"。

这个大环境的转变为特朗普总统向中国发起减少巨额贸易逆差的贸易战做了铺垫。2018年3月22日，美国宣布对价值500亿美元的中国商品加征关税；7月6日贸易战全面展开，价值340亿美元的中国商品被加征25%的关税，与此同时，第一轮针对500亿美元商品的关税也开始生效。在中国报复了等值的美国商品之后，7月10日，特朗普政府宣布额外对2000亿美元的中国产品加收10%的关税。8月1日，特朗普政府进一步施加压力，将原先提议的10%关税率提高至25%。当美国对价值160亿中国商品加收10%关税于8月24日生效时，中国回击了等值的美国商品。以牙还牙式的贸易战如火如荼地展开了。

美国发动贸易战的目的是减少赤字并使美国的工作岗位回流。据估计，"除非中国更改其产业政策，给予美国公司对等的市场准入，否则关税将促使美国公司撤离中国回流美国，或从其他不会长期威胁到美国安全的国家进口商品"。更重要的是，贸易战是为了防止中国以牺牲美国为代价来提升其高科技产能。2017年12月特朗普政府发布的《美国国家安全战略报告》指控每年都有价值上亿的美国科技被非法地转让到中国。特朗普政府将技术能力与国家安全联系起来，增加了中国对美国科技投资的限制，并扩大"战略贸易"的物品清单，要求企业公司按照规定筛选买家和下游终端用户，追踪整条价值链的动向。

共和党参议员约翰·康宁和民主党参议员黛安娜·费恩斯坦共同提议一项为国家安全而严控紧缩对中资和其他外商投资筛选过程的法案。美国海外投资委员会已经阻止了美中企业之间越来越多的收购、合并和许可协议。不久以前，这些强硬的政策还会引起美国公司高层的骚动，担心报复将导致他们被中国市场拒之门外。但是，如今美国工商界的很多企业已经沉默而且赞成转变战略。2018年8月，皮尤研究中心在贸易战激烈进行时发布了一项民意调查，结果显示经济问题非常突出，更多的美国人担忧中国的经济威胁多于担忧其军事力量。

地缘政治也在竞争中占据显著位置。结构现实主义学者约翰·米尔斯海默曾告诫，美中之间的力量对决是不可避免的。尽管几年前人们认为这个理论过于简单化，但类似的新理论，如"修昔底德陷阱"论、权力转移论、新冷战等，却在今天日渐盛行。格雷厄姆·艾利森援引修昔底德的"雅典的崛起及其在斯巴达引发的恐惧使得战争无可避免"，他写道："如果修昔底德在观察的话，他会说中国和美国正在按剧本梦游般走向一场或许成为历史上最大的冲突中。"科里·斯盖克根据权力转移理论，断言中国将推进其认同的价值而破坏美国领导的秩序，而美中两国间明显不同的文化可能会造成暴力性权力转移。

有学者认为美中对峙导致了新的两极世界的出现。在这个新的两极世界里，不同于前苏联，中国是一个参与全球竞争、极具活力的经济体，有能力竞争并且赢得胜利。有学者将美中两国之间的大国对抗和意识形态竞争描述成第二次冷战。在第一次冷战中，苏联是一个军事对手而非商业对手，而日本则是商业对手而非军事对手。不同于第一次冷战，第二次冷战中的中国既是一个军事对手又是一个商业对手。因而美国需要放弃其70年以来所采取的地缘政治与地缘经济分离的政策，转为采取传统意义上的大国行动——协调军事、外交和贸易三种手段的全面大国战略。另有学者建议美国"放弃过时的双边办法，在亚洲采取多边的方式建立以价值为基础的共同防御同盟"，因为"就如苏联在 1991 年以前对欧洲国家是威胁一样，中国在今天也是亚洲国家的共同威胁"。该建议与米尔斯海默的呼吁如出一辙。米尔斯海默长期以来主张美国应遏制崛起中的中国，包括用美国强大的军事能力围堵中国，创立类似于北约的同盟对抗中国，在经济上孤立中国，并让中国为做出违背美国利益的事情付出代价。

一定程度上，特朗普政府的国家安全战略反映了一种思路，它认为不是恐怖主义而是国家间的战略竞争，成为今天美国国家安全的最重要关切。印太被确定为一个至关重要的区域，是"自由与压迫的世界秩序之间展开地缘政治竞争的地方"。美国呼吁建立自由与开放的印太，明确表达对中国展示铁腕力量将美国挤出该地区的做法感到担忧。虽然前国防部长马蒂斯抱怨"没有任何敌人能像预算控制法案中国防开支的削减更能打击美国军队的敏捷度"，但美国国会还是通过了高达 7160 亿美元迄今最大额的"2019 财年国防授权法案"。特朗普总统在签署国防法案时表示，这项国防法案是为了对抗俄罗斯、中国及其他国家的侵略行为。法案限制了中国在美国大学出资建立中文传播项目，限制中国参与联合军演，呼吁增强美国与印度和台湾的关系，并紧缩中国对美投资的国家安全审核。曾经出现在奥巴马政府 2015 年国家国防战略中的美国欢迎"中国稳定、和平与繁荣的崛起"的表达，已经一去不复返了。

特朗普在维系美中关系的基本战略要求和接触政策之间进退维谷，其在任期第一年的作为令人难以捉摸，"摇摆于强硬和绥靖这两种极端中，一个具有升级的危险，另一个则是极端的幼稚；一个政策太强硬以至于面临战争危险，另一个政策太温和而几乎等同于纵容"。特朗普比以往的总统更加不稳定，传达的意思自相矛盾，在制造混乱中企图争取更有利的成果。在任期的第二年里，特朗普政府选定了一种好斗的方式，最大限度向中国施压。

特朗普政府从不忌讳宣布对华政策的转变。白宫亚太事务资深主管马特·波廷格在中国驻美大使馆的一次发言中说："特朗普政府已经更新了对华政策，将竞争的概念放在了最前列。"在一个重要的演讲致辞中，彭斯副总统宣布美国将在所有方面对中国予以强有力的反击。彭斯指责前任政府对中国的行为熟视无睹，甚至怂恿教唆，表示现任政府将会坚定发声、站起来、斗争，并获得胜利。彭斯的演讲被认为是"新冷战的宣言"。但特朗普总统对中国的态度从根本上说是交易性的，一直没有找到一个能替代接触政策的全面战略方案。

当2016年的竞选结束之后，候任总统特朗普接听了台湾地区领导人蔡英文的祝贺电话。这是台湾地区领导人与现任或即将就任的美国总统之间近40年以来的首次接触，是对美国所承认的"一个中国"政策立场的挑战。虽然这种行为容易引起中国的强硬对抗政策，但特朗普总统在2月份突然扭转了事态，在通话中告诉习近平主席他会尊重"一个中国"政策。时任国务卿蒂勒森在3月首次正式访问北京时，一字不差地重申了习近平主席提出的"中美新型大国关系"原则并同意尊重各自的核心利益和重要关切。该措辞被认为暗示美国接受中国反对其干预台湾和人权等问题的立场。美国研究中国问题的专家对美国公开接受了中国的提议感到意外，认为蒂勒森可能陷入了中国政府的宣传和外交陷阱中。

4月6日，特朗普—习近平佛罗里达州会晤后，两国关系快速缓和。特朗普对亚洲历史认知不足，不足以应对最敏感的问题，他全盘接受了习近平主席所说的西藏、台湾和朝鲜问题的观点，并且表示他们之间有很好的默契，认为中国在解决朝鲜问题上极其重要。两国随后宣布了美中经济合作的"百日计划"，贸易协定涵盖了农业、金融服务、投资、能源等领域。特朗普总统不再将"一个中国"原则视为讨价还价的筹码，拒绝了蔡英文"不排除再次与美国沟通"的提议，暗示他在与台湾领导人交谈之前会先与习近平主席商讨。

从简单化的反华立场转变为同样简单化的亲华立场，特朗普总统在经历由强烈批评中国到接受中国的一个大转弯后，又拐了一个弯——2017年5月24日，他派"杜威号"导弹驱逐舰进入了中国南海美济礁的12海里范围内。6月28日，美国参议院军事委员会通过决议允许美国海军舰艇例行停靠台湾。6月29日，美国财政部宣布间接制裁资助朝鲜政权的中国实体；同日，美国批准价值14亿美元的对台军售。7月2日，"斯特西姆号"驱逐舰在中国重新规划的西沙群岛中建岛周围巡航。出于对中国以投资获取军用和商用前沿技术的忧虑，特朗普政府9月拒绝了一个中国支持的投资者收购莱迪思（Lattice）半导体公司。该公司专门生产用于通信、计算和军工用品的可编程芯片。

然而，特朗普总统11月8日至9日到北京进行国事访问再次发出混乱信号。出发前特朗普总统抱怨中国的不公平贸易行为和巨大的对华贸易逆差，但在习近平主席给予其"国事访问+"的接待规格和签署价值超过2500亿美元的中国商品进口协议后，又将责任推卸到前任美国政府而非中国身上。特朗普的言行很快在美国国内引起批评。《纽约时报》报道指出，特朗普对中国表现出一种从未出现在出访美国总统身上的遵从姿态，标志着一种"角色的颠倒：比起中国需要美国，美国现在好像更需要中国的帮助"。回到美国后，特朗普又改变姿态。特朗普政府向世界贸易组织（WTO）表达了美国反对给予中国市场经济地位的立场，以便华盛顿维持它对中国商品征收高额的反倾销税政策。2018年1月，特朗普政府发布关于中国履行WTO承诺情况的报告，指出"美国错误地支持中国加入WTO，当初谈的条件未能有效确保中国接受一个开放、以市场为导向的贸易体制"，中国依然是一个国家主导的经济体，并利用WTO成员国的资格成为国际贸易的主导者。这种严厉批评为特朗普政府在第二年实行的好斗策略奠定了基础。但是特朗普并没有因此改变交易式的行事风格。2018年3月发起贸易战后，他以为可以轻易胜出。习近平主席在4月10日的博鳌亚洲论坛上许下一系列承诺，包括开放中国的银行业和汽车行业、增加进口、降低外资在制造业的持股限制和扩大知识产权保护。特朗普总统将上述"美言"视为让步，并声称"我们将共同取得重大进展！"

尽管特朗普将以往的对华谈判贬低为美国收获甚微的无意义交谈，他还是与中国展开了谈判。5月4日，美国政府向中国派遣了由财政部部长姆努钦率领的高级代表团，要求北京削减2000亿美元的贸易赤字，并更改包括强制技术转让在内的产业政策，但代表团空手而归。5月19日，在华盛顿举行的后续谈判达成一项联合声明，宣布双方就避免贸易战达成共识。5月21日，特朗普总统宣称谈判成功，他在推特写道，隔阂将"第一次得到消除"，中国将"购买我们美国伟大农民能生产的几乎所有农产品"。然而，过几天后他又改变主意，拒绝签署协议。尽管特朗普总统加剧贸易战，但在与习近平主席通话后，他又亲自改变对中国电信巨头中兴通讯的罚款做法，该公司涉嫌违反美国政府的贸易禁令，非法输送产品给伊朗和朝鲜。

与此同时，特朗普总统发起全方位的攻击，甚至与自己的盟友争执不休，而没有向美国的伙伴和盟友伸出团结合作的橄榄枝以联合向中国施压。在2017年7月1日的一则采访中，特朗普攻击欧盟"跟中国一样坏，只是比较小……最重要的是，我们还在北约花了一大笔钱去保护他们"。他将欧盟当成美国"目前全球范围内最大的敌人"，随后又补充"俄罗斯在某些方面是敌人，而中国是经济上的敌人"。北约前任秘书长抱怨道："特朗普似乎准备破坏美国长期以来对其盟友的基本战略认知。"因此，"美国快速并毫不犹豫地离弃了其全球联盟体系的领导地位。美国长期的盟友感到困惑不已，在'美国第一'转变为'美国唯一'的新世界秩序中无所适从"。美国在国际社会中变得越发孤立，特朗普总统在2017年12月发出威胁，任何国家若支持通过一项谴责他承认耶路撒冷为以色列首都的联合国决议，美国将中断对该国的援助。但相关国家无视特朗普的威胁，联合国以压倒性优势通过了该决议。

这些混乱的信号和不稳定的行为是大战略缺失的迹象。待遇没比中国好到哪里去的美国盟友和其他贸易伙伴纷纷丢下美国继续商谈合作协议。代表超过全球经济四分之一的欧盟和日本签署了一个全面的"经济伙伴关系协议"。《跨太平洋战略经济伙伴协定》（TPP）本是为了巩固不安的中国邻国间的联系和集中谈判力量为美国提供打开中国市场的经济杠杆而提出的，在特朗普总统宣布退出TPP之后，11个国家重新在没有美国参与的情况下签订了一个新的协议。这是一个显示各国如何在没有美国领导下继续前行的强有力信号。

因为美国侮慢轻蔑其盟友，这些国家转而试图与中国开展更多商业合作。德国和日本都增加了对华投资，土耳其也在"一带一路"倡议框架内与中国开展合作。尽管北京和欧盟在诸如技术转让和知识产权保护等问题上意见不合，2018年7月在北京召开的中国—欧盟峰会发表了一项联合声明，宣布双方坚定承诺抵制保护主义和单边主义、提高贸易投资自由化与便利化。中日关系经历动荡起伏，但如今两国与美国之间的贸易摩擦促进了这两个亚洲老对手接近。2018年10月，日本领导人时隔七年首次正式访华之际，习近平主席对日本首相安倍晋三表示，两国关系如今"重回正轨"，两国"有了更多的共同利益和关切"。

二、美中两国纷争的缘由

自从1979年美中建交以来，两国之间的合作与竞争利益一直存在。多年以来，两国领导人一直希望用合作利益定义竞争关系。但是近些年来，竞争的利益正在日益突出并定义合作。

2009年的全球金融危机是一个转折点。因为中国摆脱危机影响并迅速发展，中国开始公开指责西方国家"不合理的宏观政策"和他们"不可持续的发展模式"。中国提出"四个自信"，即道路自信、理论自信、制度自信、文化自信。在特朗普政府背离自由主义模式后，习近平主席指出，中国特色社会主义"给世界上那些既希望加快发展又希望保持自身独立性的国家和民族提供了全新的选择"。

北京的自信来自过去40年来的快速经济增长使其成为一个崛起的强国。清华大学的胡鞍钢以2014年中国的国力在包括经济实力、技术、整体竞争力和能力等各方面都超过美国的论断而闻名。在推广中国成功的宣传活动中，2018年3月由央视制作的90分钟纪录片《辉煌中国》，宣传习近平主席执政后中国在世界科学、技术、基础设施和军事中领先的成就，成了中国历史上最赚钱的纪录片。在此前一年，《战狼2》，一部讲述一名中国特种部队特工从西方雇佣兵手中拯救一个受战火蹂躏的非洲国家的电影，创下中国史上最高票房纪录；其次是《红海行动》，一部关于中国海军在一虚拟阿拉伯国家从恐怖分子手中营救人质的电影。

从经济上看，中国政府强化了国有企业的地位并引导了关键行业中的高科技发展。上海的李世默认为，"中国利用了西方对全球经济秩序的错觉，以优惠条件有效谈判加入了世贸组织。然而，中国不会且或许永远不会接受一个普世的自由民主意识形态，它充满活力的市场经济有别于资本主义"。曾是接触政策强有力支持者的美国商业界，如今抱怨中国窃取了他们的商业机密，使美国公司在华投资条件恶化，中方执行对外国公司的歧视性规定，继续实施早该降减的高关税政策，以及拦截美国的互联网公司。很多美国评论者批评美中经济竞争规则对美国不公平。美国经济被挖空，技术被公开或隐秘地强迫转让到中国。

在国际上，中国的"一带一路"倡议和亚洲基础设施投资银行挑战了美国的全球领导地位。尽管随着国力强大，中国开始呈现崛起大国的行为并不意外，但一些美国人却担忧中国要通过重建"中华王朝"，执意怀揣着百年耻辱的憎恨和威胁弱小邻国来追逐大国梦。中国政府不再生活在愤怒的孤立中，而成为"一条国家重商主义的巨龙，利用其广阔的市场力量来恐吓和驯服资本主义竞争对手，扭曲和破坏以规则为基础的秩序，并将美国驱向亚太地区的边缘"。

因此，接触政策遭到质疑。一位称其为"世纪之赌"的学者认为，华盛顿和其他自由主义者都误判了北京维持甚至扩张其威权主义做法和重商主义政策的决心。富裕而强大的中国离美国越来越远，这让很多美国专家感到沮丧。就如两位美国前任官员抱怨的："美国的军事力量和地区平衡策略都没能阻止北京挑战美国及其领导的世界秩序，自由主义世界秩序也没能像预想的那样强有力地吸引或束缚住中国。"

中国的美国问题专家王缉思承认，中国历来在塑造双边关系中发挥决定性作用。"中国再一次以其力量和行为导致双边关系发生变化。美国人对中国全球影响力的扩张感到震惊，例如'一带一路'倡议、中国在经济和社会领域中国家角色的强化、中国共产党的领导及意识形态得到巩固。"

与此同时，"9·11"恐怖袭击事件发生后美国的转变也加速了错位共识的崩塌。冷战结束之后，美国人欢呼自由民主的胜利，但其狂妄浪费了这场胜利。为了维持"单极"的辉煌时刻，美国倾其国力，在伊拉克和阿富汗进行徒劳无益的战争，成为海外的不稳定因素。贪功冒进造成巨大的财政亏空和债务，威胁美国履行国内外职责的能力，并使公众对美国的建制派感到失望。由于党派僵局阻碍了政府有效行动，美国人在许多政策议题上深陷分歧，对"功能失调的民主"产生信任危机。自越南战争以来，美国从未出现如此两极分化的局面。

分裂的美国国内政治与其国际义务相冲突，诞生了一位"美国优先"的总统，他实行孤立主义政策以减少美国的海外承诺，退出全球领导地位。美国对改变中国已失去信心，所以现在转向利字当头、交易性的政策。冷战结束后，美国曾宣称自由主义才是历史的正确选择，要求中国朝此方向靠拢；但是美国在"9·11"事件之后，便不再是民主与普世价值的典范。20世纪90年代初对自由民主充满自信的弗朗西斯·福山写道："不同政治和经济模式的声望在21世纪的头十年内发生了戏剧性的逆转。"美国在20世纪90年代掀起一股向往民主的浪潮，美国也因此占据道义制高点，但十年后美国所暴露的缺陷使所有的景仰都让位给了一个更为微妙和批判性的看法。王缉思指出，美国常常要求中国遵守"以规则为基础的自由主义国际秩序"，但华盛顿现在已经抛弃或暂停了过去提倡的这样一些相同规则。"中国的外交决策者越来越难辨别出美国自己到底想要什么样的规则，想要别国遵守什么样的规则，想要维持什么样的世界秩序，而在重大国际问题上华盛顿的立场又在哪里？"

现实主义学者约翰·米尔斯海默认为，美国在冷战结束后追求的自由主义霸权注定是要失败的。美国依据自己的形象重塑世界，包括在世界范围内传播自由民主，构建开放的国际经济和国际机构的政策，本应是为了保护人权、促进和平与创造一个民主安全的世界。然而，美国却最终成为了一个高度军事化的国家，参与破坏和平的战争，损害人权，还威胁自由主义价值观——因为国内的民族主义和现实主义几乎总能打败自由主义。因此，华盛顿不得不采取一个基于民族主义和现实主义的更为克制的外交政策。

但有些美国人却诿过于他国，包括中国。特朗普总统将美国几乎所有弊病都怪罪到外国人身上。拿中国来当替罪羊，可以帮助政客避免面对作为全球化输家的这一难题。这个转变在特朗普总统对中国展现敌意之前就已经发生，并助长了反华的经济民族主义。一位资深的中国问题研究者因此分析道，为了应对中国对美国利益的侵蚀，美国政治中的民粹主义热潮要求将本国利益放在更优先的地位，而美国的对华政策也因此发生了五十年来最为消极的转变。

三、接触政策是美中良性竞争的基础

自 1979 年关系正常化以来，美中关系经历了风风雨雨、上下起伏。在 20 世纪 80 年代，哈里·哈丁称美中关系为"脆弱的关系"；90 年代，戴维·兰普顿则将其描绘为"同床异梦"。进入 21 世纪，美中关系在频繁的危机与动荡中越发起伏不定。尽管动荡不稳的循环造成过较严重的对峙僵局，美中关系还是顺利度过了许多波折。两国虽不是天然伙伴，却也并非必然的敌人。在深远的意义上，两国的关系同时是合作伙伴和竞争者。尽管美国和中国对这样的关系感到难以适应，但也都担不起与对方脱钩的后果。《第二次冷战》的作者指出，虽然历史上大国间由衷热忱的和平极为罕见，但冷和平或缓和却是一个切实可行的目标。"作为接下来几十年里的两大强国，美国与中国别无他选，只能想办法'和平共处'。"

尽管美中竞争加剧了，接触政策仍然是健康竞争的基础。不管接触政策遭受如何广泛的批评，很多美国人仍在坚持接触政策。戴维·兰普顿说得好："美国发挥自己的经济、军事和意识形态力量建立了造福全球经济增长和避免大国战争的机构、联盟和管理机制。这样做的同时，它也促进了一系列新兴大国的崛起，其中最瞩目的是中国，这是它现在必须要应对的。如果美国要维护好自己的利益，华盛顿就必须赢得北京的合作而非试图逼其服从。"宾夕法尼亚大学沃顿商学院（特朗普的母校）院长杰弗瑞·嘉瑞特表示："中国与美国确实不同。我们所能做的最重要的事，是保证美中之间的差异分歧是力量的来源、经济增长的来源、商业机会的来源，而不是冲突的来源。创造这种历史的最好方式是通过更多的接触、更多的文化交流、更多企业与企业间的纽带、更多的理解。因此，更多的接触才是处于 21 世纪最重要的关系中的我们的正确道路。"

继续坚持接触政策的人是有理由的。第一，虽然接触政策有时很难实行，但它比孤立中国的企图更符合美国利益。史文（Michael Swaine）认为，中国直到 20 世纪 70 年代和 80 年代初还是一个很大程度上封闭的国家。"尽管最近有所挫折，今天的中国比起接触政策之前依旧有极大改观，更加开放、全球化和宽容了。"最重要的是，接触政策产生了一种深刻的相互依赖，使两国共生共荣。努力工作的中国根据比较优势向美国市场提供成本低廉的商品，使收入受限的美国消费者能够在痛苦的滞胀年代维持生计。自那以后，中国制造的商品使美国消费者受益无穷。美国从中国巨大的储蓄储备中获益，弥补了本国储蓄短缺加剧和不负责任的财政政策的危害。作为过去十年里全球增长的最大贡献者，中国惊人的经济增速也是美国繁荣的原因之一。中国需要美国市场来发挥其出口和在供应价值链上的比较优势，而美国的利益则在于维持和加深在中国市场现有的生产链和经营业务。

尽管存在贸易逆差的问题，中国自 2015 年以来取代加拿大成为美国头号贸易伙伴和第三大出口市场。从 2007 年至 2016 年，美国对华商品出口增长了 86%，而对世界其他地方的出口仅增长了 21%。美国对华服务贸易出口增长了 12%，而对世界其他地方的出口却缩减了 0.6%。特朗普总统强调工作岗位的流失，却无视对华贸易所创造的工作岗位。中国贸易的增长支撑了 2009 年至 2015 年间美国最大的就业增长。美国的对华贸易赤字确实可观，但是很大一部分美国的对华进口是来自于其他地方，包括美国的转口贸易。如果基于增值来计算贸易赤字，结果将减少接近 40%。另外，美国有巨额的对华服务贸易顺差：2015 年 500 亿美元、2016 年 380 亿美元。在 2016—2017 学年度，有超过 35 万的中国学生赴美留学，占外国学生总量的三分之一以上。中国游客也成为对美国旅游产业发展至关重要的因素。2016 年中国游客在美消费达到了 332 亿美元，比其他任何国家都要高很多。与中国打贸易战不仅伤害中国经济，还因扰乱美国公司供应链而对美国经济产生很大伤害。当中兴通讯因违反美国制裁而导致其在美营业牌照暂时被吊销和无法获取美国技术时，一系列连带伤害也广泛传递到了高通、谷歌、刺槐通信公司和众多小供应商等美国伙伴中。世界银行的一项研究表明，在美国与中国间加征 25% 的贸易关税可以降低高达 3% 的全球出口量和高达 1.7% 的全球收入；而中国和美国可能各自下跌 3.5% 和 1.6%。尽管两国可以宣告胜利，但贸易战在此过程中却可能会消耗大笔财富，最终使双方得不偿失。

当特朗普政府在 2018 年 3 月 22 日宣布对中国发起 500 亿美元的关税制裁后，道琼斯工业平均指数猛跌 724 点，即 2 个百分点，传递出强烈的信息。随后，习近平主席在 4 月 10 日的致辞中，在贸易上表现出的安抚基调暂时平息了贸易战的紧张气氛，道琼斯指数推高了 1.6%。虽然特朗普政府满怀信心认为美国在贸易战中占上风，但关税抬高了美国各种进口商品的成本，带来了通胀压力和利率提升，进一步加重美国贸易逆差和美元强势。美国政府在 2018 年 3 月宣布贸易战后，美国的对华贸易赤字继续攀升，8 月份高达 386 亿美元，比上年增长 10.5% 并创下了最高的月度对华赤字纪录。

尽管中国经济对美国贸易的依赖程度高于美国对中国，但中国政治经济体制比美国的民主选举制更有能力抵御贸易战的后果。随着美国生产者遭受到贸易战带来的痛苦，越来越多的立法者对提高关税的影响持谨慎态度。美国参议院以 88∶11 的投票通过了一项象征性的决议，试图在 2018 年 7 月 11 日——即政府宣布对 2000 亿美元中国商品实施新一轮征收 10% 关税的次日——抵制特朗普总统的关税令。特朗普总统在 8 月宣布了加征中国 2000 亿美元的商品关税措施后，参与贸易代表办公室听证会的 355

名厂商中有95%的人表示反对这些关税。2018年9月13日，美国全国零售联盟、石油协会、玩具协会和由全国最大的农业商品集团支持的团体"农场主支持自由贸易"及80多个其他组织，联手组建了"支持自由贸易美国人联盟"。联盟致信立法者，抱怨"无论大小公司都因为提高关税和接二连三的报复行为而受到伤害。这类事例举不胜举"。

成百上千的美国公司游说政府将他们的产品划出特朗普的关税清单外。因为游说活动的影响，贸易代表办公室后来豁免了年度进口价值74亿美元左右的商品。南卡罗来纳州参议员林赛·格雷汉姆（Lindsey Graham）是最支持特朗普总统打击中国的人之一，但他在幕后代表7家从中国进口的南卡罗来纳州化学和纺织品公司展开交涉以避免贸易战的伤害，其中4家的进口材料从特朗普关税清单上撤销了。

由于两国的可持续性增长都有赖于对方，美国对华民意一直没有太大变化，反映出一种谨慎态度。2018年芝加哥全球事务委员会的民意调查数据显示，过去40年来美国对中国的态度保持稳定。只有31%的民众将中国的经济力量、39%的人将中国的军事力量视为对美国的严重威胁。这将中国的威胁远远置于了其他国家对美国的威胁之后，如朝鲜（78%）和俄罗斯（47%）。回应中国在世界各地日益增长的影响力，42%的美国人认为中国应该在亚洲承担更大的责任。相比之下，只有24%的人认为美国应该承担更多责任；28%的人认为美国应该少承担责任；47%的人支持美国继续维持目前承担的责任。

尽管许多美国厂商对中国的经营环境不满，但在支持特朗普保护主义和接受旷日持久的贸易战的后果上，他们的态度并不明确。上海美国商会2018年4月10日至5月10日进行了一项调查，发现尽管公司对各种监管和经营挑战颇有怨言，但只有8.5%的受访者支持使用关税手段，而69%的受访者反对使用关税手段。41.5%的人赞成将对等投资作为在中国获得更大市场准入的工具。在贸易紧张局势不断升级时，中国美国商会和上海美国商会于2018年8月29日至9月5日联合对其会员企业进行调查。超过60%的受访者表示，美国和中国最初发起的加征500亿美元商品关税都对其公司产生了负面影响；而预计受第二轮加征 2000 亿美元商品关税负面影响的公司比例跃升至 74.3%。联合关税的实际影响反映在盈利损失（50.8%）、生产成本上升（47.1%）和产品需求减少（41.8%）三个方面。

第二，接触政策不仅结束了两国间 23 年的外交疏离，还为越南战争后的亚洲和平繁荣奠定了基础。该地区的大多数国家寻求能从美中两国获得最大限度好处、降低得罪任何一方的风险、维持自身独立的战略，都希望美国不要在亚洲和中国脱钩。当中国与亚洲其他国家经济相互依存度增加时，他们担心特朗普政府抽身而去、对多边机构不屑一顾。2016 年东亚区域内的贸易份额上升至 57.3%，而与美国的贸易下降。欧盟，日本和美国共占东亚国家出口总额从 1990 年的近 50% 下降到 2015 年的 29%。作为该地区的主要生产基地，中国成为日益增长的区域内贸易中心。

中国利用这些潜在的变化，增强了其力量并改善了其形象。越来越多的亚洲国家被拉向中国的轨道。由于这种地缘政治转变正在积聚动力，一些国家倾向于向中国接近，低调处理领土争端和分歧，以及为了弥补美国的脱离而加入中国的倡议。大多数亚洲国家都参与了中国主导的亚洲基础设施投资银行和"一带一路"倡议。虽然美国的军事能力仍然在亚洲占主导地位，但中国的影响力却越来越大，甚至拉近了和美国长期盟友的关系。例如，菲律宾总统杜特尔特为寻求中国投资而搁置了对北京声索南中国海领土主权的法律挑战。中菲关系升温的一个迹象是，杜特尔特在 2017 年 5 月视察了一艘停靠菲律宾的中国海军舰艇，这是中国军舰多年来首次对菲进行此类访问。在马尼拉主持召开 2017 年东盟首脑会议时，杜特尔特在较早的首脑声明草稿中删除了中国对有争议水域岛屿军事化的提法，以及"紧张局势"和"活动升级"的说法。杜特尔特通过在大国间巧妙周旋，从这两个大国获得了实惠。中国人向杜特尔特提供了有利的投资待遇，而美国人减少了杜特尔特对同盟的义务。

在这种情况下，正如杰弗瑞·贝德尔所指出的，就算美国沿着"与中国脱钩的道路继续走下去，追求无节制的竞争，也不会出现与苏联冷战的重演，尽管当时有许多西方和民主国家加入了美国的阵营孤立苏联。"经济上与中国深深地相互依赖，"即使那些警惕中国的国家，如日本、印度和澳大利亚，也不会拿与中国的经济联系去冒险，不会加入这场由西方重新竖起'竹幕'的争斗中。我们将孤身战斗，只能靠自己"。

第三，尽管中国的崛起不可避免地加剧了摩擦，但接触政策让中国成为与邻国及美国关系中的利益相关方，从而帮助避免了潜在灾难性的美中对抗。与美国维持关系符合中国的利益，因为中国还远未具备像美国一样承担起全球领导者角色的能力。全球领导力的代价高昂，它意味着一国需要挺身而出为他国的福祉做出贡献而派士兵到远离家乡的地方战斗甚至死亡。中国崛起并不意味着美国衰落。虽然美国在亚洲维持主导地位变得困难，但对中国来说，要在短期内将美国赶出亚洲也同样困难，甚至会越来越困难。中国对美国的支配地位感到不安，尽管如此，它还是从美国领导的秩序所造就的该地区的稳定繁荣中获益匪浅。中国将从与美国和周边国家的友好而非敌对关系中受益。

美中对决可能会给中国的经济转型和政治稳定带来极大风险。经过多年的 GDP 高速增长，中国经历了从依赖低成本制造和出口产品到高科技创新和消费驱动型经济的艰难过渡。因此，北京明确表示，不希望打一场对中国经济损害远多于美国的贸易战。对中国出口来说，没有其他市场能替代足够大而利润丰厚的美国市场。另外，中国普通百姓支持降低进口关税，因为这意味着普通消费者能购买到更便宜的外国商品和服务。

历史上，外部的敌对压力有助于动员中国民族主义者反对做出任何被视为向外国投降的让步。随着贸易战的升级，中国媒体将经济摩擦描述为"美国阴谋论"的一部分，甚至是一个遏制中国的大战略。中国的怀疑和诉求并非毫无根据。在历史屈辱和今天强大力量的基础上，中国追求"中国梦"具有强大的民意基础。

特朗普政府认为它很容易就能在贸易战中胜出。中国的产业政策和其他举措仍在继续。产业政策曾一度帮助日本、韩国和台湾地区升级产业并带来财富和繁荣。美国政府也支持过全国的铁路系统、马歇尔计划、网络发展、胡佛水坝和空间计划。虽然政府在自由的企业制度中担任适当的角色有别于中国全面支持国有企业的产业政策，但中国不会因美国的压力而放弃其产业政策。

部分由于美国的压力，毛泽东"自力更生"的口号再次被人们想起。对中兴通讯的制裁唤醒中国政府，鼓励中国企业将高科技和关键工业品、系统和投入本土化，减少对美国的技术依赖。2018 年 1 月，美国禁止阿里巴巴的转账机构收购美国的速汇金（MoneyGram）汇款公司，理由是防止中国公司掌握数百万美国公民的私人数据。阿里巴巴使用基于区块链的技术，创造了在许多方面不同而更具创新性的产品。过去，华盛顿未能逼迫北京在大部分的争端中退让。随着中国变得更加强大，逼迫中国让步只会变得越来越难。把中国赶到角落将会促使中国变得更加强硬，中国除了反击之外别无选择，尽管两国都没有做好准备陷入一场双方均无胜算的暴力对抗中。

四、美中共同管控竞争、继续实行接触政策是不二选择

当美国开始实行接触政策时，两国之间的分歧要比今天大得多，而尽管有大的分歧，美国还是与中国接触。美国必须保持其竞争力和对其优势及价值观的信心，重建自己作为一个高效、包容和开放国家的声誉，支撑其民主和资本主义的制度，并投资于传统联盟。1972 年，随尼克松总统访华的小查尔斯·弗里曼认为，"让美国或中国再次取得伟大成功的最好办法就是不要试图阻碍对方的进步或将其摧毁。双方都要关注国内的战线，贯彻其所宣扬的价值观，提高其国家竞争力的基础因素，并在担心别人的问题之前先解决好自己的问题"。黎安友（Andrew Nathan）附和说："成功的对华政策的第一步就在于国内。我们必须恢复我们的力量并重新致力于我们的价值观，改变自己的使命比改变中国的任务更加艰难。"威廉·H. 奥弗霍尔特批评特朗普总统放弃美国自身成功的发展模式，认为"应该通过做美国最擅长的事情来确保美国的繁荣：在国内创新并与世界其他国家进行自由贸易"。

中国驻美大使崔天凯说的对，"中国和美国仍然坐在同一艘大船上，同

命运、共患难。为了保全两国的利益，他们共同的挑战是在不确定而未知的水域中驾驭好这艘船"。虽然并没有在两个庞大经济和军事大国之间展开经济和地缘战略和平竞争成功的先例，但美国和中国必须找到彼此利益的平衡点，避免不符合双方利益的暴力对抗。这种层面的接触要求前瞻性和灵活性。由于经济上的紧密联系和相互依赖、国际机制秩序的存在、有限的意识形态对抗以及二次核打击能力，两国领导人别无选择，只能寻找管控竞争和继续相互接触的政策。

国际体系中的新安全挑战：大国政策的变化

美国前总统里根特别助理

卡托研究所高级研究员

道格拉斯·班多

世界从未像今天这样日益丰富多彩，地球居民也从未拥有如此多的机遇。新知识、新技术给予我们一个更加健康、富庶的未来，人类创造力的馈赠得以更广泛地分享。但是，要享受这些有利条件必然要求各国调整适应剧变中的国际环境，包括适应经济和军事力量及有全球影响力的软实力的重要变化。

一、传统国际秩序的发展变化

当代世界以欧洲中心为基础。古代秩序的特点是王国和帝国不断出现，分别统治一段时间，然后被新的王国和帝国代替。罗马帝国的统治出乎寻常的长，但其影响力有限，对亚洲、中东、北非影响甚少，与东半球几乎没有联系。

西罗马帝国瓦解时，人们无法预知未来欧洲的统治帝国。中华帝国当时看来是全球统治的强有力竞争者。虽经改朝换代，但帝国的统治架构得以延续。然而，15世纪的明王朝选择闭关锁国，对后世中国的影响甚大。自此，内乱、内部弊病丛生等改变了帝国走向。相比而言，此时的欧洲完全向另一个方向发展。尽管受周期性危机的冲击，如"黑死病"、蒙古人入侵等，但欧洲大陆开始学着"向外看"，甚至在始于10世纪的中世纪，欧洲已开始了经济持续增长期。14世纪出现了文艺复兴，15世纪海外探险和国际贸易迅猛发展，18世纪开始的工业革命彻底改变了欧洲大陆。

财富和技术促进了军事实力的发展。进入20世纪，欧洲国家的足迹已遍及亚洲、非洲和拉美。虽然英国是当时全球最强大的国家，但令人意外的是它仅拥有有限的军事力量：英国虽统治着广大的海外殖民地，但其自身军队规模较小，依靠殖民地军队和盟军推进其政策。除失去北美殖民地之外，到二战时英国都无往不胜。中国是英国殖民扩张的受害国之一，被迫将香港割让给英国，同时将澳门和其他一些地区分别"租借"给葡萄牙和其他列强。一战期间，欧洲国家彼此协商如何瓜分殖民扩张的战利品，时常合作行动，正如在中国对付义和团那样。

二、传统国际秩序的覆灭

虽然欧洲国家在彼此间许多规模有限的冲突中保住了他们的声誉和影响力，但一战的结局却非如此。除德国以外的所有殖民国家都获得了战利品，但声誉却遭重创。这些国家经过多年厮杀，再无以前那么强大的力量来对付一些小国和寻求独立的民族。战争催生了一批脆弱的小国，战后的和平反而使欧洲变得更加不稳定。随后各种革命席卷德国、俄国、意大利及奥匈帝国。虽然英国和法国保住了在国际秩序中的主导地位，但地位脆弱、信心破灭。

到1917年，美国很大程度上仍远离世界政治、军事舞台。美国的加入使协约国获得了对付德国领导的同盟国的关键优势。1919年，美国国会拒绝批准《凡尔赛条约》，美国民众要求和平的意识觉醒，选民选出新总统，并将美国从世界领导者的角色中撤出。但是，自此美国不再置身世界事务之外。

明治维新之后，日本成为亚洲的主导国家。因为加入了协约国，日本也从协约国的胜利中分到一杯羹。然而，由于巴黎和会拒绝了日本代表在会上提出的"种族平等"、禁止民族或种族歧视的建议，日本认识到"欧洲俱乐部"仍然是封闭的。即使如此，日本仍是欧洲列强被迫在国际上公平对待的唯一的亚洲国家。

孙中山领导的革命推翻了清王朝，虽然新生的共和国依旧分裂和孱弱，但预示着重大变革的到来。中国人民终于打破了腐朽封建王朝的统治，开启了伟大变革的进程。新生的中国与日本一道，使亚洲开始脱离西方的主宰。

两次世界大战之间，欧洲强国再次激烈对抗，日本侵略中国。当欧洲正式爆发战争，亚洲与欧洲两个战场合二为一成为全球性的大战。德国和日本战败导致全新国际秩序的形成。在欧洲，只有英国仍拥有较强军事实力，但财力耗尽，帝国统治难以为继，德国战败并被分裂。法国需要处理被德国占领所带来的后果。欧洲大陆的其他地区也大多成为废墟。在亚洲，旧的国际秩序解构已近完成。日本被打败和占领。曾经的殖民地如朝鲜、越南、荷属东印度群岛等处于飘离状态，既没有了殖民统治但又未获得独立。更重要的是，中国此时从日本的侵略和占领中获得解放，旋即陷入全面内战。

由此，东西方都出现巨大的地缘政治真空。冷战爆发，美国和苏联填满了这些真空地带。接下来的40年，全球的其他地区逐步迎来老牌强国的复苏和新兴大国的崛起。欧洲、日本复兴，殖民地国家赢得独立，印度成为国际舞台上的一股外交和经济力量。最重要的是，中华人民共和国诞生，并最终战胜国内的各种挑战，迅速融入了国际市场。到苏联解体前，世界基本处于两极状态，美苏关系因两国间时而剧烈或危险的竞争不断出现起伏。

三、单极世界时刻

苏联解体留下一个由美国主导的世界秩序。这一世界秩序有多种称呼，包括"单极世界"，因为一段时间内世界上只有美国一个超级大国。美国处于优势地位，其经济和地缘政治倡议容易赢得国际社会赞同，或者至少是默许。而且，它的举动可以不用顾忌别国感受，例如将北约东扩到俄罗斯边境。此时，任何政治或军事争斗基本都是美国最终取胜。但这种情形只维持了一段时间，很难用历史的长度来衡量，所以只能称之为"时刻"。很多帝国延续了好几十年甚至几个世纪，中华帝国更长，而美国拥有类似帝国实力的时间仅 20—30 年。特朗普政府的行为让人觉得现在似乎仍是由美国主导的单极世界，但事实并非如此。

俄罗斯不再是全球霸权的竞争者，但仍是有国际影响力的地区大国。在北约东扩特别是乌克兰和格鲁吉亚问题上，俄罗斯与美国、欧洲矛盾对立。而对俄联合制裁已被证明是无用的，多个欧洲国家想尽快改变这一政策。俄罗斯还在委内瑞拉、叙利亚、伊朗等问题上阻挠美国的有关行动。在阿富汗和朝鲜问题上，普京政府也没有多大意愿支持美国。

美国在处理与其长期盟友包括加拿大、墨西哥、欧洲之间的关系时更加咄咄逼人。经济和移民问题是双方最突出的矛盾，与欧洲之间的安全矛盾也日益凸显。在古巴和伊朗问题上，美国决心利用其主导性的经济优势来落实外交政策目标，结果招致许多国家的反对。

虽然欧元的使用及成员国之间大不相同的财政政策给欧洲带来了挑战，但欧洲经济影响力已经上升。尽管欧洲人仍旧难以在达成共识的基础上解决一些国际问题，但欧洲经济实力超过中国，能与美国匹敌。欧盟扩容发展停滞，欧洲无法成为"合众国"，一体化进程受阻。欧洲能否创立一个稳固的联合政府来管理自身的财政问题、能否创立一支超越国家的军队、能否执行统一且独立的对外政策，都有待观察。如果都得以实现，届时欧盟的影响力将远超当前。欧洲与亚洲特别是中国的经济联系紧密，但在亚洲缺乏政治和军事影响力。

美国发觉自身的影响力有限，甚至对邻国亦如此。特朗普政府加紧了对古巴和委内瑞拉的制裁，但至今没有任何效果。而且左翼力量在该地区生机勃勃：墨西哥有位与美国作对的总统，阿根廷的庇隆主义者将在 10 月的选举中重新上台。

美国加强了对非洲的军事关系，2007 年正式成立非洲司令部。反恐是非洲司令部的首要任务，但诸多军事行动更多的是帮助非洲国家的政府，而非保护美国自身。然而，长期的国际竞争越来越依赖于经济和政治实力，美国官员担心在非洲竞争中落后。冷战期间，美苏通过援助、投资、贸易和军事力量等手段在非洲进行较量。目前，美国在非洲最重要的竞争对手是中国，后者通过实施"一带一路"倡议框架内的项目，稳定提升与非洲国家的经贸关系。尽管中国在非洲的介入存在争议和反复，但其在非洲的影响力正在不断上升。

中东问题耗费了美国不少精力。美国在该地区的行为表明，其有能力打败任何中小型国家，但缺少重塑这些国家和社会所必需的思维、耐心和技巧。因为美国没能在其采取行动的国家设定有意义的优先任务，所以它将大量的资源浪费在了次要甚至不重要的目标上。例如，连续三届美国政府在阿富汗和伊拉克牺牲了不少士兵、花费了大量物资和精力来尝试重建工作；在利比亚和叙利亚，奥巴马政府意在摧毁现政权，但没有慎重考虑随之而来的事情。美国卷入了沙特、阿联酋等国与也门的战争，当前还与伊朗处在战争边缘。在伊拉克和伊朗问题上，美国发现多个传统盟友并未随之起舞。最重要的是，美国还发现自己长于制造混乱，它制造的混乱就像流沙反而使自身难以逃脱。即使美国确实依赖于中东的能源，但实际上它现在更多的是在军事上与该地区绑在了一起。而每一次的军事行动都制造了许多新的敌人和潜在的恐怖分子，而对付这些人又为美国进行进一步军事干涉提供了理由。

在亚洲，美国依旧是安全方面的主导者，但正在失去其强大的经济影响力。美国选择了直接与朝鲜对抗，但在 2017 年用"火与怒"威胁之后，它又被迫尝试外交途径解决问题。目前美朝对话陷入僵局，大多数观察家认为，如果想实现半岛无核化，特朗普政府将不得不做出让步。

更为紧要的是美国企图遏制中国。虽然美国官员否认这一企图，但对美国的有关政策无法做出其他解释。特朗普政府的决策者们认为中国有咄咄逼人的意图，因此在东亚海域的领土争端上做出了强硬回应。美国加强了在该地区的军事存在，重申与日本和菲律宾的盟友关系，寻求加强与印度的安全合作。特朗普政府还强调了与台湾关系的重要性。这些举动迫使中国下定决心增强军事实力。

然而，东亚地区不仅只有美中双方的竞争。其他国家也采取了独立步骤，常与中国发生对抗。日本安倍政府采取了更加好斗的政治和军事政策。印度也更加积极主动，特别是加强了与日本、越南之间的关系。韩国与中国原本正稳步提升双边关系，却因韩方部署"萨德"系统，中国立即采取了制裁措施。目前两国关系已经改善但疑云仍存。澳大利亚与美国安全合作紧密，在其国内发起了关于中国在澳影响力的炒作。

对美国而言，与中国的经济竞争更加激烈。中国与邻国的经贸合作已超越美国与这些国家的合作。在安全上依赖美国的韩国与中国的经贸额比韩美、韩日经贸额之和都多。特朗普政府蔑视自由贸易，特别是退出了前任政府谈妥的 TPP，为中国在该地区签订双边和多边贸易协定打开了方便之门。最重要的是，美中两国目前正在打贸易战。

有人说美中两国有可能开始新的冷战。两国关系恶化，但庆幸的是还未到冷战的程度，目前还没有包括军事对抗和威胁的全球性冲突。尽管两国贸易谈判有诸多分歧，但两国间仍有大规模互利的经贸合作，双方还有人员、学术、旅游等多方面交流。这些在美苏冷战期间是没有的。而且世界上大多数国家都与美中两国保持着紧密关系，两国都深深地融入同一个国际秩序中。

四、新的世界秩序的发展

"单极时刻"明显已经结束。但很多美国的决策者还有错误幻想。在美国对外政策的辩论中，关于美国全球领导力的话题就像诅语反复困扰着这些人。美国越来越不具备能力和决心来主导全球的每个地区。美国总统和国会继续肆意妄为，不关心美国的未来。美国长期得益于美元作为世界储备货币的地位。欧元的接受度由于希腊和其他欧洲国家的债务危机减弱。由于中国的金融缺乏透明度，近年来人民币国际化程度有限。但是，今年美国的财政赤字接近 1 万亿美元，未来还会扩大。因为更多美国人退休、税收减少，而养老金和医疗费用增加，联邦政府预算日益紧张。美国向海外派兵、展示强大实力所付出的代价要比采用震慑手段进行防卫大得多。美国民众对美国在海外收效甚微的冒险政策支持度越来越低。这些都迫使华盛顿重新思考其对外政策。

主要大国未来的安全政策是怎样的？国际体系必须从如下几个方面进行改革。未来一段时期，美国仍会追求其霸主地位。它将恫吓盟友服从其领导，用军事威胁和经济制裁来迫使其他国家就范。但结果往往难以如愿。与美国友好的国家将会拒绝使用军事威胁，努力防止国际金融体系受到美国操控。例如，欧盟一直在努力维护与伊朗的贸易和与之达成的核协议。美国潜在对手将互帮互助，共同对抗美国。俄罗斯最近也表达了对伊朗的支持，中国和俄罗斯都向委内瑞拉提供了不同形式的支持。受到美国威胁的国家会充分利用其经济增长带来的收益发展军力，加强导弹、潜艇等武器装备来击退或阻止美军侵犯其领海、领土和领空。

在沉重的财政压力下，美国将紧缩影响其太大利益的开支，其他国家便会随之接管其安全责任。例如，美国很可能不再为欧洲提供安全防御。欧洲并没有面临实质性威胁，自身也有能力进行防卫。俄罗斯缺乏对欧洲动武的动机，因为这样会得不偿失。而且，欧洲人口和经济体量都比俄罗斯大。在美国的承诺中，最有可能放弃的是对欧洲的安全保证。照此，欧洲将承担更多安全责任，包括对抗俄罗斯，限制从北非和中东涌入的难民和移民，挫败来自这些地区的恐怖袭击。承担安全责任的机制将会是美国作用减小后的北约，或者是欧盟新创立的某个欧洲防务机构。目前，欧洲还无法在超出自身范围的地方投射军事实力，欧盟成员国之间的政治分歧很大、对军事投入的意愿严重不足。今后，美国可能会从中东地区收缩，因为以往干预的效果介于失望和灾难之间。而且，一个长期动荡的地区对美国而言不再那么重要。例如，美国已是能源生产大国，没有完全依靠中东石油。别的地方发现不少新的油气田，这将减小欧洲、亚洲对中东油气资源的依赖。作为美国传统盟友的以色列是地区大国，有能力击败任何敢于挑衅它的邻国。由于美国一直介入该地区的战事，支持以色列及其对巴勒斯坦的压制，这些行为引发了对美国的愤懑，导致恐怖分子袭击美国。美国从该地区抽身会使自身更安全。

该地区的局势发展结果可能是形成新的地区均势。海湾国家可能会更加公开地与以色列走近，土耳其将会非正式地与叙利亚、伊拉克和伊朗站在一起。所有国家都能在与"伊斯兰国""基地组织"等圣战武装分子和恐怖分子的战斗中找到它们自身的利益。也门等国可能会长期身处危机之中，埃及等国看起来稳定，但也面临难以预料的剧变。伊朗不大可能屈服于特朗普政府的过分要求，但也可能会与新一届美国政府和欧洲达成一个更加平衡的协议。而且，东西方的工业化国家都将面临波斯湾石油运输安全的压力。正常情况下，中东国家没有搅乱这一通道的动机，但域外因素如美国的经济制裁或武装冲突会改变局势。此外，如果美国不愿再承担维护海上运输通道安全的责任，这一责任将落在中国、欧洲、印度和日本海军的肩上。

美国从亚洲撤出将更加缓慢和慎重，因为在该地区还没有形成多边联盟。美国的伙伴们都有互相对抗的历史，特别与日本之间。中国是美国过去和现在最大的关切，它的实力使得中小邻国相形见绌。美国可能最终会转变为"离岸平衡器"的角色。新的大国，如印度尼西亚和马来西亚，将发挥更加重要的地区性作用。朝韩关系的改善将减弱美国在韩驻军的合理性。随着日本稳步提升其军事能力，美国可能会将驻扎在冲绳的海军陆战队远征军撤回，当地居民对此也要求已久。美国可能将加强与越南、印度等国的地区性军事合作。与此同时，美国可能会把防御重点从有争议的领土转向盟国的主权独立，尽管这些国家的主权独立从未受到过中国的威胁。中国的邻国如何看待它的抱负和计划，很大程度上决定着这些问题的发展。近些年，该地区的国家担心中国已经放弃了"和平崛起"的承诺，更愿意用军事力量来实现目标。这一认知促使中国的邻国更加靠近美国，改变了对日本加强军力的看法，彼此间加强了合作，还将印度引入该地区，连接起印度洋和太平洋。近期中国对台湾和香港的政策强化了这些消极的认知。如果中国的战略继续朝这一方向发展，美国撤出亚洲就应更加慎重。而且，地区国家也会及时填充美国撤出后的真空。如果中国能与邻国达成临时协议，搁置领土主权争议、实现共同开发，成功解决争端，那么美国更应准备撤出亚洲，也不需要有关国家来替代美国在该地区的军事部署和承诺。

非洲有巨大的发展潜力，但取决于各国政府所实行的政策。非洲一直都有一定的民主进步和经济增长。改革带来更大的稳定，促进了更多的投资和贸易，二者实现良性循环，给贫穷百姓带来福利。肯尼亚、尼日利亚、南非等国如果能克服政治挑战，将崛起成为有全球影响力的国家。虽然非洲面临现实的安全挑战，但这与域外大国关系不大。非洲安全挑战主要是内生性的，源自邻国叛乱分子或恐怖分子，如尼日利亚的恐怖组织"博科圣地"。因此，国际上的地缘政治竞争不再阻滞非洲的发展。相反，中美在非的经贸竞争有利于非洲大陆。

拉美的情况与非洲类似。虽然拉美的国际影响力不大，但该地区有三个具有重大潜力的国家：阿根廷、巴西、墨西哥。所有国家都面临着自己造成的创伤，也都可以进行改革，在基本不考虑美国因素和自身对外政策的情况下都能取得成功。当然，美国与拉美国家近在咫尺，自然主导了它的邻国，但古巴与委内瑞拉是例外，美国对它们的影响较小。特朗普对马杜罗政府的反应近乎歇斯底里，相对而言，委内瑞拉政府却无法对美国或其他邻国产生影响。随着近期哥伦比亚长期武装叛乱的解决，除了毒品贸易，该地区已少有其他突出的安全问题。在毒品问题上，美国长久以来都是基本的诱因，它一方面对毒品有需求，刺激了毒品生产；另一方面又通过法律予以禁止，从而使得毒品交易更有利可图。由于地理上邻近，美国不可能改变对拉美的干预政策。尽管美国在拉美投入的成本相对较低，但拉美对美国而言却至关重要。

总的来说，前文所述的世界秩序带来了总体的稳定与和平，以此趋势发展的新秩序将会比目前的世界秩序更好。虽然小规模冲突不可避免，但大国间仍能保持和平，如果它们能一起努力构筑战争防火带则更好。欧洲除了巴尔干，基本不会有任何形式的战斗。南美和非洲引发战争的可能性也较小。亚洲最为脆弱，因此这些国家的人民和政府能否努力解决导致暴力冲突的争端显得尤为重要。

五、和平与稳定面临的威胁

尽管暴力冲突时有发生，但世界还是变得越来越和平，大规模、毁灭性的战争少了。虽然叙利亚内战、沙特与阿联酋入侵也门令人难以接受，但远没有 20 世纪 30 年代的中日战争、一战、二战等战争惨烈。

因此，世界各国和各个国家集团共同反对冲突很重要，最重要的是世界大国要建立一个安全架构，有效防止大规模战争爆发。当前，中等规模国家之间的对抗非常危险，包括两个核国家印度和巴基斯坦，沙特与伊朗，朝鲜与韩国。有关国家、世界大国、国际组织应一道努力应对这些问题。客观而言，特朗普与金正恩的会晤缓和了最严重的对抗，为实现朝鲜半岛和平稳定带来希望。

更为危险的对抗在大国之间，所幸很少。美国对中、俄有诸多抱怨和指责，中、俄也与美对抗，但它们之间的对抗并不涉及到彼此的核心利益。它们为了影响力而竞争，并非领土、人口或生存，也没有发动战争的传统借口。

美国面临的最大威胁来自恐怖分子，因为这无法用传统的战争解决，而且入侵或占领其他国家只会增加对美的恐怖袭击。中国、俄罗斯与别的国家有更多源自领土纠纷的直接对抗，如中国与印度、日本、菲律宾、越南；俄罗斯与格鲁吉亚、乌克兰。

美国惯常做出的安全保障承诺已成为导致大国冲突的传感器。美国一直支持北约扩容，甚至希望将格鲁吉亚和乌克兰纳入跨大西洋联盟。特朗普政府重申了在亚洲有关领土争议问题上的防务承诺，如钓鱼岛问题。美国充当了以色列、沙特和阿联酋王室的保护人，所有这些承诺都可能导致冲突。虽然美国的防务承诺有助于震慑外来干预，但也助长了被保护者的鲁莽，迫使美国在这些威慑手段失败时不得不介入。所以，美国在承诺因出现重大问题而为盟友提供核保护的同时，又要约束盟友的行为。

在这些问题上避免大国冲突的最佳途径是和平解决与美国防务承诺有关的争端。例如，对俄，美国可以提出停止北约扩容，特别是可以探讨邀请俄罗斯和格鲁吉亚都加入北约的可能性。作为回应，俄罗斯可以宣布放弃对乌克兰分裂势力的支持，在克里米亚问题上举行有国际监督的公投。

在亚洲，美国可以选择从已经找到和平方式来预防潜在冲突的有关国家领土争端问题上脱身。有的情况下，美国还有能力帮助解决冲突，如在朝鲜半岛问题上同意实行可核查的军控和开展经贸合作。此外，切实解决贸易争端等次要但会累积紧张氛围的问题，将有助于构筑额外的预防冲突的防火带。

在中东，美国可以继续支持盟友，但不应干预与自身利益关系不大的问题，而且还可放弃维护中东稳定的责任，这吃力不讨好且效果不彰，对维护美国和其他大国的和平安全亦无多大必要。虽然这些举措不能保证不再发生冲突，但会使爆发战争的可能性大大变小。

六、实现未来的和平必须构筑新的安全架构

今天的民众比祖先们生活得更美好，即使是中等收入的人比过去最为富有和有权势的人都过得更方便与富足。现代医疗、发达的交通、互联网等，使这个时代变得美好。但是，冲突和战争的威胁在全球范围依然存在。最糟糕的情形是大国之间爆发冲突，那将造成大规模的伤亡与毁坏，甚至威胁到国家的生存。过去已经发生多次这样的惨剧，如二战（结束仅74年）、朝鲜战争（结束仅66年且至今未签订和平条约）、越南战争（结束仅44年）等。这些大战之后虽然也有过一些惊心动魄的冲突，但大国之间爆发战争的风险已经降低。

随着"单极时刻"的结束，世界各国人民和政府必须寻求建立新的安全架构，以争取一个更加稳定、和平的未来。这个未来世界不是命中注定的，而需要付出艰辛努力。一旦我们开始承担起这一使命，正如人们常说的，"只能成功不能失败"。只有成功才能避免使我们物质丰富的世界陷入灾难。

百年变局视野下的中美摩擦与全球安全

中国社会科学院世界经济与政治研究所

国家安全研究室主任、研究员

冯维江

2019 年上半年以来，中美贸易摩擦在美方层层加码下日趋激烈，吸引了国内外学术界、外交界、企业界等各方面投入大量关注和资源。实际上，已有多项对贸易摩擦经济后果的评估都表明，中美贸易摩擦对双方经济增长的直接影响不大。各方担心的是由贸易摩擦到全球产业链断裂，甚至滑向货币、金融等多领域制裁与反制裁，乃至陷入更严重的安全冲突或全面对抗状态的风险。如果放宽观察的视野，从世界所处的百年未有之大变局来看，不难看出贸易摩擦只不过是"东升西降"的长期地缘政治运动中的小片段。

2017 年初，习近平主席在联合国日内瓦总部演讲时，发出"世界怎么了、我们怎么办"之问。当年年底，他在接见 2017 年度驻外使节工作会议与会使节时的讲话中指出，"放眼世界，我们面对的是百年未有之大变局。21 世纪以来一大批新兴市场国家和发展中国家快速发展，世界多极化加速发展，国际格局日趋均衡，国际潮流大势不可逆转。"这个"百年未有之大变局"就是他对"世界怎么了"之问的凝练解释。2018 年 6 月，他在中央外事工作会议上以辩证观点详细阐述了百年未有之大变局的特征。此后，习近平主席又多次在涉及军事、国家安全、经济、外交等问题，以及对青年人、领导干部、其他国家的领导人及民众的讲话或署名文章中阐述如何看待和因应世界百年未有之大变局的论断。

百年未有之大变局，从国际关系看，主要是世界多极化加速发展、国际格局日趋均衡，国际形势处于新的转折点，各种战略力量分化组合、国际体系加速演变，大国关系深入调整，同时霸权主义、强权政治的威胁依然存在。

从经济来看，主要是以中国为代表的一大批新兴市场和发展中国家快速发展，经济全球化持续深入发展、世界经济格局深刻演变，同时美国等内顾倾向、保护主义、单边主义不断抬头。经济上的大变局直观表现为中国在经济规模上对美国的赶超。

国际货币基金组织（IMF）数据显示，2014 年中国 GDP（按购买力平价指数即 PPP 计价）的世界占比为 16.5%，超过美国的 15.8%，这是 19 世纪末美国超过英国以来首次被其他国家反超。预计到 2024 年，中美两国 GDP 的世界占比分别为 21.4% 和 13.7%。

当然，从其他指标（如现价计算的 GDP 或人均 GDP 等）来看，这个过程要迟缓和复杂得多。按现价计算 GDP 来看，中国从 2021 年至 2024 年的经济增长率虽然较此前会有所下降，但仍然维持在较高水平，从而保持对美国赶超的势头；但由于美国经济体量较大，直到 2024 年，美国仍将保持全球第一大经济体的角色。

从人均 GDP 看，欧洲议会预计，到 2035 年中国按 PPP 计价的人均 GDP 将由当前的 10000 美元左右增加至 21000 美元左右，但仍然不到欧盟水平的一半。IMF 对中国人均 GDP 增长的估计更乐观一些，认为到 2024 年中国按 PPP 计价的人均 GDP 就将达到 22419 美元，与欧盟之比将达到 53.7%，与美国之比也达到 37.7%，接近当前发达国家水平的下线（2018 年发达国家中按 PPP 计价人均 GDP 最低的希腊为 25887 美元）。俄罗斯科学院世界经济与国际关系研究所（IMEMO）的预测则显示，到 2035 年，中国按 PPP 计价人均 GDP 将达到 37400 美元，与美国之比为 43.3%；中国按汇率计价人均 GDP 将达到 21400 美元，与美国之比为 24.8%。尽管人均水平仍存在较大差距，但由于中国人口规模巨大，人均水平向发达国家迈进折射出背后的整体实力的大幅度上升。

从安全来看，大变局下，国际环境总体稳定但国际安全挑战错综复杂，战乱恐袭、饥荒疫情此伏彼现，传统安全和非传统安全问题复杂交织。尽管全球战略稳定面临美国退出《中导条约》等行动的威胁，但大国之间，或者说中美之间滑向严重冲突而带来全球系统性安全风险的概率不大。无论是对中国还是对美国，最具破坏性的预期损失可能都不会是两者直接发生严重冲突所造成。正如美国兰德公司在《与中国开战——想不敢想之事》报告所言，"核武器应该不会被使用，即使是在高强度的常规战争中。没有一方会认为其战争代价如此之大、前景如此可怕，或者其赌注如此重要以致要冒着遭受核报复的风险来发动先发制人的核打击。"

从文化来看，大变局意味着各种文明交流互鉴、不同思想文化相互激荡，在文化多样化深入发展的同时，"文明冲突"的论调也沉渣泛起，并向着"自我实现的预言"的方向产生影响。例如，2019年4月，时任美国国务院政策规划司司长斯金纳在华盛顿一场安全论坛上表示，美国当前和中国的较量与"冷战"情况不同，美国与苏联之间的竞争是"西方家庭的内部斗争"，苏联所信奉的马克思主义也源于西方政治理念，而与中国发生的则是"很不同的文明和意识形态之间的斗争，美国没有经历过这种情况"。这是"美国第一次面对非白人种族的强势竞争对手"。斯金纳还表示，美国正在制定基于"文明冲突"的对华关系框架。尽管此论一出，即受到美国国内不少政治和外交学者的严厉批评，但我们不能把此番言论当成个别美国政府官员并非深思熟虑的偶然失言，而忽视其背后的支持势力和可能的配套行动。

从科学技术看，大变局的时代是社会信息化深入发展、新工业革命风起云涌的时代。各国都明白，谁占据了科学技术领域的制高点，谁就在大变局中掌握了更高的主动性和更大的发言权。支撑经济力量格局深度调整的科技、制度、人口这三大支柱中，人口结构是慢变量，仅可能通过移民政策等作出边际上的调整，并且容易引起国家内部的分裂；制度竞争是高成本竞争，很难通过强制措施要求对方或对方"阵营"的国家更弦易张，而要争取（或"收买"）中间地带的制度性支持，也是所费不菲、难得易失；科技竞争可能成为影响百年变局的主战场之一。

人类社会经历了高度依赖劳动力要素投入的一维经济，以及资本要素以边际替代率递减的方式替代劳动的二维经济，正在迈向科学技术要素以全新面目强化劳动生产率和资本产出率的三维经济。三维经济条件下，可以实现的战争方式或将发生颠覆性的变化。一是战争场域大为拓展。在先进技术支持下，三维经济条件下的战争出现由传统海陆空拓展至太空、由宏观空间发展至微观空间、由物理世界延展至虚拟世界、由战斗场景扩展至生活场景等转变。二是对抗手段更加丰富。定向能、生命科学、人工智能、网络、高超音速等领域技术在军事应用方向上的发展，可能让战争的指挥、实施及效果检验方式多样化。三是战争伦理发生变化。在一维及二维经济下，无论是要通过战争来获取人口，或者要消灭有生力量，都反映出人作为劳动要素的提供者本身是有价值的。尽管也存在资本或技术对劳动（人口）的替代，但一般来说低维经济服从边际替代率递减的规律，即随着资本或技术投入规模的上升，每增加一单位资本或技术可以替代的劳动的数量是下降的，这意味着资本或技术理论上不可能完全取代劳动。三维经济下，随着人工智能等技术的发展，边际替代率递减规律被打破，劳动可以被非人力的运动完全取代，作为劳动载体的劳动者的价值可能变得无足轻重。人与人的矛盾将由一部分人对另一部分人的剥削转变为一部分人对另一部分人的无视。剥削范式下，剥削者承认被剥削者的价值，在特定条件下还能达成某种"同情之理解"，就像农民对他赖以耕种的老牛，虽然不时策之以长鞭，但闲来也会为之梳毛抚背并以老伙计相称。无视范式下，富裕人口不再视富余人口为同伴，甚至借宗教、种族、文化、籍贯、阶层等标签将后者划归另类，而无感于后者的喜怒哀乐，就像科学家对他实验所用的老鼠，电击水淹、开肠破肚也不会有半点犹疑愧疚，而后者的价值也不待其主观能动性的发挥，而只剩下任前者摆布或宰割的用途。基于虚拟现实的远程作战技术和无人作战平台的兴起，可能加剧参战者对人类生命的无视从而增加战争的残暴性。

世界大变局下经济社会发展的基本特征是，少数大国正在竞相迈向三维经济世界，同时希望各自的主要竞争对手长期处于低维状态。竞争的基本逻辑是发起降维攻击，通过经贸投资、军事行动、外交折冲、国际规则等手段，约束主要竞争对手由 2.5 维经济向高维的进一步发展，最好能迫使其退回并维持在低维经济状态。如果以美国为代表的发达国家将中国等主要新兴经济体的经济形态降维并锁定在二维经济状态，断绝其技术维度升级发展的可能，则"东升西降"的态势可能停滞甚至逆转。

应对百年未有之大变局是一个长期过程。这个过程中，上升与下降所产生的持续挤压之力在中美两国（以及其他相关国家）内部造成的紧张、焦虑、慌乱带来的应力，作用于内部宗教摩擦、民族矛盾、贫富分化、环境污染、腐败问题、干群关系、劳资冲突等脆弱性不等的领域，而在其特别脆弱的一处或若干处出现断层线，进而诱发造成经济崩溃、社会失序、政治倾覆等严重问题，以及各国特别是大国为了暂时缓解这些问题而将矛盾指向外部从而引发高科技背景下的全球性动荡或安全危机，可能才是真正具备破坏性之处。从这个意义来说，联合"一带一路"沿线发展中伙伴及参与"第三方合作"的发达伙伴共同拓展开放空间，以深度改革开放防御各种"灰犀牛"，应当置于防范中美贸易摩擦滑向失控的"黑天鹅"同等重要的位置。

中美安全关系新变化

英国剑桥大学教授、高级研究员

马丁·雅克

当前，很多人希望自 20 世纪 70 年代末开始的全球化和多边主义时代继续存在下去。彼时，中美关系相对稳定，合作是两国关系主要特点。然而，这种稳定以两个因素为前提：第一，中美关系存在极大不平等，美国始终是占据优势的一方；第二，按照美国的错误思维，中国实现成功的唯一途径是成为像美国一样的国家。事实证明，这两点现在都不成立。在全球经济史上最引人注目的 40 年里，按照购买力平价计算，中国已经超越美国成为最大经济体，但中国也永远不会成为美国。因此，美国误判了形势，成为傲慢的受害者，如今转向强势政策来应对中国崛起，以一种近乎绝望的方式试图遏制或迟滞中国发展。美国深知中国崛起的根本动力是经济发展，因此从贸易战入手是合乎逻辑的，但美国不会止步于此，或将在多个领域引发争端，这只是时间问题。中美谈判或将取得实质成果，但不宜太过乐观，因为中美关系相对稳定的 40 年即将结束，中美关系新态势或将持续 20 年乃至更长时间。

中美之间不会爆发"新冷战"。当前局势与冷战时期相比只有两个相同点：美国是其中一方；共产党是另一方的执政党。但是中国共产党和苏联共产党有着本质区别。中美关系紧张并不意味着冷战。第一，美国所处发展阶段不同。冷战时期，美国是崛起中大国。当前，美国国家实力下降，美国人愤怒而焦虑，努力维持自己所创造和拥有的一切，而中国实现了人类历史上最伟大的经济发展，目前仍处于上升趋势。第二，中美对国力支撑的理解不同。冷战期间，美苏争霸对抗主要聚焦于军事。当前，美国仍追求强大军事实力，中国军事实力也发展迅速，但其战争观、和平观与美苏时期截然不同。中国古代著名军事家孙子虽著兵法，却讲究"慎战""不战"，主张谈判解决问题，反对进行战争。此外，中国人认为最重要的两种权力模式是经济和文化，主张从长计议，面对问题具有耐心和定力。例如，中国对待特朗普始终保持坚定而克制，保持沟通渠道畅通。种种做法表明，中国是一个非常不同的强国。

美国攻击华为是出于对中国崛起的恐惧。如今，中国经济增长率是美国的三倍，经济创新能力取得巨大进步。五年前，西方还在质疑中国缺乏创新，如今没有人再提这个问题了。阿里巴巴和腾讯已成长为行业巨头，位列全球技术公司第一梯队。华为是全球电信行业领跑者，特别是在5G技术方面优势突出。许多中国公司虽在生产力上远落后于美国公司，但其发展势不可挡。中国已成为技术大国，这是最让美国震惊的一点。美国攻击华为的根本动机与安全关切没有太大关系，而是面对中国这一巨大挑战时内心恐惧。

美国或将是贸易战最大输家。由于征收高额关税、追求单边主义，美国经济竞争力有所下降，未来或因保护主义上升而进一步受损。美国前财长亨利·保尔森（Henry Paulson）早前在英国《金融时报》的一篇文章中亦表示，美中两个经济体都将受损，但从长远来看，美国经济很可能是更大的输家。

美国是影响全球安全的最不确定因素。美国发展伴随着侵略和战争，而中国坚持走和平发展道路，始终保持战略定力。面对国力衰退，特朗普的选择是进行独断式政策转向，破坏民主，让美国信誉下滑，导致美国社会分裂和倒退。美国完全没有对自身衰落做好准备。希望美国应对自身衰落的过程不会给本国民众及世界其他国家和地区带来太多痛苦。

美国与中国："斗"的逻辑与"和"的理念

暨南大学国际关系学院院长

张振江

2019 年 6 月 18 日，美国总统特朗普致电中国国家主席习近平，表示希望在 G20 大阪峰会期间举行两国领导人专门会晤，就当下的中美关系进行直接沟通和交流。习近平主席表示愿意会晤。由此，前几天特朗普发布的一则推特所引发的关于中美领导人会晤的沸沸扬扬之传闻暂告一段落。特朗普总统曾发推特表示，如果 G20 峰会期间见不到习近平主席，他将启动对中国商品的新一轮关税措施。特朗普总统这种隔空喊话率性直为，不顾外交应有的协调委婉，也不考虑中方如何理解这一信息。

结合特朗普总统之前的诸多做法和他独特的行事风格，很难预期危机重重的中美关系会因此而峰回路转。很大的可能就是，特朗普先给世人一个夸张的惊喜，然后给大家抛出一个接一个意想不到的"炸弹"。近期的中美关系就是这样被特朗普总统反复变化的推特信息一会儿"推上峰顶"，一会儿"踢到山谷"。过去几年来，中美双方都进行了一系列的"出招"和"接招"，特别是美国方面，加之特朗普总统独特和难以捉摸的个人行事风格，使得中美关系看起来犹如坐过山车：忽上忽下，波谲云诡，惊心动魄，难以把握。

要理解当下眼花缭乱的中美关系，需要穿过众多的谜面走入谜底。美国和中国在认知和处理两国关系时体现了两种截然不同的世界观：美国"斗"的逻辑与中国"和"的理念。

美国的逻辑很清楚，那就是"非我族类，其心必异"。"异质"的中国之崛起一定会危及和挑战美国的现有地位。从 20 世纪 70 年代中美关系缓和开始，"接触"还是"围堵"的争论就一直与之相生相伴。"接触"的目的是希望把中国变成美国认同的"族类"与国度，变成自己团队的一员。但随着中国的发展与自立以及美国优势地位的相对衰落，美国觉得难以掌控中国这个"异质"的国家。由此，"接触"慢慢转向"围堵"。特别是从无视国际政治正确的特朗普总统开始，在美国政府的公开话语中，中国迅速成为美国"对手"和"敌人"，中美之争甚至成为"文明之争"。

追根溯源，美国"斗"的逻辑有着丰厚的历史实践和思想基础。基督教关于上帝与撒旦的截然二分，是西方和美国看待他人与国际关系时难以摆脱的思维定式和思想指导。德国著名政治学家卡尔·施密特就明确指出，西方政治的最根本问题就是界定敌友。在历史实践上，目前称霸世界的美国就是不停地寻找、界定并打败一个个"敌手"而不断生存、发展与壮大的。就此而言，美国对中国达成超越两党与朝野之分的罕见共识并不意外。

中国的理念和政策也是一以贯之：秉持和平发展的原则与和谐世界的目标，既不挑战美国的地位，也明确表示不会称霸世界。即使中国的力量足够强大，中国也致力于建设一个"己所不欲，勿施于人"的以理服人的和谐世界，致力于推动构建人类命运共同体。如果用中国古人的描述，那应是一个王道而不是霸道的世界。此外，中国传统哲学主流强调阴阳、善恶之间的相互转化，很少用黑白是非截然二分、完全对立的有色眼镜看待自己与他人的关系。实际上，在这种错与对、是与非的具体争论之上，一个更重要的理念是"和"之秩序的维持和延续。

中国"和"的理念也来自于中国的历史实践。汉唐盛世、"五胡乱华"、蒙古统治、康乾盛世等等，民族"融合"终将取代族群冲突而成为中国历史的大势。即便是在被西方指责为不平等的"华夷秩序"或"朝贡体系"中，历代中国政府都对直接干预他国非常谨慎，更鲜见出兵征讨、采取将"非我族类"归化于中华的行动。按照西方的逻辑，郑和下西洋时，凭借中国船队的实力，完全可以把海洋诸国纳入中国版图，但实际的结果与90年后哥伦布与麦哲伦地理大发现后整个世界成为西方殖民对象的结果完全不同。很多西方人依然把中国的"一带一路"倡议与"马歇尔计划"相提并论，但二者最根本的差别是，"一带一路"的目标是建设一个联通的世界，"一带一路"倡议没有对手，没有敌人，而"马歇尔计划"却是为了帮助美国的盟国强大起来，对付共同的敌人。

"斗"的逻辑与"和"的理念，使得中美两国在众多问题上，特别是在对各自的认知与判断上产生一系列误解和纠缠。从根本上看，"和"的思路可以学习，可以转化，可以稳定，但"斗"的逻辑却是伤害很大，它甚至可以摧毁当前两国共存的基本态势，瓦解"和"的未来可能。就此而言，未来的中美关系，美国该承担更多的责任。所谓的"修昔底德陷阱"主要是针对斯巴达的，如果雅典崛起是一个不可逆转的客观事实，那么如何认知与理解这一事实至关重要。遗憾的是，斯巴达认定雅典是敌人和对手，恐惧由此而生，结果发生了希腊神话中的俄狄浦斯效应，悲剧不可避免。

"和"的理念可以引导中美关系走向另一番景象。但在具体实操方面，"和"并不在与"斗"的互动过程中占有明显优势。在未来的中美关系建构中，中国应当更加积极主动和有所作为。中国不但能够走出美国"斗"的逻辑并抵御其挑衅滋事，保持斗而不破，更需要积极释疑解惑，减少误会。正如习近平主席强调，我们都应该努力避免陷入"修昔底德陷阱"，强国只能追求霸权的主张不适用于中国，中国没有实施这种行动的基因。

把"斗"的逻辑引向"和"的理念，将是一个艰苦卓绝的历程，但也将是中国之幸，美国之运，更是世界之福。

美中竞争对阿根廷和拉美国家的影响

阿根廷国际关系理事会学术秘书长

国防大学教授

胡安·巴塔来梅

我的思考基于两个观点。第一，我们这个时代两大强国之间的竞争和对抗源于它们各自"保障未来"的目标。第二，为了实现这一目标，它们必须确保在"自由国际秩序"日益破裂的情况下获得一个机动空间。美国自1945年起确立的现状即将面临改变。

美中两大强国的竞争影响了中小国家的外交政策视角。阿根廷因此在成为国际体系稳定伙伴的进程中面临非常复杂严峻的局面，实现自身安全和繁荣目标的自主性也受到影响。而且阿根廷的情况远非个案，所有拉丁美洲国家都受到同样影响。阿根廷在目前的局势中左右为难。在商业和金融方面，阿根廷既需要美国也需要中国；阿美、阿中双边关系中都不存在直接的安全问题，而且阿根廷在任何情况下都不涉及任何国家的安全关切。

然而，美中关系开始在商业和安全领域出现僵化，并从经济和政治角度影响阿根廷。中国对拉美地区的影响越来越深，引发美国忧虑，这就形成了一种三角关系，并进一步引发安全担忧。长远看，阿根廷将因自身脆弱的国际地位而在其中受到影响。

处于崛起大国和守成大国之间，迫使像阿根廷这样脆弱的国家积极考虑自身在面临直接或间接压力时的定位。保持中立的空间比以前小多了。阿根廷从2015年底开始实施"与世界进行有智慧地接触"政策，现在应根据在相互依存的世界中谋求自主的需要进行调整。在一个复杂的世界里，自主不仅是增加自身机动性，也要在一个多重互联的世界中通过增强实力、谋求福祉来追求国家利益，这其中包含广泛的相互影响，不同的行动者可能做出难以预料的封锁行为。

从拉美的政治现实中可以看到，胁迫、吸引和封锁政策使某些国家变得强大，并被用来达到某些目的。委内瑞拉的悲剧提醒我们，国际体系中最脆弱的国家遭受大国及大国竞争伤害的速度有多快。

从技术上讲，我们正处于获取新技术的竞争阶段。在 21 世纪下半叶，我们将生活在 21 世纪上半叶的成功和错误带来的后果中。获取的不仅包括自然资源，还意味着释放那些可以推动物质转化、生命创造和向一个可预期的、迅猛发展的未来跃进的"无形"力量。到目前为止，我们还没有掌握获取类似力量的正确工具，所以很难实现这一目标。就技术而言，正如赫拉利（Harari）在《未来简史》（Homo Deus）中所指出的那样，我们正在迈向下一次进化飞跃。

然而，新技术在各国权力分配方面产生的一个问题是，大国和部分商界人士意图限制对新技术的获取。首先是针对那些可能有害利用这些技术的行为者，其次是针对那些希望窃取他国军事或公民安全发展成就的国家。这使技术开发人员、用户、政府和公司之间产生紧张关系。从政治角度看，战略考虑开始取代经济考虑，而这种取代为当前的技术发展踩了刹车。

如果技术能够确保进入不同的空间，并推动特定类型的全球化，那么它还可以允许制定一些政策，以预防并禁止潜在竞争对手未经授权地进入或访问这些空间。"北美自由全球化"项目使美国有了优先准入权，但随着时间推移，一些国家为实现本国利益，利用全球化手段推进实施一些具有相反效果的项目，损害了这种"准入权"。正如法雷德·扎卡里亚（Fareed Zakaria）在他的《后美国世界》（The Post-American World）中所展示的那样，这些国家没有自由主义精神，但它们有着同样的雄心壮志，要最大限度地为世界提供服务，同时获取新的竞争技能和效率所带来的好处。

我们可以理解，这一时期的紧张局势是由于各国通过了一个以普遍或全球共识为中心的国际秩序，而这一秩序允许推进一系列共享规则，所有自认为是国际社会一部分的人都受到这种规则的影响。奥巴马政府试图在自由主义秩序的基础上，给中国戴上"负责任大国"的帽子，而这种自由主义秩序正逐渐暴露出弱点，这些弱点来自于美国犯下的错误、竞争性大国的成功、各国权力日益分散，以及一些行动丧失合法性。美国实力的削弱，以及不同于西方的其他政治力量崛起，使国际秩序暴露出更多弱点。虽然存在一些关于"国际失序"的讨论，但当前的形势与兰德尔·施韦伦（Randall Schwellen）在谈到国际体系时给出的定义非常接近：鉴于有序和无序状态都没有优势，我们宁愿生活在一个永久"波动"的状态中。

"文明冲突"、战略能力和卓越的竞争对手，凸显出所有大国在确保未来安全方面都存在困难，因此，中国设计了诸如"一带一路"这样的合作倡议，却得到来自西方强国的不同反应。在亚洲，因为各国之间相互关注度上升，误解和不信任也在加深，技术在其中发挥了不可忽视的作用，"黑客"不仅存在于计算机系统中，也存在于人们的意识形态中。

我们可以把战略竞争的目的归结为一句话：保障未来。今天，我们发现强国在地缘政治（包括外层空间）、地缘经济和网络空间准入的竞赛中开展竞争。这三种竞争相互交织，并在国际社会引发恐慌，开展竞争的各领域驱动力不一，导致紧张局势加剧。

1. 军事上，在东南亚，中国和美国形成不稳定均势，并转化为军事力量投射战略，比如美方提出的"空海一体战"（ASB）、反介入和区域拒止武器（A2/AD）等。可以看出，这两者实质上都是零和博弈。

2. 地缘经济竞争虽然是开放的，不同主体之间存在明显的相互依赖和依存关系，但合作的可能性和领域在不断缩小，零和博弈更加突出。美中两国互相指责对方对弱国进行剥削。正如《经济学人》杂志在其文章《新殖民主义者》（The New Colonialists）中指出的那样，这种日益增长的经济渗透加剧了区域内的紧张局势，因为外来者开展的经济活动在当地社区引发一些阻力和反抗。这种情况使中国的两个主要论点遭到严重质疑，一是和平崛起，二是和谐世界。然而，也存在许多对这些批评意见的限制，因为对许多国家来说，中国仍是其实现发展愿望的主要伙伴。

3. 网络空间已成为不稳定的根源，人们对其中存在的零和博弈已有清晰认识。中美两国相互指责对方从事间谍活动、窃取工业机密、开展专利战等。两国认为在此领域缺乏合作空间，双方控制和利用网络空间的模式也存在很大差异，担忧不断上升。此外，正如作家肖莎娜·祖博夫（Shoshana Zuboff）所指出的，"平台经济"具有微妙的侵入性。目前还不清楚谁将从这场竞争中获得最大利益，但有预测显示，在未来较短的一个时期比如到2030年左右，中国将处于更有利的地位。

要保障未来，就需要了解如何应对这三种竞争，这将确定美中两国在其中的结构性地位，因为除了相互联系之外，它们还创造了不同的战略、军事和经济优势。2007年，许多国家参与了迈克尔·克拉雷（Michael Klare）所提到的在北极或南极争夺剩余利益的竞争。而现在我们正处于一场更复杂的竞争中，我们可称其为"接下来会发生什么"。

"接下来会发生什么/下一次的破坏是什么"是根据进化步骤来思考的，就像是一次新的"登月竞赛"，或是由第四次工业革命导致的战略性变革，主要涉及机器人技术、空间技术、通信技术、人工智能技术和数字生物学技术等。就像我们无论在短跑或长跑比赛中，第一次冲刺是非常重要的。特朗普政府抱怨中国在专利使用方面的缺陷，并在当前贸易战中与中国在这一点上发生冲突。正如格雷厄姆·艾里森在其《注定一战：中美能避免"修昔底德陷阱"吗？》一书中所说，美方认为自己在从事研究和开发，而中国同行从事的则是研究、开发与偷窃。

保障未来意味着做出最佳战略选择。美国和中国的选择是开放的，但美方表现出越来越多的限制。两国都追求"再次伟大"，但基于各自在国际体系中扮演角色的不同，两国有不同的立场和考虑。美中都知道当前的国际秩序是人为建构起来的，也都明白现有国际秩序已经过时。中国巧妙地以不同方式提升与世界的关系，为所有人呈现一个"辉煌"的未来。美国则是从安全和风险角度看待问题，这就限制了合作，产生了紧迫感。美国人提供的是安全，而不是未来，这对拉美人来说适得其反，因为拉美人充分意识到美国在该地区的作用，以及美国在整个20世纪对该地区进行的干预和分裂。虽然中国不为人知，地理位置遥远，但来自中国的移民越来越多地与当地社区互动，表现出友好的形象，带动中国与拉美国家关系日益密切。

美国的大战略已从离岸平衡转向"和解战略"（可能包含绥靖选项），再转向目前国际参与度较少的战略。其中每一项战略都有批评者和支持者。美国国家安全战略认为，21世纪的主要目标是与俄罗斯和中国竞争。特别是在探测、定向能武器、自动武器、量子探测、核防御和核武库现代化等敏感问题上，面对俄罗斯和中国日益增强的能力，必须保持一定程度的技术领先优势。这方面的一个例子是建立太空部队并装备进攻性武器。

特朗普总统终止了前几届政府的部分激进政策，认为这些政策是对"真正"竞争的干扰。布什和奥巴马政府进行了不同类型和强度的战争，对别国进行了近20年的公开干预，并延续了前任政府未完成的行动，其中比较突出的是继续阿富汗战争。"选择性接触"道路似乎是美国维持其在国际体系中地位的唯一出路，民主党人也开始为争取大选获胜而展开类似讨论。事实证明，斯蒂芬·沃尔特（Stephen Walt）所称的"自由至上"战略代价高昂、不计后果，而且效率低下。

美国政府采用各种手段使技术领域价值链脱节，只会带来一个更为僵化的世界。美国的大学以及所有处于美国家安全核心的科技公司等都因此重新考虑与中国的关系。尽管这使中国更容易寻求与其他国家建立伙伴关系，但美国同时让潜在伙伴知道，与这个亚洲巨人关系密切有损于与华盛顿的关系，并让这些国家做出选择。目前看，还不清楚这些国家会站在哪一边。

兰德公司《美中军事积分卡》报告显示，在危机中动用军事力量的可能性似乎不大。该报告指出，美中在常规军事能力的9个领域中，有6个领域是对等的（对基地的攻击、对地面部队的攻击、取得优势防止对手发射天基武器等）。未来15年，中国将能够抵挡住美国的军事优势。美国在网络战和核稳定问题上保持着优势。美国年度军费支出约为6000亿美元，如果不对美整体预算产生负面影响，其波动幅度不会太大。中国年度军费支出超过1,000亿美元，并有足够的继续增长空间。美国不仅担心力量的相对变化，也担心这些变化背后的意图。

在当今相互依存的世界中，中国和美国都试图强化其他国家对自身的依赖。因此，贸易战使中美在一定程度上脱钩后，又将限制国际政治中次要参与者的选择。随着时间的推移，大国之间不断加剧的分歧也会给次要参与者的行为带来更多结构性限制。在 21 世纪后半叶，第三世界国家的自主权将会有更大幅度削弱。

在这种情况下，2011 年阿根廷做出了一项外交政策决定，将阿根廷与中国的军事太空综合体联系起来，改变了阿根廷在 21 世纪以来一直保持的相对中立、不参与权力竞争的传统政策。同样，中国不仅在阿根廷，在整个拉美地区的影响力也越来越大。中国巧妙介入该地区涉及两个关键问题，一是要与所有与其国家利益相关者相处。二是重视价值观的作用，但也认识到在多极世界中，价值观的普遍性是有限的。

新兴大国崛起的动力和国际政治格局的变化影响着各国的机动性能。地区各国应当共同确定地区性议程并将它们相互联系起来，并设法了解其可能对双边关系产生的不利后果，解决利益分歧将是实现地区自主的核心要素。阿根廷既需要美国，也需要中国，未来我们需要找到应对大国竞争的有效方法。

第二编

地区安全秩序新调整

努力构建更加和平稳定的地区安全秩序

越南和平发展基金会副主席
越共中央对外部原常务副部长

陈得利

冷战结束以来，东亚地区保持了近 20 年的和平稳定。在这期间，美国从该地区撤出了第七舰队，放弃了在菲律宾的军事基地，减少了在该地区的军事存在。随着中南半岛从战场变为市场，柬埔寨恢复和平，东盟成员国逐渐从 5 个扩大到 10 个，并向建立单一共同体的目标迈进。中国奉行"和平发展"政策，改善同地区国家关系，同东盟签署并落实《东南亚友好合作条约》（TAC）和《南海各方行为宣言》（DOC）。尽管有关各方在领土主张上仍存在分歧，但南海局势保持相对和平稳定。虽然世界各地发生了包括亚洲金融危机在内的诸多动荡，但和平与合作始终是世界和该地区发展的主流。全球化和一体化进程加快，贸易和投资不断扩大，多边主义势头增强。毫无疑问，东亚地区所有国家都从中获益，这也使该地区成为世界经济发展最具活力和领先的火车头。

然而，区域稳定的"美好时代"好景不长。此后南海冲突和军事化加剧，朝鲜半岛局势不稳，导致地区局势严重紧张和战略不信任，引发国际社会高度关注。美国通过实施"亚太再平衡"战略和"印太战略"，将战略重心转向该地区。中国在南海采取新举措，对该地区采取了新的战略方针。主要大国增加了在该地区的军事存在，许多国家的军费开支显著增加。恐怖主义、网络犯罪、气候变化、极端民族主义日益抬头，对地区稳定构成越来越大的威胁。

最近美中之间发生的一切表明，这两个全球第一、第二大经济体之间，不仅存在类似于 20 世纪 80 年代美日之间曾发生过的贸易冲突，而且已从合作与竞争并存的态势，向战略遏制与反遏制的地缘政治对抗的方向发展，这其中包含了许多冷战的元素，对该地区和整个世界的未来构成了非常严峻的挑战。

当前，东亚地区安全稳定面临三大挑战。一是地区主要大国之间，尤其是美中之间存在战略竞争与对抗。二是全球性威胁对地区和平、发展与稳定产生不利影响。三是域内国家之间的战略不信任和核心利益冲突导致诸多地区内部问题，特别是南海领土争端。

东亚地区正处在一个十字路口，面临着是走向和平稳定还是冲突、合作还是对抗、遵循多边主义和国际法还是采取单边行动的抉择。历史和现实清楚表明，对抗对任何人都没有好处，只会带来共同损失。特别是中东局势反复证明，外部干涉和强加于人只会给地区和世界各国人民带来混乱和灾难。

在全球化的今天，贸易、投资、交流、人员往来把各国联系在一起，相互依存更加紧密。任何国家都不能在孤立状态下实现发展，安全对所有人都不可或缺。面对恐怖主义、气候变化、传染病、网络犯罪、跨国犯罪等全球性威胁，国际社会需要携手合作。当今时代需要更多的政治智慧，而不是武力。我们的选择应该是所有人共享的和平与稳定之路、合作与发展之路。

尊重各国独立主权、不干涉内政、和平解决一切争端和冲突、不使用武力或以武力相威胁等国际法核心原则应得到严格遵守。一国的发展繁荣不应建立在损害别国利益的基础之上。这在很大程度上取决于各大国的行为，以及该地区所有国家的共同努力。

中美这样的大国在这一进程中发挥着最大的作用，因此也负有主要责任，它们的行为和双边关系将影响本地区和整个世界。衡量一个国家的伟大与否，要看它能为人类的和平、发展与繁荣作出什么贡献，而不是看其显示的实力和霸权。我们生活在一个不应该也不能被分割的地区和世界上，有必要共同努力，避免任何形式的第二次冷战或"文明的冲突"。希望大国成为遵守国际法和多边合作的榜样，避免采取损害他国利益或共同安全与繁荣的单方面行动。

维护本地区的和平、安全与稳定需要制定和遵守足够的规则与行为准则，以及有效的预防冲突机制。正如冷战期间，欧洲是两个阵营对抗的中心，军备集中程度最高。赫尔辛基进程的结果是签署《赫尔辛基协定》和成立欧洲安全与合作组织（OSCE），这有助于预防冲突和维护地区和平。

不幸的是，虽然当前亚太地区面临非常严峻和日益增长的安全挑战，我们仍然缺乏这样的规则和机制。因此，我们需要共同努力来填补这个关键的空白。我们可以制定集体协议，规范军备、军事部署和演习，确保航行和航空自由与安全，打击恐怖主义、网络和跨国犯罪，同时保护环境、应对气候变化以及所有其他对地区安全与稳定的威胁。我们可以共同建立维护地区和平、防止冲突的集体安全机制。我相信，如此我们将能增强战略互信，确保该地区的长期和平、安全与稳定。

幸运的是，我们已经签署了许多重要而有用的协议来推动这一进程，比如《东南亚友好合作条约》（TAC）、《和平、自由和中立区宣言》（ZOPFAN）、《东南亚无核武器区条约》（SEANWFZ）和《南海各方行为宣言》（DOC）等等。此外，还存在一些可以加强和进一步发展的机制，如东盟地区论坛（ARF）、东盟防长扩大会议（ADMM+），特别是东亚峰会（EAS）。与由两个对立集团建立起来的欧洲集体安全体系不同，我们的机制应由所有相关方共同建立。在这一进程中，东盟的中心作用将非常有益和重要。在当今相互依存的世界上，这一机制应向所有相关方开放。

南海问题对地区的和平、安全与稳定至关重要。南海是所有沿海国家的传统生存空间，也是最重要的国际海上通道之一。海洋领土主权是沿海各国的核心利益，南海的和平稳定、航行自由与安全是影响整个国际社会的根本利益问题。各方在南海的行为特别是对现有争议的处理，对各方建立战略互信、维护地区政治安全具有决定性影响。正因如此，解决南海问题在地区和平与安全进程中至关重要。

我相信，和平、稳定、合作、发展是我们的共同利益。从历史上看，世界各国各地区的经验表明，争端可以得到和平解决，而不一定非要引发冲突或对抗。我相信，只要我们有足够的诚意和政治智慧，就能共同努力，把南海建设成为和平、友好、合作的地区。

亚太地区安全秩序构建的历史经验与现实挑战

中国人民争取和平与裁军协会常务理事
中国社会科学院台湾研究所所长
杨明杰

相较于世界其他地区而言，亚太地区近三十年来一直保持相对稳定繁荣的整体态势，区域内的热点安全问题尽管此消彼长，但基本得到比较合理的危机管控。区域内从双边到多边的安全对话与合作机制建设也取得卓有成效的进展。这一安全态势的塑造和维护得益于本地区相关国家在经济上谋求自由开放、共同繁荣；安全上谋求综合施策、合作共赢；战略上谋求增信释疑、求同存异。然而这一良好安全态势正在遭受严峻挑战，亚太地区安全秩序的构建又到了新的历史拐点。

一、从历史经验看，亚太地区相对繁荣稳定局面的获得受益于该地区战略与发展和安全之间所形成的良性互动，共同、综合、合作、可持续的安全观在稳步践行中

第一，区域国家对经济与社会发展的重视和追求成为地区安全的重要基石。以发展谋安全、以发展促安全，在很大程度和相当范围内成为区域国家的共识。特别是亚洲地区的经济发展在近几十年中一直处于世界经济的前列，该地区的经济增长占世界经济增长的60%以上。经济的繁荣不仅有利于各国内部稳定和社会治理，而且向外传导，助推了区域经济合作的积极势头。共谋发展、共享繁荣理念指导下的各层次经贸合作机制在一定意义上也成为了地区安全关系的"压舱石"。区域和次区域层面上的各类经济合作架

构向安全领域传导着源源不断的正能量。

第二，安全领域的互信措施和机制化建设受到高度重视，并开始向经济和社会发展领域拓展。亚太地区虽然面临着不少安全上的分歧与难题，但在过去相当长的时间内，区域主要国家能以国家和地区利益的大局为重，积极构建不同渠道、不同方式的多层次安全对话渠道和互信机制。这些渠道和机制比较有效地削弱了相关国家在战略上的疑虑与具体问题上的分歧，并对一些敏感的热点难点问题进行了相对有效的危机管控。区域间的新型安全合作机制不仅在反恐、打击跨国犯罪等非传统安全领域取得实效，而且一些机制开始纳入经济与社会发展合作内容。发展与安全的结合发挥了促进地区稳定的能量倍增效应。

第三，主要大国虽存在不同程度的战略分歧，但普遍将对话与合作作为主要战略选项。区域内主要国家之间的结构性与非结构性矛盾长期存在，在一定时间和空间内甚至有所激化，但相关国家基本坚持不轻易触碰对方底线和红线，即使在危机过程中依然立足于战略管控。主要国家间这种战略选择的默契对地区安全稳定态势做出了积极贡献。

二、目前，亚太地区相对稳定的安全态势正在遭遇深层次战略威胁和挑战。战略与安全和发展之间所形成的良性互动有逆转的可能

一是在全球经济复苏乏力、全球化进程受阻的背景下，个别国家出于单边考虑疯狂挑战基于自由开放的地区经济合作秩序。正在进行区域经济一体化新进程的亚太合作前景被投下巨大阴影。经贸领域的单边主义、保护主义和霸凌行为不仅外溢到安全领域，而且对亚太地区人文交流产生极大的负面影响。基于这一地区人民共同追求的经济与安全观念遭受挑战。

二是安全合作架构的极端化认知和行为严重冲击现有稳定态势。一方面，个别国家拼凑新的以针对第三国为目标的盟国和伙伴关系网络，无端增加地区的紧张。另一方面，对已有的传统军事同盟提出新的要求，增大了地区盟友的战略选择难度，甚至制造了新的安全议题。

三是个别国家安全战略重回传统的大国对抗窠臼，加剧了地区紧张，并将对话与合作为主的战略选择调回对抗和压制为主。

面对新的威胁与挑战，我们必须认真总结历史经验，结合当前安全形势的发展，不断加强区域间的经济与安全对话和合作，联合抵御单边主义霸凌行为，反对某些大国战略选择的冒险和极端行为，重塑地区安全良性互动的新格局。

携手应对地区安全局势新调整

巴基斯坦前外秘
伊斯兰堡战略研究所所长
艾扎兹·乔杜里

　　二战以来所形成的世界秩序正在迅速瓦解。随着中国成长为经济巨头，其他一些国家寻求发展经济和军事实力，一个多极化的世界正在兴起，需要达成新的权力平衡。这一点在亚太地区尤为明显。中美关系正在转向以竞争为主，美国将中国视为"战略竞争者"甚至是敌人。一场"新冷战"正在萌芽。

　　美国特朗普政府奉行"美国优先"政策，多边主义日益被边缘化，狭隘民族主义、民粹主义抬头。福山认为，认同感是一个关于"我是谁"的综合性概念，国家、宗教、宗派、种族、性别等因素构成认同感的不同层面且相互影响。如今，不同群体间的隔阂加深，交流减少。

　　但全球化并未走向末路，国际社会中仍有推动世界向包容化方向发展的关键力量。如中国通过"一带一路"倡议和亚洲基础设施投资银行与欧亚国家开展经济合作。"一带一路"倡议希望提供互利共赢的经济和商业机会，实现60多个国家的互联互通。美国指责中国实施所谓的"债务陷阱外交"以拓展其在亚洲地区的影响力，宣称中国的野心是主导亚洲，但美国没有提供相关证据，难以服众。无论如何，中国领导人使全世界相信，全球化和互联互通最终将惠及全人类，有助于构建人类命运共同体。许多国家积极响应中国提出的互联互通倡议。上海合作组织也发展成为地区国家解决共同挑战的重要平台。

一、中美之间是否会有一战？

2018 年 1 月，美国发布《国防战略报告》，诬称中国追求实现军事现代化，把追求印太地区霸权作为短期目标，进而取代美国成为全球领导者。对此，中国外交部敦促美国立即停止此类故意歪曲中国战略意图的行为，抛弃冷战思维和零和博弈的旧观念。

中美贸易战持续升级，成为中美关系的"症结"，直接关乎两国能否实现国家安全目标。中美领导人都曾强调，经济安全就是国家安全。目前，中美贸易谈判陷入停滞，激进的民族主义言论增多。

美国还指责中国强制技术转让、盗窃知识产权、从事网络间谍活动以及其他不公平的贸易行为。最近几个月，华为事件使中美关系更为复杂。美西方国家认为，华为的技术将为中国政府预留入侵别国国防和安全系统的后门，必须予以抵制。但中国并未将这些举措单纯视作西方的安全关切，而更多认为是在遏制中国的发展。

美国领导人正在讨论要将军事重心从中东和阿富汗等地区冲突转向大国竞争。2019 年 6 月香格里拉对话会期间，美国指责中国试图通过军事现代化、提升影响力、对他国开展掠夺性和压迫性的经济行为来重塑地区秩序。在中美贸易争端背景下，此类言论无疑将进一步损害两国间的互信基础。

研究表明，对于彼此意图的误判将使两国跌入危险的"修昔底德陷阱"。两国要采取必要措施，避免冲突达到战争临界点。这需要成熟的领导力，谨慎处理两国关系面临的各类危机。

二、亚太地区成为全球地缘政治博弈的焦点

亚太地区地缘政治关系复杂，依旧是大国进行地缘战略和地缘经济竞争的主要场所，还未形成能够有效预防冲突的地区安全机制。多个权力中心并存的现状为美国等域外势力插手地区事务提供了便利。

未来，亚太地区或将呈现以下三种趋势：第一，中美战略竞争引发"新冷战"。美国将重塑中国在南亚、中亚和东亚地区的邻国，形成遏制中国之弧。而中国将采取相反策略跳出亚太地区，通过"一带一路"倡议开展域外经济合作，加强自身战略力量。同时，在朝鲜半岛问题和反恐政策上，中国依旧与美国保持对话与合作。第二，美国离间中俄关系防止形成反美同盟。一旦俄罗斯知晓美国战略意图，可能在中美之间寻求平衡，扩大自身在中亚和中东地区的影响力。第三，中美俄三国在亚太地区合作打击跨境恐怖主义，特别是打击伊斯兰极端主义。

南亚、中亚、东亚和中东（西亚）等地区，都已出现明显转变，以下调整更为突出：

南海地区：中国对美国在南海和西太平洋地区主张的航行自由极度关切。2019年上半年，美国、日本、菲律宾和印度在南海地区举行海军演习。南海地区的货物贸易额高达5万亿美元，其重要性不言而喻。美国支持和鼓励菲律宾、文莱、马来西亚、越南等东南亚国家在南海地区采取更为激进的手段寻求自由与开放，同时还支持印度在南海地区增加海军军事力量。

南亚地区：美国公开支持印度发展，以平衡中国的地区影响力。因此，美印都希望通过法律战、经济遏制政策和次常规战争战略将巴基斯坦变得更为中立化，避免巴阻碍印崛起。巴基斯坦则试图平衡中美利益，不希望加入反对中国的阵营。对于美印来讲，中巴对他们设计的亚太地区秩序构成挑战。阿富汗已经让美国陷入历时最久的战争之中，美国利用巴基斯坦为阿富汗问题降温。其他国家如孟加拉国、尼泊尔和不丹等，则屈从印度利益大幅调整其地区政策。

南亚地区紧张局势的主要根源在于印巴之间互不信任。作为拥核国，印巴都对维持南亚地区战略稳定负有责任。不幸的是，印度常常试探核威慑的红线，狂热扩充军备，奉行激进的战争宗旨，如"冷启动"、先发制人快速打击等作战理论，弱化不首先使用核武器的立场。近来，印度对巴基斯坦实施非常危险的动作，以发动外科手术式打击相威胁，2019年2月26日对巴方发动空袭。美印核协议使印度更具胆量，印度在2008年获得核供应国集团给予的特别豁免权，允许其在国际核市场上进行交易，并与英国、法国、日本和美国签署了民用核能合作协议。美印之间已经签署了《后勤交换协议备忘录》（LEMOA）和《通信、兼容与安全协议》（COMCASA），两国可以使用对方特定的军事设施，进一步增强了印军后勤与通讯能力。印度还拥有核潜艇，具备二次打击能力，给印度洋地区带来核武器威胁；加大弹道导弹防御技术研发，并于近期进行了反卫星试验。

上述事实清楚表明，印度的地区和全球野心正在膨胀，毫不顾忌南亚地区的战略稳定。而巴基斯坦始终严格实施可信任的最低核威慑，不愿被卷入军备竞赛的漩涡中。巴方认为，两个相邻的拥核国应采取负责任的行为方式。巴方致力于实现最高水平的核安全，从严进行出口管制，健全控制指挥系统。那么巴方保持克制、负责任地发展核项目，印度为何要如此激进地发展核项目？是因为印度图谋地区霸权，或希望成为全球性大国，或简单地选择了不负责任的核行为，抑或三个原因都有？

印度发动的普尔瓦马行动很能说明问题。印方不断降低核门槛，并将印巴传统对抗升级。2019年2月26日，印度军机入侵巴基斯坦领空，向一块空地投掷炸弹。2月27日，两架印度军机再次入侵，被巴方空军击落，一名飞行员被俘。试想一下，若巴方以牙还牙将会如何？印方是否考虑到这一行为可能引发的后果？与印方毫无责任感且违反国际法和国际规则的行为形成鲜明对比的是，巴方成熟应对，释放飞行员，展示和平姿态，避免局势升级。但印方领导层在接下来的竞选活动中依然继续威胁巴方。

更大的问题在于，拥核国如此不负责任的行为是否合理？印度希望国际社会相信自己是负责任的拥核国，但其在普尔瓦马威胁巴方主权和领土完整的行动，是否符合负责任拥核国的标准？美国及其他大国应客观公正地评价印度所作所为，切实推动南亚地区的和平与稳定。

中亚地区：中亚地区自然资源丰富，地处亚洲中心，战略位置重要，传统上被视为俄罗斯的后院，但现在成为中美角逐的另一战场。近来，中国在中亚地区投入巨额资金落实"一带一路"倡议，通过经济手段将这些国家与中国的不同省份连接起来。俄罗斯对中国在该地区的战略延伸提供支持。对美国来说，想要绕开俄罗斯影响力打入该地区并不容易（俄罗斯曾于2004年至2005年成功逆转了该地区的"颜色革命"）。俄罗斯与中亚各国在反恐与能源改革方面开展合作，扩大其影响力。

中亚各国希望其能源市场更为多样化，向南延伸至印度，向东延伸至中国。美国支持这一多样化举措，以降低俄罗斯对该地区的影响力。

中亚地区的热点问题是阿富汗问题，目前局面仍很混乱。当前，美国与塔利班就阿富汗和平进程举行谈判。破局点出现在美方原则上同意从阿富汗撤军，但具体时间表需进一步商议。塔利班承诺其控制的领土不会被恐怖主义利用。这是巨大的进步，但通往和平的道路依旧充满严峻挑战：第一，阿富汗各派系必须一致同意达成和平协议。为此，阿富汗内部对话至关重要。第二，阿富汗需要保持停火状态，而且各方必须作出停火承诺，建立执行机制。第三，阿富汗邻国和其他国家必须就阿和平达成一致，形成地区性共识。长期以来，阿富汗是代理人战争的受害者。美国主导下的阿富汗和平进程已经取得了积极进展，美国、俄罗斯、中国、巴基斯坦和其他国家都支持阿富汗和平进程。前进的道路尽管存在障碍，但阿富汗和平符合该地区利益。巴基斯坦已经深受阿富汗动乱之苦，和平、稳定和繁荣的阿富汗符合巴方利益，必将积极推动。

东南亚、东亚和太平洋地区：这是中美战略竞争最为激烈的地区，许多热点问题相互交织，主要包括：南海问题、朝鲜半岛问题和台湾问题。中国在该地区的应对也最为激烈。三个热点问题近期都有向军事行动发展的趋势，恐将爆发更大规模的冲突。此外，东南亚地区扼守马六甲海峡，中国、日本和其他国家进口的石油和天然气大多经过此地。

该地区经济活力充沛，保持了高速增长。在全球经济低迷的背景下，东南亚因其成本优势成为制造业的聚集地。由此，东盟国家的地区事务话语权增加。

在东亚地区，美国试图让朝鲜保持冷静，但实际效果有限。在台湾问题上，中国向外界发出了其坚定维护一个中国原则的承诺。美国多次挑战中国忍耐限度，但至今未跨越中方设定的红线。

中东地区：中东局势依旧动荡，巴勒斯坦危机悬而未决，恐怖主义持续泛滥。伊拉克、叙利亚和利比亚政局不稳，暴乱时有发生。也门爆发代理人战争。伊朗和沙特的紧张局势引发地区国家关注。近期美伊僵局让中东地区处于战争边缘，美国退出《关于伊朗核计划的全面协议》（JCPOA）是多边外交的倒退。美国持续对伊朗施加制裁阻碍了伊朗与地区和全球的经济与商业往来。

俄罗斯积极介入叙利亚危机，在中东的影响力有所提升。尽管中东地区与中国在地理上并不相连，但后者依赖波斯湾地区的能源供给。在这一地区，中国的影响力仍维持在较低水平，似乎希望加大与波斯湾地区的经济联系，美欧则继续享有在该地区的重要影响力。

三、亚太地区安全局势前景的三种可能性

影响地区安全秩序的主要因素包括：全球性大国与地区大国间的关系、地区大国对强权政治的态度、全球性大国对地区大国决策的影响力。从上述三个要素出发，我们看到，中美竞争将引发地区安全新挑战，对亚洲各国产生直接影响。在缺乏地区安全架构的情况下，所有亚洲国家都有责任为维护地区安全与稳定作出贡献。

未来，亚太地区安全局势或将产生三种可能情况：第一，中美两国在南海或台湾海峡擦枪走火，爆发有限冲突。近段时间以来，两国军舰已发生数次危险对峙。同时，地区紧张局势正在加剧，美国领导的海军演习恐成为有限冲突的导火索。中国应将关注重点从发展转移至预防冲突上来。第二，地区进入所谓的"冷战"状态，既无战争，也谈不上和平。中美两国仍能在战略层面管控分歧，但亚太地区将出现新形式的隐蔽战争，地区国家被迫选边站队。印度已经先行一步，升级对巴基斯坦的战争和恐怖主义威胁。第三，达成特朗普所说的"世纪交易"，中美两国协商谈判，重新划定各自在新的全球权力平衡中的角色和责任。中国已不时向美发出信号，希望与美合作应对全球问题。中美两国间互信水平降低，中美合作需要美国内政或中国经济

出现重要变化，或由其他不可预测因素予以推动。

　　此外还有其他可能性。当下，世界或者是亚太地区面临的最大现实威胁是民粹主义和极端民族主义的兴起，目前还未找到有效的应对方法。因此，我们或许应为更加不稳定的地区安全形势未雨绸缪。

泰国视角下的地区安全秩序新调整

泰国国家研究院泰中战略研究中心主任

退役陆军上将

苏拉西·塔纳唐

当前，亚太地区安全秩序正在发生深刻变化。美国特朗普政府的亚太战略已经转向。在"美国优先"政策指导下，美国高举单边主义和贸易保护主义旗帜，突出军事力量优势和威慑作用，打破国际多边贸易体制和规则，对中国发动贸易战。这不仅给其亚太盟国，也给地区安全带来更大的不确定性。美国和印度、日本、澳大利亚等地区重要国家根据各自能力和利益，参与并发起了"印太战略"等各种地区安全与发展议程，正在改变该地区的地缘政治格局。

在东南亚，由于国情和自然禀赋的差异，各国内外政策存在既竞争又合作的关系。与亚太秩序演变的不确定性相反，面对新的机遇与挑战的泰中关系显示出较强的互信和韧性。我们秉持"泰中血脉相连"的理念，全面理解和推动"一带一路"合作。自此，泰中两国在国际和地区多边机制中加强交流与相互支持，在人文交流中加强风险防控与危机管理，从更宏观的视角看待和发展泰中关系，使双边关系行稳致远，也为地区稳定与繁荣作出贡献。

纵观亚洲安全形势发展变化，可以看到中美力量均势导致的四大主要现象，这些现象可视为新的地区安全观在亚洲产生的新影响：一是"2.0版华盛顿共识"使美国在世界地缘政治中扮演重要角色。二是美国未能遏制中国崛起，亚太地区出现"中印轴心"。三是在美国仍然控制世界霸权的情况下出现了"多极力量平衡"。四是中国影响力的增强导致"新两极化"出现，但未来仍将面临诸多问题和挑战。

由于东盟不是一个主权国家，许多地区"安全智囊团"都在探讨对"新的地区安全观"的看法，并暗示美中这两个超级大国一直在相互竞争，通过"印太战略"和"一带一路"倡议传播其影响力，以便在世界各地获得竞争优势。来自"印太战略"和"一带一路"倡议的影响既包括美中力量均势带来的好处，也包括美中两国为争取东盟对自身战略和倡议的支持，而向东盟提出不同建议所带来的好处等等。然而，大多数东盟成员国都在"印太战略"和"一带一路"倡议的不平等和缺乏透明度，以及部分东盟成员国的理念和行动影响东盟统一性这样的局面中受到不利影响。泰国作为一个小国，必须管理好有关双边关系和与"印太战略""一带一路"倡议相关的谈判，这可以使各方共同获益，而不会引起东盟与域外国家的冲突。

地区安全秩序新调整可聚焦人类社会发展合作的新目标和新方式，而不是"权力竞争"。

共建"一带一路"反映了人类对美好未来的共同期待，但部分地区和国际社会仍未认同"一带一路"所倡导的构建人类命运共同体理念。有人质疑这是否是"华人共同体"？实际上，构建人类命运共同体理念符合世界经济发展的需要和世界文明进步的方向。

在东盟国家，"一带一路"倡议正在成为地区互联互通的重要平台。"一带一路"倡议充分体现了非竞争性和非排他性，反映了国际社会对建立一个公正、平等、开放、包容的全球治理体系的要求，是面向当今世界的重要公共产品。正如联合国秘书长古特雷斯所指出的，"一带一路"倡议与联合国千年发展目标有着共同的目的，都是向世界提供公共产品。共建"一带一路"不仅促进了国际贸易和人文交流，也增进了各国之间的了解，减少了文化壁垒，最终将实现和平、和谐与繁荣。

基于民族思想与和平行动原则的"智慧竞争"，是共享未来地区安全和世界和平的关键途径和手段，关于这一点还存在争议。孔子的"和而不同"可被看作是"多样之美"，这是人与自然的现实。生活的艺术则指引人们如何在多元文化中和平共处，在世界许多地方被证明是可行的，中国和泰国就是一个例子。"东方智慧"强调好好思考、好好说话、好好做事，也意味着

"己所不欲、勿施于人"。

展望未来，地区安全秩序调整应更多注重以下几个方面：

第一，建设法律体系。法律体系是地区安全合作中不可逾越的道德原则和法律红线。在联合国有关国际公约和双边条约的基础上开展法律合作，为双方在国家层面的经济合作提供制度保障，有效营造积极友好的国际投资和营商环境。

第二，拓展沟通渠道。由于世界各国联系日益紧密，相互理解就变得更加重要。经济的崛起、社会的颠覆、非传统的挑战都会给人类带来越来越多的不利条件。应在地区内部和国家层面建立或恢复横向与纵向联系，这不仅有利于经济社会发展，而且有利于整个地区安全。

第三，促进人文交流。人文交流日益密切，加深了各国人民特别是"一带一路"沿线国家人民的相互了解。本地区各国应该建立多层次的人文交流机制，加强在历史文化遗产保护、对外开放和文物保护、联合考古等方面的合作。最后特别重要的是，我们应该加强政党、非政府组织、妇女和青年之间的交流，以促进包容性的地区安全发展。

安全理念的演变与东北亚安全治理

俄罗斯国际事务委员会研究员

尤里·库林采夫

东北亚是亚洲的一个次区域，指与太平洋接壤的东北大陆和岛屿。它包括东亚核心国家及其邻国，这些国家在历史、地理、经济、政治、文化方面都相互联系。从这个意义上讲，东北亚的核心国家是中国、日本、蒙古、朝鲜和韩国。大多数情况下，鉴于该地区的共同问题及其相互渗透影响，东北亚与美国和俄罗斯远东地区的联系被单列出来，这既扩大了东北亚概念本身的内容，也对该地区国家战略方针的形成与发展产生了特殊影响。

为建立一个全球安全体系，最好在理解该地区时区分几个层次，即宏观区域层面和次区域层面。前者包括蒙古高原、东北平原、朝鲜半岛和俄罗斯远东的山区，西起勒拿河，东至太平洋，再加上美国西北海岸；后者包括日本列岛、朝鲜半岛和中国东北地区在内的范围，从历史和地理上看，具体指的是中国、朝鲜、韩国和日本。这种区分，可以更准确地界定次区域国家与其周边国家间可能存在的互动关系，而这些周边国家在亚太地区也扮演着权力中心的角色。

一、概述

2011—2012 年开始的亚洲转型进程，严重破坏了亚太各国本已脆弱的政治权力平衡。尽管仍然存在不断出现的新威胁，以及对外部因素和域外行为体的高度依赖，这些进程也凸显了形成一个更稳定的地区体系的新机遇。

大规模杀伤性武器扩散威胁、永久性冲突、国际恐怖主义、国家危机是亚洲各国面临的主要挑战。域内主要行为体之间互信程度低，以及域外行为体在该地区的永久性存在仍然是关键问题。目前，尚未建成能够解决东北亚各国发展问题的有效地区性机构，特别是缺乏维持和加强安全局势的区域内体制基础。尚未解决的领土争端以及朝鲜半岛核问题是加剧这种不稳定的主要因素。克服这一局面需要朝鲜与其邻国建立和加强互信，当然也必须考虑到所有亚洲国家的利益。因此，有必要尽一切努力来建立和发展全球安全治理体系。

尽管这一倡议包含着积极的信息，但建立这样一种体系将引发许多争议。这在很大程度上是由于参与该地区事务的国家（中国、俄罗斯和美国的同盟国）在建立和发展安全体系的途径和方法上存在显著差异。域内国家之间现有的关系将对这一进程产生重大影响，这些国家在危机时刻所选择的优先事项也将起到决定性作用。然而，当今世界，特别是东北亚国家所面临的威胁和挑战，使该地区整体复杂的体系结构发生了一定变化。

二、东北亚安全治理中涉及的问题

东北亚主要国家都面临着同样的安全威胁，其中最重要的是朝鲜半岛核问题。另一个挑战是东北亚国家需要适应中国经济的增长及其影响。由于西方国家对俄罗斯的制裁，俄美合作跌至有史以来最低水平，而且这种情况还在恶化。然而，尽管这些国家在安全理念和全球治理体系的处理方式上存在差异，但也存在许多共同利益，在这些有共同利益的领域开展合作对本地区和域内各国都是有益的。

许多专家认为，未来十年内，亚太地区将成为世界上最重要的经济和政治中心。不能把该地区的长期稳定与和平视为理所当然，许多安全挑战都可能破坏这种稳定。

该地区的主要热点是朝鲜半岛核问题。外国军事介入（美国领导人已宣布这是可能的选项）代价太高，后果严重，因而不可接受。以下几个理由也可说明这一点：首先，军事行动不被联合国安理会批准，只会破坏目前由联合国保障的国际秩序。其次，它会给参与国和周边国家造成巨大的人道主义灾难和经济损失。最后，从安全理念的角度看，这将终结该地区持续了50多年的和平局面，可能促使其他国家将来也把使用武力作为选项之一。这意味着，成功的军事行动即使不会立即引发全面军事冲突，也可能在未来引发更激烈的战争。

与此同时，朝鲜成功利用了2018年平昌冬奥会开启的机会窗口。2018年4月底，朝韩领导人举行了会晤，随后在新加坡举行了具有历史意义的朝美首脑会晤。朝鲜领导人与韩国总统文在寅、中国国家主席习近平举行了一系列会晤，并与美国总统特朗普在河内举行了第二次会晤，与普京总统在符拉迪沃斯托克举行高级别会谈，证实了朝鲜外交政策的活跃性，也给国际社会带来了希望，全球战争不太可能爆发。但目前尚难确定这些事件是国际安全治理的突破，是朝鲜半岛长期稳定的标志，抑或只是暂时正常化的迹象。

另一个值得东北亚国家关注的安全治理问题是中国的崛起及其日益增长的经济、政治和军事实力。日本和美国认为这是对全球秩序的挑战。在讨论安全理念时，应考虑到全球秩序变化和亚洲国家日益增长的责任可能产生的长期后果。一些专家认为，如果中国决定挑战美国主导的世界秩序，那么该地区的安全平衡将发生变化。

东北亚地区国家关系的特点是体制基础薄弱。违反国际机构制度和条例限制了合作的机会，并对东北亚各国之间的互信、力量平衡和国家共存产生了破坏性影响。该地区的问题表现为长期存在"无法解决"的冲突。地区国家之间也存在破坏性竞争。由于该地区缺乏明确的"领头羊"，渴望获得地区领导权的国家之间的竞争给地区总体安全带来了消极影响。

我们还必须承认，全球治理机构（主要是联合国）在解决东北亚问题上存在弱点。在解决地区危机方面，联合国往往既拿不出统一的做法，也没有有效手段来监控局势和执行已通过的决议。由于缺乏辅助性的地区机构，联合国的任何行动都会遇到不断出现的障碍而无法推进。另外，我们也应认识到该地区资源缺乏、制度多样、各国发展目标迥异的现实。

战略平衡和安全治理对东北亚地区至关重要。2014年乌克兰危机后，特别是 2016 年美国总统大选被指受俄罗斯干扰后，俄美矛盾进一步加剧，这些都不利于维护该地区安全局势，不利于构建区内互信。

三、在东北亚地区塑造全球安全治理体系的条件和机遇

今天，该地区内外环境都在发生变化，这可能对在一个广义的东北亚地区建立全球安全体系的谈判产生不同的推动力。建立由地区国家领导人组成的临时工作组（或采用类似形式）似乎是最合适的解决方案。从战略上讲，最恰当的选择是建立一个全面的安全体系，在这一体系框架内的生产活动很大程度上与发展一体化项目有关，其中与经济和基础设施建设有关的国家间项目将是至关重要的。

各国都对加强当前的区域多边合作形式、机制评估、促进国际对话，以及防止将具体问题政治化持积极立场。

在解决东北亚安全治理问题时，应优先考虑以下目标：缩小"安全困境"，恢复国家间互信；促进广义的东北亚地区的和平与稳定；促进该地区不稳定国家的有效政治过渡。

全球安全治理的优先任务包括：为参与塑造全球安全体系的国家之间建立信任措施创造条件；加强核不扩散体系，建立无核区；确保各国之间、新地区体系与联合国之间的互动，以确保全面安全；监测"实地"情况；确保冲突后人口非军事化，以及包括大规模杀伤性武器在内的军备控制。

先前指出的东北亚国家之间缺乏互信是发展地区内和地区间关系的严重障碍。在东北亚建立全球安全体系，可直接与加强现有地区机制联系起来，比如亚洲相互协作与信任措施会议（CICA）、上海合作组织（SCO）和亚洲合作对话（ACD）。这些平台都可用于就加强东北亚全球安全治理前景开展工作讨论。

俄中两国支持维护和坚持国家主权平等原则，支持加强联合国和多边机构在推动普遍参与国际多边合作方面的作用。此外，专家们呼吁要防止对其他国家事务进行非法国际干预，要使核技术既不能出口给潜在的恐怖主义组

织，也不能出口给亚洲地区其他国家。

俄罗斯在东北亚的国家利益是由其远东地区发展需要所决定的。普京总统指出，发展远东地区是俄 21 世纪的国家优先事项，这意味着与中、韩、日等地区主要国家保持和平友好关系是俄远东经济发展的前提。俄外交政策的主要纲领性文件——《国家安全战略》（2015）和《俄罗斯外交政策理念》（2016），都确认朝鲜半岛是世界紧张局势的发源地之一。与此同时，俄方立场与美日两国相反，美日指责朝鲜是造成紧张局势的唯一过错方。俄方一贯主张朝鲜半岛无核化，并将以一切可能的方式推进半岛无核化。俄方还宣布将以政治对话作为唯一可能的手段，努力降低对抗水平，缓和朝鲜半岛紧张局势，推动建立半岛和平机制，推动发展南北合作。

无论是俄罗斯政治领导人的任何声明，还是任何计划文件，都不包含担忧中国崛起的观点。相反，俄罗斯优先任务之一是促进与中国在所有领域的合作。俄中都认为，多极世界比美国霸权下的单极世界更可取。

俄日两国在安全治理领域的关系遇到一些困难。一方面，日本效仿西方国家于 2014 年对俄实施制裁。另一方面，专家们认为，这些制裁是象征性的，对双边经济关系几乎没有影响。此外，2016 年日本首相安倍晋三访俄和俄罗斯总统普京访日，以及两人在不同国际场合的多次会晤，都显示了两国关系的积极发展态势。2017 年两国恢复"2+2 会晤"（国防部部长和外交部部长），确认两国将安全治理讨论和军事领域合作作为重要目标。过去几年来，俄日关系有所加强，但在缔结和平条约和解决领土争端方面仍然存在问题，要解决这些问题还有很长的路要走。

朝鲜半岛安全治理的一个途径是支持对话和相互停止进攻性行为。最好的例子是俄中提出的"双暂停"倡议。另一种处理办法是美国提出来的。美方希望在朝鲜建立无核区，以将朝鲜遭受核打击的威胁和实际可能性降到最低。美方战略是将对话和施压结合起来。特朗普因其轻率的言行受到批评，因为这些言行可能带来严重后果，但他明确表示其目标不是推翻朝鲜政权。这意味着现任美国总统不像其前任那样，卷入类似中东地区旷日持久、代价高昂的冲突。特朗普不想在乌克兰危机的背景下，与任何地区国家发生冲突，就像俄美之间曾经发生过的一样。从中可以看出，俄美解决半岛问题的方法差别更多存在于战术层面而非战略层面。

任何一体化倡议都应以各国领土完整和平等原则为基础，同时预设地区内和不同地区间互动的可能性。在继续支持无核化谈判努力的同时，有必要落实外交倡议，协调朝鲜最高领导人与韩国政府的立场，为朝鲜半岛政治过渡创造必要条件。

亚洲危机的多重性增强了其影响的累积效应。没有一个全面的集体性措施，就不可能解决这些危机。在特定区域内出现的这种"多要素"安全挑战，可以为旨在克服危机的联合行动奠定基础。

全球安全治理将推动地区与全球和平稳定的整个发展进程，为解决地区各国面临的发展任务创造条件。尽管东北亚国家的信任危机不断恶化，安全问题日益突出，但建立全面的安全治理体系似乎是稳定该地区局势的最有效办法。

美国的印太战略与亚洲安全秩序

中国人民争取和平与裁军协会理事
北京大学国际关系学院副教授
韩华

2017 年 11 月，特朗普总统在越南举行的亚太经合组织峰会上的讲话中第一次明确提出了美国印太战略的轮廓与构想，这标志着特朗普政府亚洲政策的出台，也让在政策圈中酝酿 10 年之久的"印太"概念正式在美国政府官方政策中得到体现。2019 年 6 月，美国国防部发表《美国的印太战略报告》全面系统地阐述了美国的印太战略，至此印太战略正式取代了奥巴马政府时期的"亚太再平衡"成为特朗普政府的美国亚洲战略。作为一个将印太地区视为战略重心的世界霸权国，美国对该地区战略的制定与调整势必对该地区政治、经济及安全等各个领域带来重要影响，亚洲安全秩序也会因此发生变化。

一、特朗普的印太战略

印太的概念在 2007 年前后就时常出现在印度、澳大利亚等国的智库报告或学者文章中，但除了日本首相安倍晋三将印太概念提升到日本官方的印度洋太平洋两洋战略并在 2007 年访问印度期间向印度推销该战略外，印太概念一直没有成为有关国家的官方战略。奥巴马政府期间，美国虽然显示出对印太概念的兴趣，但官方文件中仍以"亚太与印度洋"称呼这一地区。

特朗普上台后即对该概念产生兴趣，将其引入到自己的亚洲战略中。在2017 年亚太经合组织越南峰会的发言中，"印太"的构想成为特朗普发言的基调。如果说特朗普在越南的讲话更多是从经济与贸易的角度阐释美国的印太构想的话，美国国防部发表的《印太战略报告》则从安全的角度阐释美国印太战略。特朗普讲话与《印太战略报告》构成了美国印太战略的基本内容，主要包括：

第一，在历数美国与印太地区的紧密联系和美国在该地区强有力的政治、经济、军事存在的基础上，强调该地区是美国未来最重要的区域，并宣示美国在该地区的利益与维护这些利益的决心，同时提出美国倡导的原则，即以规则与原则为基础的国际秩序，经济上强调公正与相互性，安全上强调开放与自由。

第二，在列举了该地区各种不同的安全挑战的基础上，突出地缘政治的挑战与威胁，并将中、俄、朝定性为对印太安全的挑战者。其中，强调中国试图通过其军事现代化、战略行动及经济杠杆对其他国家实施强权，以期改变地区秩序。为了应对这些地缘政治挑战，美国宣誓会通过加强竞争、威慑以及赢得战争来维持地区秩序。

第三，在重申美国在该地区的盟友与战略伙伴的重要性及其对盟友、战略伙伴的安全承诺、加强彼此间合作的同时，要求这些国家承担与所获安全承诺相应的成本。

第四，在对安全威胁重新评估的基础上做出军事能力、人力、物力的重新配置、制定新的战法、提出各种倡议以及加强美国与其认为重要国家之间的关系。

从以上内容来看，特朗普印太战略有以下几个主要特征：第一，特朗普的印太战略是在美国战略界对当今美国整体实力相对下降的大背景下应该在战略上"积极介入"还是"理性收缩"争论的一个妥协产物。特朗普提出的"美国优先"与他反复强调美国盟友应承担自身安全责任的主张反映了某种战略收缩的态势，但其强调如今是大国竞争的时代又使美国需要在世界地缘政治的中心扮演积极角色。因此，印太战略所采取的态势介乎于在印太维持美国的强势存在与该地区盟友要适当分摊安全责任之间。特朗普政府在印太战略框架下构建起的"四国安全对话"（The Quad）机制从某种程度上就是这种分担安全责任的安排。其中，日本与澳大利亚可以在亚太地区为美国做战略协助，将印度拉入美国的印太战略也是期待印度在印度洋扮演安全上的"净提供者"的角色。第二，大国竞争是特朗普印太战略的主要目标与利益所在，反恐及其他非结构性的安全问题不再是主导美国亚洲政策的主要依据。其中，中国和俄罗斯被视为印太地区的主要对手，中美、俄美关系中的对抗性明显增加。过去 20 年美国对华政策中的"接触""两面下注"的成分逐渐减弱，遏制色彩明显增强。第三，地理上，印太是亚太的扩展，是奥巴马"亚洲再平衡"战略空间的扩展。美国将在印度洋与太平洋——比亚太地区更大的空间内形成对中国的牵制（如果不是围堵的话）。如果奥巴马的"亚洲再平衡"战略的重心是南中国海及邻近区域的话，特朗普的印太战略的重心则是太平洋与印度洋以及中国"一带一路"的沿线地区。第四，特朗普印太战略将更多地通过在该地区建立美国与盟友和战略伙伴之间的合作"网络"加以实施。这就是说，美国在加强与其亚洲盟友、伙伴合作与协调的同时，强调加强盟友与伙伴之间的合作与协调，以此打造印太安全的"天罗地网"。

二、现有亚洲安全秩序

在许多人眼中，亚洲缺乏地区性的安全安排与机制，因此，有人对亚洲冷战结束以来没有发生过战争的事实极为不解，至少一些人认为亚洲的和平与稳定充满不确定性。然而，尽管与欧洲的安全秩序显著不同，亚洲确实存在着其特有的秩序。

冷战结束后的 30 年，亚洲安全架构由两个并存的系统构成。一个是美国建立起来的以美国为中心、以美国与亚洲盟友之间双边安全同盟为主要形式的"轮轴—辐条"的安全体系。其中，美日同盟被视为美国亚洲安全战略的基石，外加美韩、美澳、美菲等双边同盟与伙伴关系。这一双边同盟为主的体系中，美国以自己的军事实力优势为支撑，为盟国提供安全保障，包括核保障。这种安排使美国在亚洲安全事务中扮演着支配角色，也成为美国人视其为亚洲安全保障者的主要依据。30 年来，尽管亚洲国家提出过地区性安全倡议，但都不足以撼动美国的这一"轮轴—辐条"的安全体系。

在美国主导的安全体系外，亚洲还存在一个以东盟为主导的亚洲安全体系，这一体系与欧洲的安全体系有着显著的区别。与欧洲以"北约"为主要机制、以正式同盟条约约定的成员国担负安全义务的安排不同，亚洲的安全机制更多的是强调"合作性安全"。合作性安全没有条约绑定的成员国义务；没有特定的敌人；以"宣示性"外交为主要协调形式。这一体系通过亚太经济合作组织、东盟地区论坛、"东盟10+"的形式加强安全问题的协调与沟通，也取得了中国、美国与其他大国的支持或接受。尽管一些人对这种安全架构的效力存有质疑，但在冷战结束以来长期存在并得到发展，成为小国联盟主导、大国协调的合作性安全实践。

三、特朗普印太战略对现有亚洲安全秩序的影响

如上所述，特朗普政府的印太战略呈现出新内容与特征，这些新内容与特征不仅是特朗普政府根据其对当今国际关系新现实进行评估基础上对前一届美国政府亚洲政策的调整，也意味着这一新战略对现存亚洲安全秩序产生深远影响。具体表现在以下几个方面：

1. 印太战略对美国原有的"轮轴—辐条"的亚洲秩序产生冲击。由于美国对亚洲安全挑战的来源有新的解读，中、俄、朝（在亚洲更多的是中国）成为美国地缘政治上不同层级的对手，美国政策界的一些人认为，原有的以美国的双边同盟为主的同盟体系已经不能应对新的安全挑战，要对盟国体系进行重新构建。重新建构从奥巴马政府时期美国试图使美日、美韩同盟三边化的尝试中得到了某种体现，尽管这一努力没有成功。如今，特朗普政府对亚洲同盟体系的重新构建又出现了新的取向。第一，美国提出重新启动并构建美日澳印"四国安全对话"机制。这一尝试虽然出现过曲折，其努力是否能成功也备受质疑，但近期美国推动该机制发展的力度在加强。最近，四国外长在参加联合国大会期间进行会晤，使这一长期维持在司局级层面的

对华机制首次提升到部长级。第二，美国鼓励美国的盟友与战略伙伴之间加强协调与沟通，由此打造以美国为主的安全伙伴网络，以这一网络制衡中国的继续崛起。

2. 由于特朗普的印太战略是应对"大国竞争"所提出的，因此，大国之间的地缘政治之争成为印太地区的"主旋律"，这客观上影响了以东盟为代表的小国在该地区舞台上原有的显著角色，因而弱化了"东盟主导、大国协调"的地区安全体系。不仅如此，随着中美之间相对实力的逐渐接近，美国政策圈中"中美权力转移"的言论日益流行，中美关系中对抗性日益明显。结果是，小国发现自己越来越多地被迫在中美之间选边。中美之间的回旋余地正在缩小，小国维持原有平衡外交空间的努力越来越艰难，出现了小国在经济上倾向中国，安全上倾向美国的两难抉择。这种结果间接使亚洲原有的"合作性安全"架构面临诸多挑战。

综上所述，自特朗普执政后，对奥巴马的"亚太再平衡战略"做出了大幅度的调整，将再平衡战略中显示出的"大国竞争"色彩进一步加强，将中国等国更清晰地界定为"修正主义"国家并视为对美国治下的亚洲秩序形成挑战的对手。在此基础上，提出了一系列应对"挑战"的对策与政策，包括对原有的同盟体系进行重构，并将应对挑战的地区从传统的亚太地区扩展到印度洋。这些新发展对亚洲现有的安全秩序构成了冲击，也对该地区的和平与稳定产生了负面影响。

日本"自由和开放的印度洋—太平洋战略"的演变

日本中曾根康弘世界和平研究所高级研究员
庆应义塾大学法学系教授
细谷雄一

一、概述

自 2016 年 8 月 27 日日本首相安倍晋三在第六届东京非洲发展国际会议（TICAD VI）开幕式上提出新的外交政策理念以来，日本"自由和开放的印度洋—太平洋战略"（FOIP）引发了对未来印度洋—太平洋地区秩序的更广泛辩论。

此前，从未有日本首相提出过如此全球瞩目的外交政策愿景。如果安倍能继续执政到 2019 年 11 月 20 日，他将超过桂太郎（Katsura Taro），成为日本立宪政府历史上任职时间最长的首相。由于在日本国会拥有稳定的多数席位，安倍有能力致力于实现 FOIP 这样一个长期的外交政策愿景。

安倍在当今国际政治中的作用十分重要。他已成为 G7 峰会上任职时间第二长的领导人，仅次于德国总理默克尔。此外，安倍在维护以规则为基础的国际秩序方面发挥着重要作用。特朗普当选美国总统后不久，普林斯顿大学教授约翰·伊肯伯里（John Ikenberry）为《外交事务》杂志撰文写道，自由国际秩序的未来"将落在日本首相安倍晋三和德国总理默克尔的肩上，目前只有这两位重要领导人支持这一观点"。同样，兰德公司安全专家杰弗里·贺南（Jeffrey Hornung）认为，"在安倍晋三首相领导下，日本在支持国际秩序方面的作用尤为显著"。贺南还指出，"这是安倍更广泛的自由和开放的印太战略的一部分,特朗普政府后来支持了这一战略,这让日本在保护该地区的自由、法治和市场经济方面承担起更大责任"。

另一方面,日本的 FOIP 也招致了多方批评。美国卡内基国际和平基金会中国问题专家迈克尔·史文(Michael Swaine)警告说:"FOIP 可能产生相反的效果,激怒北京,使其他亚洲国家感到恐慌,并使该地区面临高度紧张的零和博弈。"

FOIP 是一个模糊的概念。阿布扎比哈利法大学教授阿什·罗西特(Ash Rossiter)指出,"关于 FOIP 实际上意味着什么,人们几乎没有共识,更不用说它可能影响日本未来外交政策的方式"。本文虽然承认罗西特的观点,即 FOIP 确实是一个模糊的概念,但日本目前版本的 FOIP 不同于安倍曾在其文章中提出的"亚洲的民主安全钻石"。由于日本目前版本的 FOIP 对抗性较低,分歧较小,与中国的合作意愿也更明显,因此它应该被称为"2.0 版FOIP"。

二、1.0 版 FOIP 的起源

日本政府在 2016 年 8 月首次发布"自由和开放的印度洋—太平洋"概念之前,从未正式使用过这个词。然而,2006 年 9 月安倍就任日本首相后,日本政府经常暗示印太地区民主国家之间的合作应成为该地区秩序的核心。

1.0 版 FOIP 源自 2007 年 8 月 22 日安倍首相在印度议会发表的政策演讲。安倍认为,"通过日本和印度以这种方式走到一起,这个'更广阔的亚洲'将发展成为一个横跨整个太平洋、包括美国和澳大利亚在内的巨大网络。这个开放透明的网络将允许人员、货物、资本和信息自由流动。"安倍在讲话中提到了 FOIP 的重要组成部分,如开放、自由、更广阔的亚洲以及美国、澳大利亚、印度和日本之间的合作。安倍还在演讲中提出了有关"两洋交融"的愿景。他说:"这个新的'更广阔的亚洲'正在印度洋和太平洋的交汇处形成,当务之急是位于这两个大洋沿岸的民主国家应在各个可能的层面上加深人民之间的友谊。"

　　与此同时，安倍政府推行了一项名为"自由与繁荣之弧"的长期战略。"这一战略是以价值观为导向的外交，旨在促进欧亚大陆的民主、自由、人权和法治，在普世价值观的基础上构建一个富裕和稳定的地区。"这在地缘政治上与 FOIP 所指的区域有很大程度的重叠。

　　我们也可以从日本官员人选方面找到一些线索。安倍首相国家安全顾问、日本国家安全保障局（NSS）局长谷内正太郎，曾在安倍首任政府（2006—2007 年）中任外务省事务次官，NSS 副局长金原信胜（Nobukatsu Kanehara）曾任外务省政策协调局局长。2006 年 10 月"自由与繁荣之弧"的起草者都是安倍第二任政府期间 FOIP 的主要设计者。

　　日本的这些举措可被视为对中国迅速崛起的回应。日本的政策制定者正试图塑造一个地区秩序，而不是由中国来塑造。日本认为，美国、印度、澳大利亚和日本应该成为这一地区架构的主要参与者，因为它们拥有民主、自由和法治等共同的核心价值观。因此，日本政府在此期间开始推动与澳大利亚和印度的安全合作。2007 年 5 月，在安倍首相和时任美国副总统切尼的倡议下，启动了第一次"四方安全对话"（QUAD）。

　　QUAD 面临几个困难。首先，中国政府认为这种安全合作是包围中国。因此，中方通过加强与日本和澳大利亚的双边合作，对这一倡议提出批评。澳大利亚麦考瑞大学的拉维娜·李（Lavina Lee）指出，"日本首次试图在日本、澳大利亚、印度和美国之间建立更深入的战略合作，2007 年的'四方安全对话'是一次短暂的实验，最终因为中国的强烈反对和澳、日、美当政者的下台而失去动力"。李还指出，"安倍首相被广泛认为是 QUAD 背后的主要人物，得到了美国布什政府，特别是时任美国副总统切尼的坚定支持"。之后不久安倍卸任，日本新一届政府把 QUAD 搁置起来，开始加强与中国的合作。日本时任首相福田康夫和时任澳大利亚总理陆克文都认为发展与中国领导人的友好关系比推进 QUAD 更为重要。

　　第二，一些东盟国家对 QUAD 的发展表示严重关切，认为这似乎违背"东盟中心地位"的基本原则。在此之前，亚洲区域合作一直以东盟为中心，东盟国家不希望看到该地区出现大国主导的局面。

第三，奥巴马领导的美国政府开始将美中双边关系放在优先于 QUAD 的位置。美国政府内部有一种乐观的看法，认为美国可以与当时作为世界第二大经济体的中国发展友好的双边伙伴关系。当时正值美日双边关系陷入困境，部分原因是时任日本首相鸠山由纪夫在普天间美军基地搬迁问题上处理失当。

2008 年以来，中国开始变得更加自信，特别是在中国南海和东海问题上。2010 年 9 月，中国渔船在钓鱼岛（日本称尖阁诸岛）附近海域与日本巡逻船相撞，成为日本官方和公众舆论风向的重要转折点，日本政府开始更加警惕中国在周边地区的活动。奥巴马政府注意到与中国建立合作关系有困难，日本也意识到有必要用不同方式来应对中国崛起。

大约在这个时期，一些专家开始撰写关于印太区域新概念的文章。例如，迈克尔·奥斯林（Michael Auslin）在为美国企业研究所撰写的一份报告中写道："印太地区的经济实力、军事实力和政治活力，将使其在未来几十年成为世界上最重要的地区，其影响力将遍及全球。"奥斯林鼓励美国及其盟友制定印太地区战略。2011 年，澳大利亚罗伊研究所的罗里·梅德卡夫（Rory Medcalf）和拉乌尔·海因里希斯（Raoul Heinrichs）也在文章中强调印太概念的重要性。同样，大卫·斯科特（David Scott）2012 年在为《亚太评论》杂志撰写的文章中写道："印太地区的政治实践涉及将两个大洋紧密联系在一起的制度框架和国家间行动。"

在日本，日本防卫学院教授神谷万丈（Matake Kamiya）等安全专家开始关注印太地区对安倍政府外交政策的重要性。2013 年 2 月 22 日，神谷在华盛顿发表演讲时指出了安倍首相运用印太区域概念的重要性。安倍晋三可以说是第一个明确"印太"区域新概念重要性的政治领导人。

2012 年 12 月，当安倍晋三重返首相职位时，他在为世界报业辛迪加杂志（Project Syndicate）撰写题为《亚洲的民主安全钻石》的文章中重提 QUAD 概念。回顾五年前在印度议会的演讲，安倍写道："太平洋的和平、稳定和航行自由与印度洋的和平、稳定和航行自由密不可分。"他在印度说，印日两国政府有必要联合起来，作为太平洋和印度洋航行自由的守护者，承担起更多的责任。

安倍的两个重要思想，即"两洋交融"和"亚洲的民主安全钻石"成为1.0版FOIP的核心。1.0版FOIP的基本特征是针对中国的竞争战略。庆应义塾大学的神保谦（Ken Jimbo）教授认为，日本的印太愿景显然既有"竞争战略"的维度，也有"合作战略"的维度。由于1.0版FOIP具有更强的"竞争战略"特征，所以日本的倡议自然会招致一些亚洲国家的批评，因为它似乎在印太地区制造分裂和对抗。鉴于存在这些批评，安倍首相自那以后一直避免使用"亚洲的民主安全钻石"这一概念。

三、从1.0版FOIP到2.0版FOIP

1.0版FOIP面临一个明显的困境，即没有多少亚洲国家乐意看到中国与美国及其盟友之间的分裂日益加剧。如果日本的倡议被视为企图在印太这一更广泛的区域内孤立中国，那么大多数亚洲国家将会犹豫是否要参与这一倡议，因为中国是它们最大的贸易伙伴。

此时，中美竞争，尤其在中国南海的对抗日益加剧。马尼拉外交事务分析家理查德·贾瓦赫达里安（Richard JavadHeydarian）写道："如果安倍的政策得以实施，将把日本卷入北京和华盛顿之间日益激烈的太平洋海上霸权的争夺中，并引发新的关注。尤其在中国，人们将认为日本军国主义死灰复燃。"

自2014年11月10日安倍首相与习近平主席首次会晤以来，日中双边关系逐步恢复。安倍表示希望在基于共同战略利益的互惠关系理念基础上重建两国关系。自那以后，安倍首相领导的日本开始与中国发展稳定的双边关系，而将领土问题搁置起来。

当安倍在内罗毕举行的第六届东京非洲发展国际会议（TICAD Ⅵ）上提出"自由和开放的印度洋—太平洋战略"时，日本需要保持与中国的合作关系。在他的演讲中，安倍强调了两大洋以及两大洲融合的重要性。安倍说："只有两个自由开放的海洋和两个大陆的融合带来的巨大活力，才能给世界带来稳定和繁荣。"他暗示了"两个自由开放的海洋的融合",即印太地区的重要性。

日本外务省 2017 年 4 月发布的一份简报称,"日本将推动战略性和有效性的发展合作,以推进其外交政策,包括'自由和开放的印太战略'"。"国际社会稳定与繁荣的关键是'两大洲'和'两大洋'的融合所带来的活力。"这份简报解释说,"日本将以尊重非洲国家主权的方式,在发展、政治和治理领域提供国家建设支持。"

日本 2017 年外交蓝皮书有一个关于 FOIP 的专门章节。文中解释说:"日本认为国际社会稳定和繁荣的关键是由'两大洲'—— 实现显著增长的亚洲和充满潜力的非洲,以及'两个自由开放的大洋'—— 太平洋和印度洋之间的协同作用所产生的活力。"日本把这些大陆和海洋看作是一个统一的区域,打算开辟日本外交的新疆域。FOIP 旨在扩大日本的经济利益,并为印太地区的和平与稳定作出贡献。对中国来说,由于这一外交倡议更加倾向于合作而非竞争,这应该被视为 2.0 版 FOIP。

2017 年 6 月 5 日,安倍首相首次在演讲中明确表示愿意支持中国的"一带一路"倡议。他说:"我期待'一带一路'倡议能够充分体现这一共同思路,与自由公正的跨太平洋经济区和谐共处,为地区和世界的和平与繁荣做出贡献。"《日本时报》社论认为,安倍首相改变立场,表示日本愿意在一定条件下与中国的"一带一路"倡议合作,推动跨大陆的基础设施建设。

在 2017 年 7 月 8 日举行的日中首脑会议上,安倍首相和习近平主席一致认为,"日本和中国将讨论如何为地区和世界的稳定与繁荣做出贡献,包括'一带一路'倡议"。同时,日本政府努力协调两项外交举措,即中国的"一带一路"和日本的 FOIP。尽管有几个障碍需要清除,但两国政府开始避免批评各自外交愿景。2.0 版 FOIP 不同于 1.0 版,后者被视为一种拒绝中国外交倡议的竞争战略。

因此,日本国际协力机构(JICA)前主席田中明彦批评称,"媒体经常解释说,FOIP 是日本反击中国'一带一路'倡议的外交手段"。"仅仅为了对抗其他国家而对印度—太平洋这样广阔而有希望的地区制定战略,是短视的行为。融合两洋的'印太'概念的出现，反映了全球经济的长期发展趋势。"

大卫·布鲁斯特（David Brewster）指出，"日本的愿景包括开发从太平洋到印度洋再到非洲的新的经济和交通走廊。顾名思义，其重点是建立一个开放的、非排他性的基础设施体系"。

2018年1月22日，安倍首相在国会发表演讲，明确提出"自由和开放的印太战略"。他说："广阔的海洋从太平洋一直延伸到印度洋。自古以来，这个地区的人民就从这片广阔而自由的水域中获得富裕和繁荣。航行自由和法治是基石，我们必须确保这些水域成为公共产品，在未来使所有人不受歧视地享有和平与繁荣。为此，我们将推进自由开放的印太战略。"他表示无意将印太地区划分为两个集团，强调包括"所有人"在内的重要性。在自由开放的印太地区，中国自然也能享有这样的和平与繁荣。

四、结论

日本 FOIP 面临的一个最重要问题是，这一外交倡议经常与美国的"印太战略"相混淆，后者的核心是侧重以军事为导向的 QUAD。特别是 2017 年《美国国家安全战略报告》指出，"在印太地区，一场自由与压迫的世界秩序愿景之间的地缘政治竞争正在发生"。读过这份战略报告的人自然会有这样一种印象：印太地区被分为两个阵营，即美日同盟的"印太战略"和中国的"一带一路"。然而，日本对自由开放的印太地区的态度比美国在《美国国家安全战略报告》中所写的更加全面、包容与合作。

在中国和一些东盟国家，部分专家此前曾对印太地区未来的分裂表示担忧，谴责 FOIP 是分裂该地区的工具。然而，正如本文所述，日本 2.0 版 FOIP 一直在小心翼翼地避免给人留下日美打算遏制中国的印象。日本推动这一外交倡议的时期，很大程度上与日中友好时期重叠。随着特朗普政府强化与中国的对抗，中国政府对日本的态度变得比以往更加缓和。

安倍对中国采取更加合作的态度，受到包括中国在内的更广泛的欢迎。

安德烈·布林扎（Andreea Brinza）在《日本时报》上撰文指出，"安倍所采取的措施可能会给该地区带来和平，也可能会让日本加强在亚太地区的存在"。"通过这种方式，日本的 FOIP 将能够被东盟国家接受，也能够被印度和澳大利亚接受，而这两个国家与中国的对抗程度不及美国。"因此，日本FOIP 从 1.0 版向 2.0 版发展是回应亚洲国家呼声的必要演变。

日本视角下的地区安全秩序新调整

日本中曾根康弘世界和平研究所高级研究员

日本法政大学法学系教授

森聪

亚太地区战略形势的主要变化之一是美国对华政策由"接触"转变为"竞争"。2017 年 12 月出台的《美国国家安全战略报告》指出，中国不太可能成为潜在的负责任的利益相关方，而是"修正主义大国"，大国竞争已经恢复。同时，《美国国防战略报告》认为，"对美国繁荣和安全核心的挑战是长期战略竞争的再现"。

在这种情况下，将会出现两种对地区有重要影响的美中竞争。第一，在发展下一代军事、工业和信息力量的基础上开始了美中双边竞争。中国的崛起恰逢第四次工业革命，从人工智能到合成生物学等领域的许多先进技术几乎同时取得突破。美中等国正在为工业目的开发这些技术，以推动经济增长，提升经济的国际竞争力。中国出台的《中国制造 2025》就是例证。而且，防务和军事部门也在开发利用尖端技术，谋求成为军事强者。美国国防部正在进行防务创新，人工智能就是被选中用于军事应用的技术之一。中国力推军民融合战略，从国家层面努力使军事和商业技术创新形成合力。美中两国正进行直接的综合国力竞争，这一竞争实质上是关于谁能在军事、工业和信息等领域应用尖端技术方面领先。

新兴和重大技术的出口管制及中国 5G 技术的使用已经成为竞争焦点，本地区的国家将不得不做出选择。美国的盟友如日本将与美国协调行动。日本决定采取网络安全措施，保护网络和关键设施，免受恶意攻击和操控。

第二，为在第三国争夺地缘战略影响力而展开的竞争，至少包括三个方面：海上竞争、基础设施融资竞争、数字网络竞争。当前正在进行的数字网络竞争，既是关于与下一代信息技术相关联的专利和知识产权的经济竞争，又是谋求全球数字数据主导权的战略竞争。中国提出的"数字丝绸之路"，基本囊括了中国出口通信设备和基础设施、海底光缆、移动网络、云计算系统、电子商务和智慧城市等技术产品所做的努力。美国在很大程度上遵循市场规则，允许其私营企业在全球不同的市场展开自由竞争。在"印太战略"框架下，相关国家正在通过一系列努力，构建数字互联互通和网络安全的伙伴关系。当前讨论的关注点在于如何将华为从一些国家的5G供应商中排除，以及这样做在多大程度上会影响5G基础设施建设的成本，诺基亚、爱立信、三星等其他5G设备供应商是否有能力弥补排除华为留下的空白。

美中之间的地缘政治竞争已在印太地区及其之外的范围展开。本地区的国家担心美中贸易战产生的经济冲击，然而美国的安全政策似乎在印太地区受到普遍欢迎。日本、澳大利亚和印度在该地区实行同多方接触与合作的政策，目的是打造基于规则的包容性的秩序。日本所推行的区域内安全合作，为本地区的国家提供了另外的选择，使它们不至于在依赖中国还是美国的问题上陷入两难处境。

"东盟中心地位" 与地区安全

菲律宾国防学院院长

退役海军少将

罗贝托·埃斯蒂奥科

亚太地区安全环境正在演变，权力平衡已被打破，新的安全挑战日益逼近。各国无论大小，都应携手合作共同维护地区繁荣与稳定。在"安全观念演变与全球安全治理"议题下，我将重点围绕"东盟中心地位"发表看法。这—特定的安全概念已经影响了安全治理。

一、如何理解"东盟中心地位"

东盟，全称东南亚国家联盟，可以说是全球差异化最大的地区性组织。东盟有 10 个成员国：文莱、柬埔寨、印度尼西亚、老挝、马来西亚、缅甸、菲律宾、新加坡、泰国和越南，各国政治传统和经济发展阶段存在巨大差异。

东盟成立于 1967 年 8 月 8 日，其标志是发布《曼谷宣言》，主要目标是：尊重正义、法治和恪守联合国宪章的宗旨和原则，促进该地区的和平与稳定。东盟始终遵循协商一致原则，并在不同条约中予以体现，如《东南亚友好合作条约》《东盟宪章》等。《东南亚友好合作条约》规定缔约各方在处理相互间关系时需遵循下列基本原则：相互尊重独立、主权、平等、领土完整和各国的民族特性；任何国家都有免受外来干涉、颠覆和制裁，保持其民族生存的权利；互不干涉内政；和平解决分歧或争端；反对诉诸武力或以武力相威胁；缔约各国间进行有效合作。

《东盟宪章》也就地区合作规定了如下原则：

1. 尊重所有东盟成员国的独立、国家主权、平等、领土完整和国家认同；

2. 共同承担推进区域间的和平、安全和繁荣的承诺和集体责任；

3. 放弃使用武力或以武力相威胁及其他任何违背国际法的行为；

4. 以和平方式解决争端；

5. 不干涉东盟成员国内政；

6. 尊重每个成员国抵抗外部干涉、颠覆和胁迫以维护其自由生存的权利；

7. 就涉及东盟共同利益的事宜加强磋商；

8. 坚持法治、良政、民主和宪政原则；

9. 尊重基本自由，促进和保护人权以及推动社会正义；

10. 支持《联合国宪章》和国际法，包括东盟成员国签署的国际人权法；

11. 不受任何东盟成员国或非东盟成员国、非国家行为体影响参加任何威胁到成员国主权、领土完整或政治和经济稳定的活动，包括使用其领土；

12. 尊重东盟国家各民族的不同文化、语言和宗教，强调求同存异；

13. 推进东盟在对外政治、经济、社会和文化联系中的中心性，保持积极参与和开放包容的态度，不采取歧视政策；

14. 在市场经济中坚持多边贸易规则和以东盟规则为基础的体制，履行经济承诺，消除区域经济一体化的障碍。

东盟在地区多边事务中的地位和作用有目共睹。互不干涉和协商一致原则使得东盟在成员国差异较大的情况下，仍发展成为包容性的国际组织，而其他地区合作平台的作用却有所下降。

二、地区安全架构中的东盟角色

在后冷战时代，东盟日渐成为亚太地区的"调停人"，特别是为解决非传统安全问题提供了对话与合作的平台。

东盟在全球安全治理方面发挥了两大作用。一方面，就其成员国而言，东盟具有广泛代表性。虽不是全球性平台，但其伙伴关系囊括全球主要行为体，特别是美国、中国、欧盟、俄罗斯等。另一方面，东盟能够主导议题设置，特别是在非传统安全合作领域。

以东盟地区论坛、东盟防长扩大会议和东亚峰会三个多边平台作为重要依托，东盟在地区安全与合作方面始终处于中心地位。

东盟地区论坛是东盟在印度洋—亚洲—太平洋地区领导的最具包容性的平台，其目标是就共同关心的政治与安全问题举行建设性对话和磋商，推动亚太地区建立信任，并推进地区预防性外交。该论坛成立于1994年，成员国（组织）包括：澳大利亚、孟加拉国、文莱、柬埔寨、加拿大、中国、朝鲜、印度、印度尼西亚、日本、老挝、马来西亚、蒙古、缅甸、新西兰、巴基斯坦、巴布亚新几内亚、菲律宾、韩国、俄罗斯、新加坡、斯里兰卡、泰国、东帝汶、美国、越南和欧盟，这充分体现了东盟倡导的包容性原则。朝鲜和韩国均为东盟地区论坛成员国，还有中国、印度、巴基斯坦等，历史上这些国家间曾爆发过冲突。这足以说明东盟是促进开放性地区主义的践行者。

东盟防长扩大会议成立于2010年，是地区安全合作的重要平台。东盟地区论坛由各国外长参加，而东盟防长扩大会议，就像其名称所指一样，是由东盟成员国和来自澳大利亚、中国、印度、日本、新西兰、韩国、俄罗斯和美国等东盟伙伴国家的防长参加。其目标如下：（1）发挥东盟各国所长共同应对安全挑战；（2）扩大对话和透明度，建立互信；（3）促进国防与安全合作应对跨国安全挑战，推动地区和平与稳定；（4）践行《第二巴厘宣言》构建东盟安全共同体，将东盟打造成和平、稳定、民主和繁荣的地区，各成员国共享和平；（5）加快推动《万象行动纲领》落地，建立和平、安全和繁荣的东盟，实施外向型对外战略。为实现这些目标，东盟防长扩大会议成立7个专家工作组，涉及人道主义救助与灾难援助、海洋安全、军事医学、反恐、维和行动、人道主义排雷行动和网络安全等议题。

东亚峰会成立于2005年，除东盟成员国外，还包括：澳大利亚、中国、日本、印度、新西兰、韩国、俄罗斯、美国。第一届东亚峰会在马来西亚举行，发表了《吉隆坡宣言》，明确了东亚峰会的优先事项：（1）推动政治与安全问题的战略对话与合作，确保东盟成员国享有公正、民主与繁荣的国际环境；（2）通过加强技术转移、基础设施建设、能力建设、善治与人道主义援助、金融和贸易往来，扩大投资和开放，促进发展，维护能源安全，推动经济增长与一体化，消除贫困，缩小东亚地区发展差距；（3）深化文化理解，扩大人文交流，推动民生领域合作，增进团结互信，在环境保护、传染病防治和减灾方面开展合作。

东盟地区论坛、东亚峰会和东盟防长扩大会议的主席国与东盟主席国保持一致。

三、多边主义前景

不可否认，印度洋—亚洲—太平洋地区的主要权力关系正在发生转变。

在充满不确定性的地区权力转移过程中，东盟能够起到"稳定器"的作用，具体而言：一要以东盟三大共同体（政治安全共同体、经济共同体和社会文化共同体）为支柱推动制度化建设；二要秉持东盟宪章精神，推动东盟式外交。东盟宪章在东盟发展中具有里程碑意义，东盟因此变得更加团结，政府和非政府行为体的外交活动得以强化和规范化。东盟共同体建设不仅包括各国政府等官方外交渠道，也包括议会、企业、智库和非政府组织等。东盟在地区事务中无处不在，受到各成员国肯定。随着共同体建设在关键领域持续推进，东盟宪章中提及的增加凝聚力的目标正逐步实现，东盟的地区话语权不断增强。内部一体化建设为加强东盟地区领导力提供了必要的外交筹码，增加了东盟作为中立方运筹大国关系、维护世界和平与稳定的可信度。权力转移自然而然会使地区利益相关者之间的关系紧张，但是，如果东盟能够始终保持团结，合力应对冲突，保留外交解决渠道，那么即便面临最恶劣的政治气候，东盟依旧能以其坚强的领导力通过外交手段将他国从暴力的边缘拖拽回来。因此，支持东盟共同体建设符合各大国的利益。这样一个遵循通过磋商解决问题的、团结的地区组织能在多边外交中发挥高效、中立、不对抗的领导作用。

东盟对于开放性地区主义的主张是对建设包容性印度洋—亚洲—太平洋地区的有力补充。东盟及其领导的多边平台始终对各方持开放态度。或许正是由于成员国间政治传统和经济发展水平存在差异，东盟自始至终都是包容性的，愿意通过磋商解决问题，并欢迎非东盟成员国甚至是全球大国加入。在许多场合中，东盟呼吁建立互信、不干涉内部事务、不因政治制度和发展水平差异而区别对待任何行为体。这种开放性姿态有利于通过外交解决问题，使各方远离媒体聚光灯，摒弃鼠目寸光的短见。

南共体视角下的地区安全秩序新调整

南非丹尼斯·赫利和平研究所前所长

达尼沙·库马洛

国家和地区安全已经上升为全球大部分国家的优先选项。过去几十年，国家对安全的重视程度与日俱增。恐怖主义在全球扩散使安全担忧不断增加，军事政变、政局动荡、内战、社会动乱等时有发生。随着安全风险积聚，南部非洲也触发了诸多安全问题。本文将重点关注南部非洲发展共同体（简称南共体），其成员国包括安哥拉、博茨瓦纳、科摩罗、刚果（金）、莱索托、马达加斯加、马拉维、毛里求斯、莫桑比克、纳米比亚、塞舌尔、南非、斯威士兰、坦桑尼亚、赞比亚和津巴布韦。

总体而言，对于如何处理南共体地区的安全问题还未达成共识。南共体各国中负责安全的各部门财政预算充足，如国防、情报、警察、海军、空军等。根据2018—2019年财政预算，博茨瓦纳的安全部门经费占总预算的14.4%，纳米比亚为17.2%，赞比亚为9.1%，莱索托为12%，毛里求斯为10%。

当前，南共体地区面临的外部威胁较小，更大的威胁来自区域内部，如艾滋病、移民、轻武器扩散、腐败和埃博拉病毒等。倘若仅讨论南共体国家间关系和国内外安全问题，或将忽视南共体国家面临的最突出的威胁。津巴布韦、赞比亚和南非的警察腐败现象严重，已损害公众利益。作为地区性组织，南共体的权力因领导人内斗而遭到削弱，治理赤字成为地区动荡的根源。尽管大多数南共体国家相对稳定，但仍面临武装叛乱、治理危机、经济社会发展迟滞等挑战，而南共体各国对此准备不足，应对不力。许多非洲国家的欠发达状态为地区和平与安全埋下长期隐患。有人曾这样描述非洲的和平与安全环境："失败国家的制度缺陷和与之相伴的治理缺失及日益扩大的贫富差距交织在一起。冲突逐渐成为常态，而非洲的环境因冲突、动乱和执政乏力变得动荡。"

国家或地区安全与经济发展无法割裂。为此，非洲成立了多个经济团体来解决不同地区的特定经济问题，如：阿拉伯马格里布联盟（简称马盟）、东部和南部非洲共同市场（简称科迈萨）、萨赫勒-撒哈拉国家共同体、西非国家经济共同体（简称西共体）、东非共同体、中部非洲国家经济共同体、政府间发展组织（简称伊加特）、南部非洲发展共同体（简称南共体）等。

刚果（金）等国家的武装军事行动仍很频繁，这也成为南共体地区面临的主要安全威胁。目前，联合国规模最大的维和部队驻扎在刚果（金）。此外，过去几年，莱索托、津巴布韦、斯威士兰、马拉维等国的政治体制相对脆弱。

一、南共体的安全关切

1992 年 8 月，《南部非洲发展共同体条约》在纳米比亚首都温得和克签署，其宗旨是稳步推进、建立真正公平的地区一体化，目标是实现经济一体化，加强在地区发展方面的合作，涉及七个方面，最后一项是：政治、外交、国际关系、和平与安全。尽管安全议题并非南共体成立之初的首要目标，但随着安全威胁增多，该地区必须妥善应对。南共体是地区性组织，其前身是南部非洲发展协调会议，成立于冷战结束和纳米比亚独立后。劳里·内森（Laurie Nathan）指出，南共体没有建立共同安全制度，导致维和力度不够。原因有三点：一是成员国间共同价值观缺失，不利于建立信任关系、制定共同政策、培育内部凝聚力和共同应对危机；二是各成员国不愿向共同安全制度让渡主权，无法制定有约束力的规则和进行有效决策；三是各成员国在经济发展和行政管理上存在弱点。但也有一定成果，如南共体 1998 年为刚果（金）内战进行调停；同年，南非和博茨瓦纳调停莱索托军事叛乱。

必须指出的是，南共体在地区内设有经济、政治、文化、社会和安全等方面的保证原则。就安全保证而言，南共体政治、国防和安全合作机构（简称安全机构）于1996年成立，但没有明确安全机构的主席（成立时主席为穆加贝总统）如何与南共体领导机构相融合。安全机构的功能包括预防国内和国家间冲突，并寻求冲突解决方案，但缺少明确任务、责任和权力范围的法律文件。南非被誉为地区外交的推动者，特别是在注重"增长"和"发展"的大背景下强调"善治"和"民主"。

二、关于2001年南共体《政治、防务和安全协议》

南共体地区爆发过多起冲突，例如莱索托内部动乱、刚果（金）内战等，由南共体各成员国认可和支持的《政治、防务和安全协议》旨在保护地区民众免遭冲突造成的动荡之苦。历史上，安哥拉政府军与反政府组织争取安哥拉彻底独立全国联盟（安盟）间的内战破坏了地区稳定。南共体领导人察觉到冲突导致普通民众的生活每况愈下，由此达成该协议。协议目标是"促进地区协调，提升防务、安全、冲突预防、管理等方面的合作，落实共同防御条约应对外部军事威胁；加强成员国执法机构和安全部门的合作"。根据协议安排，在成员国面临威胁时，南共体须团结一致，而非各行其是。南共体领导人也希望协议能进一步提升南共体能力，合力阻止政变或颠覆合法政府的行为。这也有利于消除南共体面临的恐怖主义威胁。

南共体2003年提出了防御条约，聚焦冲突解决、军事准备、集体自卫、减少不稳定因素和争端解决。南部非洲面临的主要挑战是大部分地区发展落后，因此亟须营造"和平、稳定与民主"的环境。安全机构可视为一驾马车，能够带领南部非洲驶向这一理想的发展环境。该地区也需要加强彼此团结。

三、南共体处理地区安全事务乏力

前文已经阐述南共体领导人在建立地区安全支柱方面所作的努力。南共体作为一个地区机构，在面对某些成员国的政治行为可能有损地区稳定时，能够发挥的作用十分有限。

南共体成员国可以运用不同方式对地区架构施加压力。南非作为南共体中最大的经济体，其科技水平也更为先进，有能力对南共体议程设定产生重大影响。南共体秘书处居弱势地位，超过40%的预算经费来源于捐助，大多数项目都能获得良好的资金支持，但和平与安全项目除外。这导致南共体自主权较低，易受成员国左右。秘书处总体上是一个办事机构，执行成员国领导人在峰会上达成的决议。

最后，由于成员国同时加入其他地区组织，南共体的作用也有所削弱。刚果（金）和安哥拉两国同时是南共体和中部非洲国家经济共同体成员，坦桑尼亚也是东非共同体成员，导致这些国家在各个组织内都不能充分发挥作用。此外，身份的重叠意味着成员国需要践行不同的原则，很难在承担义务方面达成共识。

四、南共体可能面临的安全威胁

抛开南部非洲公民面临的安全威胁来谈地区安全秩序显然是不合理的。艾滋病已成为南共体地区的安全隐患。联合国艾滋病规划署资料显示，东部非洲和南部非洲受艾滋病影响最为严重，艾滋病患者数量占全球45%，艾滋病毒携带者占比53%。异常严峻的形势需要南共体成员国加大关注力度。埃博拉病毒在刚果（金）和乌干达肆虐，影响东部非洲和南部非洲安全，亟须进行边界管控和建立疾病控制机制。移民是正常现象，但强制迁徙给输入国带来安全威胁。南非是南部非洲国家和其他国家进行强制迁徙的主要接受国。统计数据显示，2011年人口普查时，南非已经有220万移民。南部非洲各国相连，人们很容易跨越边境，大量移民涌入会造成输入国资源紧张。

五、南非在南共体地区危机管理中的作用

谈及地区和平与稳定问题，需关注南非的作用和影响。南非是地区最发达的经济体，拥有最先进的安全部门，同时还是金砖国家中唯一的非洲国家代表，这足以说明南非的实力。但南非没有利用其经济、政治和社会优势介入困扰南共体或非洲地区的冲突。南非奉行"温和外交"策略，如2000年，南非时任总统姆贝基践行该策略与津巴布韦领导人协商，而不是将南非的国家意志或既定政策强加于他国。

南非还坚持"以非洲方式解决非洲问题"，受到非盟的支持。近期，南非鼓励地区组织如南共体和非盟等主导地区危机管理，南非在此框架内与他国进行合作。南非尊重他国主权，这一原则不因国家大小和军事实力强弱而异，也不愿被视为"大哥"过多介入地区危机。

"以非洲方式解决非洲问题"的理念得到拥护，特别体现在和平与安全领域。"非洲方式"意味着唤醒自我意识——非洲人民要自力更生、承担责任、有自豪感和自主性；意味着提出解决危机的非洲倡议。这也能遏制域外大国介入非洲危机的企图。

南共体地区安全秩序需要进行调整，并建立"互查机制"，充分发挥潜力，以维护地区安全。

第三编

新兴科技与全球安全

全球安全治理视域下的新兴科技与全球安全

联合国裁军研究所首席研究员

约翰·珀利

新兴科技与全球安全主要涉及导弹防御系统、高超音速武器和其他先进远程武器、反卫星武器、无人机武器系统、网络、人工智能和机器学习等。其中，机器学习虽然不是一种新技术，却是"有用的武器"。这些技术单独或综合发展对核平衡以及难以预测的危机都有实际影响。

这些技术是世界四大风险源之一。其他风险分别是：核武器国家的不确定性；一些国家之间关系紧张；国际组织及国际准则遭到破坏。美国和俄罗斯的双边核裁军进程停滞不前，裁军谈判会议 20 多年来一直陷于僵局，《不扩散武器条约》正尽力阻止因核裁军进展缓慢而不断加剧的政治分歧。

尽管前景黯淡，但基于新技术的军控措施可能有助于形势稳定。加强战略对话、澄清核能利用和加强危机管控，可降低核武器风险，有助于各国建立互信，走向无核武器世界。

这些新技术的发展涉及到全球安全中的两个问题。第一个问题是对核平衡的影响，这些技术是美国、俄罗斯、中国和印度战略武器现代化和军备竞赛的产物和动能。第二个问题是，尽管有几项技术表面上意在加强威慑，但在危机升级的情况下，它们的实际效果难以预测，并可能导致更大的危机和不稳定性。这正是在美俄中和中印巴这两个主要的三方核关系中需要加强军控协议的重要原因。此外，在这些战略关系中，如果不加强裁军与防扩散，将很难防止权力冲突和核战争。

一、新兴技术与核不稳定

1945 年美国在日本引爆原子弹后，核武器成为与以往所有战略技术有本质区别的武器，难以有效应对。核战略正是基于这个可怕的、不可避免的事实应运而生。尽管"相互确保摧毁"从来不是美国的官方政策，但它捕捉到了核威慑的敏感性，预见到了核报复带来核灾难的绝对确定性。1972 年美苏签订了《反导条约》，可以看出苏联实际上承认了这一点。《反导条约》消除了一方由于另一方发展导弹防御而失去对其进行核打击能力的风险，这为削减战略武器开辟了道路。

今天，核战争的策划者对"战略稳定"的把握不如以前。新技术使基于相互脆弱的核威慑出现了新的不确定性。核计划针对的是最坏情况下的突发事件，如果某些突发事件导致重大事故，那么牺牲不可避免（例如，"蓝色闪电"攻击将摧毁或"斩首"国家核指挥和控制系统，使核威慑无效），必须采取措施加以预防。这就是"现代化"核武器改进质量的一个原因，这也有助于解释国家之间保持军备竞赛的动因。在危机情况下，为提高核威慑能力而研发的战略性技术可能会引发不确定反应。

二、哪些技术具有战略意义？

（一）导弹防御

美国自 2002 年退出《反导条约》以来，已研发出更先进的导弹防御系统以拦截弹道飞行路径上的导弹。尽管本土导弹防御系统的进展仍然有限，但随着技术进步，以保护军事资产和军队为重点的战术级和战区级导弹防御已成为越来越多国家的重要能力。美国、俄罗斯、印度、法国、以色列和中国都发展了导弹防御系统，美国已经向其盟国提供了导弹防御系统，包括中东的沙特阿拉伯和亚洲的日本和韩国等。

随着导弹防御系统的发展，它们正逐渐成为更为一体化的"系统体系"。

这意味着以前针对非核导弹和核导弹拦截系统的区分可能会逐渐弱化。俄罗斯表示，在东欧部署导弹防御系统可能会削弱其二次核打击能力。2018年3月，俄罗斯总统普京指出，由于美国退出《反导条约》，俄罗斯已启动新武器系统的研发工作。中国部署的核导弹数量相对较少，可能会因此更加担忧。

（二）高超音速武器和其他先进远程武器

高超音速武器飞行速度超过音速五倍多。几个国家正在积极研制新型远程可操控武器，其中最引人瞩目的是装有高超音速滑翔机（HGV）的高超音速助推滑翔系统。高超音速滑翔机在分离后无动力，在助推阶段后不遵循弹道飞行路径。由于其机动性以及低弹道特性，它们可能有更强的能力克服导弹防御系统。今天，美国、俄罗斯、中国和法国都有积极的采购计划。据报道，其他国家也对这项技术感兴趣。美国打算将助推滑翔技术与常规或动能弹头结合使用。目前还不清楚俄罗斯和中国的系统是否会装备核武器。

尽管高超音速滑翔机的军事用途尚不清楚，但相关军备竞赛正在展开。高超音速滑翔机弹头性质的模糊性以及其预期目标的不确定性，意味着导致战略误判的可能性极大。发射载有高超音速滑翔机的导弹，可以被理解为发生核攻击。即使高超音速滑翔机的最终影响是常规性的，核国家也可能认为其针对的目标是它们的核预警、指挥和控制系统基础设施，会使核国家面临"要么使用，要么失去"的困境。鉴于这些模糊性，高超音速滑翔机的出现可能促使一些核国家修改其政策，以扩大使用核武器应对高超音速滑翔机的必要条件，或将其核力量置于更高的警戒状态。

先进远程导弹的发展也可能给核理论和战争计划带来压力。俄罗斯和中国一直认为，常规巡航导弹可能会破坏战略平衡。近年来，美国生产并向一些盟国出口空对地导弹，这是一种雷达截面小的空中发射常规巡航导弹，于2018年4月在叙利亚首次使用。这种新版本的导弹射程约为1000公里，从敌方防御最为严密的空域外发射，由于其隐身特性，可以避开空中防御，打击核指挥控制系统和移动核发射器等战略目标。与HGV一样，一个相关的问题是，用常规巡航导弹系统发动的打击可能会被目标国误认为是空射核巡航导弹的攻击。

（三）反卫星武器

各国长期以来都认识到外层空间的重要性，包括通信、监视、核攻击的早期预警，许多军事行动依赖卫星接入。1967 年的《外层空间条约》禁止在空间部署核武器，中俄提出谈判禁止在太空部署其他武器的条约，但未能引起广泛关注。西方国家声称这是不可核查的，而且在任何情况下，都没有必要把武器放在太空中，而且还威胁到其他空间物体。事实上，迄今为止，3 个国家（美国、中国和印度）已经测试了地面发射的反卫星（ASAT）拦截能力。然而，不仅这种导弹拦截器，而且各种"非动能"网络和电子空间对抗能力都可以破坏或摧毁卫星。任何空间物体都有碰撞的危险。这使得共轨无人机技术日益受到国际社会的普遍关注，尤其是在碰撞即将来临之前很难确定近程机动的意图。

为什么反卫星武器受到战略关注？最明显的原因是，各国将空间技术更多地用于民用和军事目的。即使各国没有在空间部署明确为武器的物体，也没有故意碰撞或炸毁彼此的资产，但非动能攻击性空间行动实际上已经进行了一段时间。美国和印度组建国家"空间力量"，反映出其对天基系统基础设施脆弱性的担忧。然而，这可能导致更加公开的竞争和军备竞赛：如果部署探测导弹发射和飞行路径的天基系统，将反过来增加对反卫星能力的需求。此外，使用反卫星摧毁空间物体所产生的碎片可能会造成重大破坏，并可能使空间在一段时间内不能被有效利用，这将对地球上数十亿人的日常生活造成重大影响。

（四）无人自主武器系统

2013 年，联合国人权理事会提交了两份重要报告。一份是关于无人机（或武装无人机），另一份是关于所谓的"致命自主机器人"。这些文章引起了国际社会对这些议题的关注。首先，国际社会对遥控无人机在常规战场以外的秘密行动中的作用感到不安，因为在常规战场以外的秘密行动中并不总是能明确适用哪些法律规则。然而，这些担忧尚未在国际上形成集中的讨论。这些议题在《联合国常规武器公约》的讨论中被提到，谈判仍在继续。

这里提出的问题包括机器选择目标和攻击人类的含义、这类系统能否充分预测或可靠、自主武器是否合乎道德等。

尽管到目前为止，武装无人机和自主武器系统还没有产生太大影响，但在战争升级或危机的情况下，可能会引发一些问题。从运营商的角度看，某些军事力量对其更感兴趣，因为它们比载人平台更具吸引力（例如，即使可能被拦截和摧毁，也能被送入有争议的空域或水域收集情报）。然而，有证据表明，使用者和受到影响者在如何看待无人系统上仍然存在分歧，这些分歧可能导致误解和事件升级。在 2013 年一次涉及中国无人机的事件后，日本表示，它制定了新的交战规则，以击落其领空上出现的任何无人机。中国表示，任何对无人机的攻击都是"战争行为"，如果发生这种情况，中国将"反击"。尽管设计师和运营商尽了最大努力，但由于无人机具有更高的反应速度和坠毁速度，在紧张局势或危机中，这些因素会增加额外变量。

（五）网络

包括现代军事系统在内的现代生活依赖于在网络上创建、保存、管理和移动的数字数据。利用代码进行黑客攻击、诈骗、网络钓鱼、窃取、破坏甚至更改数据已在过去的十年里成为主要安全焦点。现在，尽管很难归罪于黑客，但是几个主要军事大国对彼此以及其他国家进行攻击性的网络操作是几乎公开的秘密。网络攻击行动越来越普遍和持久，在国家间的进攻行动、间谍活动、盗窃和敲诈活动中，平民设施往往是受害者，因为两者之间的界限是模糊的。

在两种情况下，网络攻击能力会上升到战略关注的水平。第一种是黑客或其他网络干扰核预警、指挥和控制系统或决策支持系统，或在目标国制造恐惧。目标国称其已受到网络威胁，这可能导致核升级，在极端情况下，可以想象会出现"使用它，或失去它"的情况。第二种情况涉及到侵略者使用网络攻击手段破坏敌方所依赖的关键社会基础设施。2019 年 6 月，有报道称，美国和俄罗斯都在深入调查对方的电力设施，植入恶意软件，破坏其国家电网。美国在 2018 年的《核态势评估》中，明确拒绝排除对"非核战略攻击"的核反击，比如重大的网络攻击。因此，网络威胁似乎已经影响到各国的核使用理论。

（六）人工智能与机器学习

人工智能（AI）的巨大进步正在产生广泛的社会影响。基于算法的机器系统在各种技术性能的自我优化方面变得越来越出色，其中许多与模式识别和数据匹配相关。这将提高机器系统执行各种关键军事任务的能力，使其具有更大程度的自主权，如从通信、后勤到网络防御、火力控制、情报分析支持，甚至包括选择目标和发动攻击。各方担心美国和中国之间可能出现"人工智能军备竞赛"或"威胁我们所有人的人工智能冷战"。

关于人工智能将人类排除在冲突决策之外的想法可能有些言过其实，但至少目前是这样。最新研究发现，机器学习驱动的人工智能应用和自主系统在设计上过于脆弱，会带来更大的风险："当它们面对的任务或环境与它们接受过培训的任务或环境略有不同时，它们可能会失败得惊人。它们的行为也是不可预测的，因为它们使用不透明的算法。人类很难解释它们是如何工作的，也很难解释它们是否怀有偏见。它们也可以通过网络攻击甚至简单的传感器欺骗手段击败智能对手。在核武器系统的背景下，如不慎重采用人工智能最新技术，可能会造成严重的后果。"

同时，基于算法的系统越来越成为军队必不可少的系统。有两个原因需要特别注意，即加强军队指挥链对自动化的依赖，对核武器或其他战略武器进行预警和探测。首先，随着这些技术在核环境中的发展，机器学习和其他人工智能相关技术的预测能力可能会影响核报复能力，从而影响当前的战略平衡。第二，人工智能的使用将是一个持续的过程，对核预警、指挥和控制系统中的人类决策过程产生不同的影响，即使发射核武器的最终决定总是由人类作出的。然而，从冷战危机中得到的一个教训是，人的情景感知对于避免在若干场合使用核武器至关重要。当人类决策者依赖人工智能时，他们能做出正确的决定吗？

（七）更多"可用"的核武器

这里提到了更多可使用的核武器，虽然不是严格意义上的新技术，但它们正在成为一些国家考虑的战略技术组合的一部分，一些核武器国家正在讨论部署更多"可用"的核武器。使用这种武器可能在战术上有用，甚至可能会吓阻对手。

事实上，以这种方式部署核武器将导致不稳定性。目前，拥有核武器国家对威慑性核武器非常谨慎，只有在自卫的极端情况下才使用。这导致了核使用规范的产生。更多"可用"的核武器倾向于破坏《不扩散核武器条约》中的不扩散准则。在和平时期，它要求改变核使用的政策，这种改变可能会加剧紧张局势，实际上降低了核使用的门槛。

三、为什么新兴技术需要军备控制

以上概述的每一项技术发展都对核平衡或对难以预测的危机有实际影响，或两者兼而有之。这影响了全球安全，因为没有什么比核危机或使用核武器更具"全球性"。

当然，对于学者或决策者来说，很难预见这些技术和其他因素将以何种精确方式相互作用，也很难预测是否有其他技术和因素将影响世界主要战略竞争对手。在缺乏战略信任的情况下，这种不确定性往往会导致军备竞赛和进一步的不稳定。世界主要战略竞争对手如何才能找到摆脱困境的方法？

现代战争是不断加快速度的过程，计算机微处理器技术及相关技术的应用通常有助于压缩人类的决策时间。现在迫切需要确保在涉及使用核武器的情况下，人类决策者不只是在危机中随波逐流。正在发展或考虑发展本文所讨论的技术的各国的决策者，需要进行对话，以确保他们理解这些含义，并能够弥合分歧。

这种交流是降低核武器风险的战略对话的一部分。降低风险的框架、要素和途径已经成为研究机构关注的重点，降低核风险最近在《不扩散核武器条约》讨论中得到了广泛支持。作为其中的一部分，应注意在此讨论的新技术对核理论、战略、行动和透明度的影响，这比《不扩散核武器条约》的五个核武器国家之间的定期交流要深入得多。有一系列实际措施可以帮助减少核风险，包括更好的危机沟通手段，不仅是双边的，而且要包括美俄中、印巴中三方机制。

　　降低核风险措施有助于为制定具体的军备控制措施铺平道路，这些措施涉及到本文讨论的新技术的各个方面，并有助于增强战略信任。联合国秘书长在 2018 年 5 月裁谈会上呼吁，必须朝着无核武器世界的目标发展。虽然这对某些人来说可能是乌托邦式的，但更乌托邦的观点认为核威慑可以无限期地进行，而不会发生事故、误算或导致核使用的其他情况，尤其是在当今复杂多变的战略环境中。有时人们会忘记，军备控制诞生于 20 世纪 50 年代的一场核军备竞赛，在这场竞赛中，氢弹、洲际弹道导弹、卫星被引进，两个超级大国之间的信任度很低。军备控制无论是为了"稳定"还是为了更持久的安全条件，都是一个理性的利己主义问题。今天，随着战略平衡的转变，它还需要超越华盛顿和莫斯科的主动性和领导权。中国应发挥重要的建设性作用。

高新技术发展及对全球战略稳定性的影响

中国人民争取和平与裁军协会常务理事
中国工程物理研究院战略研究中心副主任、研究员

伍钧

当前，以人工智能为代表的高新技术突飞猛进，将对未来战争决策和战争的模式产生影响，有些技术和装备的使用在某些方面可替代核武器的部分功能，将影响全球战略稳定。但从破坏能力上看，能够对人类造成毁灭的还是核武器。人工智能武器、网络武器与核武器系统发生关联（破坏核指挥系统、攻击核设施和攻击核武器发射系统等）都会对全球造成灾难性后果，因此必须尽快制定网络武器和人工智能武器的行为规则。本文从人工智能和网络武器发展入手，讨论了它们的军事应用及对全球战略稳定的影响，提出如果肆意发展人工智能武器和网络武器对核设施的攻击能力，将会对全球产生灾难性的后果。为保证核武器不被使用，拥有核武器的国家应该尽快采用不首先使用核武器的政策，降低核武器的警戒水平。

一、当前新兴科技发展

随着社会进步，全球融合，特别是科技领域的合作，新兴科技得到飞速发展，给人类生活带来很多便利，创造了巨大价值，特别是人工智能、网络和外空技术的发展，使我们的生活无比便利。同时，它们的巨大军事价值，也受到世界各国重视。这些新兴技术的军事应用可能破坏全球的战略稳定，给人类带来灾难，需要提前预防。

（一）以人工智能技术为代表的高新技术的发展

在 1997 年"深蓝"国际象棋大师后，2017 年"阿尔法狗"（Alfa Go）升级版 Master 战胜柯洁等诸多围棋高手，显示出人工智能在快速处理大容量数据并学习有用信息方面取得重大进展。自主学习的方式和大数据在学习中的应用使人工智能技术的未来应用发生颠覆性变化。考虑未来的发展，计算机处理器的储存容量几乎可以不受限制，机器通过自我学习，不断改进。同时机器人不知疲倦，对外界的反应比人类快很多。因此，在人类生活的诸多领域，人工智能机器人替代人类的活动将成为一种趋势。

在军事安全领域，机器人的使用可能使未来战争发生根本性变化，在阿富汗战场，美国士兵使用的"大狗"机器人帮助作战人员实施伴随保障，颠覆了战场后勤保障的模式。人工智能装备下的无人机可以自主规避雷达和导弹攻击，通过图像识别系统，定点打击重点关注的目标，使战争模式发生变化。

人工智能的战场感知手段与信息融合处理能力在战场上有极大的优势。在人工智能辅助下，人在战场的反应时间大幅缩短，可以做出更准确的判断和动作，从而取得战场优势。事实证明，用人工智能辅助的飞行员在空战演练中对无人工智能辅助的飞行员拥有压倒性优势。

自主学习型的人工智能，掌握信息全面，通过对历次战例的学习，利弊得失计算准确，能在未来战场决策中发挥重要作用，特别是在军事计划、后勤组织保障、战场实时信息获取、分析、目标图像分析等方面，可能发生颠覆性变化。

致命性自主武器系统，是信息系统、人工智能、机器人、无人系统和传统武器平台技术交叉融合的产物，可以独立发现、定位、识别、打击目标，具有高度智能化。当前，随着自主技术快速发展，致命性自主武器和智能化武器系统发展迅猛。

目前，人工智能及致命性自主武器在军事中的应用，尚处于发展演进阶段，没有明确的物理形态和能力特征；不同国家发展水平和应用能力不同，理解认识还存有偏差。因此，目前国际社会尚未对人工智能武器及致命性自主武器系统形成明确定义和一致认识。

（二）网络空间战场化、武器化趋势加速，网络攻击手段已开始实战化运用

网络空间的广泛应用给人类生活带来无限便利，创造了巨大价值。网络空间与国家安全和战略利益的关联日益紧密。公开资料显示，全球已有100多个国家发布网络空间安全相关战略和政策，40多个国家发布了与网络空间相关的军事计划或建立了相应的组织机构和军事力量，其中近20个国家明确发展进攻性网络作战力量。2016年6月，北约正式将网络空间确定为与陆、海、空、天并列的作战域，并强调要将网络空间防御融入联盟的行动规划和作战任务中。网络空间战场化态势日益凸显。

美国为捍卫其在网络空间的利益，势必要确保在网络空间的优势地位。2017年1月以来，美国发布了一系列有关网络安全的战略文件，凸显了网络安全在美国国家安全的重要地位，以及美国要捍卫其在网络空间的绝对优势地位的决心。

美国国防部2016年计划在5年之内斥资347亿美元加强网络空间安全建设。其中，143亿美元用于网络空间活动，支持进攻性网络空间行动和在网络空间的防御性军事行动等。2016年2月25日，美国国防部向众议院提交2017年预算案，计划增加9亿美元用以提高网络空间作战能力，实现威慑"最强大对手"的目的。2017年3月16日，美国总统特朗普发布2018年"美国优先"联邦预算计划，国防预算同比增长10%，达到6390亿美元。该预算显著增加了应对网络攻击威胁等方面的经费。

2018年5月4日，美国网络司令部正式升级成为独立的联合司令部，与印太司令部及欧洲司令部同级，执行任务可直接向国防部长报告。2018年5月17日，美国国防部网络司令部官员称，美国网络司令部下的133支网络任务部队已全部具备全面作战能力，网络空间力量建设和机构设置进一步完善。美国频繁组织各类网络空间安全相关演习活动，旨在提升各类网络安全人员在网络空间的进攻和防御能力，提高机构间协作及应急响应能力，并培养网络安全人才。

当前，网络已经成为各方激烈对抗的领域，网络攻击时有发生，特别是有些攻击针对民用基础设施，如对伊朗的"震网"病毒攻击，也有消息称俄罗斯的电网基础设施被安装病毒。这些都表明当前的网络攻击已经达到实战应用的地步。

二、新兴技术发展有可能动摇业已形成的战略稳定

人工智能和网络技术给人类带来方便的生活，提升人类生活的品质，但因其军事应用不可避免，将对国际安全产生影响。随着技术的不断发展，"人工智能系统的欺骗性和破坏性难以预测和理解，将会对国家安全和关键基础设施带来巨大风险"，但从破坏能力看，人工智能武器和网络武器不可能替代核武器。

当今世界处于和平时期，反对战争已经成为世界各国共识。而人工智能的快速进步和新材料的应用，将极大压缩战争成本；同时，人在战场上的作用将会下降，并且人员的伤亡也将减少。因此，决策者在权衡得失时，顾虑会减少，人们对战争形态的认识将发生变化，可能会降低战争的门槛，使暴力回潮，世界可能变得更加动荡。

现在，一般认为人类干预在人工智能决策过程中至关重要，但随着学习型人工智能的不断进步，在绝大多数情况下，出错的概率很小。其后果是人类对人工智能的依赖越来越大，习惯于依赖人工智能进行决策，主动退出参与对人工智能机器人的控制。这样可能产生严重后果。

人工智能的使用门槛不高，任何非政府组织或个人都可能使用人工智能进行破坏活动。随着人工智能的进步，这些破坏作用可能很严重。

人工智能可能破坏已经形成的战略稳定。比如，移动导弹发射装置被一致认为可以提高导弹的生存能力，但随着人工智能在情报、监测、侦查和分析系统发挥关键作用，使移动导弹发射器容易受到先发制人的打击。美国的《导弹防御评估报告》提出要发展装载激光的无人机，要在导弹发射前进行打击。这也是人工智能破坏战略稳定的一个体现。

人们在日常生活中已经不能离开网络，因此网络攻击对国民经济的破坏可能不次于一场大规模战争，这种破坏作用已经得到验证。有媒体报道，美国在俄罗斯电网中植入病毒，试图在关键时刻控制俄罗斯电网。如果实施，可能产生严重后果。特别是如果网络攻击核指挥系统，影响指挥决策系统，后果将不堪设想。

三、制定人工智能和网络空间行为规则是当前的重要工作

2016年5月，七国集团峰会发布了《G7网络空间原则与行为》，主张加强成员国间网络安全合作，共同保护关键基础设施，鼓励更多国家加入《布达佩斯网络犯罪公约》，共同打击网络犯罪，支持现行国际法适用于网络空间，制定国际网络空间稳定性战略框架等。

网络空间军控已开始成为世界主要国家维护自身安全、推进安全和外交战略的重要手段。国际交流平台已开始涉及很多相关问题。各国政府及专家学者对网络空间军控问题的研究日益深入，开始着手制定更加具体的网络相关军控措施。制定人工智能行为规则十分重要。国际社会应共同努力，使人工智能向有利于人类的方向发展。拥有核武器的国家应让人工智能远离核战争的任何领域。

从技术角度看，当前尚没有任何武器能够替代核武器。核武器依然是维护全球战略稳定的重要力量。人工智能技术和网络空间技术的快速发展，导致现有核武器系统变得脆弱，可能搅乱现有战略平衡，以致产生严重后果。为防止人工智能对人类的破坏作用，拥有核武器国家应该最大限度地降低核武器的作用，奉行不首先使用核武器的政策，确保未来不会发生核战争。

总之，新技术发展给人类带来生活便利，同时也给世界带来许多不确定性。正如习近平主席指出的那样："新一代人工智能正在全球范围蓬勃兴起，为经济社会发展注入新动能，正在改变人们的生活方式。把握好这一发展机遇，处理好人工智能在法律、安全、就业、道德伦理和政府治理方面提出的

新课题需要各国深化合作，共同探讨。"这也是以人工智能为代表的新兴技术面临的重大问题，世界各国应该紧密合作，共建有利于人类幸福美满的人类命运共同体。

新兴科技与全球安全

瑞典席勒研究所所长
乌尔夫·桑德马克

当前，现有世界秩序正在逐渐瓦解，国际法越来越不受尊重。《联合国宪章》确立的主权平等原则是当代国际关系的基本准则，联合国每一个成员国的主权都应受到尊重。实际上，准则中不仅规定了"被动"的不干涉内政的和平政策，而且还规定了"主动"的和平政策，即促进"他者的利益"，这种促进和平的积极理念在中国推进"双赢"合作新范式的政策中得到了充分体现。

在当今世界，我们看到很多反面例子。所谓的反恐战争已经成为超越国界部署无人机、特种部队、情报机构和进行军事干预的借口。地缘政治学的"伪科学"已重新启动，不但未给其他国家带来和平，反而给地区带来了不稳定因素。瑞典也存在通过人道主义援助支持所谓的"武装斗争"，以迫使叙利亚政权更迭的现象。瑞典政府和其他西方国家政府一样，拒绝承认其代理人战争已经失败，拒绝与叙利亚实现关系正常化，从而延长了灾难性的战争。英国和美国地缘政治学的理念是基于对欧亚大陆中心地带的控制，将其与欧亚大陆边缘地区隔离开来。西方国家无视国际法准则，导致了国际秩序的崩溃，也导致了贸易战、极端紧张局势和大国之间的危险战争。如同普京总统所说，美俄关系"每时每刻都在恶化"。

大国主导的旧安全观念已无法应对新的安全形势，调整安全观念刻不容缓，否则安全秩序将陷入混乱。为了在各国之间建立新的合作范式，我们需要从更高的层面来解决人类面临的紧迫问题，如贫困、食品、卫生服务、教育、住房、水电问题和核武器的威胁等。从这个层面而言，国际社会可通过发展新兴技术，找到一条通向全球安全的有效途径。

事实上，人类不仅面临核扩散的严重威胁，而且还面临小行星或各种形式的彗星、太阳耀斑、宇宙辐射等来自太空的危险。圣彼得堡州立大学天体力学系发布的最新报告指出，小行星阿波菲斯将在 2029 年、2036 年、2068 年出现几次近地飞行，2029 年的飞行距离仅为地球与月球距离的十分之一。俄罗斯和美国已经就小行星撞击地球开展防御合作进行了认真的讨论。

空间科学十分重要，某种程度上，空间科学将使人的心灵得到升华，并能够超越人类所有文化障碍。太空探索本身并不是最终目的，它体现了人类探索宇宙的创造性潜能，是一种从根本上加速科技创新的手段。中国和巴基斯坦在航空航天领域建立的合作关系是利用新兴技术建立长期合作的典范。中国在嫦娥四号项目中与德国和瑞典都开展了科学载荷方面的合作，见证了科学在超越政治冲突和促进技术交流方面的作用，被看作是欧中太空合作的新象征。

展望未来，我们可以构建一个能源和原材料安全的世界。通过开采氦-3，能够在地球上生产核聚变能源。核聚变能源将为人类提供空间科学、医疗、天体研究等方面的更好条件。这种新兴技术将从根本上改变原材料的可用性。核聚变能源是一种几乎无限的能源，将使开采岩石以获取矿物甚至开发利用海水盐成为可能。核聚变技术将有助于驳斥地缘政治零和博弈的理论。由于生产力大幅提高，征服和战争将更加"无利可图"。中国在开发利用核聚变能源方面正在付诸实际行动。

习近平主席在 2013 年提出了"一带一路"倡议，这是一种先进的理念，极大促进了世界的联通性。"一带一路"并不是将世界划分为孤立经济区的地缘政治，而是致力于发展全球基础设施网络，并正在创造一个新的经济合作平台。这个更先进的经济合作平台使世界经济达到更高生产力水平成为可能，同时让投资更加有效和安全。"一带一路"倡议有利于推动新兴科技的国际化应用，建立更安全的经济金融体系，有利于推动人类命运共同体建设，建设人类更加美好的未来。

人工智能军事化及其安全、伦理及法律挑战

国防科技大学国家安全与军事战略研究所所长、研究员

朱启超

近年来，随着大数据的快速增长、算力的显著提升和深度学习算法的进步，人工智能在经历了两起两落的起伏后，迎来了第三次发展浪潮，正深刻影响各国政治、经济、军事、社会、文化等各个领域。世界各国尤其是军事大国都在加快推进人工智能的军事应用，战争性质和形态正在经历深刻变化。作为一种新的颠覆性技术，人工智能将使未来战争形态呈现出怎样的图景？将如何推动新一轮军事变革？人工智能的军事应用将带来哪些挑战和隐忧？本文试就这些问题做一个初步探索。

一、人工智能驱动战争形态发生历史性演变

战争是人类社会的一种特殊活动，指"敌对双方为了一定的政治、经济目的，有组织有计划地使用武力进行激烈的军事对抗活动；是解决阶级、民族、政治集团、国家之间矛盾冲突的最高斗争形式；是政治通过暴力手段的继续"。克劳塞维茨指出，战争是"政治交往通过另一种手段的继续"。战争形态是指在战争这一事物所表现出来的外在形式或其内在的本质的必然联系的外在表现，它由这一时期的经济状况、政治性质和军事发展水平等因素所决定。技术形态的变化影响着军事形态的变化，进而推动战争形态的转型。换言之，一个时代的标志性（颠覆性）技术的突破与应用唯有推动军事系统的结构与功能发生根本性变革，即作战主体、作战工具、作战空间、作战样式、军队体制编制、军事理论等方面出现质变，才能推动军事系统发生

质的跃升，战争形态也随之转型。这样看来，战争形态的基本要素就包括战争主体、战争工具（武器装备）、战争空间（战场）、战争样式（战法）、战争理论、军队编成等具体方面。战争形态的转型就意味着这些要素中的部分或全部发生了显著变化，促使战争向另一种形态跃升。

纵观历史，重大科技的突破和应用往往给战争带来革命性变化。从古至今，人类社会大致发生了四次重大军事革命。第一次军事革命是青铜、铁等金属兵器取代棍棒等木石兵器的金属化军事革命；第二次军事革命是热兵器取代冷兵器的火药化军事革命；第三次军事革命是机械化装备出现和普及所带来的机械化军事革命；第四次军事革命则是由信息技术革新带动信息化武器装备进入战场的信息化军事革命。第三次和第四次之间还穿插着核武器为标志的军事革命。不难看出，这四次军事革命的触发都离不开那一时代颠覆性技术的出现与发展。从冶炼技术到火药技术、机械化技术、原子能技术，再到信息技术，四次军事革命的发生都贯穿着技术革命的核心作用。与四次军事革命相适应，人类社会分别经历了冷兵器战争、热兵器战争、机械化战争以及信息化战争等四大战争形态。从人类正式战争的出现到 19 世纪初属于冷兵器战争时代，这一时期主导的武器装备是刀、斧、棒、矛、弓、弩等冷兵器，武器装备释放能量的主要方式是将体能转化为机械能，主要考验作战人员的体能。热兵器战争时代大致处于 19 世纪初到 20 世纪初，这一时期主导的武器装备是以火药为基础的枪、炮等热兵器，武器杀伤方式主要是将热能转换为化学能，主要考验作战人员的技能。机械化战争时代大致处于 20 世纪初至 20 世纪中叶，这一时期飞机、坦克等机械化武器装备平台开始登上战争舞台，能量释放方式主要是化学能转换为机械能。20 世纪中叶至今，精确制导武器等信息化武器装备逐步登上历史舞台，人类社会逐步进入信息化战争阶段。

当前，人类仍处于信息化战争时代。与此同时，随着人工智能技术的飞速发展，与军事智能化相关的概念和武器装备不断涌现，各国都在积极调整现有军事理论和体制编制，战争形态向智能化转型的趋势愈发明显。战争主体将由原来的由人构成的军事组织、国家及国家联盟向由人构成的军事组织、非军事组织、非国家组织以及机器人部队等转变；军事革命形态将由金属化、火药化、机械化向信息化、智能化、无人化等方向转变；战争博弈的主导因素将由原来的物质、能量向信息、智能转变；战争样式将由原来的冷兵器格杀向机器人战、网络中心战、算法战、认知战等转变，混合战争的特征更加丰富；对抗样式将从原来的武器对抗、平台对抗向体系对抗、人机编组之间的对抗转变；战场空间将从原来的陆、海、空等物理空间进一步向太空、网络、电磁、生物、认知等领域拓展，跨域作战成为常态；军队兵种将在传统兵种力量的基础上不断增加网络部队、太空部队、机器人部队等新型兵种力量。

二、人工智能推动新一轮军事变革

一般认为，当新的军事技术、武器装备、作战理念和组织编成相互作用显著提升军事作战能力时，将促动新的军事变革的发生。人工智能在军事领域越来越广泛的应用，正成为军事变革的重要推手，催生新的战争样式，改变战争制胜的内在机理。一方面，运用人工智能将可能塑造颠覆性的军事能力，带来战斗力的倍增或大幅跃升，另一方面，也将为军事理论创新和军事能力实践带来新的挑战。

（一）冲击传统战争观念

人类战争史经历了冷兵器时代、热兵器时代、机械化时代、信息化时代，人工智能使得智能化时代加速到来。对于军事能力建设而言，如果说机械化是基础，信息化是神经和血液，则智能化体现的是人类智能之间的终极对决。智能是否可分为高阶智能和低阶智能？拥有高阶智能化水平的军队对于低阶智能化的军队是否具有压倒性优势？如果说战斗力是人、武器以及人与武器的结合，那么智能化战争时代的人、机器人和智能信息系统之间的关系该如何界定？如果说人的"机器化"和机器的"人化"是两个必然的发展趋势，会思考的机器人代替人类拼杀是否有悖于传统的战争伦理？人工智能使得战场感知能力和信息处理能力空前提高，在高技术化的战场上战争的

"迷雾"是否仍旧存在？对于这些问题的理解认识，要求军事领域必须来一场头脑风暴式的观念更新。

（二）推动武器装备和指挥决策智能化

在智能化武器装备上，一方面，人工智能作为一种"使能技术"，将嵌入传统武器装备体系，提升其智慧程度和作战效能。另一方面，人工智能还会催生出新的武器装备，比如高度自主的无人机、无人车、无人潜航器等新型无人作战平台和"无人蜂群"、仿生机器人等。在智能化指挥控制上，各国军队通过开发各种军事信息系统，构建功能强大的栅格化网络信息体系，从而提高智能化评估和辅助决策能力。近年来，美军建立并升格网络司令部，大力加强网络攻防能力建设，重点基于云计算、大数据分析等技术研发针对网络入侵的智能诊断信息系统，能够自动诊断网络入侵来源、己方网络受损程度和数据恢复能力。此外，美军正在推动人工智能用于国防情报分析，辅助国防部和其他军队层级做出战争决策，提升情报分析和决策的科学性、有效性和可靠性。2017 年 4 月 26 日，时任美国国防部副部长罗伯特·沃克签署备忘录，授权建立"算法战跨职能小组"，旨在"将国防部拥有的海量数据迅速转变为可用情报，有效促进人工智能、大数据、机器学习等技术在军事情报领域的应用"。不难预见，人工智能将逐步进入战争设计、战略方针、作战指挥等关键领域，人机融合模式将成为未来指挥决策的基本形态。

（三）促进军事理论创新

战争的物质技术基础不断更新，战争形态和战争样式不断演化，自然为战略理论和作战概念创新开辟了新的空间。比如，信息技术的蓬勃发展，其催化剂、粘合剂和效能倍增器的作用日益凸显，不断催生人工智能领域新的颠覆性技术，但另一方面，也使得处于技术优势的一方为模仿跟随者提供了"战略诱导"和"技术欺骗"的可能；精确打击弹药、无人化装备与网络信息体系的组合应用，催生了"分布式杀伤""母舰理论""作战云""蜂群战术"等新的智能化作战理论；凭借己方的信息优势和决策优势，如何在去中心化的战场网络中切断和迟滞对手的信息与决策回路，成为智能化战争中克敌制胜必须解决的核心问题。可以预见，"无人集群作战"和"人机协同作战"有望成为未来的主流作战样式。分布式作战的无人集群系统具有侦察监视和自主攻击等"察打一体"的作战能力，且性价比高并可回收，用于对敌方的饱和攻击拥有巨大的优势。美军正在加紧推进以"小精灵"等项目为代表的"无人蜂群"研究，验证和评估低成本无人系统集群技术的可行性。此外，人机协同作战也日益受到各国军队青睐，与士兵协同作战的"勇士"排爆机器人已经在阿富汗和伊拉克战场上大显身手。

（四）更新军事教育训练手段

人工智能在军事领域的广泛应用，将引发军事教育与训练领域的新的变革。战场制胜的武器装备和系统越来越具有智能化的特征，与科学家群体、前沿技术实验室、作战实验室的连结越来越紧密，科学家设计战争、军事家指挥战争、人工智能打赢战争的局面将会到来，传统的教育训练科目将被进一步压缩。打游戏式的智能化训练平台、体验式的虚拟现实技术及增强现实技术将给军事训练提供新的手段，而以超大规模计算、云计算、大数据技术为支撑的知识挖掘和数据挖掘过程对于人工智能系统而言，本身就是能力训练的重要组成部分。人工智能技术的发展也将为军事人员物理技能、生理机能、心理效应等各层次的教育训练评估提供新的手段。2018 年 6 月 18 日，美国国会正式通过的《2019 财年国防授权法案》专设"将先进技术纳入职业军事教育"一节，强调要加强人工智能等先进技术在职业军事教育中的应用，要求国防部长在 2018 年 12 月 1 日前向国会汇报将人工智能等技术嵌入职业军事教育项目的可行方案，具体包括考虑建立适当的职业军事教育院校机构、扩大职业军事教育机构在民间招生等方面。

三、人工智能军事化的安全、伦理与法律隐忧

人工智能正在向军事领域加速渗透，这既给军事变革带来巨大的机遇，同时也潜藏着诸多风险。概括起来，主要有以下几个方面。

（一）安全隐忧

人工智能军备竞赛与战略不稳定性。"战略稳定性"是指当潜在对手认识到如果与对方发生冲突难以得利，双方便不会轻举妄动，从而产生战略稳定。根据攻防平衡理论，当防御占优时战略稳定性会增强，而进攻占优时战略稳定性会削弱。致命性人工智能武器的出现和应用会对战略稳定性产生极大的负面影响，威胁地区和国际安全。具体而言，人工智能武器可能会增强进攻方面的主导地位，并产生一系列严重后果，包括先发制人将成为获取战略优势的最佳手段，最佳的防御策略就是发动先发制人打击，这将降低国家间武力使用的门槛，提高军备竞赛的可能性。此外，人工智能武器的使用会让使用武力的责任归属成为巨大难题，容易因此造成战略误判，破坏战略稳定性。再者，人工智能武器走向战场还会放大国家间武装冲突的不对称性。拥有先进技术且有能力开发、采购和部署人工智能武器的国家与没有这些能力的国家之间的差距在今后很有可能会继续放大武装冲突的不对称性。此外，大国战略稳定很大程度上建立在"相互确保摧毁"的核威慑基础上，即双方都拥有慑止对方先发制人的二次核打击能力。然而，目前快速发展的传感器技术可能使得潜艇、机动导弹系统等报复性武器装备更加容易被发现、定位和摧毁，增大二次打击力量的脆弱性，由此侵蚀核威慑体系的根基。据报道，美国防部正在资助一项旨在运用人工智能帮助识别和预测核导弹发射，以及追踪和瞄准朝鲜和其他国家的移动导弹发射平台的技术。如果属实，无疑会极大破坏战略稳定性。兰德公司的一份报告甚至认为人工智能可能会在 2040 年前引发一场核大战。

人工智能武器装备的扩散与被恶意使用的风险。人工智能是一个中立的技术，但是使用者却并非中立，因此存在被恶意使用的风险。此次人工智能浪潮大都出现于私营领域，人工智能技术本身具有明显的"军民两用性"和"易扩散性"，人工智能软件能够以几乎为零的成本进行复制和传播，这也降低了使用者获取此类技术的门槛和难度，只要拥有足够的资金便能有效提升自己的网络攻击能力，而不需要太高的技术要求。人工智能技术和武器装备的诸多优势对于恐怖组织、跨国犯罪集团等非国家行为体具有巨大吸引力，因为它能够成倍增强武力强度，有效降低攻击成本，节省自身战斗人员，使其更加有能力发动恐怖袭击。例如，目前已经开发了运送爆炸物的无人机的技术，一旦此类技术落入恐怖主义手中，将为独狼式恐怖袭击提供新的手段和方法，从而更难防范和追溯责任。因此，人工智能武器研发可能加剧恐怖主义威胁，恶化全球或区域不稳定状况。此外，研究表明，人工智能技术不仅能够用于搜集和分析数据，也能用于制造包括自动生成的图像、视频以及文本等虚假信息。不难预见，人工智能所具有的制造"假新闻""假情报"等虚假信息的能力一旦被恶意使用，势必为战争蒙上另一层"迷雾"，在未来的战场上真假信息将会愈加难以分辨。

人工智能的局限性。人工智能技术虽然有很多优点，但是也存在诸多局限性。可以将之分为内部固有的局限性和外部局限性两个方面。内部的局限性主要有三点：一是"狭窄性"。目前的人工智能技术基本属于"弱人工智能"或"狭义人工智能"范畴，它尽管能够在规则确定、信息完备的系统中展现出强于人类的极大优越性，但是在解决可编程范围外的战争问题时仍旧需要人类的理性分析能力、灵活应变能力、道德分辨能力等，在这一方面人工智能无法取代和超越人类智能。换言之，目前的人工智能技术和系统缺乏理解广义语境的能力，缺乏人类常识和随机应变的灵活性，这也是人工智能领域的"莫拉维克悖论"。二是"脆弱性"。这意味着，一旦真实世界的环境发生变化，人工智能系统就可能会失效甚至发生错乱，从"超级聪明"退化为"超级愚蠢"。如果将此类人工智能系统运用于高度变化的军事战场领域，一旦发生错乱而操作者又未能及时制止，就可能带来灾难性后果。比如，自动导弹预警系统错误预警而发射导弹，将可能带来误伤甚至危机升级。三是"难以解释性和难以预测性"。不同于传统的信息技术，人工智能技术具有极高的复杂性，也更加容易带来不确定性和不可预测性。具体而言，人工智能存在"算法黑箱"的固有缺陷，其作用机制难以为设计、部署和操作此类机器的人类所完全理解，结果也更加难以预测和保证。此外，由于系统自我交互等引起的系统故障很难排除，当不同方案和系统组合或者系统和代码互动速度过快时，这类风险可能会加剧。另一方面，外部的局限性主要来自于人机交互错误、网络攻击（比如遭遇敌方黑客攻击、数据注毒等带来灾难性后果）。人工智能武器装备需要依托电脑软件和系统才能运行，而软件和系统恰恰容易被敌方网络攻击，在战场上出现失能甚至临阵倒戈的风险。

（二）伦理隐忧

1942年，著名美籍俄罗斯裔科幻作家艾萨克·阿西莫夫在《惊奇科幻小说》中首次提出机器人的伦理问题，并设定了"机器人三定律"，以约束机器人行为，使之遵守保护人类的强制性道德准则。如今，人工智能的快速发展使机器人的自主性日益提升并逐步走向战场，也对传统战争伦理构成了巨大挑战。

日益自主的武器装备将冲击传统人机关系。人与技术支撑的武器装备的关系在历史中不断演变。从人类社会战争产生至今的很长一段时期，武器装备不管怎么发展只不过是人手中的工具，只是在杀伤性、复杂性和精密性上有所不同罢了。换言之，这一时期人类始终是武器装备的绝对控制者，武器装备只是人的体力和智力的延伸和拓展，对人类这一整体并不构成直接挑战。如今，快速发展的人工智能技术可能使得武器装备的自主性越来越高。长期来看，如果战争机器人进化出自我意识，拥有与人类类似甚至超越人类的判断和决策能力，从技术性替代转换为决策性替代，将对人类这一整体的生存构成主观威胁，严重冲击人类传统的伦理道德和人的尊严。近期来看，如果技术上可行，是否应当将"生死决策权"让渡给没有生命的机器，使之能够在战场上自主发起攻击决定人的生死？这一问题将对阿西莫夫"不得伤害人类"这一定律构成严重挑战。是否应该将人类的伦理道德规范植入日益智能化的机器？植入什么样的伦理道德规范以及如何植入？是否应该限制致命性自主武器的研发？这些问题都将成为人工智能走向军事应用后不得不面对的难题。

智能化武器装备挑战传统战争伦理。在人工智能武器不断走向战场的趋势下，传统的开战正义、交战正义、终战正义等战争伦理都将受到严重挑战。具体而言，在开战正义方面，越来越多的非国家行为体也能获得廉价而易扩散的人工智能武器装备，一旦向国家行为体发起攻击将冲击合法权威、正当理由这些要素。此外，随着人工智能支撑的无人化武器装备越来越多地走向战场，人员伤亡在国家战争选项中的顾虑弱化，战争的门槛也可能显著降低，以无人作战平台为主导的小型战争更可能爆发。在交战正义方面，目前的人工智能武器还难以做到区分军人和平民以及军用设施和民用设施，一旦投入战场使用将可能造成大规模误杀误伤，致使平民无辜伤亡。更为甚者，如果没有人类监督的致命性自主武器走向战场，由于其高度的自主性、致命性以及无情感性，杀戮生灵不会有任何愧疚感和怜悯之心，这将严重冲击人类的伦理道德底线。在终战正义方面，人工智能武器装备的军事应用可能会造成战争责任主体困境。以往的战争中，只有人才是战争中的唯一合法主体和责任承担者，但是随着战场机器人和智能系统的自主性越来越高，机器能否成为道德主体和责任主体，承担战争行动中的非正义不合法责任？这一问题将日益凸显。

（三）法律隐忧

除了安全和伦理方面的隐忧，人工智能军事化也带来了诸多法律问题。

战争问责问题。人工智能武器装备的研制和使用可能会带来"问责空白"问题，造成这一问题的主要原因在于责任归因将变得越来越困难。对于人工智能武器系统尤其是无人系统作战引发的不当行为，其责任的追究和分配可能涉及国家行为体、个人和武器系统本身等多个层次，覆盖系统的研制、生产、装备与应用这一整个过程。因此，涉事武器系统的操纵者、制造者、程序员、采购员、军火商、军事指挥员、设备保障人员乃至武器系统本身都难辞其咎，追溯和分配责任的难度将大大提升。如何进行相关责任的分配？是否应该追溯机器人犯罪的法律责任？武器系统如果没有生命和自主意识，又如何能够感受到惩罚和威慑？追溯其责任又有何法律和现实价值？这些问题目前依然悬而未决。未来，"人的机械化"和"机械的人化"这两大趋势将愈发明显，届时战争责任分配可能面临更大的困境。

国际人道法的核心原则将遭受重大挑战。在人工智能日益走向战场的背景下，国际武装冲突法中的必要原则、区分原则、比例原则和人道原则等核心原则都将受到严峻挑战，面临着如何适用和调整的问题。具体而言，必要原则是指为了使敌人屈服而采取的必要作战行动是正当的，但显然不必要的军事行动则是禁止的；比例原则是指在对军事目标发起攻击时，要尽可能减少对平民和民用物体的偶发或附带损伤。在军事行动中造成的附带损伤，不能超过为取得预期的直接和具体的军事优势所造成的破坏；区分原则是指在武装冲突中要区分作战人员和平民，保护受害者；人道原则是指对所有人员均应给予人道待遇。目前，战场机器人仍然无法有效区分军人与平民，一旦投入战场使用而造成滥杀无辜将对区别性和人道性原则构成重大挑战；机器人战场使用所带来的附带杀伤将挑战比例原则和人道原则；无人装备泛滥推动战争门槛降低将对必要原则构成挑战。目前的国际法无疑都是以人为中心的，但机器人是否能够成为法律主体？现有的国际武装冲突法是否足以规制当前和日后日益自主的人工智能武器？是否需要修改或者制定新的国际人道法？如何制定？这些问题都需要进一步研究和探讨。

客观看待人工智能军事化可能带来的安全、伦理及法律挑战，是我们理解人工智能、发展人工智能、管控人工智能的前提。人工智能本身的特点，为人们理解人工智能带来了难度甚至障碍。客观看待人工智能军事化可能带来的安全、法律与挑战，需要树立正确的思维理念。**一要秉持科学的态度**。人工智能带来的安全挑战既可能来自于技术不成熟，也有可能由于人为管理管控上的疏失，必须用科学的态度，进行实事求是的分析。一般来说，人工智能引发的安全问题可以分为三个层次：一是某行业某领域或某系统内安全操作规程管理方面的安全风险；二是国家安全层面对于政治、经济、金融、科技、国防等领域带来的安全挑战；三是由于人工智能技术的跨国使用引发的网络安全、太空安全、核安全、反恐行动乃至国际安全治理等方面的挑战。人工智能在不同层面带来的安全挑战具有不同的特点及应对要求，需给予区别对待，而不能"一锅煮"甚至张冠李戴。**二要坚持发展的态度**。总体上看，人工智能带来的安全挑战仍处于可控的范围，人们对人工智能未来发展的担忧，主要在于人工智能作为一项技术可能触发更多的安全问题。历史上，每一次工业革命或技术革命的到来初期，由于人们对于技术的认知与实践体验相对缺乏，都曾引发过一定程度的恐慌。比如第一次工业革命初期作坊工人对于机器的抵制与破坏，第二次工业革命初期人们对于电力使用不当造成人员伤亡的恐慌。作为不断发展演进的人类文明的产物，需要我们用发展的眼光看待人工智能的正面作用和可能引发的安全挑战，既充分发挥人工智能的潜力造福人类，又能够未雨绸缪管控人工智能可能引发的安全危机。人们越是能够客观看待人工智能带来的安全挑战，就越能够开辟人工智能安全科技与安全产业创新的蓝海。**三要坚持合作的态度。**人工智能技术与信息技术的发展紧密相关，尤其是移动宽带通信、大数据、云计算、物联网等领域的技术突破，将促进人工智能相关技术和产业的成熟。从技术特点看，人工智能与信息技术类似，都具有低成本、易扩散、难封控的特征，并且技术一旦成熟，市场的边际成本将大大降低，甚至被认为属于"零边际成本"的技术。这使得人工智能可能引发的安全问题也将具有易扩散、难封控的特点。比如，若监管缺失，一个黑客就有可能运用新的人工智能算法及入侵技术破坏一个国家的电网、公共交通指挥网络等的正常运转，引发大面积的灾难性后果，甚至殃及无辜。从理论上说，社会信息化智能化程度越高，对技术体系就愈加依赖，而一旦原有的技术体系受到冲击，将产生新的不确定性和脆弱性。在信息技术、人工智能技术等大发展的时代，我们面临的安全挑战呈现出技术复杂性、体系脆弱性的双重特征。正因如此，必须坚持开放合作的态度，国家政府部门、社会行业领域及公民个体等应共同加强对人工智能的技术认知和实践体验，共同应对人工智能可能带来的安全挑战，那些"各人自扫门前雪"独善其身的想法已与这个时代越来越脱节。

　　总之，对于人工智能军事化的发展浪潮，既不能只见其利而盲目追捧，也不能因为其潜在的安全、伦理及法律挑战而踟蹰不前。必须客观认识人工智能的发展应用，人类只要能够在未来实践中避免对人工智能相关安全问题的误解、误判和误用，就仍然能够掌控自己的命运。

巴西视角下国际安全中的科技因素

巴西国际问题研究中心学术和项目协调员

莫妮克·戈德费尔德

巴西国际问题研究中心项目分析员

加布里埃尔·托雷斯

巴西国际问题研究中心是拉丁美洲顶尖的国际安全智库，研究领域涉及国际体系运作及其主要问题，每年与康拉德·阿登纳基金会巴西办事处合作主办科帕卡巴纳国际安全会议，得到欧盟驻巴西代表处的支持。

一、巴西有关安全与国防领域的研究力量正逐步壮大

2004 年至今，每年 9 月份，我们会在里约热内卢举办科帕卡巴纳国际安全会议。按惯例，巴西国防部长会在开幕式上致辞。会议主要目的在于讨论、展望和传播欧盟、南美地区在国际安全问题上的战略与行动，针对全球地缘政治、地区安全的突出特点、挑战和未来可能性等议题，汇聚来自外交界、军事界、学术界、政界的不同观点。

同时，科帕卡巴纳国际安全会议也是国际关系及相关专业本科生和研究生的重要学习平台，他们作为听众参与其中。会议还有助于拓展和加强巴西在安全与国防领域的研究，数个研究机构和项目陆续成立，如巴西防务研究协会。

科帕卡巴纳国际安全会议、巴西防务研究协会已把对安全和国防的讨论由军界拓展至全社会，让尽可能多的民间角色参与其中。就科帕卡巴纳国际安全会议而言，它已积累了良好的媒体资源，可针对特定议题引导公众

观点。

起初，科帕卡巴纳国际安全会议主要聚焦于制定国际安全领域的公共政策，推动地区合作。近年来，会议讨论的议题更为多样化，如美国大选对国际安全局势的影响、和平建设行动、多边主义，以及巴西的作用和影响等。会议还重视讨论国际安全领域的科技因素。

二、科帕卡巴纳国际安全会议与科技安全议题

科帕卡巴纳国际安全会议召开前将举行两次预备会议，一个是闭门圆桌会，另一个是面向公众开放的研讨会，发言人的文章将结集出版。虽然会议在 9 月份召开，但对特定议题的讨论可持续一整年。每年 2 月份，主办方会联合确定会议主题。

联合国贸易与发展会议 2017 年报告显示，巴西互联网用户数量全球第四，达到 1.2 亿，仅排在美国、印度和中国之后。巴西社交网络的用户数量也非常庞大，拥有全球第二大 Facebook 用户群体。然而，在国际电信联盟 2017 年发布的全球网络安全指数（GCI）中，巴西只排在第 38 位。

巴西相当一部分网络安全技术由军方掌控，如国防部下设的网络防御中心和内阁安全机构等。在民用领域，里约科技与社会研究所、国际关系与对外贸易研究所都针对网络安全议题举办会议或发表评论。

2017 年，网络安全议题正式进入科帕卡巴纳国际安全会议及其预备会，主题是"安全架构：南美与欧洲的交流互动"。讨论中，各方都强调了在全球秩序转型期安全架构面临的挑战，其中就包括网络安全挑战，由此引出大会第一个分议题——安全架构与网络威胁，分析了在管理网络危机时国家和地区政策的进步与挑战，突出强调数据保护与尊重隐私面临的困境。

2018 年，科帕卡巴纳国际安全会议的主题围绕国际危机管理，聚焦当下移民和环境危机。4 月举办的第一场预备会议则重点关注科技问题，集中了来自国营和私营部门、学术界和民间团体代表，议题为"竞选期间的网络安全和国家利益"，讨论假新闻和垃圾邮件对公众舆论的影响，以及政府、媒

体和民间团体应发挥的作用。会议还关注外部势力干预及其对选举结果可信度的影响，认为需制定政策预防、制止和回应网络攻击。

会议讨论遵循"查塔姆宫规则"（Chatham House rule），不透露发言者身份，汇编成指导文件为 9 月份召开的全会提供参考。文件主要目标为解决大选期间的安全问题，并以 2014 年巴西大选为例，当时巴西网络服务器平均每秒受到 20 万次网络攻击，引发人们对假新闻和垃圾邮件影响的关注和思考。我们看到，在 2018 年巴西大选中，这些影响变得更为显著。文件指出，自 2016 年起，全世界广泛讨论、研究网络攻击，公开指控网络攻击，甚至出现"妄想症"。巴西已举办多次全球性重大活动，2016 年举办的里约奥运会遭受严重的网络安全威胁。此前，巴西已成功举办了 2007 年泛美运动会、2011 年世界军人运动会和 2014 年世界杯。

据参会者介绍，2016 年奥运会期间，共计触发了约 4000 万次网络犯罪警报。事实上，里约奥运会组委会早已通过加强协调政府力量保护敏感信息系统和阻止网络攻击，并于 6 年前成立了一休化操作中心，采用大数据分析，使用最新一代软件，从市内交通、安全漏洞到网络攻击等方面对里约奥运会进行全方位监测。

里约奥运会前夕，巴西正式通过反恐法，明确将为可能发生的恐怖袭击所做的准备行动定为犯罪。反恐法的首个应用案例发生于奥运会开幕前，主要犯罪行为是操控话题标签。一群人因涉嫌与"伊斯兰国"有关，密谋在奥运会期间发动恐怖袭击而被捕，此前他们的通信软件已受监控。这一逮捕行为虽因缺少实际证据而受到合法性质疑，但也说明社交媒体和网络通信不仅可用于组织和策划恐怖主义活动，也可用于阻止类似安全事件发生。

2019 年，科帕卡巴纳国际安全会议的主题是"第四次工业革命对国际安全局势和全球秩序重塑的影响"。第一次预备会议重点关注了网络安全和人工智能问题，汇集了军事院校的高水平专家。讨论重点为第四次工业革命的安全隐患，应对网络安全挑战的战略，技术竞争对重塑全球秩序的影响，以及冲突中自主性武器应用带来的风险和机遇等。9 月份全会拟对这些议题进行拓展讨论。专家们普遍认为，学术界应加强合作，深入讨论科技对安全与国防的影响。关键的问题是，如何应对科技领域日趋紧张的竞争态势？如何应对混合战、网络战和非对称冲突？我们应优先发展何种防御力量？

三、结论

巴西和巴西国际问题研究中心充分利用科帕卡巴纳国际安全会议这一平台加强在安全与国防领域的研究。

巴西日益关注科技因素对国际安全的影响，特别是自 2016 年里约奥运会以来，这一趋势更为明显。网络安全隐患在 2014 年巴西大选已有显现，而 2018 年大选更为突出。

我们看到，巴西相关立法工作仍处于初期阶段，应对科技带来的安全挑战主要以军方研究机构为主。虽然这一议题越发紧迫，但学术研究和社会关注度还不够。网络等问题不仅事关大国角逐科技领域主导权等地缘政治之争，也是巴西面临的紧迫问题。例如，无人机参与城市暴力行动应受到何种约束？如何利用科技手段取得情报以有效侦查或破获国家或跨国犯罪组织网络？

总之，这是一个极富前景的研究领域，当下问题比答案更多。

第四编

安全观念演变与全球安全治理

共谋全球安全之道

俄罗斯联邦公众院副主席

联合国原副秘书长

谢尔盖·奥尔尼忠启则

在新兴的多极化世界格局中，围绕规则制定权的竞争越发激烈，这一趋势在很大程度上决定了现阶段国际关系的发展。如今，我们清楚地看到，某些国家企图独占全球事务决策权，甚至不惜动用一系列令人望而生畏的手段向竞争对手施加制裁。普适性的国际法规范和原则被束之高阁或被选择性使用，多边机构的作用遭到人为削弱。这些因素加大了战略不确定性，导致互信缺失、国际合作空间不断缩减。在此背景下，全球安全与战略稳定面临诸多挑战。

一、国际核裁军体系遭到严重损害

某些国家采取进攻性外交政策，致使一些弱小国家认为只有拥有核武器才能保障国家主权不受外来军事干涉，由此破坏了核不扩散机制。此外，我们遗憾地看到，现有的国际核军控条约体系出现动摇，核武器扩散的危险势头逐步上升，特别是美俄等核大国间签署的条约失去约束力。

2014 年，美国宣布暂停与俄罗斯一切军事合作，有关军控与核不扩散的讨论急转直下。特朗普总统曾多次对普京总统表示希望两国共同控制军备竞赛的势头，但美国政府却挑衅地退出《中导条约》，而非建立双边对话机制。美国谴责俄方违反条约规定，却从未提供任何证据来佐证其对俄指控，又拒绝回应俄方合理的关切。2019 年 2 月 2 日，美国政府正式宣布暂停履行《中导条约》相关义务，并于 6 个月后正式退出。

日前，白宫还未决定是否延长《美俄关于进一步削减和限制进攻性战略武器措施的条约》（新 START 条约）。俄方一直完全履行和遵守条约义务，美方公布的数据证实俄削减了相关武器。与此相反，美国重新部署了 56 架三叉戟 II 型潜射洲际导弹发射器，41 架 B-52H 重型轰炸机随时待命，没人能够肯定这些设施不会转为搭载核弹。

美国 2018 年发布的《核态势评估报告》公开点名俄中两国，核对抗成为现实的政治选项，引发全世界严重关切。我们也看到，美国一直呼吁中国加入美俄核军控谈判，这一立场十分牵强且毫不公平。若类似的核军控谈判一定要包含所有拥核国，那么美国的军事盟友英法更应加入谈判进程。

二、外空军事化动向值得高度警惕

美国为确保其在外空领域的主导优势，实施具有破坏性的计划，部署天基反导武器，危害全球安全。一旦某国将武器部署到近地轨道，就如同打开了潘多拉的盒子，外空军备竞赛将变得一发而不可收拾。因此，国际社会必须通力合作开展外空军备控制。俄中两国已将不首先在外空部署武器决议草案提交联合国大会审议，这一举动有助于防止外空军备竞赛。

三、网络空间国际合作面临障碍

新型社会文化、政治生态和史无前例的技术进步加剧了大国间的传统竞争关系。网络安全问题与新技术发展息息相关，已对当今世界构成严峻挑战。如今，网络攻击可以瞄准任何国家的关键基础设施，摧毁其防御能力。俄罗斯已充分认识到信息通信技术的潜在威胁，在双边和联合国等多边场合多次提及网络安全问题。如俄罗斯积极与上海合作组织成员国合作，参与制定国际网络空间行为规范；2009 年，上海合作组织签署《上海合作组织成员国保障国际信息安全政府间合作协定》；2015 年，上海合作组织向联大提交"信息安全国际行为准则"。

与此同时，在信息通信技术领域，某些国家不愿履行任何国际义务，甚至指责他国在网络空间实施激进行为。美国及其盟友妄想在网络空间维持主导权，从不支持俄方提出的任何倡议，特别是对俄方提出确保互不使用网络技术干涉他国内政的建议，奥巴马政府视而不见。

我们大大低估了信息通信技术领域的安全风险，这亟须汇聚全球力量来应对该挑战。2018年10月，俄罗斯正式向联合国大会提交信息安全决议草案，涉及三个重点议题：国家在网络安全领域应承担的责任、国际法在信息领域的适用性和帮助发展中国家保障网络安全。草案中提及的原则得到了除美国及其盟友以外的大多数国家支持。2018年12月，联大采纳俄方建议，决定2019年成立信息通信技术安全开放工作组，使联合国在这一领域的谈判过程更加民主、包容和透明。从1998年开始，俄方就已开始采取建设性的、和平的措施以促进信息安全，但均被美方反复地、直截了当地予以否决。

四、共同打击恐怖主义的政治意愿需转化为实际行动

随着原教旨主义意识形态的蔓延，恐怖主义成为21世纪最紧迫的安全挑战之一。出于政治利益考量，某些国家通过其代理人对恐怖组织进行资助，类似行为不可接受，也是不负责任的。国际社会必须明确谴责恐怖主义，尽最大努力携手应对恐怖主义的挑战。尽管俄美双边关系面临复杂局面，但两国间的反恐合作仍在继续，这向国际社会传递出积极信号。俄美两国于2002年成立了反恐工作组，但2014年因美国对俄罗斯制裁而陷入停滞，现在我们正在考虑重建反恐工作组。2018年12月13日，双方在维也纳进行了第一次会谈；2019年3月26日，俄美专家讨论会也在维也纳举行。这充分表明只要有政治意愿，俄美就有可能开展合作。

总之，战略稳定缺失、多极化受到挑战给当今世界发展带来负面影响。但我们必须认识到，以联合国为代表的现有国际体制仍是人类在20世纪最

伟大的成就，至今无法替代。尊重国际法的基本原则和规范，巩固联合国作为国际政治"稳压器"的权威性，促使国际关系朝着更加合理的方向发展，符合绝大多数国家的利益。我们有必要尊重所有国家的文化、历史、文明、价值观和利益，摒弃零和博弈、双重标准和结盟思维，顺应时代大势，维护全球安全。

世界上不存在"天选之国"，我们必须共谋全球安全解决之道。

建立基于规则的国际秩序是艰难而漫长的过程

中国人民争取和平与裁军协会副会长
中共中央对外联络部原副部长

于洪君

近年来，世界形势复杂多变的特点分外突出，国际关系，特别是大国关系走势不明，令人倍感忧虑。建立基于新规则的国际新秩序，正在成为人们研讨国际关系的焦点和重点。

人类社会的历史，归根到底，就是从无规则无秩序到有规则有秩序，再到建立新规则新秩序，循环往复以至永远的发展历程。公元前14—前13世纪，雄踞北非的埃及帝国与统治叙利亚地区的赫梯王国经过百年霸权争夺战，最终签署了旨在缔造永久和平、彼此和睦相处的友好条约，开创了大国实行自我约束、谋求共同安全的古老范例。但是，人类社会当时不可能建立普遍公认的相互关系准则和具有普遍约束力的行为规范。《埃及—赫梯和约》问世后，人类社会仍然生活在弱肉强食的丛林法则之下。人类发展进步的路径一再被列强争雄、国强必霸所打乱。

进入资本主义发展阶段后，历经30年宗教战争的欧洲人，切身感受到在不同民族国家之间划分边界、建立规则、维护秩序的必要性，著名的《威斯特伐利亚和约》于1648年应运而生。从此，以国家主权相互平等为重要前提，以不干涉内部事务为基本原则，以保证国家领土和独立不受侵犯为共同准则，以多边会议为争端解决机制的国际秩序初具雏形。

200多年后，欧美国家开始切实考虑共同安全、共同发展问题，其着眼点首先是人类社会普遍关心的人的生命与尊严问题，其次是各国共同关注的技术进步及其管理问题。1863年，红十字国际委员会宣告成立；1864年，瑞士、法国等 12 国签署有关改善战地伤病员境遇的《日内瓦公约》；1865年，国际电报联盟宣告成立；1874 年，欧美地区 20 多个国家成立邮政总联盟，1878 年，该联盟升格为万国邮政联盟；1889 年，各国议会联盟亮相于世界；1899 年和 1907 年，欧美国家在荷兰海牙先后召开过两次国际和平会议，当时影响很大。会议不仅通过了以《和平解决国际争端公约》为主要内容的《海牙公约》，而且还建立了世界上第一个常设仲裁法院。

当时，人类社会对国际关系和国际秩序等问题的认识还相对幼稚，相关各方在执行和约的过程中随心所欲，甚至剑走偏锋的情形时有发生。威斯特伐利亚和约体系仍不足以有效应对国际力量对比变化和大国关系重组带来的新挑战。资本主义时代各种矛盾的积累，特别是欧洲两大国家集团的形成，终于在 1914 年引发了第一次世界大战。

第一次世界大战带来了巨大破坏和可怕后果。于是，在美英法等战胜国主导下，1919 年召开了著名的巴黎和会，后来又召开华盛顿会议，有了《特里亚农条约》和凡尔赛体系，有了空中航行国际委员会之类的新型多边合作组织。甚至还有了《非战公约》，有了国际联盟，有了常设国际法院，有了国际刑警组织（当时称国际刑警委员会）。那时，国际社会为这些政府间组织的建立和运转而欢欣鼓舞，美欧大国为打造出它们主导的国际关系体系和世界秩序而踌躇满志。

然而，此时已成为世界强国的美国，由于主导世界的意图未能充分体现，拒绝参加它所发起成立的国际联盟。苏联则因社会制度和意识形态有别于西方，被排斥在国联之外许多年。美英法三国为维持对外用兵权，对《非战公约》做了重大保留。1932 年的世界裁军会议由于日德退出而短命夭折。正是因为美国缺位于国联，苏联被拒于国联，《非战公约》成为废纸，世界裁军大会成了南柯一梦，凡尔赛体系和国际联盟实际上仍弱不禁风。后来事实也充分证明，凡尔赛体系和国联没有遏制住德意日法西斯的崛起，未能约束英法两国的绥靖政策。1939 年第二次世界大战全面爆发。战事之激烈，牺牲之惨痛，远远超出了人们的想象力和承受力。国际社会开始重新考虑制定新的国际关系准则、构建更为广泛的政府间合作组织等问题。1944 年秋的敦巴顿橡树园会议，勾勒出联合国的大致蓝图。1945年2月美苏英三国领导人的雅尔塔会议，就战后世界格局、大国利益分配、国际秩序安排，特别是成立联合国等问题做出了最后决定。

1945年10月，完全不同于旧国联的联合国组织呱呱落地，象征国际新秩序的历史性文件《联合国宪章》隆重签署。此后，联合国系统下属机构及相关组织大量涌现。其中许多机构和组织，如国际法院、关贸总协定、世卫组织、国际货币基金组织、世界银行、联合国教科文组织、国际原子能机构等等，在建立和维护二战后国际政治经济秩序、推动和平发展进程、处理重大问题和危机、应对全球性挑战等方面，发挥了不可否认的重要作用。

与此相适应，二战前已存在的国际法文件，如《日内瓦公约》《海牙公约》等，经过修改补充，成为新的国际法体系的重要组成部分。一系列以《联合国宪章》为指导的新的国际法文件，如《世界人权宣言》《维也纳外交关系公约》《不扩散核武器条约》等，陆续诞生。这些反映时代变化特点，符合人类进步方向，并且得到普遍认可的新文件，覆盖面大大超过了凡尔赛体系和国联时期的文件。这是国际社会相向而行、共同努力的宝贵成果。

但是，战后初期世界分裂为东西方两大阵营。美国由于拥有独一无二的综合国力，在联合国系统以及其他各大多边组织中的地位极为突出。美国所代表的西方价值观和国际政治思维，仍在国际事务中起支配作用。20世纪40年代后期美国施行的欧洲复兴计划，即马歇尔计划，加速了欧洲分裂。它所建立的北大西洋公约组织、巴黎统筹委员会以及短命夭亡的东南亚条约组织、巴格达条约组织等，将冷战之风吹向了整个世界。对此，美国恐怕难辞其咎。

二战后成为第二超级大国的苏联，与美国分庭抗礼，打造了华沙条约组织和经济互助委员会。双方不仅在联合国系统，同时也在全球范围展开了战略角逐。20世纪80年代末90年代初，东欧剧变，苏联解体，华约崩溃，引导战后几十年国际关系发展变化的雅尔塔体系宣告破裂。在这种情况下，国际关系需要重新调整，国际法体系亟待更新，国际社会呼唤新的政治经济秩序，世界安全格局应有新的安排。全球治理从理念到实践，都有必要创新发展。

遗憾的是，在国际战略格局由两极向多极转换、经济全球化向纵深发展、社会制度与道路选择日益多样化的大过渡时期，"一超独霸"现象意外生成。近30年间，个别大国冷战思维严重，强权政治和霸权主义有新的发展。作为冷战工具的北约，不但没有随着冷战结束退出历史舞台，反而全力东扩，并且还参与了美国主导的科索沃战争。俄罗斯与美欧的关系进入不同以往的另一个复杂进程，欧洲安全格局和形势依然扑朔迷离。结果是，中东之乱祸水外溢，恐怖主义成为人类公敌，发展失衡更加突出。孤立主义、单边主义、民粹主义、种族主义、极端民族主义等极端思潮，此生彼长，浊浪翻腾。

目前，人类社会正处在一个非常重要的历史当口。如何调整现行国际关系准则，如何完善以《联合国宪章》为主的国际法体系，如何构建稳定发展的大国关系，如何构建新的世界秩序，各种建议主张莫衷一是，名目繁多的区域性全球性会议和论坛如雨后春笋。广泛建立并日益活跃的多边机制涵盖了人类活动的所有领域，已经残缺不全的雅尔塔体系，因此得到一定程度的修补。

冷战结束以来，中国一直主张超越意识形态分歧，超越社会制度差异，共同推动世界多极化、经济全球化健康发展，推动建立公正合理的国际政治经济新秩序。习近平主席提出了构建人类命运共同体的新理念和建立总体稳定均衡发展的大国关系框架的新主张，形成了既有中国政治智慧，又蕴含时代精神，并且又为国际社会广泛认同的新时代观、新文明观、新发展观、新合作观和新安全观。中国通过大力推进"一带一路"建设，引领世界各国走向发展联动、安危与共、前途与命运休戚相关之路。

正是由于中国和广大发展中国家的积极参与，冷战后联合国的声望和作用明显加强，联合国机构的地位和影响进一步显现；关贸总协定改组为世贸组织后也有了新的发展；亚太经合组织领导人非正式会议在推动区域合作方面发挥了重要作用；二十国集团成了国际社会寄予厚望的"经济联合国"。

就这一点来说，传统大国与新兴大国携手整个国际社会，共建国际新规则和世界新秩序，还是有所成就、有所建树的。

近两年来，国际形势复杂多变的特点更加突出。美国国际战略与对外关系大幅调整，国际社会构建基于新规则的新秩序，面临意想不到的冲击和挑战。鉴于大国对人类和平发展负有特殊责任，相互尊重、彼此包容、互惠发展、共谋安全、继往开来、推陈出新，应当成为各大国构建新的国际关系体系，亦即基于新规则的新秩序的共同选择。历史和实践终将证明，这是世界格局转换之际，世界各国特别是主要大国所能做出的唯一选择。对此，我们既要进行全局性战略性的深入思考，也要准备进行艰难而曲折的长期博弈。

合作构建更加公正合理的国际新秩序

法国欧洲前瞻与安全研究院院长

伊曼纽尔·德佩

美俄相继宣布退出《中导条约》，并加大在叙利亚、伊核问题上的战略博弈，欧美关于军费开支、能源供应的分歧难解，欧美关系面临更多不确定性。现有的国际安全秩序难以适应新的形势，亟须加以重塑。近年来，中国越来越多地参与联合国维和行动，在叙利亚问题、气候变化、维护地区稳定方面发挥了重要作用，特别是通过和平外交手段为解决朝核危机作出了贡献。法中应携手共同构建更加公正合理的国际新秩序。

中欧在秉持多边主义立场上有一致性。多边主义是新型安全观的重要特征，多边主义坚持合作、共同安全、开放包容的新观念。联合国安理会改革、加强以联合国为代表的国际多边机制建设、全球及地区安全秩序构建等必须坚持多边主义原则，确保各方平等参与安全事务的权利。同时，多边主义还要关注非国家行为体，并对国际组织进行相应重组以强化多边国际机制。

在促进经济发展、维护世界和平方面，中国作出了重大贡献。自2009年以来，中国在美国的直接投资增加了5倍，与非洲大陆的贸易额已接近2200亿美元，而法国加上欧盟的其他26个伙伴与非洲之间的贸易额才从"不多的"540亿欧元增加到1000亿欧元。通过保持军费稳步增长、积极参与联合国事务，中国已成为一流的安全维护者。法中在"一带一路"框架下的合作具有广阔前景。这条新的"丝绸之路"对未来几十年全球经济发展意义重大。2013年9月，习近平主席在纳扎尔巴耶夫大学的演讲中提出了"一带一路"倡议。"一带一路"经过中亚、高加索、巴尔干和中东，使中国与欧洲和非洲实现互联互通。"一带一路"倡议覆盖全球60%的人口，将帮助沿线国家弥补基础设施建设方面的缺口。新的"丝绸之路"是一条共赢之路，展现出中国更加务实的态度。中国借此将确立世界大国地位。

尽管无论在军事预算方面，还是产品占世界贸易份额方面，中国目前都难以超越美国，但是自2014年年底法定资本1000亿美元的亚投行签约以来，中国已经在亚洲基础设施建设方面取得极大进展。亚投行实际上已经吸引了世界各强国的参与，有实力与美国和欧盟进行可持续竞争。在中亚和东亚，一个新的世界秩序正在形成。在这个秩序中，"合作"外交的概念、关于"人的发展"政策得到广泛讨论。

法国与中国之间具有巨大互补性。中国近年来大幅减少温室气体排放量，对应对气候变化做出了坚定承诺。法中应建立生态命运共同体，共同应对全球性气候挑战。法中还应在非洲开展三方合作。通过多领域合作，法中关系将产生新的活力。

安全理念的演变与全球治理的未来

印度和平与冲突研究所所长

退役陆军中将

阿尔文德·兰巴

一、二战后安全理念的演变

自第二次世界大战以来，全球安全经历了许多问题和挑战。二战后，世界分裂为北约和华约两个阵营，美国和苏联分别主导这两个组织与地区国家的关系，而日本则受制于一项禁止其恢复军事力量的战略协议。

世界大战的结束，见证了战争的维度从常规战争范式转变为确保彻底摧毁敌人的核战争。这两个大国展开军备竞赛，引发了对核武器数量的竞争，使核武器发展轨迹和规模失去控制，进入相互确保摧毁（MAD）的状态。核武器和运载系统的扩散在两个阵营间肆无忌惮地升级，其数量令人震惊。

全世界迫使核大国减少核武器数量和核战争威胁。《限制战略武器条约》（SALT）和《削减战略武器条约》（START）谈判试图控制核武器，使其不再成为大规模杀伤性武器，数量也从条约规定的最高数量减少到限制的数量，从而逐渐下降为威慑级别的力量。《反导条约》（ABM）和《中导条约》（INF）设置了一些限制武器系统数量的规则，确保销毁一类导弹或全部导弹。

当今世界的地缘政治已经发生重大变化，《反导条约》、新的《削减战略武器条约》《中导条约》以及其他条约面临被签约国践踏的挑战。

联合国和联合国安理会是唯一可信的全球性机构和机制，尽管其拥有引导世界走向和平与裁军的权力，但却无法将其引导作用施加于全球安全与稳定。

苏联、华约相继解体后，北约却坚定存在并不断扩张，使美国比以前更加强大。有史以来，世界第一次以清晰和直观的方式见证了单极世界的建立。美国不仅成为全球发展的驱动力量，也成为重新定义全球版图的超级大国。

冲突转而发生在世界多个地区，主要是第三世界。1962 年中印边境自卫反击战，以及 1965 年和 1971 年印度和巴基斯坦之间爆发的两场战争，使南亚成为最容易发生冲突的地区。伊拉克入侵科威特、第一次伊拉克自由行动和第二次伊拉克自由行动奠定了西亚的基本框架。阿富汗成为美俄冷战的中心，为以美国为首的单极世界回归创造了决定性的条件。

到 20 世纪末，中国以其巨大的军事和技术实力、核能力震惊了世界。中国崛起的影响是重大的，主要体现在经济方面，其次是其在周边地区就有争议领土、南中国海以及世界其他地区事务上采取了更加坚定自信的战略。中国的空前崛起成为对单极世界的首要挑战。

21 世纪以来，人类历史经历了三次重大演变。中国的空前崛起对现有世界秩序带来新挑战，美中之间的直接军事竞争日益激烈，恐怖主义也在兴起。

从单极向两极和多极的转变具有重要意义，世界面临着一个充满挑战的前景：中国正在崛起，俄罗斯正在复兴，美国打算遏制中国。正如英国剑桥大学马丁·雅克教授所指出的，冲突的产生是由于美国的过分干预和中国的过度反应，双方在冲突中都采取了一系列对策，并打算针对当前局势向对方提出指控。

二、战争性质的演变

战争的性质随着以武力为中心的常规战争的演变而改变，这种演变包括部队实战，以及高技术战、信息战、人工智能战等战争形式的出现，这些战争不可预见，找不到根源，难以确定发起者。它们改变了以往战争可以被控制和监控的性质。

现在，核武器在区域和次区域一级占据了中心地位。在军方为政策主要制定者的国家，或在那些不仅支持将恐怖主义作为战争的替代选择，而且使恐怖主义成为综合战争机器一部分的国家中，国家行为体和非国家行为体发动核战争的风险都很高。考虑到可能会出现"理性的非理性"（Rational Irrationality）政治选择，这些地区通常有格外高的战争风险。

三、关于恐怖主义

恐怖活动是一种新"武器"，它为超越常规的冲突增加了一个特殊层面，即通过在世界范围内进行非理性破坏和杀戮威胁来表达实力。恐怖活动规模的大小成为区别恐怖组织、个人以及实施恐怖活动的国家的正式标签。

冷战后，非国家行为体参与全球事务，引发权力关系、经济一体化及不同问题和领域政策的剧烈变化。极端主义和社会动荡将持续加剧，原因是在人类发展进程中国家内部和国家之间的经济不平等。在恐怖主义灾难和核裁军方面，需要有一个全球性立场，以防止相关国家和国际社会的安全受到威胁。

四、关于未来全球治理

全球治理的基本原则正在经历范式转变。尽管美国仍然是当前全球治理体系的主导力量，但中国及其合作伙伴正在寻求改革全球治理体系。美国和中国将继续作为政治影响力、对外关系和军事体系等方面不同层次的竞争对手展开激烈博弈。

必须尊重联合国、联合国安理会、国际法院和国际货币基金组织、世界银行等传统国际机构的权威，而不能为了权力和政治利益去挑战它们。必须防止安理会内部的政治分歧和派别利益，特别是一些常任理事国使用否决权，这已经对国际社会应对叙利亚局势、恐怖主义威胁和难民涌入造成了影响。

印度和欧盟很可能在不久的将来成为强大力量，而俄罗斯一旦复兴，则可能成为具有重大军事影响的国家。印度的崛起不仅是可以预见的，而且是可以感知的。崛起的印度被视为充满活力的、领先的游戏规则改变者。

主权、领土完整和人类争取权力与公平的斗争，正在以非常多元的方式塑造国际关系和全球治理。全球领导人和国际社会必须有效应对国际关系的范式转变。第三世界小国的外交衰退、军事化加剧、互信减弱以及核战争威胁增加了冲突的可能性，并对全球治理提出了重大挑战。尽管双边关系仍将是国家关系的核心力量，但武器系统的获取、不同架构军事系统的集成等跨领域的战略问题将进一步加剧地区层面的激烈竞争。

五、关于外交战略和政策

传统上讲，外交战略和政策是合理保密的，或至少在一定范围内是模棱两可的，而如今，这些政策和战略却在《国家安全政策和战略》（National Security Policy and Strategy）或在白皮书中被阐明，从而导致了不合理的解释和分析。

当前，外交正屈从于各国领导人在国际局势中和面临挑战时所采取的立场，以及领导人在国际舞台上的抱负。糟糕的外交或战略领导能力，可能比其他由于误判政治和军事形势而做出非理性行为造成的威胁更加严重。特朗普总统最近在退出伊核协议后威胁对伊朗发动战争的外交灾难，给西亚的和平与稳定增添了巨大的不确定性。

战略伙伴关系是除联盟以外双边交往的新准则，在这种情况下，大国与地区中小国家/集团之间的交往对全球稳定具有非常复杂的影响。

印太概念无论多么不被大国认可，都改变了该地区局势。安全威胁和经济压力正迫使地区集团和组织摆脱大国参与。另一方面，大国必须停止通过操纵进入这些集团。如果地区集团和组织仍不能占据主导地位，域外势力将变得更加突出。

在全球层面，美中在亚洲的竞争和中国在南中国海和印度洋地区日益增强的自信，正在重新定义地区和全球的和平与稳定。

印度被许多国家视为一股有益的力量，这是显而易见的。印度与美国、中国、俄罗斯和东盟、东亚、中亚、上海合作组织等各大国和地区组织的伙伴关系日益密切，印度的外交手段和外交实力也在不断增强，这也在一定程度上升级了现有矛盾，阻止了印度与他国合作和改善关系。

六、结论

权力竞争加剧，导致合作与对话破裂。我们正在经历一个消极的时代。只有发挥好外交、外交政策和国家领导人的既有作用，才能实现良好的全球治理。

中国在争取全球利益的意志和战略上具有更大的一致性。中国正在通过合作与讨论推进国际体系重大变革，正在成为发展、太空、贸易、国际合作和多边协调的贡献者。中国认为，国际社会支持中国发挥更负责任的作用，如果这种看法得到证实，将极大地促进全球和平与稳定。

得到新兴大国支持的美国、俄罗斯和中国，将需要重新调整它们在地区事务中的介入程度，并在新的全球形势下，在核裁军、限制性谈判、遵守条约以及恐怖主义问题上表明立场，以实现良好治理以及地区和全球稳定。

作为另一种选择，随着大国竞争加剧，印度、日本和欧盟等新兴的、强大的国家和组织实现显著增长并在国际社会得到积极认可，可能是时候率先建立新的机构，以确保实现更好的全球治理。

总之，必须扭转从战略稳定到危机稳定的范式转变，这种转变极有可能升级为冲突。

可持续安全观与全球安全治理

中国人民争取和平与裁军协会常务理事

清华大学国际关系研究院教授

刘江永

2019 年是新中国成立 70 周年，也是中国国家主席习近平提出共同、综合、合作、可持续安全观 5 周年。当前，就可持续安全观与全球安全治理进行研讨，很有意义。

一、中国提出可持续安全观五年来取得的成效

2014 年 5 月 21 日，中国国家主席习近平在上海举行的第四次亚洲相互协作与信任措施会议峰会上首次提出，"我们应该积极倡导共同、综合、合作、可持续的亚洲安全观，创新安全理念，搭建地区安全合作新架构，努力走出一条共建、共享、共赢的亚洲安全之路"。这一新安全观写入会议发布的《上海宣言》，成为与会各国的重要共识。

2015 年 9 月，习近平主席在联合国大会的讲话中重申，要树立共同、综合、合作、可持续安全的新观念。从那时起，中国倡导的可持续安全观便不局限于亚洲，而是具有全球意义。越来越多的国家开始意识到，可持续安全追求的是，通过共同安全、合作安全、综合安全，以较低的安全成本获取较高质量安全的可持续性。这是引领全球安全治理的科学的安全观。

五年来，全球、地区和各国安全局势的发展变化进一步证明，可持续安全观是当今时代全球安全治理的一盏指路明灯。这一新安全观顺应了当代国家安全与国际安全的基本规律，与世界各国人民的安全利益诉求相吻合，对

157

于世界各国正确的安全决策具有重要参考价值。

五年来，可持续安全观在中国周边各国得到积极响应，正成为各国安全决策的指导思想，并逐步落实到安全政策的制定与安全合作的实施上，迅速而有效地改变了中国周边的国际安全环境。从东北亚、东南亚、南亚到中亚地区，中国同几乎所有接壤邻国及周边国家都就可持续安全达成共识，并初步尝到了共同安全的甜头。

五年来，中国是可持续安全观的倡导者与实践者。可持续安全观已成为当代中国治国方略的重要内容。2017年中共十九大报告指出：推动构建人类命运共同体，"必须统筹国内国际两个大局，始终不渝走和平发展道路、奉行互利共赢的开放战略，坚持正确义利观，树立共同、综合、合作、可持续的新安全观，谋求开放创新、包容互惠的发展前景，促进和而不同、兼收并蓄的文明交流，构筑尊崇自然、绿色发展的生态体系，始终做世界和平的建设者、全球发展的贡献者、国际秩序的维护者"。

五年来，立足可持续安全观，中国在改变长期处于危险紧张状态的朝鲜半岛局势方面发挥了重要作用，取得明显效果。在2017年朝鲜半岛剑拔弩张的情况下，中国强调朝核问题的解决要考虑有关各方的安全关切，即共同安全；在坚持朝鲜半岛无核化大方向的同时，支持朝鲜发展经济改善民生，即综合安全；提倡和平的多边主义，鼓励朝鲜半岛和平机制的建立与实现无核化"双轨并进"，即合作安全；主张朝韩双方通过对话协商实现民族和解，反对使用武力或武力威胁，即着眼于可持续安全。结果，在有关各方特别是朝韩双方的共同努力下，2018年以来，朝鲜半岛形势发生70多年来前所未有的可喜变化。

五年来，遵循可持续安全观，中俄全面战略协作伙伴关系明显加强，上海合作组织发挥着越来越重要的作用，亚信峰会凝聚起更多可持续安全的合力。2017年7月，中俄发表联合声明宣布，双方将继续在亚信、东亚峰会、东盟地区论坛、东盟防长扩大会、亚欧会议等区域组织框架下开展协作，推动以恪守国际法、共同、综合、合作、可持续安全和建立在合作基础上的平等不可分割安全、和平解决争端、不使用武力或以武力相威胁为原则，构建开放全面透明的亚太地区安全架构。作为可持续安全的重要法律措施，2017年6月9日有关六国领导人共同签署《上海合作组织反极端主义公约》。2019年6月15日在塔吉克斯坦首都杜尚别举行的第五次亚信峰会上，与会各国领导人均表示将继续践行可持续安全观。亚信第五次峰会宣言重申：谋求共同、综合、合作、可持续的安全，促进发展和进步。实践证明，凡是可持续安全观得到认同和践行的地区，国家间安全合作与相互信赖的纽带就越牢固。

五年来，可持续安全概念已成为东盟国家安全合作的重要概念。2019年7月10日在曼谷举行的第13届东南亚国家联盟国防部长会议主题即是"可持续安全"。这次会议对国际社会进一步普及可持续安全观，促进可持续安全国际合作实践都具有特殊意义。因为这是国际多边安全合作会议第一次使用"可持续安全"这个关键词作为会议主题；参加这次会议的东盟10国防长11日签署《东盟防长关于可持续安全的联合宣言》，也是第一个关于可持续安全的多边国际联合宣言。可持续安全联合宣言强调，为实现东盟国家的可持续安全，要进一步加强东盟内部、东盟与对话伙伴国的合作，共同应对非传统和跨境安全威胁。东盟各国意识到，随着地区安全环境快速变化、地区一体化和互联互通不断增强以及技术进步，本地区面临复杂多变的非传统安全威胁和跨境安全威胁，且发生频率和严重程度都在上升，东盟需要加强内部以及与对话伙伴国的合作。东盟各国在边境管理、军事医学交流、防范海上风险、反恐情报交流等领域要加强合作。这次会议证明，共同、综合、合作、可持续安全的新安全观，已成为东盟国家指导安全合作实践的重要安全理论。未来东盟国家可持续安全战略的实施，不仅有利于东盟地区安全治理，还将通过与东盟对话伙伴国的合作，使东盟的可持续安全效应辐射到更广阔的范围，为全球安全治理提供新范例、新经验、新路径。

二、当前全球安全治理面临的挑战

(一) 全球安全面临的威胁日趋多元化、专业化

持久和平是人类的共同理想。对于世界上大多数国家来说，21 世纪以来，在和平状态下的安全问题更加突出。有关这一点，欧洲的哥本哈根学派有比较早的认识。遗憾的是，冷战后，北约成员国采取暴力多边主义的方式，在中东地区发动了多场局部地区战争或军事打击。结果导致欧洲近年来接连受到难民潮、恐怖袭击、民粹主义和离心倾向抬头的严重困扰。欧洲一体化进程、欧洲多边安全机制和欧元的地位均受到削弱。

与和平问题相比，安全议题具有更大的涵盖面、普遍性、多样性和专业性。既有热点敏感问题，又有民族宗教矛盾、恐怖主义、跨国犯罪、环境安全、网络安全、能源资源安全、重大自然灾害等带来的挑战。传统安全威胁和非传统安全威胁相互交织，安全问题的内涵和外延都在进一步拓展。太空安全、海洋安全、极地安全等是全球安全治理的重大课题。对于太平洋岛国来说，气候变化直接威胁着其生存空间，而由战争引起的碳排放和植被减少，实际上可能远远超过工业碳排放。

正因如此，习近平主席在提出可持续安全观的同时，于 2014 年 4 月 15 日，首次提出要坚持总体国家安全观，其中涉及政治、军事、国土、经济、金融、社会、文化、科技、网络、生态、资源、核能安全等诸多领域。总体国家安全观与可持续安全观中的综合安全是交叉概念。总体国家安全观主要针对中国国内的国家安全战略而言的，而可持续安全观则更多涉及国际安全与全球安全治理范畴的问题，两者相互支撑。

(二) 贸易保护主义对世界各国发展的外部环境造成威胁

美国总统特朗普要使美国"继续伟大"无可厚非，但是如果越来越多地以牺牲别国的安全、发展利益为代价，就会受到普遍的质疑。

美国决策者的安全战略思维基本上仍是信奉传统的现实主义权力政治，而不了解包括美国在内，21 世纪的人类社会需要共同安全、综合安全、合作

安全与可持续安全。美国为确保控制别国的权力，往往不择手段。结果，美国不仅难以成为全球安全治理的贡献者，反而经常成为"麻烦制造者"，到头来必定坑害美国人民和自身安全利益。二战结束以来，这种例子不胜枚举，冷战结束以来愈演愈烈。

2018 年以来，美国把权力政治的思维逻辑从军事、外交领域，带入经贸、科技、人文交流领域，直接冲击了中美关系。在经贸领域推行单边主义，通过加征关税发动贸易战；以所谓安全隐患为由，动员国家力量对中国的华为公司 5G 系统进行打压、封杀。这些做法严重危害了自由贸易体系及市场规律。对此，2019 年大阪 G20 峰会成员国大都表示担忧，并发出维护多边主义和自由贸易的呼声。

（三）地缘战略博弈与军事安全风险上升

这主要表现在三大板块：一是北约东扩与俄罗斯之间的地缘战略矛盾加深，特别是美俄退出《中导条约》后，欧洲军备竞赛与安全对抗可能加剧；二是中东地区，美国退出伊朗核协议后，叙利亚、也门的战火硝烟尚未平息，美国、以色列和伊朗之间又剑拔弩张；三是美国推行"印太战略"，视中国为主要战略竞争对手，把多国海军力量引入南海，企图建立美国主导的海洋霸权。

美国在中东地缘战略的核心目标是拿下伊朗，控制波斯湾，进而控制中、日、欧海上石油通道，并进一步北上控制里海地区等原苏联的能源腹地。这些必然对中国与"一带一路"沿线国家的合作带来某种不确定性和潜在风险，同时也会导致美国安全成本和代价上升，安全质量下降，具有破坏性。与其相反，中国的新安全观和共建"一带一路"倡议则具有建设性。可持续安全的地缘政治与地缘经济理论，奉行的是"共商、共建、共享"的海陆和合论，而非海陆争霸论。

三、21 世纪全球安全治理的出路

可持续安全观与可持续发展观同等重要，堪称是具有普世价值的科学安全观。五年来，可持续安全观得到越来越多国家的认同，具有强大的生命力。1953 年 12 月，周恩来在接见印度代表团时首次提出和平共处五项原则，并得到印度、缅甸等国的赞同，后来成为中国外交和处理国家间关系的基本准则。亚信峰会确认的共同、综合、合作、可持续安全的新安全观，也具有同等重要的意义。经过实践检验，可持续安全四原则也可成为全球安全治理的准则。

第一，坚持可持续安全四原则，包括中美两国在内，在各国之间确立共同、综合、合作、可持续安全的共识；在双边安全对话过程中形成可持续安全共同文件；减少传统权力政治、地缘战略旧思维带来的零和博弈与对抗；增强共同安全意识，提高综合安全能力，拓宽合作安全领域，降低可持续安全成本，打造国际安全命运共同体。

第二，坚持可持续安全四原则，在全球热点、难点安全问题或安全领域，理论联系实际，积累成功案例，努力将可持续安全观转化为国家的可持续安全战略、政策和具体措施，切实解决实际安全问题。

第三，坚持可持续安全四原则，在以联合国为首的多边国际安全组织、机制、论坛，列入可持续安全议题。联合国维和行动、裁军领域合作，都有必要引入可持续安全观。联合国安理会可考虑下设可持续安全委员会，发挥类似联合国可持续发展委员会的作用，系统研究和提出全球可持续安全的有效治理方案。建议联合国会员国从各自国防经费中划拨 0.1% 或哪怕 0.01% 捐赠给联合国，用于设立联合国可持续安全专项基金。

代　跋

中国人民争取和平与裁军协会顾问
中共中央对外联络部副部长王亚军
在研讨会闭幕式上的总结发言
（代跋）

第二届万寿国际安全研讨会即将落幕。借此机会，我谨代表中共中央对外联络部和中国人民争取和平与裁军协会，对参加本次研讨会的各位嘉宾和代表，对所有为研讨会成功举办做出重要贡献的朋友们表示衷心感谢！

本次研讨会期间，中国全国政协副主席、和裁会会长马飚发表主旨讲话，呼吁来自世界各国的政治家、安全研究专家、和平组织代表牢记和平初心，担负时代使命，为维护世界和平与安全做出不懈努力。中联部部长宋涛主持开幕式并指出，当今世界面临百年未有之大变局，国际形势不稳定不确定因素更加突出，各国只有秉持共同、综合、合作、可持续的安全观，才能共建人类和平与安全的家园。来自俄罗斯、美国等国的政要、前政要也就维护世界和平与安全发表了演讲。

中外嘉宾和代表聚焦"大变局下的全球安全"这一主题，围绕"大国安全关系新变化""地区安全秩序新调整""新兴科技与全球安全""安全观念演变与全球安全治理"四个议题进行了热烈讨论，分享了对国际和地区安全形势的真知灼见，并达成诸多共识。

第一，当前国际安全形势已经发生了重要变化并正在继续发生深刻复杂变化，不稳定性不确定性不可测性更加突出。改革和完善基于规则的国际秩序，为当今世界注入更多稳定性和正能量，努力建设持久和平、普遍安全的世界日益成为各方的共同呼声。

第二，国际力量对比发生重大变化，一些国家的不安全感、对别国的疑虑和焦虑感上升，单边主义与多边主义、保护主义与开放包容激烈较量。面对多元复杂的安全威胁，坚持和平解决争端、反对武力和武力威胁，坚持多边主义原则、反对保护主义和强权政治，坚持联合国在维护国际和平与安全中的核心地位，仍是国际社会的主流声音。

第三，大国安全关系发生新变化，在合作的主流下，竞争、对抗的一面较前突出，对现有国际秩序和国际规则带来冲击，影响全球战略安全稳定，牵动世界发展走向，攸关人类前途命运。大国合作对国际安全至关重要。大国对世界和平与安全负有更大责任，应在维护和平、安全与稳定中发挥重要引领作用。

第四，当今世界面临多元、复杂的安全威胁，地缘政治、军备竞赛等传统安全问题依然突出，恐怖主义、网络安全、气候变化、移民难民等非传统安全威胁日益凸显，二者相互交织、叠加共振，给世界带来严峻挑战。各国应秉持共商共建共享原则，将共同、综合、合作、可持续的新安全观作为加强全球安全治理的指导原则，将构建人类命运共同体作为全球安全治理的战略目标，加强多边安全合作，以对话谋和平、以合作促安全，共同推进全球安全治理进程。

第五，新兴科技的"双刃剑"效应更加明显，科技进步在给人类带来福祉的同时，也带来严峻的安全挑战。国际社会应兼顾各方利益和关切，趋利避害、善加管控，在太空、网络、大数据、人工智能等新兴领域制定监管新规则、建立对话新机制、打造合作新平台，应对好这一新的共同挑战。

第六，发展是和平的基础和前提。实现共同发展繁荣是各国人民的普遍追求，但军事冲突、武力威胁、恐怖主义、保护主义等仍在严重阻碍世界经济发展。各国应顺应时代发展潮流，化解矛盾分歧，构建开放型世界经济，让各国人民都过上幸福美好的生活。

第七，坚持开放包容，加强文明互鉴，有助于维护世界和平与安全。文明多样性是世界丰富多彩的重要表现，也是人类发展繁荣的不竭动力，不应成为冲突和对抗的根源。各方应拆除思想的藩篱和桎梏，推动文明共存和互鉴，为促进国际安全与稳定营造有利氛围。

当然，由于历史文化背景、学术专业领域以及所处角度的不同，大家在观点和看法上也存在一定分歧，但这并未妨碍我们畅所欲言、各抒己见、坦诚交流、凝聚共识。正因为与会各方本着相互尊重、相互理解、相互启迪的精神，才使得本次研讨会开成了一次友好、务实、高效、专业的国际安全会议。

总的看，此次研讨会日程安排紧凑有序，代表发言积极踊跃，研讨互动充分深入，得到大家的一致肯定和高度评价。人民日报、新华社等中国主流媒体和重要新媒体对本次研讨会进行了全方位、多样化报道，向世界展示了各方维护和平与稳定的决心，传递了期盼安全与安宁的愿望，扩大了本次研讨会的国际影响。

今后，和裁会将努力把万寿国际安全研讨会打造成国际知名、务实高效、高端专业的安全研究对话品牌。我们也希望继续得到各方的积极参与和大力支持，欢迎中外专家 2020 年继续来华参加第三届万寿国际安全研讨会，为建设更加和平与安全的世界贡献智慧和力量！

后　记

后 记

　　当今世界正处于百年未有之大变局。世界多极化、经济全球化、社会信息化、文化多样化深入发展，各国相互联系日益紧密，和平发展大势不可逆转。与此同时，当前国际安全形势正在发生复杂变化，大国竞争博弈加剧，地区安全秩序深刻调整，传统安全与非传统安全问题相互交织，安全观念交锋激荡，新兴科技对全球安全的影响日益凸显，全球动荡源和风险点增多，不稳定性不确定性不可测性更加突出，国际安全环境更趋严峻，加强全球安全治理成为国际社会的普遍关切。

　　2019 年 7 月 1—3 日，中国人民争取和平与裁军协会（简称和裁会）主办的第二届万寿国际安全研讨会在北京举行。研讨会以"大变局下的全球安全"为主题，下设"大国安全关系新变化""地区安全秩序新调整""新兴科技与全球安全"和"安全观念演变与全球安全治理"四个分议题。全国政协副主席、和裁会会长马飚出席开幕式并发表主旨讲话，中共中央对外联络部部长宋涛主持开幕式。俄罗斯联邦公众院副主席谢尔盖·奥尔忠尼启则、老挝国会副主席宋潘·平坎米、美国前总统里根特别助理道格拉斯·班多、上海合作组织秘书长弗拉基米尔·诺罗夫及来自俄罗斯、美国、英国、法国、奥地利、瑞典、日本、韩国、印度、巴基斯坦、越南、泰国、菲律宾、南非、巴西、阿根廷等 20 多个国家的国际安全问题专家、和平组织代表，以及中国社会科学院、中国工程物理研究院、中国国际问题研究院、北京大学、清华大学、国防大学、国防科技大学、外交学院、北京航空航天大学、国际关系学院、暨南大学等单位的国际安全问题专家共 50 余人参加会议。

　　与会中外方代表围绕主题议题畅所欲言、各抒己见。中外代表普遍认为，尽管当前国际和地区安全形势存在不稳定不确定因素，但求和平、促安全、谋发展仍是大多数国家的战略取向和利益诉求。大国要积极承担国际责任，加强协调，管控分歧，建设更富包容性和建设性的伙伴关系，营造和平稳定、健康和谐、合作共赢的国际安全环境；地区国家要增进战略互信，努力构建符合地区实际、满足各方需要的地区安全架构；各方要紧跟科技发展前沿，趋利避害，维护共同安全，更好应对新一轮科技革命带来的安全风险；各国要旗帜鲜明反对冷战思维和零和博弈，践行共同、综合、合作、可持续的新安全观。

第二届万寿国际安全研讨会高度契合国际社会对全球安全的关切，充分反映了世界各地区及主要国家对当前国际安全形势的主流看法，达到了增进理解、求同存异、凝聚共识的目的。为进一步体现第二届万寿国际安全研讨会成果，扩大社会影响，我们对部分专家的发言和提交的会议论文整理编辑后结集出版。

和裁会秘书长安月军、副秘书长陶涛对论文集进行了策划和审稿，陈晓涵、侯红育牵头负责组稿和统稿，羊蕾、宋一鸣、沈芳、孙博文、王清、牛娜等同志做了一些翻译和编辑工作。

论文集收录文章所涉看法，均为作者本人观点，仅供读者参考。

编者
2019 年 9 月

Global Security under Great Changes

——Anthology of the 2nd Wanshou Dialogue on Global Security

Wang Yajun；Chief Editor

An Yuejun，**Tao Tao**；Executive Editors

当代世界出版社
THE CONTEMPORARY WORLD PRESS

Acting Prefaces

A speech at the Opening Ceremony of the 2nd Wanshou Dialogue on Global Security (Acting Preface 1)

Ma Biao

Vice Chairman of the National Committee of the Chinese People's
Political Consultative Conference,
President of the Chinese People's Association for Peace and Disarmament

I am very pleased to meet with our friends in Beijing. I would like to take this opportunity, on behalf of the Chinese People's Association for Peace and Disarmament, to extend our warm welcome to the distinguished guests and representatives attending the Second Wanshou Dialogue on Global Security.

President Xi Jinping points out that the world today is facing profound changes unseen in a century. Currently, the mega-trend of peaceful development is irreversible. However, the competition among major powers is obviously intensified, the regional security order is profoundly readjusted, the impact of newly emerging science and technology on global security is getting increasingly prominent, security concepts are interacting one another, traditional security issues and non-traditional security issues are intertwined, and sources of global turbulence and risky spots are increasing, humankind still faces many common challenges. We should adhere to the primary idea of peace, shoulder the responsibility of the times, and contribute our wisdom and strength to maintenance of international and regional peace, security and stability. I would like to share some views with you:

First, we should become a booster of security cooperation among major countries. Today's relations among major powers in the world are generally stable, their dialogues, exchanges and cooperation are continuing. However, precaution, antagonism and even confrontation among major countries are becoming increasingly prominent. Wrongdoings such as blackmail, pressure and sanctions are frequently seen. The international security architecture is still in the process of profound adjustment.

Major countries bear special responsibilities for world peace. We hope that the major powers will strengthen coordination, manage and control differences, enhance mutual trust, build a framework for major power relations featured by overall stability and balanced development,build more inclusive and constructive partnerships, and promote cooperation among major powers to jointly respond to international security threats.

Second, we should become coolants for regional hot issues.In today's world, wars, conflicts and instability still plague many regions; terrorist activities are rampant; people in many countries, especially children, suffer from the devastation of war. Hot issues such as Korean Peninsula nuclear issue, Iran nuclear issue, issues of Syria, Palestine and Afghanistan need to be properly settled.

Regional hotspots have become the wound of human civilization. We hope to have conflicts and disputes settled peacefully, oppose provoking incidents and intensifying contradictions for selfishness, and oppose beggar-thy-neighbor and benefiting oneself at the cost of others. We should strive to explore a security framework that meets the real situation of the region and the needs of all parties, and promote the realization of cooling and relaxation of regional hot spots.

Third, we should become a think tank for dealing with security challenges. The vigorous development of the new round of global technological and industrial revolutions has brought both development opportunities and security challenges. Non - traditional security challenges are increasing, militarized employment of newly emerging technologies has brought huge negative impacts on global security, as well as competition and game-play in the fields of cyber network, outer space and artificial intelligence are reshaping security order and security governance model.

Security challenge is a hard problem facing mankind. We should keep pace with the times, keep abreast with the development frontier of new science and technology, study the general trend, command the direction, and seek advantages and avoid disadvantages. In emerging domains such as the cyber network and outer space, we should actively promote countries to jointly establish new mechanisms, formulate new rules, and create a new platform for win-win cooperation.

Fourth, we should become a leader in practicing the new concept of security. Nowadays, various security concepts collide with each other fiercely, populism, protectionism, isolationism and other thinking trends continuously emerge. Some countries still adhere to the Cold War mentality of "either winner or loser" and zero-sum game, promote unilateralism and power politics, thus, global security

178

governance faces many difficulties.

The new era calls for a new concept of security. We should extensively publicize the concept of peace and practice a new concept of common, comprehensive, cooperative and sustainable security. We need to take a clear-cut stand against unilateralism and protectionism and pursue a win-win, multi-win and all-win concept. We should strengthen communication and exchanges and mutual learning among civilizations, and firmly adhere to the global governance concept of extensive consultation, joint contribution and shared benefits, so as to pursue peace and promote security with cooperation and inject stable and positive energy into the uncertain world.

In the age of globalization, we share security and insecurity together. As ancient Chinese saying goes, a drop of water cannot make a sea while a single tree cannot make a forest. I wish all the distinguished guests and representatives to have in-depth exchanges, brainstorming, consensus building and strength pooling during the seminar to make a positive contribution to the construction of a world of lasting peace and universal security.

A speech at the Opening Ceremony of the Second Wanshou Dialogue on Global Security (Acting Preface 2)

Sergey Ordzhonikidze

Vice President of the Civic Chamber of the Russian Federation,
Former UN Under-Secretary General

Thanks to our Chinese host for organizing this important international seminar, which enables us to think and exchange views together. We wish to share our consensus with all the governments and peoples of the world.

At present, the international situation is in a critical period, and global security and strategic stability are facing many serious challenges. The game-play situation of various countries determines the development of international relations, and a multipolar world is taking shape. However, certain countries pursue unilateralism. Some countries try their best to build up exclusive small circles, strengthen military alliances, weaken international mechanisms, defy international law and norms, and try to use various means to put pressure on other countries to achieve selfish ends. Such actions have led to the lack of mutual trust among major powers, the damage to normal relations between countries, the intensification of trade conflicts, the increase of economic instability and the increase of global security challenges. At the same time, non-traditional security challenges such as the increase of migrants and refugees, terrorism and climate change remain serious.

Recently, President Putin and President Trump have repeatedly stressed the hope that Russia and the United States can reach consensus on a series of international issues, but the U.S. administration is slow to take action, which leads to variable relations between Russia and the United States, thus it is difficult for either side to make progress in international affairs. Although Russia and the United States always express their willingness to cooperate in reducing the arms race, but they have not established a dialogue mechanism. The United States announced its withdrawal from the INF Treaty, and Russia followed. The collapse of the international nuclear disarmament system one after another will bring greater uncertainty to the world. The Treaty on Measures for the Further Reduction and Limitation of Strategic Offensive Arms (the New START) between the United States and Russia will expire in 2021, but the United States has not yet made a clear commitment to extend, which is of great concern to Russia. The United States wants to build a space force, and some European members of NATO decide to join the process. There is an urgent need to control the arms race in space and establish legally binding codes of conduct for the use of weapons in space. If the United States deploys weapons in space, the space arms race will be hard to stop and will affect global strategic stability.

To cope with complex challenges and safeguard the interests of the vast majority of countries, we need to adhere to rule-based multilateralism, support the United Nations and other international organizations to play a greater role and promote the democratization of international relations. There is no "chosen citizen" in the world. People of all countries have equal rights, both in the United Nations and around the world. All civilizations should treat each other as equals and be inclusive of each other. Although the Charter of the United Nations was adopted in 1945, it still has guiding significance for today's world and still needs to be followed and maintained.

A speech at the Opening Ceremony of the Second Wanshou Dialogue on Global Security (Acting Preface 3)

Somphanh Phengkhammy

Vice President of National Assembly,
President of the Lao Committee for Peace and Solidarity

On behalf of the Lao Committee for Peace and Solidarity, I would like to thank the Chinese People's Association for Peace and Disarmament for inviting me to attend the Second Wanshou Dialogue on Global Security held in Beijing. Not long ago, the G20 leaders' summit just concluded, and leaders of various countries have focused on major issues such as humankind peace and development. This is the right time for the Chinese People's Association for Peace and Disarmament to hold this important meeting, which I highly value and appreciate. The meeting provides a valuable platform for peace organizations of various countries and regions to accurately study and judge the international situation and put forward cooperation measures.

I highly value China's positive contribution to maintaining international security and stability in all historical periods under the leadership of the Communist Party of China. Especially in the new era, under the leadership of Xi Jinping, General Secretary of the CPC Central Committee and President of China, China has played an important role in promoting the international community to solve the problems of peaceful development, climate change and famine, etc.

Today's international situation is undergoing profound and complex changes. Our world is still threatened by force, political contradictions, war conflicts, terrorism, territorial disputes as well as existence of ethnic, religious, human rights issues and others. Natural disasters and infectious diseases also constitute major obstacles to development. These problems cannot be solved by one country alone, and strengthening international cooperation is the only choice under the current situation. Various countries should strengthen communication, share information, exchange views and build mechanisms to build our world into one of lasting peace and universal security, and create good conditions for common development

182

of all countries.

Laos has suffered from several hundred years of war and is the most bombed country in the world. There can be no development without peace. The Lao people have experienced war and know the precious value of peace. Laos, within its capabilities, is willing to work with the international community to promote world peace, stability, prosperity and development, so that people all over the world can live in an environment of common development and free from fear.

The Lao Committee for Peace and Solidarity and the Chinese People's Association for Peace and Disarmament have maintained good cooperative relations for a long time. Every year, we exchange work experience and views on the international situation, reach many important consensus, and contribute to the maintenance of world peace and stability. It is hoped that during this conference, the participants will actively and candidly exchange views and share wisdom on the institutionalized cooperation for the maintenance of world peace and stability.

A speech at the Opening Ceremony of the Second Wanshou Dialogue on Global Security (Acting Preface 4)

Vladimir Norov

Shanghai Cooperation Organization Secretary General

Holding *the Second Wanshou Dialogue on Global Security* by *Chinese Peoples Association for Peace and Disarmament* with the participation of prominent political figures and leading experts on international security issues is extremely important and relevant in the current complex, turbulent international situation. In today's world, factors of instability are increasing, there is a danger of a new round of arms race, and conflicts in several regions are escalating, there are growing threats from international terrorist and extremist organizations to peace and stability in the vast Eurasian space, and a tendency to merge terrorist groups with transnational criminal associations. New methods of financing the activities of terrorist organizations through drug business, illicit arms trafficking and corruption are emerging. The Shanghai Cooperation Organization (SCO) countries face the danger of various insurgents returning from the "hot spots" of the Middle East who are ready to continue terrorist and extremist activities against the SCO Member States. Under these conditions, the SCO's role in coordinating the development of collective and effective approaches of the world community in countering regional and global challenges is growing.

The SCO Member States reaffirm their support for the efforts of the United Nations as a universal multilateral organisation and advocate strengthening of the key role of the UN Security Council, which, in accordance with the UN Charter, is entrusted with the primary responsibility for maintaining international peace and security. The SCO Member States are convinced that the unilateral and unlimited buildup by individual countries or groups of states of ballistic missile defense is detrimental to international security and destabilizes the situation in the world. They consider inadmissible attempts to ensure their own security at the expense of the security of other states.

The SCO, as an influential and responsible participant in the modern system of international relations, will enhance its participation in efforts to ensure peace and security, consistently advocating the resolution of international and regional conflicts by exclusively peaceful political and diplomatic means, based on the principles of equality, respect for sovereignty, territorial integrity and non-interference in the internal affairs of other countries, the non-use of force or the threat of force. In order to implement the Program of Cooperation in Combating Terrorism, Separatism and Extremism, the SCO Member States are actively working to curb crimes of terrorist and religious extremist nature, neutralize clandestine terrorist cells.

Joint military antiterrorist exercises "Peaceful Mission" are regularly held with the participation of all SCO Member States. The Member States call on the international community to promote global cooperation in combating terrorism with the central role of the UN by fully implementing corresponding UN Security Council resolutions and the UN Global Counter-Terrorism Strategy in compliance with the UN Charter and the principles of international law without politicisation and double standards and with respect for the sovereignty and independence of all countries, as well as to work towards a consensus on adopting the Comprehensive Convention on International Terrorism.

An important condition for ensuring security in the SCO area and in the world as a whole is the stabilization of Afghanistan. Member States highly appreciated the results of the third meeting of the SCO-Afghanistan Contact Group (Bishkek, April 18-19, 2019) and the signing of the roadmap with the Afghan side on the further actions of the Contact Group at the SCO Summit on 14 June in Bishkek. The SCO Member States emphasize the absence of an alternative to resolving the conflict in Afghanistan through political dialogue and implementing an inclusive peace process by the Afghans and under the leadership of the Afghans themselves, call for increased cooperation of all interested states and international organizations with the central coordinating role of the UN in order to stabilize and develop this country.

Special attention is being paid by the SCO Member States to cyber security. Countering information attacks, fighting against the use of internet for propaganda of terrorism, separatism and extremism, as well as preventing the undermining of political, economic and public security is an important task in the SCO region. We consider it necessary to develop universal rules, principles and norms for the responsible behavior of states in the cyber space, while providing in this area a number of measures to ensure information security of the SCO Member States.

Over the past 18 years, the SCO has stood to the test of new developments in international security, conducted fruitful practical cooperation, and received universal recognition from the world community. Especially after the membership of India and Pakistan, the international influence and cumulative powers of the SCO have increased, while the inter-state relations of the Organization members show exemplary format. The key to this development of the SCO is, of course, the guiding rule of the "Shanghai Spirit", characterized by "mutual trust, mutual benefit, equality, consultation, respect for the diversity of civilizations, pursuit for the common development".

Developing common security, the SCO will continue to adhere to the principles of non-alignment with the blocs, the absence of counteraction and non-targeting to third parties. I am confident that the further development of cooperation within the SCO will increase the level of mutual trust, and will also allow the Organization to significantly expand the possibilities to counter the modern challenges and threats to security in the SCO space.

A speech at the Opening Ceremony of the Second Wanshou Dialogue on Global Security (Acting Preface 5)

Douglas Bandow

Former Special Assistant to U. S. President Ronal Reagan,
Senior Fellow at the Cato Institute

Today's world is both good and dangerous. The world is more prosperous than ever, but there are many problems within and among some countries. The two sides of new technology are more prominent, which can improve human life, but also bring security risks. The world is full of political variables and populist leaders come to power in many countries. The wars in Syria, Libya, Yemen and other countries are still going on, and leaders of some countries have not given careful consideration when coming to war decision-making.

We should pay more attention to the relations between major powers, which have unparalleled influence on the economy, military affairs and the number of nuclear weapons possessed than other countries. The relations between major powers determine whether the world is going to peace or war, and major powers can drag small countries into war, and handling well the relations between major powers will help to create a world of peace and security. The world is changing towards multipolarity, full of instability and uncertainty. This requires great powers to give full play to their leadership, adjust regional security structure and strengthen exchanges between countries.

Emerging technologies affect the relationship and interaction between various countries. We need to pay attention to the challenges brought by emerging technologies. Space and cyber security are new challenges. New technologies improve people's lives, but they also bring risks. We should seek benefits and avoid disadvantages, and learn to control the emerging technologies.

At present, there are some problems in the international system led by the United Nations. International and regional security challenges are more complex and diverse, such as security in the Middle East, Asia-Pacific security, nuclear non-proliferation, energy security, migrants and refugees and other issues. In order to solve the common challenges faced by mankind, we need to further discuss whether we should improve the existing mechanism or create a new multilateral mechanism.

Session I
New Changes within Security Relations among Major Countries

New Changes and Prospects of the Current Security Relations among Major Countries

Meng Xiangqing

CPAPD Executive Council Member,
Professor with the School of National Security,
PLA National Defense University

The relationship among major countries is the framework of the world architecture, which decides the trend of the world architecture to a considerable extent. The security relations among major countries are the most core, sensitive and important part of the relations among major countries, and in a sense are also the barometer of the relations among them. It is almost 30 years since the end of the Cold War, compared with the previous 20 years, a basic fact is obvious and is beyond any doubt that the security relations among major countries have entered a new stage of instability and uncertainty, and intensifying competition and confrontation. The new changes in the security relations of major powers and their future trends are not only related to the trend of the world architecture, but also to world peace and development.

I. The competition and confrontation in the current security relations of major countries is the main characteristic

For quite a long period after the end of the Cold War, relations among major countries were relatively stable. There are both cooperation and competition among major powers, with cooperation as the mainstream on the whole. With the increasing common security threats and the expanding common security interests, extensive and close security coordination and cooperation among major powers have become normal. In the post-Cold War, the security relations among major countries have basically gone through three stages. The first stage is the period of relative stability and coordination in the 1990s. The end of the Cold War and the collapse of the bipolar structure have brought both opportunities and challenges to the security relations of major powers. Although there were some major negative events in early 1990s, such as the economic sanctions imposed by the United States and the West on China, the Taiwan Strait Crisis in the middle of 1990s, the bombing of the Chinese Embassy in Belgrade in the late 1990s, the NATO's eastward expansion on squeezing Russia's strategic space in the 1990s, and the Iraq war and the Kosovo war, etc. The major country relations witnessed twists and turns, but generally speaking, the general trend of the improvement of major power relations had not changed. The upgrading of dialogue and communication, and managing and controlling crisis to spiral in the security area is the mainstream. Cooperation and confrontation coexist, but cooperation is the main factor.

The second stage is from the 9/11 terrorist attacks in 2001 to the 2016 election of Trump as US president. In a sense, this stage can be called the "honeymoon period" of security relations among major powers. The 9/11 terrorist attack is a major turning point. The request for security cooperation among major powers was increasing, and the institutionalization of cooperation was increasing. The cooperation of major powers in non-traditional security fields, such as counter-terrorism, non-proliferation, climate change and response to piracy, had reached a new height and experienced a very rare "honeymoon period" of security cooperation.

The third stage is from 2017 till now, major changes have taken place in the security relations of major powers, turning from cooperation to intensified competition and confrontation. Several major events during this period have directly affected the trend of security relations among major powers. Firstly, when Trump came to power, he "withdrew from groups" and vigorously implemented unilateral and protectionist policies. Secondly, the Ukraine incident emerged. Thirdly, the United States introduced the "Asia-Pacific rebalancing strategy" and "Indo-Pacific strategy". Trump's unilateral and protectionist policies almost destroy the security relations with all major powers, and even the relations with its allies. The Ukraine incident worsened relations between the United States and Russia and catalyzed tensions between Europe and Russia. The "Indo-Pacific strategy" intensifies the security confrontation in this region. In an overall view, cooperation and competition coexist, and dialogue and confrontation coexist in the current security relations among major powers, but there is an indisputable fact that the strategic competition and confrontation have increased significantly. In recent years, there are four noteworthy changes in the security relations of major countries:

Firstly, the geopolitical games among major countries get intensified. In

Europe, the U. S. -Russian and Europe-Russian trial of strength around the NATO's Eastward expansion continues, and the United States and Russia struggle sharply on the issue of Ukraine, Syria and Iran, etc. , so a risk of escalating the conflicts increases. Meanwhile, European countries, swept by the waves of populism and non-liberalization, have serious differences, and the geopolitical risks brought by Brexit have become more and more fierce. In the Asia-Pacific region, the United States has continuously intensified its all-dimensional suppression and containment of China in the fields of politics, diplomacy, economy, science and technology, military, culture and so on, leaving the Sino-U. S. relations seriously regressive, and increasing the risk of military friction between the two countries or escalating into conflict due to involvement in regional crises.

Secondly, the military competitions among major powers get strengthened. In recent years, the world's major military powers continue to increase military spending. According to the 2018 Global Military Spending Analysis Report released by the Swedish International Peace Research Institute (SIPRI), the world military expenditure in 2018 reached about $ 1. 822 trillion, the highest level since the end of the Cold War. In 2019, the military budgets of all major countries increased substantially. Among them, the United States reached $ 716. 3 billion, an increase of 11. 9%, exceeding the total of the top nine countries in the world. The world's major military powers compete sharply in the fields of artificial intelligence, directional energy weapons, advanced unmanned weapon systems, space weapons, cyberspace warfare and hypersonic weapons, etc. Earlier this year, the United States released an upgraded version of the Missile Defense Review Assessment Report, announcing a comprehensive updating of the missile defense system, and claiming that it would "ensure that any missile launched at any time and anywhere against any target in the United States be detected and destroyed". The new version of the "Star War Plan" which "shows the Cold War posture" has intensified the strategic precautions among major countries and caused serious damage to the security and mutual trust among various countries.

Thirdly, there is fierce competition among major countries in emerging realms. In the emerging fields of space, cyber, deep sea and polar regions, from the debate on values to the development of technology still to the competition for international rules-making and discourse, major countries have unfolded comprehensive competitions, showing an increasingly fierce trend. The relationship among major powers in emerging areas reflects the change of power pattern in real space, which will have an important impact on the adjustment of international security order and the building of new security relations.

Fourthly, the security cooperation of the major powers in various fields go backwards if not going forward. A series of reports issued by the United States, such as the National Security Strategy report, the National Defense Strategy report and the Indo-Pacific Strategy report, show that the United States no longer regards terrorism as the main threat to its national security, but the competition among major powers as the main threat. Compared with the past, in recent years, the momentum of security cooperation among major powers in such important areas as anti-terrorism, regional security, arms control and disarmament, response to climate change, counter-piracy and smuggling is obviously insufficient, some of which is weakened and some even goes backward.

There are three main reasons for escalating of competition and confrontation in the security relations among major powers: One, the change in the power balance of major countries is a fundamental reason. Particularly, the gap between China and the United States in some areas such as GDP and international influence is gradually narrowing, causing serious concern and anxiety in the United States. The core issue here still remains: how to look at China and how to view the rising China? If the United States does not treat China's rise correctly, fairly and justly, but still has a strong Cold War mentality and is committed to suppression of and containment of China from hegemonic logic, then, confrontation can hardly be avoided. Two, there is profound readjustment of the national security strategy of major powers, especially that of the United States. In recent years, the world's major countries have issued a series of new strategic reports, re-positioning the traditional relations among major countries, highlighting the position and role of competition among major powers in international security. Particularly, the United States emphasizes reshaping the international security order and the pattern of major powers with "America First". In recent years, the United States frequently withdraws from multilateral agreements, provokes frictions with major countries in the world, and intensifies regional tensions, leading to a comprehensive escalation of contradictions and conflicts among major countries. It can be said that a series of major adjustments of the U. S. security strategy are the root cause of the increasing instability and uncertainty in international security. Three, the confluence of de-globalization and populism has poisoned the atmosphere of security cooperation among major powers. The trend of de-globalization thinking is the product of the negative factors of globalization. In recent years, populism and nationalism have risen simultaneously in international politics, and the confluence of these three has seriously impacted on the stability of international security and major power relations. Since he came to power, President Trump has taken initiative to cater to populism, unilateralism and trade protectionism, and taken "de-globalization" actions under the pretext of trade frictions, and has frequently imposed tariffs on China, the European Union, Japan, India and many other countries. The wrong practices of the United States further exacerbate the risks of competition among major countries and the turbulence of the international situation.

Under the above circumstances, although there are dialogue and cooperation among major powers of the world, yet, precaution measures and frictions emerge one after another, and the risk of conflict increases, which presents a trend of long-term phenomenon. Therefore, in the future period to come, how to manage and control well risks and prevent crisis from escalating into conflict will be the theme of security relations among major powers.

II. Restructuring and reshaping a new type of security competition and cooperation relationship on the basis of healthy competition is the general trend and the aspiration of the people

In the foreseeable future, there will be three main prospects for the development of security relations among major powers. Firstly, the differences and frictions among major powers continue to escalate, resulting in the overall vicious competition and even towards the new Cold War. Secondly, a military conflict and even a war may be caused by misjudgment or accidental discharge of a gun or the fierce geopolitical game. Thirdly, Restructuring and reshaping a new type of security competition and cooperation relationship on the basis of healthy competition. Currently, the first two prospects are relatively impossible, but are on the rise, which is very worrying and must be given high vigilance. The third prospect is more likely, i. e. after a period of friction and collision among major powers, which try their best to avoid big conflict in the game-play and gradually find ways and means of benign competition so as to form a new mutual adaptation to each other, thus, building a new security competition and cooperation relationship. The reasons why this prospect is more likely are mainly the following:

First, it is shaped by the trend of globalization and the development of science and technology. With the continuous progress of globalization and science and technology, some new factors have emerged. The boundaries between countries have become difficult to distinguish in more and more emerging domains such as the cyber network, space, finance and so on. Meanwhile, transnational and global security challenges are also increasing, to which the public goods provided by the hegemonic countries become difficult to effectively respond. This makes it necessary for a country to take into account the interests of its strategic counterparts and cooperate with other countries in order to safeguard its own interests.

Second, with the power diffusion brought about by the continuous emergence of non-state actors and the rapid development of cyber information technology, the nature of major country relations has changed fundamentally compared with the past. The interests of nations are intertwined and intricate, and the zero-sum thinking of "either peace or confrontation" becomes more and more inappropriate. Only by relying on traditional power politics or armed conflicts, it is more and more difficult to safeguard national interests effectively, and the general trend is that non-zero-sum games continue to rise in international relations.

Third, the balance of nuclear terrorism and the common demand for non-proliferation are fundamentally difficult to be weakened. Some basic elements, such as cross-border and cross-regional linkages, are still being strengthened to play a comprehensive role, so that the strategic balance among the major powers, including China and the United States, can be maintained.

Fourth, the call for a new model of global security governance to address global security issues through partnership, dialogue, consultation and common development is growing, and is increasingly recognized by the international community. The international security coordination and international security governance need to expand constantly, and many countries start taking actions.

Fifth, in the face of the rising strategic competition between China and the United States, the Chinese Government and the strategic academia believe that strategic competition is not the whole content of the Sino-U. S. relations, and Sino-U. S. relations should never be simply positioned as a strategic competition relationship. The Chinese leaders and the Chinese Government have made clear for many times that China is determined to make long-term and unremitting efforts to promote the Sino-U. S. relations in the spirit of coordination, cooperation and stability. China's policy will play an important impact on the direction of the future strategic competition between the two countries and the major power relations.

Sixth, various important countries in the world do not want major countries to move towards confrontation and conflict. New-typed major power relations and new-typed international relations based on cooperation and win-win results are in the interests of the overwhelming majority of countries and peoples.

III. Managing and controlling risks well and preventing crisis from escalating is a pressing matter of the moment

First, currently, various major powers should do their utmost to maintain dialogue and exchanges, and maintain cooperation especially in the field of non-traditional security, which will help the major powers to manage and control competition, reduce misunderstandings and misjudgments, and prevent escalation of crisis.

Second, major powers should resolutely avoid moving towards a global arms race and vicious competition. We should fully recognize the rising military security risks in major power relations. The urgent task is to further improve and strengthen the crisis management and control mechanism among major powers, prioritize the crisis prevention, and implement the existing dialogues and communication and exchanges mechanisms.

Third, the world's major powers should jointly maintain, strengthen and improve multilateral cooperation mechanisms, safeguard globalization, actively promote the shaping of an open world economy, build a community with a shared future for human kind, promote transformation of the global governance system, and strive to control its negative aspects.

Fourth, China and the United States should not and cannot decouple their economic & trade and science & technology exchanges, let alone confronting each other. The two sides should strive to shape economic and technological competition on the basis of international laws and regulations and market economy, and strive to form a virtuous circle, so as to maintain economic and technological cooperation between the two sides and play a stabilizing role in world peace and development.

Major countries always shoulder greater responsibility for world peace and development, and should assume more obligations. The security relations among major powers determine the stability and prosperity of the world to a considerable extent. Currently, major powers' security cooperation is full of challenges, but also share new opportunities. Peace, cooperation and win-win situation are the general trend of the times and the aspiration of the people. Restructuring and reshaping a new type of major power security competition and cooperation based on healthy competition is the historical mission entrusted to the major powers by the times.

New Changes in Major Country Security Relations: The Emerging U. S. −China Rivalry under the Trump Administration

Suisheng Zhao

Member of the National Committee on US-China Relations,
Professor of the Josef Korbel School of International Studies,
Director of the Center for China-US Cooperation of the University of Denver

The U. S. policy toward China has undergone a fundamental change from engagement toward an emerging rivalry. No longer seeing China as a transitional nation converging with American values and interests, the Trump Administration has declared China a strategic competitor and revisionist power challenging the United States and escalated a trade war to a full-frontal clash with China.

I. The Emerging U. S. −China Rivalry after President Trump Came to Office

Although the U. S. -China relationship had been in trouble for some years, the rivalry has been intensified after President Trump came to office. The heightened U. S. -China rivalry has centered on economic areas. During the 2016 Presidential election, Donald Trump accused China of its economic growth caused by unfair currency policy and the exports at rock-bottom prices. He pledged to adopt a more confrontational approach, not least to impose a 45 percent tariff on Chinese exports to the United States. Trump's rhetoric tapped into an underlying strain of thought in the United States. As former Secretary of Commerce Pritzker explained to his Chinese counterpart, Americans were told for years that China was a developing country and shouldn't necessarily be held to the same standard as developed nations. But China's success severely undercut that line of reasoning. The world's low-cost manufacturer was rapidly becoming a global technology hub. Facing the profound and growing disconnection between rhetoric and reality, Americans felt that at least some of China's success had come at their expense. China wasn't playing fairly, consistently violating its international commitments and tilting the playing field to advantage Chinese firms. "With or without Trump, the U. S. -China relationship was moving quickly toward a crossroads. "[1]

Stephen K. Bannon, once Trump's chief strategist, was at the forefront of the crusade. Blaming China's exports financed by the American working class and middle class, Bannon declared an economic warfare against China. While Bannon is a Republican hawk, many others across the political spectrum agree that Bannon is right: China is beating up America economically, and neither the U. S. government nor U. S. businesses have done much about it for years. Even some of leading globalists like Madeline Albright, Tom Friedman and Fareed Zakaria have registered growing angst, and believed China has become an export powerhouse, but limiting market access for foreign products.

David Lampton, known for his pro-engagement position, complained that China has bilateral trade surplus with the United States because Beijing seized the opportunities of openness abroad without providing reciprocal domestic access to the United States and others. Consequently, the issues of 'reciprocity' and 'fairness' had moved to front in U. S. -China relations. Morris Greenberg, former Chairman of American International Group (AIG) and strong supporter of China's entry to WTO earlier, agreed that "China cannot expect to continue receiving favorable trade and investment terms in foreign markets when it is unwilling to reciprocate. " John Pomfret found that "A backlash is brewing against China in the United States and it goes well beyond Trump. " The shifting sentiments set the stage for President Trump's trade war to reduce the trade deficit with China. With the announcement of tariffs on $ 50 billion Chinese products on March 22, 2018, a full-fledged trade war started on July 6 when the 25 percent tariff on $ 34 billion worth of Chinese goods, the first round of the $ 50 billion tariffs, went effective. After China retaliated on the same amount of U. S. goods, the Trump Administration announced 10% tariffs on additional $ 200 billion Chinese products on July 10. Ratcheting up pressure, the administration doubled its proposed tariffs to 25% on August 1. When the 10% US tariffs on $ 16 billion of Chinese goods kicked in on August 24, China

---

[1] Penn y Pritzker, " The great disconnect between China the 'developing country' and China the great power, " *Chanel NewsAsia*, August 17, 2018, https://www. channelnewsasia. com/news/commentary/ trade-war-donald-trump-resentment-behind-tariffs- 10620880, accessed September 12, 2018.

retaliated on the same amount of U. S. goods. The tit-for-tat trade war escalated in full swing.

The trade war is to reduce the deficit and bring American jobs back home. It is calculated that "Either China will revise its industrial policy to allow U. S. companies reciprocal market access, or the tariffs will cause U. S. companies to disengage from China and bring manufacturing back to the United States, or source imports from countries that do not pose a long-term threat to U. S. security. "[1] More importantly, the trade war is to prevent China from advancing its high-tech capacity at America's expense. The Trump Administration's National Security Strategy (NSS) in December 2017 accused that billions of dollars of US technology were nefariously conveyed to China every year. Linking technological capability to national security, the Trump Administration has increased restrictions on Chinese investments in American technology and export controls and expanded the list of "strategic trade" items that require businesses to methodically screen buyers and down-stream end-users and trace the movement throughout value chains.

Republican senator John Cornyn and Democratic senator Dianne Feinstein co-sponsored a bill to tighten the screening of Chinese and other foreign investments for national security. The Committee on Foreign Investment in the United States (CFIUS) has blocked an increasing number of acquisitions, mergers and license agreements between Chinese and U. S. firms. Not long ago, these saber-rattling policies would have triggered uproar from corporate chieftains, worried about reprisals that would shut them out of China's markets. But American business community has been silent with many favoring a shift in strategy. A Pew poll published at the height of the trade war in August 2018 found economic issues featuring prominently in the list of concerns, and more Americans are concerned about China's economic threat than its military strength.

But geopolitics is lurked prominently behind the economic rivalry. While John Mearsheimer's structural realist warning about the inevitable U. S. -China power showdown was dismissed as too simplistic some years ago, similar theories, such as the Thucydides trap, power transition and new Cold War, have gained popularity. Citing Thucydides Trap that "It was the rise of Athens and the

---

[1] Drew Thompson, "US-China Trade War Is a Win-Win for Washington," *South China Morning Post*, September 20, 2018, https://www.scmp.com/comment/insight-opinion/united-states/article/2164833/us-china-trade-war-win-win-washington-least, accessed October 14, 2018.

fear that this inspired in Sparta that made war inevitable," Graham Allison wrote that "if Thucydides were watching, he would say that China and the United States are right on script sleepwalking towards what could be the grandest collision in history. "[1] Drawing on power transition theory, Kori Schake asserted that the distinct absence of cultural affinity between China and the United States could make the transition violent because China would promote its alternative values to undermine the American-led order.

Discovering a bipolarity of the U. S. -China standoff, one study argues that while it was unimaginable for the Soviet Union, China has built a dynamic economy to become globally competitive. China has ways to compete or win. [2] Using the term, Cold War II, one scholar describes a great-power struggle and ideological contest between China and the United States. Different from Cold War I in which "the Soviet Union was a military rival but not a commercial rival, and Japan was a commercial rival but not a military rival. In Cold War II, China is both a military and a commercial rival. Because of this, the U. S. needs to break with its 70-year policy of separating geopolitics from geo-economics and adopt the classic great-power practice of treating the military, diplomacy, and trade as three coordinated instruments of a single strategy. "[3]

One scholar, therefore, suggests the United States "abandon the obsolete bilateral approach and adopt a multilateral approach to form a values-based, grand mutual defense alliance in Asia" because "China is as much a common threat to Asian nations today as the Soviet Union was to Europe before 1991. "[4] This suggestion resonates with John Mearsheimer's long-standing call for America to contain a rising China by surrounding China with powerful American military capabilities, creating NATO-like adversarial alliances, isolating it economically, and imposing costs when it did things the United States did not like.

---

[1] Graham Allison, "How Trump Could Stumble from a Trade War to a Real War," *National Interest*, April 20, 2018, http://nationalinterest. org/feature/how-trump-could-stumble-trade-war-real-war-china-25481? page = show.

[2] Øystein Tunsjø, *The Return of Bipolarity in World Politics: China, the United States, and Geostructural Realism*, Columbia University Press, 2018.

[3] Michael Lind, "Cold War II," *National Review*, May 10, 2018, https://www. nationalreview. com/magazine/2018/05/28/us-china-relations-cold-war-ii/.

[4] Miles Maochun Yu, "It's Time To Change America's Alliance Approach In Asia," *Military History in the News*, Hoover Institution, December 5, 2017, https://www. hoover. org/research/its-time-change-americas-alliance-approach-asia.

In this context, the Trump administration's National Defense Strategy (NDS) states that inter-state strategic competition, not terrorism, is now the primary concern in U. S. national security. The Indo-Pacific is identified as a region of critical importance in which "a geopolitical competition between free and repressive visions of world order is taking place. " Calling for the free and open Indo-Pacific, the United States has made clear its concerns about China's muscular use of power to push the United States out of the region. While former Secretary of Defense James Mattis once complained that "No enemy in the field has done more to harm the readiness of the U. S. military than the combined impact of the *Budget Control Act's defense spending cuts* , " *the US Congress passed the largest ever* $ 716 *billion National Defense Authorization Act for FY* 2019. Signing the *Defense Bill*, President Trump stated that this measure was to confront the aggressive behavior of Russia, China, and others. The Bill limits Chinese funding of language programs at U. S. universities, restricts Chinese involvement in joint military exercises, calls for bolstering U. S. ties with India and Taiwan, and tightens U. S. national security reviews of Chinese investment in the United States. Long gone is the phrase in the Obama Administration's 2015 NSS that the United States welcomes "the rise of a stable, peaceful, and prosperous China".

Struggling between the strategic imperatives and the engagement policy, President Trump in his first year, avowedly unpredictable, swung between "two extremes of inchoate and inscrutable, one is dangerously escalatory and another is curiously naive; one policy is so tough it risks war and another so soft it resembles acquiescence. "[1] Dancing more erratic than his predecessors, sending conflicting messages, and creating confusions in the attempt to strike better deals, the Trump administration in the second year has settled on a bellicose approach to put maximum pressure on China.

The Trump administration has publically unveiled the shift in U. S. policy toward China. Matt Pottinger, senior director for Asia and Pacific in the White House told an audience in the Chinese Embassy in Washington D. C. that "We at the Trump administration have updated our China policy to bring the concept of competition to the forefront. " In a high-stake speech, Vice President Pence announced that the United States will fight back vigorously on all fronts against China. Accusing previous administrations of having ignored or even "abetted" China's abuses, he insisted that the Trump Administration will speak up, stand up,

---

[1] Rush Doshi, "Trump's China Policy: A Tale of Two Extremes," April 3, 2017, http://nationalinterest. org/feature/trump-must-choose-between-hard-line-china-strategy-soft-20002? page=2.

fight, and win. Pence's remark is regarded as "the declaration of a new Cold War". [1] But President Trump's personal approach to China is fundamentally transactional and hardly amounts to replace engagement with a grand alternative.

After heated rhetoric on the campaign trail, President-elect Trump took a congratulatory call from Taiwan leader Tsai Ing-Wen, the first contact between Taiwan's leader and an incumbent or incoming U. S. president in nearly four decades, challenging the default American position on the "one China policy". While this provocation could easily settle on a tough approach, President Trump abruptly reversed course in February when he told President Xi that he would honor the "One China policy". The then Secretary of State Rex Tillerson in his first official visit to Beijing in March repeated in verbatim of the tenets of President Xi's new model of big power relations and agreed with Xi that the two countries should respect each other's core interests and major concerns. The phrase had long been understood as implying U. S. accommodation to China's position against U. S. interference on issues ranging from Taiwan to human rights. Openly accepting China's framework surprised many China experts in the United States whether Tillerson fell into a diplomatic trap for repeating Chinese government platitudes.

The softening speeded up after Trump-Xi Summit in Florida on April 6. Without enough knowledge of Asian history to push back on most sensitive issues, Trump took what Xi said at face value on Tibet, Taiwan, and North Korea and came out with a high regard for Xi, saying that they had a very good chemistry together and seeing China as more important than ever to help with the North Korean issue. The two countries then unveiled in a 100 day action plan of economic cooperation, including trade deals on agriculture, financial services, investment, and energy. No longer taking the "one China policy" as the bargaining chip,President Trump rejected Tsai Ing-Wen's proposal for not ruling out communication with the United States again, implying that he would talk to President Xi before a conversation with Taiwan.

Reversing the simplistic anti-China stance to an equally simplistic pro-China stance, President Trump's abrupt volte-face from strong critic of China to acceptance was followed by sending the USS Dewey to within 12 nautical miles of Mischief Reef in the South China Sea, on May 24, 2017. On June 28, the

---

[1] Jane Perlez, "Pence's China Speech Seen as Portent of 'New Cold War'," *New York Times*, October 5, 2018, https://www. nytimes. com/2018/10/05/world/asia/pence - china - speech - cold - war. html.

Senate Armed Services Committee passed a resolution to allow regular stops by U. S. naval vessels to Taiwan. The next day, the Treasury Department announced the "secondary sanctions" against Chinese entities for underwriting the North Korean Regime. On the same day, the United States approved $ 1. 4 billion arms sales to Taiwan. The USS Stethem then sailed around China's reformatted Triton Island in the Paracel (Nansha) archipelago on July 2. Worrying that China's investment could give Beijing access to cutting-edge technology with commercial and military applications, the Trump administration in September blocked a Chinese-backed investor from buying Lattice Semiconductor Corporation, which makes programmable logic chips used in communications, computing, and industrial and military applications.

President Trump's state visit to Beijing on November 8-9, however, sent confusing signals again. Complaining about China's unfair trade practices and calling the huge trade deficit with China embarrassing, President Trump cast more blame on his American predecessors than on China after his Chinese hosts presented him a royal treat of "state visit plus" and the signing show of Chinese import deals over $ 250 billion. Trump's statement drew quick criticism at home. A New York Times story found that Trump projected an air of deference to China in public almost unheard-of for a visiting American president, signaling "a reversal of roles: the United States may now need China's help more than the other way around. "[1] Returning home, President Trump changed tune again. Notifying the WTO that the United States opposed granting China market economy status, a position that could allow Washington to maintain high anti-dumping duties on Chinese goods, the Trump administration's Report on China's WTO Compliance in January 2018 stated that "the United States erred in supporting China's entry into the WTO on terms that have proven to be ineffective in securing China's embrace of an open, market-oriented trade regime". The report also said China remained a state-led economy and had used the imprimatur of WTO membership to become a dominant player in international trade. This tough criticism set the stage for the Trump Administration's shift toward bellicose strategy in the second year. But Trump does not change his transactional style. Launching the trade war in March 2018, President Trump thought he could win easily. After President Xi promised to open China's

---

[1] Mark Landler, Julie Hirschfeld Davis and Jane Perlez, " In China, Trump Places His Bets on Flattering Xi Jinping," *New York Times*, November 9, 2017 https://www. nytimes. com/2017/11/09/world/asia/trump-xi-jinping-north-korea. html.

banking and auto sectors, increase imports, lower foreign-ownership limits on manufacturing and expand protection to intellectual property in his address to the Bo'ao Forum on Asia on April 10, President Trump took Xi's "kind words" as China's concession and stated that "We will make great progress together!"

President Trump opened negotiations with China any way although he had disparaged previous negotiations with China as producing endless talk and little gain for the United States. Sending a high-level delegation led by Treasury Secretary Steven Mnuchin to Beijing on May 4, the Administration demanded Beijing to cut $ 200 billion in the trade deficit and change its industrial policies, including forced transfer of technology to Chinese businesses. But the delegation came back empty-handed. A follow-up negotiation in Washington produced a joint statement on May 19, which stated that both parties forged a consensus to avert a trade war. Promoting the talks as a success, President Trump Twittered on May 21 that barriers would "come down for the first time" and China will " purchase from our Great American Farmers practically as much as our Farmers can produce. " But he changed his mind and rejected the agreement a few days after. Intensifying the trade war, President Trump, nevertheless, personally reversed the penalties against Chinese telecom giant ZTE for violating the settlement with the U. S. government over illegal shipments to Iran and North Korea.

Meanwhile, fighting trade war with China, President Trump has lashed out in all directions, fighting wars with even U. S. allies, rather than reaching out to other allies and trading partners to form an international coalition to place common pressure on China. In an interview on July 1, 2017, Trump attacked the European Union "as bad as China just smaller···. On top of that, we spend a fortune on NATO to protect them. " Pointing to the Europe Union as America's "biggest foe globally right now", he then added that "Russia is a foe in certain respects" and that China was one economically. NATO former Secretary General complained that Trump seems ready to destroy the strategic recognition for the U. S. allies. As a result, "the United States has abandoned quickly and without hesitation its role as leader of the global alliance system. Its long-term allies are left baffled, not knowing what to do in a new world order in which with ' America first' has transformed into 'America only' ."[1] Increasingly isolated in the international community, President Trump threatened in December 2017 to cut

---

[1] Joergen Oerstroem Moeller, "The End of the Atlantic Alliance," *The National Interest*, May 28, 2018, http://nationalinterest. org/feature/the-end-the-atlantic-alliance-25993? page=2.

off aid to any country that supported a UN resolution condemning his decision to recognize Jerusalem as the capital of Israel. In defiance of Trump's threat, the resolution was passed overwhelmingly.

All these confusing signals and erratic actions are an indication of the absence of a grand strategy. Being treated not much nicer than China, U. S. allies and other trading partners have moved ahead with cooperation arrangements without the United States. The European Union and Japan signed a sweeping "economic partnership agreement" for an area representing over one-quarter of the global economy. After President Trump's withdrawal from the TPP, which was meant to help cement ties between many of China's nervous neighbors while concentrating bargaining power to offer economic leverage for the United States to open the Chinese market, a group of 11 nations signed the new TPP without the United States in March 2018, a powerful signal of how countries are forging ahead without the U. S. leadership.

As U. S. allies are spurned if not insulted, some of them have tried to do more business with China. Germany and Japan have increased their investments in China. Turkey, once a NATO bulwark against Russia and in the Middle East, has worked with China through the Belt and Road Initiative. Although Beijing and EU remain at odds over issues such as technology transfer and protecting intellectual property, the China-EU summit in Beijing released a joint statement in July 2018 that the two sides were strongly committed to resisting protectionism and unilateralism and to improving trade and investment liberalization and facilitation. China-Japan relations have experienced ups and downs, but now the trade frictions the two countries have with the United States have promoted the approach of two old Asian rivals. In October 2018, on the occasion of the first official visit of Japanese top leader to China in seven years, President Xi told Japanese Prime Minister Abe that bilateral relations are now "back on track" and the two countries "have more common interests and concerns".

II. The Causes for the Emerging Rivalry

The U. S. -China relationship has always been defined by a mix of cooperative and competitive interests since normalization in the 1970s. While the leaders in both countries have tried to define competition by shared interests of cooperation in the past, competitive interests have prevailed to define the relationship.

The global financial crisis in 2009 was a turning point. Shrugging off the crisis and rebounding quickly, China began openly blaming "inappropriate macroeconomic policies" of Western countries and "their unsustainable model of development. "[1] Proposing "four confidences", i. e. , confidence in the theory of "socialism with Chinese characteristics", China's current path, current political system, and culture, President Xi declared, in the wake of the Trump administration's retreat from touting the liberal model, that China's system offered a new option for other countries and nations who want to speed up their development while preserving their independence.

Beijing's confidence came from its massive economic growth in the past four decades, which has made it a great power. Hu Angang at Beijing's Tsinghua University became known for his argument that China's national strength had surpassed that of the United States on all fronts in 2014: including economic power, technology and in overall competitiveness and strength. In promotion campaign of China's success, the 90-minute documentary "Brilliant China" produced by CCTV in March 2018, publicized China's leading achievements in science, technology, infrastructure and military affairs in the world after Xi Jinping came to power, and became the highest paid documentary in Chinese history. The previous year, "Wolf Worrier II", a story about a Chinese special task forces saving a war-torn African country from a Western mercenary, was the highest box-return movie in Chinese history; the second was "Operation Red Sea", a movie about the Chinese Navy rescuing hostages from terrorists in a virtual Arab country.

Economically, strengthening the position of state-owned enterprises (SOE) to help Chinese firms develop advanced technologies in key sectors, China has maintained a range of restrictions on foreign firms. As Li Shimo in Shanghai admitted, "China effectively negotiated into the WTO on preferential terms by taking advantage of the West's illusion of the eventuality of a globalized economic order... Yet, China does not and probably will never subscribe to the universal ideology of democratic liberalism, and its vibrant market economy is pointedly not capitalism. "[2] The U. S. business community, once the strong supporter of engagement, has complained that China hacked U. S. industrial secrets, created obstacles for American firms investing in China, enforced

---

[1] "Chinese premier's speech at World Economic Forum Annual Meeting 2009," *Xinhua*, January 28, 2009, http://news. xinhuanet. com/english/2009 - 01/29/content_10731877. htm, access September 12, 2018.

[2] Eric X. Li, "The Middle Kingdom and the Coming World Disorder," *The World Post*, February 4, 2014, http://feedly. com/k/1e3JeDm.

regulations that discriminate against foreigners, continued high tariffs that should have been reduced decades ago, and blocked American Internet businesses. "There was widespread public perception that the Sino-American economic playing field had been unfair to Americans, with the assertion that the American economy was hollowed out, in part due to overt and covert technology transfer to China. "[1]

Internationally, the China-led Belt and Road Initiative (BRI) and the Asian Infrastructure Investment Bank (AIIB) challenge the U. S. global leadershp. Although it is not a complete surprise that a more powerful China would take on the characteristics of a rising power, some Americans are alarmed that China continues to nurture its fantasies with the attempts to re-establish a "Middle Kingdom", cherish its hates by constant dredging up the century of humiliation, and threaten its weaker neighbors. They believe the Chinese government is no longer living in angry isolation but becoming "a great mercantilist dragon, using the power of its vast markets to cow and co-opt capitalist rivals, to bend and break the rules-based order and to push America to the periphery of the Asia-Pacific region. "[2]

Calling Western leaders' wish to change China along a liberal course "the bet of the century," one scholar concluded that Washington and its liberalists misjudged Beijing's determination to maintain its expansionist behavior and mercantilist policy. A infinitely richer and more powerful China moving divergent from the United States has frustrated many American pundits. As two former American officials complained, "neither U. S. military power nor regional balancing has stopped Beijing from seeking to displace core components of the U. S. -led system. And the liberal international order has failed to lure or bind China as powerfully as expected. "[3]

Wang Jisi, a Chinese scholar and American watcher in Beijing, admits that China has historically played a decisive role in shaping the bilateral relationship.

---

[1] David M. Lampton, "A Tipping Point in U. S. – China Relations is Upon US," US – China Perception Monitor, May 11, 2015 http://www. uscnpm. org/blog/2015/05/11/a-tipping-point-in-u-s-china-relations-is-upon-us-part-i/#_ftnref5.

[2] David Rennie, "How the West got China wrong, Decades of optimism about China's rise have been discarded," *Economist*, March 1, 2018, https://www. economist. com/news/briefing/21737558 – clear-thinking – and – united – front – are – needed – they – may – not – be – forthcoming – decades, accessed September 12, 2018.

[3] Kurt M. Campbell and Ely Ratner, "The China Reckoning, How Beijing Defied American Expectations," *Foreign Affairs*, p. 61.

"Once again, it is mainly China's power and behavior that incur a shifting of the bilateral ties. The Americans are alarmed by China's expansion of global influence, exemplified by the Belt and Road Initiative, and its reinforcement of the role of the state in economy and society, as well as the consolidation of the Communist Party leadership with its ideology. "[1]

But the transformation in the United States after the terrorist attack on September 11, 2001 also helped bankrupt the mismatched bargain. The United States declared the triumph of liberal democracy after the end of the Cold War. But the American hubris squandered the victory. In the attempt to maintain "the unipolar moment," the United States massively overplayed its hand, engaging in futile and costly wars in Iraq and Afghanistan. Often becoming a source of instability overseas, the overreach has produced huge domestic deficit and debt, threatening its ability to fulfill the obligations at home and abroad and leading to public disillusionment with the political establishment. Suffering a crisis of confidence in "dysfunctional democracy" with the partisan gridlock preventing meaningful governmental action, Americans are deeply divided on the domestic and foreign policies. Not since the Vietnam War have Americans been so polarized.

A divided America with no shared vision has found its domestic politics at odds with its international obligations, producing an "America first" President,who invocated an agenda of isolationism to reduce U. S. commitments abroad and retreat from global leadership. Taking a mercenary and transactional approach to U. S. obligations, America has lost confidence to mold China off the perceived undesirable path. While the United States claimed it was on the right side of history and China should follow suite toward liberalism after the end of the Cold War, the Unite States is no longer a paragon of democracy and universal values after 9-11. Francis Fukuyama, known for his triumphalism of liberal democracy in the early 1990s, wrote that "The first decade of the 21 century has seen a dramatic reversal of fortune in the relative prestige of different political and economic models. " While the Unite States held the high ground and its democracy was seen as the wave of the future in the 1990s, the admiration for all things American gave way to a much more nuanced and critical view of

---

[1] Wang Jisi, "America and China: Destined for Conflict or Cooperation?" *National Interest*, July 30, 2018, https://nationalinterest. org/feature/america-and-china-destined-conflict-or-cooperation-we-asked-14-worlds-most-renowned-experts, accessed September 12, 2018.

U. S. weaknesses one decade later. [1] Wang Jisi complained that while Americans often asked China to follow the "rules-based liberal international order", Washington now had abandoned or suspended some of the same rules that it used to advocate. "It has become harder and harder for foreign policy makers in China to discern what rules the Americans want themselves and others to abide by, what kind of world order they hope to maintain, and where Washington is on major international issues. "[2]

For realist scholar John Mearsheimer, liberal hegemony, which the United States pursued after the Cold War, is doomed to fail. The U. S. policy of remaking the world in America's image, including spreading liberal democracy across the world, fostering an open international economy, and building institutions is supposed to protect human rights, promote peace, and make the world safe for democracy. But instead, the United States has ended up as a highly militarized state fighting wars that undermine peace, harm human rights, and threaten liberal values at home because nationalism and realism almost always trump liberalism. Therefore, Washington has to adopt a more restrained foreign policy based on nationalism and realism. [3]

But some Americans have blamed other countries, including China, for many of their problems. President Trump has blamed foreigners for all America's ills. Scapegoating China for the negative externalities of trade helped politicians to avoid facing the difficult problem of compensating the losers of globalization. This shift in rhetoric predates Trump's hostility toward China and helped create anti-China economic nationalism. Witnessing these developments, one long-time China watcher warns that because a populist upsurge in American politics demands higher priority for U. S. interests in response to China eroding covertly and overtly against American interests, the most substantial negative change in American policy toward China in fifty years has taken place. [4]

---

[1] Francis Fukuyama, "US democracy has little to teach China" *Financial Times*, January 17, 2011, https://www. ft. com/content/cb6af6e8-2272-11e0-b6a2-00144feab49a.

[2] Wang Jisi, "Did America Get China Wrong: The View from China," *Foreign Affairs*, July/August 2018, https://www. foreignaffairs. com/articles/china/2018 – 06 – 14/did – america – get – china – wrong.

[3] John Mearsheimer, *The Great Delusion*, *Liberal Dreams and International Realities*, New Heaven, NY: Yale University Press, 2018.

[4] Robert Sutter, "America and China: Destined for Conflict or Cooperation?" *National Interest*, July 30, 2018, https://nationalinterest. org/feature/america – and – china – destined – conflict – or – cooperation-we-asked-14-worlds-most-renowned-experts.

III. Engagement is the Foundation for Healthy Competition

The U. S. -China relationship has been characterized by a cycle pattern of ups and downs since the normalization of 1979. Harry Harding called it a "fragile relationship" in the 1980s. David M. Lampton characterized it "same bed different dreams" in the 1990s. It has become turbulent in the accelerating frequencies of crisis and consolidation in the 21st century. Although the turbulent cycles have brought serious stand-offs, the U. S. -China relationship has survived many roller-coasters. The two countries are not natural partners, nor are they inevitable enemies. Their relationship is profoundly strategic partners and competitors simultaneously. Neither the United States nor China has found their relationship comfortable. But neither can afford to disengage with each other. The author of the Second Cold War states, although deep and warm peace among great powers is rare in history, a cold peace rather than a new Cold War is a realistic goal. As two major countries in the coming decades, the United States and China have no option rather than trying one way or another for peaceful coexistence.

Although the U. S. -China competition has intensified, engagement is the foundation for healthy competition. As a result, in spite of widespread criticism of engagement, many Americans have continued in its defense. David Lampton made the point that "The United States used its economic, military and ideological power to build institutions, alliances, and regimes that contributed to global economic growth and the avoidance of great power war. In doing so, it fostered the rise of a new constellation of powers, China notable among them, with which it must now deal. If the United States wants to see its interests met, Washington must win Beijing's cooperation rather than try to compel it. "[1] Geoffrey Garrett, Dean of the Wharton School of Business at the University of Pennsylvania, President Trump's Alma Mater, stated that "It's true that China and America are different. The most important thing we can all do is to ensure that the differences between China and the United States are source of strength, source of economic growth, and source of business opportunity, not a source of conflict. The best way to make that history is through more engagement, more understanding, more business-to-business ties, more cultural understanding, so more engagement is just the right path for us in the most important relationship in

---

[1] David M. Lampton, "Balancing US-China interests in the Trump-Xi era," *East Asia Forum*, December 10, 2017, http://www. eastasiaforum. org/2017/12/10/balancing-us-china-interests-in-the-trump-xi-era/.

the 21st century. "[1]

There are reasons for the continuing engagement policy. First of all, although engagement has been intrinsically difficult at times, it has served U. S. interests better than attempting to isolate China would have. In defense of engagement, Michael Swaine argues that China was until the 1970s and early 1980s a largely closed power. "Despite recent setbacks, China remains vastly more open, globalized, and tolerant today than it was prior to engagement. "[2] More importantly, engagement has morphed into a deep interdependence that the two countries can only thrive in tandem. Taking advantage of the U. S. market, hardworking Chinese people provided low-cost goods that enabled income-constrained American consumers to make ends meet in the grips of wrenching stagflation years. China-made goods have been a boon for American consumers since then. Providing China growth anchors, the United States benefited from China's vast reservoir of surplus saving to sidestep the mounting perils of subpar saving and reckless fiscal policy. As the largest contributor to global growth in the last decade, China's spectacular economic growth has contributed to American prosperity. While China needs the U. S. market for its exports and the strong supply and value chain to play on its comparative advantage, the United States shares an interest in maintaining and deepening the existing production chains and operation in Chinese markets.

In spite of the trade deficit, China overtook Canada to become America's largest trading partner in 2015 and has become the third largest market for U. S. exports since then. In 2007-2016, U. S. goods exports to China grew 86 percent, while exports to the rest of the world grew only 21 percent. U. S. services exports to China grew 12 percent while to the rest of the world contracted by 0. 6 percent. [3] President Trump has highlighted job losses but ignored job creation by China trade. The increase of China trade supported jobs between 2009 and 2015 was the largest by exports to a single country. The trade deficit with China is significant, but a big portion of U. S. imports from China originate elsewhere, including America. If the trade deficit were calculated on a

---

[1]　Qian Shanming, "Senior Chinese diplomat calls on US to abandon 'power politics' " , *China Plus*, 2018 – 04 – 15, http://chinaplus. cri. cn/news/china/9/20180415/118089. html? from = singlemessage &isappinstalled = 0.

[2]　Michael D. Swaine, " The U. S. Can't Afford to Demonize China," *Foreign Policy*, June 29, 2018, https://foreignpolicy. com/2018/06/29/the-u-s-cant-afford-to-demonize-china/.

[3]　US-China Business Council, *State Exports Report*, April 2018, https://www. uschina. org/sites/ default/files/final_uscbc_state_report_2018. pdf.

value-added basis, it would decrease by about 40 percent. In addition, the United States has run a significant surplus in service trade with China: $ 50 billion in 2015 and $ 38 billion in 2016. [1] More than 350,000 Chinese students enrolled in U. S. institutions during the 2016-17 school year, accounting for over a third of all foreign students. Chinese tourists have become a crucial factor in the US tourism industry. Spending by Chinese tourists in the U. S. reached $ 33. 2 billion in 2016, significantly higher than any other country. Average spending per Chinese visitor was $ 6, 900 in 2016, the highest of all international visitors. [2] The trade war with China involves big risks not only for Chinese economy but also American economy, disrupting supply chains to American companies. When ZTE's violation of U. S. sanctions resulted in a temporary revocation of its U. S. operating licenses and the denial of access to U. S. technology, an extensive collateral damage extended to ZTE's American partners, including Qualcomm, Google, Acacia Communications and host of small first and second tier suppliers. A World Bank analysis suggests that 25 percent tariffs on all trade between the United States and China could reduce global exports by up to 3% and global income by up to 1. 7% with losses across all regions. China and the United States could lose up to 3. 5% and 1. 6% respectively. Although both countries could declare victory, the trade war would destroy a great deal of wealth along the way. Both countries lose more than either gain.

Sending a strong message, the Dow Jones Industrial Average plunged 724 points or 2% on March 22, 2018 when the Trump Administration announced $ 50 billion tariff sanctions against China. After President Xi's April 10th speech struck a placatory tone on trade and temporarily calmed the burgeoning trade war, the Dow Jones index pushed up 1. 6% . Although the Trump Administration is confident that the United States has the upper hand in the trade fight with China, the tariff increase boosts the cost of a range of the U. S. imports, add to inflation pressure and interest rates, and strengthen the dollar, which makes U. S. trade deficit even worse. After the Trump Administration declared the trade war in March 2018, U. S. trade deficits with China kept rising and hit $ 38. 6 billion in August 2018, an increase of 10. 5 percent year-on-year and the highest

---

[1] The Office of the United States Trade Representative, "US-China Trade Facts," November 207, https://ustr. gov/countries-regions/china-mongolia-taiwan/peoples-republic-china.

[2] US Travel Association, *International Inbound Travel & Country Profiles*, October 3, 2018, https://www. ustravel. org/research/international-inbound-travel-market-profiles.

monthly deficit with China on record. [1]

Although Chinese economy is more dependent on U. S. trade than the U. S. on China, the Chinese political and economic systems may be better positioned to withstand the fallout from a trade war than America's electoral democracy. As the trade war registered pain on American producers, an increasing number of lawmakers were wary of the impact of tariffs at an elevated rate. In an 88-11 vote, U. S. Senate passed a symbolic resolution in attempt to curb President Trump's mounting tariffs on July 11, 2018, a day after the administration announced a new round of 10 percent tariffs on $200 billion Chinese goods. After President Trump announced the $200 billion tariffs in August, 95% of 358 business participants at the U. S. Trade Representative (USTR) hearing in late August expressed their opposition to the tariffs. On September 13, 2018 the National Retail Federation, the American Petroleum Institute, the Toy Association, Farmers for Free Trade, a group backed by the nation's largest agriculture commodity groups, and more than 80 other organizations, teamed up to form the Americans for Free Trade coalition. The coalition sent a letter to the law-makers and complained that "companies large and small are sharing their stories of the harm the tariffs and ensuing retaliation are causing across all sectors of the American economy. "[2]

Hundreds of American companies have lobbied the administration to keep their products off the list of Trump's tariffs. The lobbying has had an impact, with the trade representative removing products with an annual import value of about $7. 4 billion from the list. Senator Lindsey Graham of South Carolina is one of the biggest proponents of President Trump's crackdown on China. But behind the scenes, he worked on behalf of seven South Carolina chemical and textile companies that import products from China in his home state to avoid the pain of the trade war and succeeded to help four of them have materials removed from a list of goods subject to Trump's tariffs. [3]

Increasingly relying on each other for sustainable growth, public opinion data

[1] US-China Economic and Security Review Commission, *October* 2018 *Trade Bulletin* https://www. uscc. gov/trade-bulletin/october-2018-trade-bulletin, accessed October 14, 2018.

[2] Rachel Layne, "Major U. S. trade groups link up in anti-tariff coalition," *CBS News*, September 13, 2018, https://www. cbsnews. com/news/major-u-s-trade-groups-link-up-in-anti-tariff-coalition/, accessed September 14, 2018.

[3] Jim Tankersley, "Lindsey Graham welcomed Trump's China tariffs, then helped companies avoid them," *CNBC*, October 5, 2018, https://www. cnbc. com/2018/10/05/lindsey - graham - welcome - trumps-china-tariffs-then-help-companies-avoid. html.

in the United States has not changed much toward China, reflecting a wary but not alarmist attitude. Polling data from the Chicago Council on Global Affairs in 2018 showed that U. S. attitudes toward China remained stable during the past 40 years. Only 31 percent of the public describe China's economic power and 39 percent see China's military power as critical threats to the United States. This puts Chinese power far behind other critical threats facing the United States, such as North Korea (78 percent) and Russia (47 percent). In response to China's rising influence around the world, 42 percent of Americans say China should take on greater responsibilities in Asia. In contrast, only 24 percent say the United States should have greater responsibilities, 28 percent say the United States should have less responsibilities, and 47 percent support keeping U. S. responsibilities the same.

Business interests are increasingly critical of China but their willingness to support Trump's protectionism and accept the consequences of protracted trade war is far from clear. A survey released by AmCham Shanghai on April 10-May 10, 2018 found that although companies cited a familiar list of regulatory and operational challenges, the use of tariffs was supported by only 8. 5% of respondents vs. 69% who were opposed. 41. 5% favored using investment reciprocity as a tool for gaining greater market access in China. Amid escalating trade tensions, AmCham China and AmCham Shanghai conducted a joint survey of member companies on August 29-September 5, 2018. Over 60% of respondents said the initial $ 50 billion of tariffs from both the U. S. and China negatively impacted their companies. The percentage of companies expecting to be negatively affected by the second round of U. S. tariffs $ 200 billion jumped to 74. 3%. The practical impact of combined tariffs was reflected in loss of profit (50. 8%), higher production costs (47. 1%), and decreased demand for products (41. 8%). [1]

Secondly, at the regional level, engagement not only ended 23 years of diplomatic estrangement between the two countries but also laid the foundation for a peaceful and prosperous Asia after the Vietnam War. Pursuing strategies to draw maximum benefit from both the United States and China, minimize risks of angering either and preserve their independence, most countries in the region have desired for U. S. engagement. They are concerned about the Trump

---

[1] AmCham China, "Impact of US and Chinese Tariffs on American Companies in China, September 14, 2018, https://www. amcham − shanghai. org/sites/default/files/2018 − 09/2018% 20 U. S. −China %20 tariff %20 report. pdf.

Administration's disengagement from the region and disdain for the multilateral institutions when economic interdependence between China and the rest of Asia has increased. East Asia's intraregional trade share rose to 57. 3% in 2016, while their trade with the United States declined. [1] The EU, Japan and the United States collectively accounted for 29 percent of emerging East Asia's total exports in 2015, down from almost 50 percent in 1990. As the region's main production base, China is at the center of this growing intraregional trade. Taking advantage of these underlying changes, China has bolstered its power and profile. An increasing number of Asian countries have been pulled toward China's orbit. As this geostrategic shift is gathering momentum, some have leaned closer to China, soft-pedaling quarrels over the territorial disputes and angling for a slice of Beijing's initiatives to compensate for the U. S. disengagement. Most Asian countries have participated in the China dominated Asian Infrastructure Investment Bank (AIIB) and BRI. While the U. S. military capabilities still dominate Asia, China has wielded growing leverage, pulling longtime American allies closer.

For example, President Rodrigo Duterte of the Philippines put aside a legal challenge to Beijing's territorial claims in the South China Sea to seek investments from China. As an indication of the warming relationship, Duterte in May 2017 inspected a Chinese naval ship docked at his hometown, the first such visit to the Philippines in years. Chairing the 2017 ASEAN summit in Manila, Duterte dropped references to land reclamation and militarization in the disputed waterway as well as references to "tensions" and "escalation of activities" in an earlier draft of the summit statement. Eluding the great powers by hedging between them creatively and brazenly, Duterte collected concessions from both powers. While the Chinese offered Duterte favorable investment deals, the Americans reduced Duterte's obligations to the alliance.

In this case, as Jeffery Bader argues, if the United States goes down "the road of disengagement from China in pursuit of unbridled competition, it will not be a repetition of the Cold War with the Soviet Union, when the United States was joined by a phalanx of Western and democratic countries determined to join us in isolating the USSR. " Deeply entangling with China economically, "Even those most wary of Beijing, like Japan, India, and Australia, will not risk

---

[1] The Asian Development Bank, " Strong Asian Intraregional Trade and Investment Improve Economic Resilience," October 25, 2017, https://www. adb. org/news/strong-asian-intraregional-trade-and-investment-improve-economic-resilience.

economic ties with China nor join in a perverse struggle to re-erect the 'bamboo curtain'. We will be on our own. "[1]

Thirdly, although China's rise has inevitably increased frictions, engagement has helped avoid potentially disastrous U. S. -China confrontation by giving China a continuing stake in the relationship with the United States and its neighbors. It is in China's interest to work with the United States because China is far from the position to step into America's shoes as a hegemonic power and take the role of global leadership. Global leadership is costly; it means asking people to contribute to others' well-being and send soldiers to die far from home. China's rise is not necessarily America's decline. While it becomes difficult for the United States to hold its primacy in Asia, it is equally, if not more difficult, for China to drive the United States out of Asia anytime soon. Uncomfortable with the U. S. dominance, China, nevertheless, benefited immensely from the U. S. -led order underpinning stability and prosperity in the region. China would benefit from friendly rather than hostile relations with the United States and nations on its borders.

A Sino-American showdown may risk dooming China's economic transition and political stability. After remarkable GDP growth for many years, China has experienced difficult transition from reliance on low-cost manufacturing and exporting products to high-tech innovations and consumption-driven economy. Beijing has made clear that it does not want to fight the trade war that would harm the Chinese economy much more than the American economy. No alternative is as big and lucrative as the American market for China's export. Ordinary Chinese consumers would welcome reduced import tariffs, which means cheaper foreign products and services for the average Chinese consumers. [2]

But external hostile pressure has historically helped mobilize Chinese nationalism against any concessions that could be regarded as surrender to foreign powers. Along with the escalation of the trade war, the Chinese media has portrayed the economic friction as part of American conspiracy and even a grand strategy to contain China. Pursuing the "Chinese Dream" of restoring China to

---

[1] Jeffery Bader, "US-China Relations: Is it Time to End Engagement?" *Brookings Institution Policy Brief*, September 2018, https://www. brookings. edu/wp-content/uploads/2018/09/FP_20180925_us_china_relations. pdf.

[2] Xie Tao, "America and China: Destined for Conflict or Cooperation?" *National Interest*, July 30, 2018, https://nationalinterest. org/feature/america-and-china-destined-conflict-or-cooperation-we-asked-14-worlds-most-renowned-experts.

wealth and power on the basis of some valid historical grievances and considerable resources, many Chinese people have accepted the government position.

The Trump Administration thought it could win the trade war easily. But China's industrial policy and other practice continue. Heavy-handed industrial policy once helped Japan, South Korea, and Taiwan upgrade and bring wealth and prosperity. The U. S. government also supported national highway system, the Marshall Plan, the internet development, the Hoover dam, and space programs. Although an appropriate government role in a free enterprise system is different from the full blown Chinese industrial policy to support SOE, China would not give up its industrial policy simply under the U. S. pressure.

The ZTE sanction was a wakeup call for the Chinese government to encourage Chinese firms to localize high-tech and key industrial products and systems and their inputs, reducing technology dependence on the United States. In January 2018, the United States barred a takeover of Money Gram, the American remittances company, by Alibaba's money transfer agency, on the grounds that the private data of millions of U. S. citizens would be compromised in the hands of a Chinese company. Alibaba created a different, in many respects more innovative, product using block chain-based technology. Washington has not been able to force Beijing back down on most of disputes in the past. As China grows stronger, it can only get harder to force China to back down. Pushing China to the corner would produce a tougher China that sees no choice but to fight back although neither country is ready to be locked into a violent confrontation that neither can win.

IV. The United States and China have no choice but jointly manage and control competition and resume engagement

When the United States started engagement, the differences between the two countries were greater than they are today. The United States engaged China in spite of these differences. The United States has to maintain competitive and confident in its strengths and values, rebuild the reputation as an effective, inclusive, and open country, shore up its democratic and capitalist institutions, and invest in traditional alliances. As Chaz Freeman, who went with President Nixon to China in 1972, argued, "The best way to make America or China great again is not to try to impede each other's progress or tear it down. It is for each side to focus on the home front, implement the values it professes, improve the factors underlying its national competitiveness, and address its own problems before worrying about those of others. "[1] Andrew Nathan echoes that the first step of a good China policy lies at home. "We must recover our strength and recommit to our values—a mission for changing ourselves that, at this moment, looks even harder than the failed mission of changing China. "[2]

Chinese Ambassador Cui Tiankai put it correctly, "China and the United States remain in the same big boat faced with fierce wind and huge waves. The common challenge is to navigate this boat through the uncertainties or uncharted waters, for the benefits of both countries. "[3] Although there is no precedent to guide economic and geostrategic competition between the two largest and deeply intertwined economies and heavily militarized superpowers, the United States and China must find a balance of interests with each other and avoid violent confrontation that serves neither interest. This level of engagement requires vision and flexibility. With strong economic interdependence, the existence of an international institutional order, limited ideological confrontation, and nuclear second-strike capability, leaders in the two countries have no choice but find ways to manage their competition and continue engagement with each other.

[1] Chas W. Freeman, Jr. , "The United States and China: Game of Superpowers, Remarks to the National War College Student Body," February 8, 2017, http://chasfreeman. net/the-united-states-and-china-game-of-superpowers/.

[2] http://www. chinafile. com/conversation/american-policy-toward-china-due-reckoning.

[3] Remarks by Ambassador Cui Tiankai at the 8th US-China Civil Dialogue, July 26, 2018, http://www. china-embassy. org/eng/zmgxs/zxxx/t1580425. htm.

New Security Challenges Within the International System: Changing Policy Among Major States

Douglas Bandow [1]

Former Special Assistant to President Reagan,
a Senior Fellow at the Cato Institute

Never has the world been richer or nor the opportunities available to its residents been greater. New understandings and technologies beckon to a future that is healthier as well as wealthier and in which the bounty of humanity's creativity is much more widely shared. However, taking advantage of this promise requires nations to adjust to a dramatically changing international environment. That includes adapting to significant shifts in economic and military power, as well as softer forms of global influence.

I. Development of Traditional International Order

The modern world has a Eurocentric foundation. The ancient order featured a succession of kingdoms and empires, which typically dominated for a time and then disappeared, losing out to newer powers. Rome remained dominant for an unusually long period, but its influence always was bounded. It had little impact much beyond the periphery of Asia, the Middle East, and North Africa. Imperial Rome had no contact with the Eastern hemisphere.

Once the western half of the Roman Empire fell, few would have bet on Europe's future dominance. The Chinese empire seemed a more likely candidate for global rule. The dynasties changed, but the imperium lived on. However, in the 15th century China's Ming dynasty chose isolation. It was a hugely consequential decision for the Chinese nation. Then, stasis, weakness, and submission ended up transforming their future.

In contrast, Europe went in a very different direction. Despite periodic crises—the so-called Black Death and Mongol invasion, for instance—the continent learned to look outward. Even during the Middle Ages, starting around the 10th century, Europe began a period of sustained economic growth. The 14th century featured the Renaissance. The 15th century began what became a torrent of international exploration and trade. The industrial revolution transformed the continent starting in the 18th century.

Wealth and technology enhanced military power. Well into the 20th century European nations reached across Asia, Africa, and Latin America. Although Great Britain was the greatest of the global states, its direct power remained surprisingly limited: Britannia ruled the waves but fielded only a modest army. London relied on local troops and allied armies to advance its policies. Other than the loss of its American colonies, it was almost always victorious through World War II. One of Britain's victims was China, which was forced to detach Hong Kong to London and grant "concessions" of Macau and related areas assorted to Portugal and other Western powers. Through World War I European governments would consult with each other on how to divide the geopolitical spoils, sometimes cooperating to enforce their will, as in China during the so-called Boxer Rebellion.

II. Destruction of Traditional International Order

Although the European states survived many limited conflicts among them with their reputations and influence intact, World War I proved different. All the colonial powers save Germany emerged from the conflict with their possessions, but their reputations had been ravaged. Countries which spent years slaughtering each other appeared less formidable to smaller states and dependent peoples. Peace brought only further instability to Europe, with the creation of a multitude of vulnerable smaller states. And revolutions of various sorts swept Germany, Russia, Italy, and the conglomerate Austro-Hungary. Although Britain and France remained atop the international order, their hold was tenuous and their confidence was shattered.

Moreover, powers both east and west of Europe were rising. Until 1917 the United States had been largely disengaged from the world politically and militarily. Joining the so-called Entente, the United States gave the latter a decisive edge against the German-led Central Powers. In 1919 the Versailles Treaty was an embarrassing repudiation of the moralistic claims underlying Washington's entry into WWI, which was rejected by the U. S. Congress, and popular disillusionment set in. Voters elected a new president who pulled America back from a leading international role. However, the U. S. no longer stood aloof from world affairs.

Transformed by the Meiji Revolution, Japan became the dominant Asian state. Having joined the Entente Tokyo benefited from the spoils of victory. However, Japan learned that the European club remained closed when the 1919 peace conference rejected a proposal by Japanese delegates regarding the "equality of nations" that would have banned discrimination based on "race or nationality. " Still, Japan was the one Asian state which European powers were forced to treat as an international equal.

Finally, in 1911 China's Qing dynasty was overthrown in a revolution led by Sun Yat-sen. Although the new republic remained divided and weak, it foreshadowed great changes to come. The Chinese people had finally broken free of the stultifying imperial order and set in motion a process of great change. The new China joined Japan in undermining Asia's position as a dominion of the West.

The inter-war years saw the revival of deadly European rivalry as well as Japan's invasion of China. When war finally came to Europe the two theaters merged into a global conflagration. The defeat of Germany and Japan yielded a completely new international order. Among the Europeans only the UK still stood militarily strong, but it was financially exhausted. Although London formally retained its empire, Britain's hold was barely a short-term lease. Germany was defeated and divided. France had to deal with the consequences of occupation by and sometime collusion with Germany. Much of the rest of the continent was in ruins and chaos.

In Asia, the collapse of the international system was almost complete. Japan was defeated and occupied. Onetime colonies, such as Korea, Vietnam, and the Dutch East Indies, were adrift, neither ruled nor freed. Most importantly, China, liberated from Japanese occupation, descended into full-scale civil war.

Thus, huge geopolitical vacuums existed in both east and west. They were filled by the United States and Soviet Union as the Cold War developed. In the succeeding four decades the rest of the globe gradually welcomed both older revived and newly emerged powers. Europe recovered, as did Japan. Colonies won independence. India became a diplomatic and later economic force. Most importantly, the People's Republic of China was born and eventually overcame internal challenges to dramatically enter the international marketplace. Still, until the U. S. S. R. collapsed the world remained largely bipolar, its relationships distorted by the sometimes violent and always dangerous competition between Washington and Moscow.

III. The Unipolar Moment

The Soviet break-up left an American-dominated order. It was called many things, including the Unipolar Moment, an apt description. For a brief time there was one hyperpower. That is, among world powers there was America and no one else. Washington was in a strong position to win international assent or at least acquiescence to U. S. economic and geopolitical initiatives. And Washington could act largely irrespective of the desires of others—expanding NATO up to Russia's borders, for instance. Any real political or military battle would end in an American victory.

However, this world also turned out to be brief, just a "moment," indeed, barely that considering the sweep of history. Other empires lasted centuries or decades, China even longer. Washington enjoyed something akin to imperial power for 20 or 30 years. The Trump administration is acting as if the unipolar moment remains, with America in charge, but the results have been disappointing—for President Donald Trump, at least.

Russia is no longer a global hegemonic competitor but remains a powerful regional power with international reach. And Moscow is sharply at odds with the United Staes and Europe over NATO expansion and especially the status of Ukraine and Georgia. However, allied sanctions have proved to be a dead-end and several European nations are pressing to change policy. Moscow also has consciously impeded American objectives in Venezuela, Syria, and Iran. In Afghanistan and North Korea the Putin government has proved less willing to back U. S. aims.

Washington's relations with long-time friends, including Canada, Mexico, and Europe, have grown more truculent. Economic and immigration issues top the list of disputes, but security questions also loom large with Europe. America's determination to use its predominant economic position to enforce its foreign policy directives has created special discontent across the continent regarding Cuba and Iran.

Europe's economic influence has grown, despite of the challenge posed by adoption of the Euro alongside radically different fiscal strategies by member governments. The continent matches America's economic strength and exceeds that of China, though the Europeans continue to find it difficult to address on a common basis international issues. The European Union has stalled well short of a United States of Europe. Whether the continent is ever able to create a more consolidated government capable of managing Europe's fiscal affairs, creating a serious trans-national military, and implementing an independent foreign policy remains to be seen. Until then, Brussels' influence will dramatically diminish further from Europe. Although the continent's economic ties with Asia, and especially China, are significant, its political and military clout in Asia is nonexistent.

The U. S. found limits to its influence even in its geographic neighborhood. The Trump administration tightened sanctions on both Cuba and Venezuela, but so far without result. Moreover, the political left remains vibrant and competitive in the region: Mexico has a president at sharp odds with America and the Peronistas could return to power in Argentina in the October elections.

Washington increasingly has militarized relations with Africa, in 2007 creating Africa Command or AFRICOM. Counter-terrorism tops its missions, but many operations are directed more at aiding local governments than protecting America. However, U. S. officials fear being left behind as the long-term international competition increasingly leans economic and political. Washington and Moscow used aid, investment, and trade as well as soldiers to compete for influence during the Cold War. Now America's most important competition comes from the PRC, which has supplemented its steadily expanding trade relationships with projects under the Belt and Road Initiative. Although Beijing's involvement has not been without controversies and setbacks, Chinese influence is growing throughout Africa.

Consuming most of Washington's attention has been the Middle East. The United States demonstrated what should already have been obvious: America is capable of defeating any small to mid-size power, but lacks the mindset, patience, and skills necessary to remake other societies. Because Washington is unable to set meaningful priorities in where and what it does, it has squandered immeasurable resources in pursuit of secondary and even peripheral objectives.

For instance, three successive U. S. administrations spent lives, materiel, and attention in nation-building exercises in Afghanistan and Iraq; in Libya and Syria the Obama administration concentrated on destroying the existing governing structures without much concern about what followed. The United States got enmeshed in the Saudi/Emirati war against Yemen and currently is teetering on the brink of war with Iran. In the cases of Iraq and Iran Washington found itself acting without many of its traditional allies. Most important, the United States found itself far better at creating chaos which, like quick sand, made escape virtually impossible. Even as America's energy reliance on the Mideast falls, Washington is being ever more tied to the region militarily. Yet every military action increases the number of enemies and potential terrorists, who then become the justification for additional military interventions, and on and on.

In Asia, the United States remains the dominant security player but is losing its strong ground economically. Washington has directly confronted North Korea but found itself forced to try diplomacy after briefly threatening "fire and fury" in fall 2017. The talks are currently deadlocked and most observers recognize that the Trump administration will have to make concessions if it hopes to achieve denuclearization.

More significant is Washington's attempt at the containment of China. Although American officials deny such an intention, there is no other explanation for U. S. policy. Trump administration policymakers assume aggressive intentions by Beijing and have pushed an assertive response regarding territorial claims in East Asian waters. Washington also has increased its military presence in the region, affirmed its alliance relationships with Japan and the Philippines, and sought to expand security ties with India. Finally, the current administration has highlighted its long relationship with Taiwan. Such initiatives have likely increased PRC determination to enhance its military strength.

However, East Asia is moving beyond bilateral rivalry between Washington and Beijing. Other countries are taking independent steps and often confronting China directly. Japan's Abe government has been adopting a more aggressive political and military policy. India has been taking a more active role, building relations with Japan and Vietnam, in particular. South Korea and the PRC steadily improved their relations until Seoul's deployment of the THAAD missile defense system, followed by Beijing's imposition of sanctions; the bilateral relations have rebounded but remain tinged with suspicion. Australia, with deep security ties to America, has hosted a bitter internal debate over China's growing influence domestically.

The economic competition for America is even stiffer. China's commercial cooperation with its neighbors has surpassed their economic relations with America. Even South Korea, dependent for security on Washington, trades more with the PRC than with the United States and Japan combined. The Trump administration's disdain for free trade, and especially rejection of the Trans-Pacific Partnership, which was negotiated by the previous administration, opened the region to bilateral and multilateral trade pacts with Beijing. Most significantly, the United States and China currently are in the midst of a trade war.

Overall there has been talk of a potential cold war between Washington and

Beijing. Relations have deteriorated, but thankfully have not reached that level. There is no global clash highlighted by military confrontation and existential threats. Despite the contentious trade talks, the two countries retain large-scale and beneficial economic cooperation. There are far more personnel, academic, tourist, and other exchanges than that during the Cold War between the United States and the Soviet Union. And most of the world retains strong relations with both the United States and China, deeply embedding both in the same international order.

IV. Development of a New International Order

The Unipolar Moment obviously is over. Despite the illusions of many American policymakers, the problem is not lack of "leadership," the constant mantra tossed about in U. S. foreign policy debates. Washington increasingly will lack the capability and determination to dominate every region of the globe. The U. S. president and Congress continue to act wildly with no concern for the future. America long has benefited from the dollar's status as the world's reserve currency. The Euro's acceptance has been slowed by the travails of Greece and other European states. The Renminbi's role has been limited by concern over China's lack of financial transparency.

However, Washington's deficit will near $ 1 trillion this year and only increase in the future. The federal government budget will be under increasing strain as more Americans retire, reducing tax revenues while increasing outlays on pensions and health care. The U. S. desire to project powerat will costs far more than deterring outside intervention. The American public is likely to have a declining willingness to underwrite the expense of what appears to be foreign adventurism for little benefit. These will force Washington to rethink its foreign policy.

What is future security policy of leading nations likely to look like? The system must evolve, perhaps broadly along the lines suggested below. For a time the U. S. will continue to pursue primacy. Washington will browbeat its allies to follow its lead, and mix military threats with economic sanctions to force others to accept its ends. The results will become increasingly indifferent. Friendly nations will resist contributing to military campaigns and work to further shield the international financial system from American control. For instance, Europe has been working to protect transactions with Iran to preserve the nuclear agreement. Potential adversaries will back similar efforts while assisting each other to resist Washington. Moscow recently offered to similarly aid Iran and both China and

Russia provided other forms of assistance to Venezuela. States that feel threatened by the U. S. will use proceeds from their growing economies to bolster their militaries, emphasizing such weapons as missiles and submarines to deny or at least hinder America access to their waters, lands, and airspace.

Under extraordinary fiscal pressure, the United States will begin cutting back affecting its influence in the Asia-Pacific, and other nations can most easily take over security responsibilities. For instance, Americans are likely to tire of defending Europe, a continent facing few genuine security threats and possessing the means to protect itself. Moscow has little incentive to attack its neighbors, for the costs would vastly outrange the benefits. Moreover, as a whole Europe possesses a much larger population and economy than Russia. Of all the U. S. commitments, the one to Europe may be most antiquated. In some fashion Europe will take on increasing security responsibilities, including confronting Moscow, if need be, as well as limiting refugee/migrant flows from North Africa and the Middle East and thwarting terrorist attacks originating in the same regions. The mechanism could be NATO with a reduced U. S. role. Or it could be a new Euro-defense agency emanating from the European Union. Still, Europe will have difficulty projecting military power much beyond its own environs. The political differences among EU members and reluctance to invest in the military are likely to remain too great. In coming years Washington also is likely to draw back from the Middle East, since the results of past interventions have ranged between disappointing and disastrous. Moreover, America no longer has much at stake in a region in which instability seems endemic. For instance, the United States has become a major energy producer and is not reliant on Middle Eastern oil. New oil and natural gas fields have been discovered elsewhere and will ease European and Asian dependence on the Middle East as well. Moreover, Israel, a traditional American concern, is a regional superpower, able to defeat any of its neighbors brave enough to challenge it. As for terrorism, Washington's constant war-making in the region and support for Israel and its oppressive rule over the Palestinians have been major grievances driving attacks on the U. S. Disengaging would make America safer.

The result is likely to be development of a new regional balance of power. The Gulf states might more openly ally with Israel, and Turkey might informally join with Syria, Iraq, and Iran. All would find it in their interest to battle jihadist insurgents and terrorists, such as the Islamic State and al-Qaeda. Some states, such as Yemen, seem destined for long-term crisis. Others, such as Egypt, look stable but might face upheaval sooner than expected. Iran is unlikely to yield to the Trump administration's extreme demands but might make a more balanced deal with a different U. S. administration and Europe. Moreover, industrialized states east and west will face pressure regarding security of oil shipments through Persian Gulf waters. Normally no Mideast state has an incentive to interrupt transit, but outside factors, such as U. S. economic sanctions or ongoing conflict, could change that calculus. If Washington finally demurred from taking on the responsibility, it would fall most obviously on the Chinese, European, Indian, and Japanese navies.

In Asia an American withdrawal is likely to be slower and more measured. There is no friendly multilateral alliance in place. Washington's partners have a history of mutual antagonism, particularly toward Japan. And China, of greatest concern to U. S. governments past and present, dwarfs its much smaller neighbors. Nevertheless, America is likely to eventually move into a role more akin to that of an off-shore balancer. New powers, such as Indonesia and Malaysia, are likely to play increasingly important regional roles. An improved relationship between South and North Korea will reduce the argument for U. S. ground forces stationed in the Republic of Korea. With Japan steadily enhancing its military capabilities Washington might bring home the Marine Expeditionary Force stationed on Okinawa, as long demanded by many local residents. The United States is likely to encourage greater regional military cooperation, including with Vietnam and India. Along the way Washington might shift its defense commitment from contested territories to national independence of allied states, which has never been threatened by the PRC.

How China's neighbors perceive its ambitions and plans will likely determine these and other developments. In recent years regional concern has increased that Beijing has abandoned its commitment to "peaceful rise" and is more willing to use military force to achieve its ends. That has encouraged neighboring states to move closer to America, change their opinion of Japanese rearmament, cooperate more with one another, and invite India to effectively connect the Indian and Pacific Oceans. Recent Chinese policy toward Taiwan and Hong Kong has reinforced these negative opinions. If Beijing's strategy continues in this direction, any American withdrawal is likely to be more limited and reluctant, and to be met by vigorous regional moves to fill the resulting vacuum. On the other hand, if the PRC and its neighbors successfully address pressing controversies—for instance, some interim agreements regarding regional territorial claims allowing shared development while postponing sovereignty decisions—Washington might be readier to leave and there might be little effort to replace U. S. deployments and commitments.

Africa has extraordinary room to grow, depending on the policies adopted by individual governments. Africa has been enjoying a modest renaissance of democracy and economic growth. Greater reform-oriented stability has encouraged more investment and trade, creating a virtuous cycle to the benefit of once desperately poor populations. If countries such as Kenya, Nigeria, and South Africa can surmount significant political challenges, they will emerge with global importance. Although the continent's security challenges are real, they have little to do with outside powers. Most involve home-grown or neighboring insurgents and terrorists, such as Boko Haram in Nigeria. Thus, international geopolitical competition no longer need hinder Africa's development. Rather, any China-U. S. economic competition should redound to the continent's benefit.

Similar is the situation with Latin America. Despite having only a modest presence internationally, the region has three potentially important international participants: Argentina, Brazil, and Mexico. All face primarily self-inflicted wounds, and could make reforms and succeed largely irrespective of U. S. and their international policies.

Of course, America is nearby and naturally dominates its neighbors. Those long outside its sway, most notably Cuba and Venezuela, matter little strategically. Contrary to the Trump administration's near hysterical reaction to the Maduro government, this regime can do little to harm anyone other than its own people, whether America or Caracas' neighbors. With the recent resolution of Colombia's long-running armed insurgency, there are few significant security issues in the region other than the drug trade. For the latter America long has been the primary problem, providing the demand driving production and imposing legal prohibition, making the trade more lucrative. In any case, given America's proximity, Washington is unlikely to substantially change its intrusive policies toward Latin America. They cost the U. S. relatively little while the region matters much to Washington.

Overall, there is no reason the foregoing world, or something similar, could not deliver general stability and peace, indeed do so better than the present international order. Although at least some smaller conflicts are inevitable, the major powers could remain at peace, especially if they work to establish firebreaks to war. Combat of any sort seems least likely in Europe, outside of the Balkans, anyway. There is little in either South America or Africa to draw in one, let alone multiple ones. Asia may be most vulnerable to conflict, which highlights the importance of its peoples and governments working to resolve disputes which could lead to violence.

V. Threats to Stability and Peace

Despite the tragedy of violence which seemingly surrounds us, the world has been getting more peaceful. There are fewer large, destructive wars. Those that occur, such as the Syrian civil war and Saudi/Emirati invasion of Yemen, are awful. However, they pale compared to many in the past, considering the Sino-Japanese conflict of the 1930s, as well as World War I and II.

Thus, while it is important to work against conflict anywhere by any state and group, it is most important to develop a security structure that most effectively discourages big wars by big powers. Among the most dangerous presently are mid-level rivalries, such as India and Pakistan, nuclear powers both. Saudi Arabia and Iran are another combustible pair. North and South Korea too. These nations, major powers, and international organizations should work on such assorted military tinderboxes. Indeed, President Donald Trump's willingness to meet with North Korea's Kim Jong-un addresses one of the most worst confrontations, offering hope of creating a stable, peaceful peninsula.

Far more dangerous are existential disputes among the major powers of which, thankfully, there are few. While the U. S. has a variety of claims and complaints against both China and Russia, and they are against America, none involve vital interests of any party. Against each other the three contend for influence, not territory, population, or existence. There simply is no traditional excuse for war among them.

The greatest threat to America comes from terrorists, for which traditional war is no answer; rather, invading and occupying other nations is likely to increase such attacks. China and Russia have more direct confrontations with others, lesser powers—both over territorial claims of sorts. China with India, Japan, Philippines, and Vietnam; Russia with Georgia and Ukraine.

Washington's tendency to promiscuously issue security guarantees has turned all into potential transmission belts of great power conflict. Washington keeps supporting the expansion of NATO and even has pushed to bring Georgia and Ukraine into the transatlantic alliance. The Trump administration also has reaffirmed its defense commitments in Asia over contested territories, such as the Diaoyu/Senkaku Islands. In the Middle East Washington has acted as general guarantor of Israel and bodyguard for the Saudi and Emirati royals. All these commitments could lead to limited conflicts. Although a U. S. defense promise helps deter foreign action, it also encourages reckless behavior by recipients and ensures American involvement if deterrence fails. Thus, Washington must attempt to restrain its allies while essentially promising to back them with nuclear weapons if anything goes wrong.

The best way to avoid major power conflict in such cases is to seek peaceful resolution of disputes involving America's defense dependents. For example, with Russia Washington could offer to halt further NATO expansion, and especially discussion of possible NATO membership for Georgia and Russia. In return Moscow could drop support for Ukrainian separatists and hold an internationally monitored referendum in Crimea.

In Asia the U. S. could disengage from territorial controversies where the parties have found peaceful means to defuse potential confrontations. In some cases Washington might be able to help solve the conflict—agreeing to verifiable arms control and economic cooperation on the Korean peninsula, for instance. Finally, resolving ancillary but tension-building disputes, such as over trade, would help build additional firebreaks to conflict.

In the Middle East Washington might backstop the survival of its allies but not promise to intervene when lesser interests were at stake. Moreover, the U. S. could relinquish responsibility for maintaining Mideast stability. It is a thankless, frankly fruitless task, and is not necessary for the peace and security of America or other important powers. Such steps would not guarantee the absence of conflict, however, such a course would make war much less likely.

VI. Conclusion

People living today live far better than their ancestors. Even those with modest incomes have conveniences and luxuries far beyond the imagination of the wealthiest and most powerful figures in the past. Amazing medical care, the miracle of travel, the wonders of the internet, and so much more. It is a good time to be alive. However, the threat of conflict and war remains very real around the globe. Worst would be eruption of conflict between major powers, which could kill and destroy on a mass scale, even threatening the existence of entire nations. We have tragically suffered through such events in the past. World War II ended just 74 years ago. The Korean War concluded 66 years ago, but no peace treaty was ever signed, and the Vietnam War ended 44 years ago, etc. . The risk of new great power wars has since eased, at least slightly although there have been other horrendous conflicts since then, but none that involved a major power or threatened to draw in major powers.

With the collapse of the Unipolar Moment, peoples and governments around the world must look for alternative security structures to provide for a stable and peaceful future. Such a world is not foreordained but will require hard work. As we embark upon this task, we should insist, as has often been said elsewhere, that failure is not an option. We simply must succeed, lest this seeming world of plenty turn into one of disaster.

Footnotes:

1. He is the author of Tripwire: Korea and U. S. Foreign Policy in a Changed World and Foreign Follies: America's New Global Empire.

The Sino-U. S. Frictions and Global Security under the Backdrop of Changes Unseen in a Century

Feng Weijiang

Director and Research Fellow for National Security Studies,
Institute of World Economic and Political Studies,
Chinese Academy of Social Sciences

Since the first half of 2019, the Sino-U. S. trade frictions have become more and more intense since the United States has announced higher and higher tariffs, having attracted a lot of attention and resources given by academic, diplomatic and business circles at home and abroad. In fact, many assessments of the economic consequences of trade frictions have shown that the direct impact of Sino-U. S. trade frictions on the economic growth of both sides is insignificant. What various sides are concerned about is the risk of trade frictions breaking up the global industrial chain, even slipping into sanctions and counter-sanctions in monetary, financial and other fields, and even falling into a more serious security conflict or full-scale confrontation. If we broaden our observations with a view of the unprecedented changes unseen in the past century in the world, it is not difficult to see that trade frictions are only a small fragment of the long-term geo-movement of "rising East and falling West".

At the beginning of 2017, speaking at the headquarters of the United Nations in Geneva, Chinese President Xi Jinping raised a question: what's wrong with the world and what should we do? At the end of the same year, when he received the delegates to the 2017 Diplomatic Envoy Conference, he pointed out that looking at the world, we are faced with great changes unseen in the past century. Since the beginning of the new century, a large number of emerging market economies and developing countries are developing rapidly, the development of multi-polarization accelerating in the world, the international pattern is becoming increasingly balanced, and the mega-trend of the international situation is irreversible. The "unprecedented changes unseen in a century" are his concise explanation of the question of "what's wrong with the world". In June 2018, he elaborated on the characteristics of the unprecedented changes unseen in a century in a dialectical perspective at the Central Conference on Work Relating to Foreign Affairs. Since then, President Xi Jinping has repeatedly expounded how to understand and respond to the great changes unseen in the past century on issues relating to military affairs, national security, economy and diplomacy, as well as in his speeches to young people, leading cadres, leaders and people of other countries or signed articles.

From the perspective of international relations, the unprecedented changes unseen in the past century are mainly as follows: the accelerated development of world multipolarity, the increasing balanced international pattern, the international situation at the new turning point, the division and reconfiguration of various strategic force, the accelerated evolution of the international system, and the in-depth adjustment of relations among major powers, meanwhile the threat of hegemonism and power politics still in existence.

From the economic perspective, a large number of emerging market economies and developing countries represented by China are developing rapidly, economic globalization continues to develop in depth, and the world economic structure has undergone profound changes. Meanwhile, the U. S. inward-looking tendency, protectionism and unilateralism are raising their heads. The dramatic economic change is reflected in China's catching up with the United States on economic scale.

According to the data of the International Monetary Fund (IMF), in 2014, China's GDP (purchasing power parity index, or PPP value) accounted for 16. 5%, which was more than 15. 8% of the U. S. share in the world economy, which was overtaken for the first time by others since the late 19th Century as the United States surpassed Britain. It is estimated that by 2024, China and the United States will account for 21. 4% and 13. 7% of the global economy respectively.

Of course, judging from other indicators, such as current-price GDP or per capita GDP, the process is much slower and much more complex. According to the current price of GDP, China's economic growth rate from 2021 to 2024 will be lower than before, but will still remain at a high level, so as to maintain the momentum of catching up with the United States. However, due to the large U. S. economic volume, the United States will still maintain the role of economic No. 1.

From per capita GDP, the European Parliament predicts that by 2035

China's per capita GDP in terms of PPP will increase from about $ 10,000 to about $ 21,000, but is still less than half of the EU level in 2035. IMF is more optimistic about China's per capita GDP growth, and thinks that by 2024, China's per capita GDP in terms of PPP will be $ 22,419, reaching 53. 7% of that of EU, and 37. 7% of that of the United States, which will be close to the current bottom level of the developed countries (in 2018, the lowest per capita GDP in PPP terms of developed countries is $ 25, 887 for Greece). The prediction of the Institute of World Economy and International Relations (IMEMO) of the Russian Academy of Sciences shows that by 2035, China's per capita GDP in terms of PPP will reach $ 37,400, which is 43. 3% of that of the United States, and China's per capita GDP in terms of exchange rate will be $ 21,400, which is 24. 8% of that of the United States. Although there is still a big gap at per capita level, because of the huge population of China, the per capita level moving towards the developed countries reflects a big rise of the overall strength.

From a security perspective, under the circumstances of profound changes, the international environment is generally stable, but the challenges of international security are complex and intricate, there are wars and conflicts and terrorist attacks, as well as rise and fall of famine and epidemic. Although global strategic stability is threatened by U. S. withdrawal from the INF Treaty and other actions, yet, there is little probability that serious conflicts between major powers, or between China and the United States, will break out to bring about systematic global security risks. The expected most destructive losses for China or the United States may not be generated by a direct conflict between the two. Just as the U. S. RAND says in the report entitled *War with China—Thinking through the Unthinkable* that nuclear weapons would not be used, even in high-intensity conventional wars. Neither side would run the risks of nuclear retaliation to launch a pre-emptive nuclear strike since the war costs are so great, the prospects are so unimaginable, or its stakes are so significant.

From the cultural perspective, the great changes mean that various civilizations exchanging with and learning from each other, and different ideas and cultures interacting one another. Meanwhile, with further development of cultural diversity, the argument of "clash of civilizations" has also become sediment coming to the surface and has pushed its impact in the direction of "self-fulfillment prophecy". For example, in April 2019, K. Skinner, Director of Policy Planning of the State Department said at a security forum in Washington that the current trial of strength between China and the United States is different from that of the Cold War. The competition between the United States and the Soviet Union is "the internal struggle of the Western family". Marxism the Soviet Union had belief in is also rooted in Western political theories, while what is happening between the United States and China is a very different struggle between civilizations and between ideologies, and the United States has never had such experiences. This is the first time that the United States faces a strong competitor from a non-white race. Skinner also said that the United States is developing a relations framework with China based on the "clash of civilizations" . Although this statement has been severely criticized by many political and diplomatic scholars in the United States, we should not regard it as an accidental and careless slip of tongue made by an individual U. S. government official and ignore the supporting forces and possible supporting actions behind it.

From the perspective of science and technology, the era of great changes is the era of deepening development of information society and the surging of new industrial revolution. Every country knows that whoever occupies the commanding height in the field of science and technology will have a greater initiative and a stronger voice in the great changes. Among the three pillars of science & technology, system and population, which support the in-depth adjustments of the pattern of economic force, the population structure is a slow variable, which can only be possible to make marginal adjustments through immigration policies, but it is easy to cause internal division within a country. Institutional competition is not only a high-cost competition, and it is also difficult to require the counterpart side or its "camp" countries to be more flexible through coercive measures, but to strive for (or to buy over) the institutional support of the intermediate zone is also costly, and difficult to gain and easy to lose. So the competition of science and technology may become one of the main battlefields that will influence the changes unseen in the past century.

Human society has experienced a one-dimensional economy highly dependent on the input of labor factor, and a two-dimensional economy in which capital elements replace labor in the way of diminishing marginal substitution rate, and is moving towards a three-dimensional economy in which scientific and technological elements strengthen labor productivity and capital output rate in a completely new way. Under the three-dimensional economic conditions, the way wars can be won will undergo subversive changes. Firstly, the domain of war is greatly expanded. With the help of advanced technology, wars under the three-dimensional economic conditions have expanded and transformed from traditional sea, land and air to space, from macro-space to micro-space, from physical world to virtual world, and from battle paradigms scenes to life paradigms scenes. Secondly, the means of confrontation are more abundant. The development of directional energy, life sciences, artificial intelligence, cyber network, hypersonic technology and other fields in the direction of military application may diversify the way of commanding, performing and testing war. Thirdly, the war ethics has changed. under the one-dimensional economy and the two-dimensional economy, whether to win the population or to destroy effective forces through war reflects that human beings themselves as the provider of labor elements are valuable. Despite the substitution of capital or technology for labor (population), generally speaking, the low-dimensional economy obeys the law of diminishing marginal substitution rate, i. e., with the growing capital or technology investment scale, the number of labor that can be replaced by one unit of capital or technology decreases, which means that capital or technology can not completely replace labor in theory. Under the three-dimensional economy, with the development of artificial intelligence and other technologies, the law of diminishing marginal substitution rate is broken, and labor can be completely replaced by unmanned operation, so, the value of laborers as labor carriers may become insignificant. Contradictions between human beings will change from exploitation of one part of it by another part to ignorance of one part of it by another part. Under the exploitative paradigm, the exploiters acknowledge the value of the exploited, and under given conditions can reach a certain "sympathetic understanding", just like those farmers who take good care of their bulls like partners although they sometimes uses whips on them. Under the ignorance paradigm, the affluent population no longer regards the surplus population as their peers, or even classify them as a different kind by the labels of religion, race, culture, native place, class and so on, without feeling the joy and sorrow of the latter, just like scientists who use rats in their experiments will not necessarily hesitate to feel any guilty at all. While the later will not be allowed to give full play to their subjective role, but only be manipulated or slaughtered by the former. The rise of long-range combat technology and unmanned combat platforms based on virtual reality may exacerbate the ignorance of human life by war-fighters, thus increasing the brutality of war.

The basic features of economic and social development under the profound changes in the world is that a few major countries are competing for stepping toward the three-dimensional economic world, while hoping that their main competitors will remain in a low-dimensional economic state for a long time. The basic logic of competition is to launch de-dimensional attacks, holding back the further development of major competitors from 2. 5-dimensional economy to high-dimensional economy by means of economic and trade investment, military operation, diplomatic hedging and international rules, etc. , and hopefully forcing them return to a low-dimensional economy and stay. If the developed countries represented by the United States reduce the dimensionality of the economic formation of major emerging economies represented by China and lock them in a two-dimensional economic situation and cut off the possible path of upgrading their technological dimensionality, the trend of "East rising and West declining" may stagnate or even reverse.

It is a long-term process to cope with the unprecedented changes unseen in a century. In this process, the pressure of tension, anxiety and panic caused by the forces of continuous extrusion resulting from rise and decline between the United States and China (as well as other countries) impacting on the areas of internal religious frictions, ethnic contradictions, polarization between rich and poor, environmental pollution, corruption, cadre-mass relations, labor conflicts and other vulnerabilities, one or a few areas of which are particularly vulnerable catalyze fault lines, which lead to serious problems such as economic collapse, social disorder and political subversion, as well as global turbulence or security crisis in the backdrop of high-tech caused by countries, especially major powers that guide these contradictions to the outside world in order to temporarily alleviate these problems, which may be truly destructive. In this sense, we should unite with the developing partners along the Belt and Road and the developed partners participating in the "tripartite cooperation" to jointly expand the open space, and deepen reform and opening up in order to prevent all kinds of "grey rhinoceros", and give equal importance to preventing the Sino-U. S. trade friction "black goose" from sliding out of control.

New Changes in the China–U. S. Relationship

Martin Jacques

Professor and Senior Research Fellow with the University of Cambridge

Currently, I am sure the great majority of us would prefer that the era, beginning in the late 1970s, of globalisation and multilateralism will continue, and that the era was characterised by relative stability and cooperation in the relationship between the United States and China. That stability had depended on two things. First, a huge inequality in the relationship, with the United States by far the dominant partner. Second, the long enduring American illusion that the only future for China, if it was to be successful, was to become like America. History has undermined both propositions. Over a period of 40 years, the most remarkable in global economic history, China overtook the U. S. economy in terms of GDP purchasing power parity. Furthermore, it is patently clear to everyone that China is never going to be like the United States. The United States hugely miscalculated, a victim of its own hubris. Its response is avolte face: a desperate search to find ways of reversing China's rise or at least slowing it down. The United States is right that the underlying reason for China's rise is economic. So it is logical to start with a trade war. But the United States will not stop at that. It seems likely that disputes will in time encompass most if not all aspects of their relationship. The China-U. S. negotiations may reach to a substantial result, but we should not be too optimistic, since the relative stable 40-year China-U. S. relations is coming to an end. And the new scenario for the China-U. S. relations is most likely to last a long time, my guess is at least twenty years, perhaps longer.

There will not be an outbreak of a new cold war between China and the United States. There are only two similarities between the current situation and that in the Cold War: the United States is one side; and a Communist Party is the governing party in the other side. (In truth, though, the Chinese Communist Party and Soviet Communist Party have barely anything in common.) So the tense China-U. S. relations does not mean a cold war. Firstly, the United States is in deferent development stage. During the Cold War, the United States was still a rising power. Now it is a declining power. The Americans are an angry and worried, desperately trying to hold on to what it had and the world which it created, while China has achieved the most remarkable economic rise in human history, and is in the ascendant. Secondly, China and the United States have different understanding of the national power support. During the Cold War, the rivalry and confrontation for hegemony between the United States and the Soviet Union focused on military competition. Currently, while military strength remains America's most coveted form of power, China's military capacity has also grown fast, but its views on war and peace are entirely different with that between the United States and the Soviet Union during the Cold War. In Chinese thinking, Chinese ancient military strategist Sun Tzu who wrote warring tactics entitled Sun Tzu's Art of War, but regarded war as something to be avoided rather than embraced, upheld negotiations rather than fighting to solve disputes. In addition, the Chinese view that the two most important modes of power, both historically and in the contemporary context, are economic and cultural. The Chinese believe in tackling matters in the long run with patience and will. We can see this in the manner that China has responded to Trump: firm but restrained, and kept the lines of communication open. All of this tells us that China will be a different kind of great power.

The U. S. response to Huawei corporation is out of its fear. Nowadays China's growth rate is still three times than that of the United States, its standout economic achievement over the last decade has been its sharply rising capacity for innovation. Even five years ago, the West was still questioning if China could ever be innovative rather than imitative. No one asks that question anymore. The speed with which Alibaba and Tencent have joined the Silicon Valley tech giants in the premier league of technology has been quite remarkable. Huawei is the global leader in telecommunications, most notably 5G. Of course, most Chinese companies lag behind their American equivalents in terms of productivity, but the direction and speed of development is irresistible. China is a technological major power in the making, above all, what has stunned the United States. The underlying motive for the attack on Huawei has not too much to do with security; above all, it is about a fear of China's competitive challenge.

The United States faces being a biggest loser with the trade war. Imposing higher tariffs and pursuing unilateralism will make the U. S. economy increasingly less competitive, as a result, it will emerge from the protectionism, whenever that might be, seriously weakened. Henry Paulson, the former U. S. Treasury

Secretary, makes exactly this point in an article in Financial Times. Both economies, of course, will suffer, but in the long term the U. S. economy is likely to be much the bigger loser.

It is the United States that is the most uncertain factor impacting the global security. The United States fought many wars of expansion during its rise. In contrast, China's rise has been characterized by an extraordinary path of peaceful development, and adherence to the strategic focus. In the face of its decline, Trump's first clear expression of and response to this process is the authoritarian turn, the erosion of democracy, drifting of American prestige, leading to U. S. social division and retrogression. America is almost totally unprepared for its own decline. One must hope that it is not a harrowing experience either for the United States or for the rest of the world.

The United States and China: the Logic of "Struggle" and the Concept of "Harmony"

Zhang Zhenjiang

Dean and Professor, School of International Relations
and Institute of Overseas Chinese Studies,
Jinan University

On June 18, 2019, President Trump called Chinese President Xi Jinping by telephone to express his hope to hold a special meeting between the leaders of the two countries during the G20 Summit in Osaka, so as to directly communicate and exchange views on the current Sino-U. S. relations. President Xi expressed his willingness to meet him. As a result, a few days ago, a tweeter release triggered several rumors about the Sino-U. S. leaders' meeting, which came to light afterward. President Trump in his tweeter said if he fails to meet President Xi at the G20 Summit, he will launch a new round of tariff measures on Chinese goods. This is the Trump's frank behavior of ignoring the diplomatic coordination and euphemism, without considering how the Chinese side understands that information.

It is difficult to anticipate the crisis of Sino-U. S. relations will turn around given President Trump's previous practices and unique style of action. It is very likely that Trump first gives the world an exaggerated surprise and then throws out unexpected bombs one after another. The recent Sino-U. S. relationship is pushed onto a roller-coaster by his twitter messages. In recent years, China and the United States had carried out a series of game-play, especially the United States, together with the unique and elusive personal style of President Trump, making the Sino-U. S. relations like taking a roller-coaster: ups and downs with surprises now and then.

To understand the current dazzling Sino-U. S. relations, we need to go through many mysteries to get to the bottom of the mystery. The United States and China show two totally different concepts when identifying and dealing with the relations between the two countries: the U. S. logic of "struggle" and the

China concept of "harmony".

The logic of the United States is very clear, i. e. those "different races" must have different minds. The rising China with a different mind will surely jeopardize and challenge the existing status of the United States. From the beginning of the relaxation of Sino-U. S. relations in the 1970s, it has been accompanied by the controversy of "engagement" or "containment". The purpose of "engagement" is to turn China into the "same category of state" recognized by the United States and a member of its team. But with the development and independence of China and the relative decline of the dominant position of the United States, the United States finds it difficult to control this "different" state. As a result, the "engagement" slowly turns to "containment". Especially from the disregard of the correct international politics by President Trump, in the language used by the U. S. government, China quickly becomes a "rival" even "enemy" of the United States, and the Sino-U. S. disputes even become a " clash of civilizations".

Tracing back to the origin, the logic of American "struggle" has a rich historical practice and ideological basis. Christianity's distinction between God and Satan is a hard-to-get-away thinking pattern and ideological guidance when the West and the United States look at other peoples and the international relations. Carle Schmidt, a famous German statesman, clearly pointed out that the most fundamental problem of Western politics is to define enemy and friend. In historical practice, the United States, which currently dominates the world, is constantly looking for, defining and defeating an "enemy" to continuously survive, develop and grow. In this regard, it is not surprising that the United States can reach a rare consensus on China that can transcend the ruling parties and the opposition.

China's concepts and policies are also consistent: upholding the principles of peaceful development and the goal of a harmonious world, does not challenge the status of the United States, and explicitly states that it will not dominate the world. Even if China's strength is strong enough, it is also committed to building a harmonious world of convincing others as the ancient Chinese saying goes that one would do not onto others as you would not have them do onto you, and is committed to building a community with a shared future for mankind. If we use the description of ancient Chinese, it should be a world of harmony instead of a world of hegemony. In addition, the mainstream of Chinese traditional philosophy emphasizes the mutual transformation between Yin and Yang, between good and evil, and seldom sees the relationship between oneself and others in either black or white way, or in completely opposite. In fact, a more important idea is to maintain and continue the order of "harmony" above this specific debate on right and wrong, correct and incorrect.

The China's concept of "harmony" also comes from China's historical practice. Prosperity of Tang dynasty, Mongol's rule, Emperors' Kangxi and Qianlong flourishing times, etc., ethnic integration eventually replaced ethnic conflicts and became the general trend of Chinese history. Even in the "Hua-Yi order" or "tributary system" blamed by the West for inequality, Chinese governments of the past dynasties were very cautious in taking direct intervention in other countries' internal affairs, and even rarely sent troops for punitive expedition and taking actions to domesticate those "different races" into China. According to the Western logic, when Zheng He took the voyage, he could bring the coastal countries into Chinese territory by virtue of the strength of the Chinese fleet. But the actual result was totally different from the fact that the whole world became a target for Western colonization 90 years later when Columbus and Magellan made the geographical discovery. Many Westerners still place China's Belt and Road Initiative and the Marshal Plan on the same par, but the fundamental difference of the two programs is that the goal of the Belt and Road Initiative is to build an interconnected world, and identifies no rival and no adversary, but the Marshal Plan is to assist the U. S. allies to get stronger to deal with the common adversary.

The logic of "struggle" and the concept of "harmony" lead to a series of misunderstandings and entanglements between China and the United States on many issues, especially on their respective perceptions and judgments. Fundamentally, the idea of "harmony" can be learning, transforming and stabilizing, while the logic of "struggle" is very harmful, can even destroy the foundation of coexistence of the two countries and disintegrate the possibility of "harmony" in the future. For this reason, the United States should shoulder more responsibilities for the future of Sino-U. S. relations. The so-called " Thucydides trap" is mainly aimed at Sparta, if the rise of Athens is an irreversible objective fact, then, how to recognize and understand this fact is very important. It is regrettable that Sparta believes that Athens is the enemy and opponent, from which the fear is incubated, having resulted in the Oedipus effect in Greek mythology, which is an inevitable tragedy.

The concept of " harmony" can lead Sino-U. S. relations to another paradigm. But in terms of concrete practice, "harmony" does not necessarily have obvious advantages in the process of interaction with "struggle". In the future building of Sino-U. S. relations, China should be more proactive and constructive. China can not only resist and get out of the logic and provocation of the U. S. "struggle", but also needs to resolve and dispel doubts and reduce misunderstandings. Just as President Xi Jinping stresses, we should all endeavour to avoid falling into the "Thucydides trap", the idea that a powerful nation only pursuing hegemony does not apply to China and China has no gene for taking such an action.

It will be an arduous course to introduce the logic of "struggle" to the concept of "harmony", but it will also be a blessing to China, to the United States and the world as well.

The Impact of U. S. –China Competition on Argentina and Latin America

Juan Battaleme

Director of Academic Department, Argentine Council for Internation Relations

We base the following reflection on two related ideas. The first one is to point out that the competition and rivalry between the two great powers of our times come from those areas they consider relevant in terms of "securing their future". The second implies that in order to achieve this objective, they must ensure and obtain a maneuvering space that as a result of the growing fracture of what we call the liberal international order. An existing alteration entails the status quo established by the United States in 1945.

This dynamic affects foreign policy perspectives of middle and lesser powers and creates severe complications in the specific case of Argentina's process to be a stable partner in the international system and begins to affect our autonomy to achieve our own security and prosperity objectives. Likewise, the situation in the country is far from unique. The whole Latin America is affected by the same dynamic of rivalry. The present situation is paradoxical for Argentina. Commercially and financially, the country needs both the United States and China. In the bilateral relationships, we do not have security issues that directly affect us, and in no case, Argentina as such represents a security concern for any of the countries involved.

However, the rigidity that the relationship between the United States and China begins to show in the field of commercial and security affects the country in economic and political terms. There is a kind of triangular relationship forming it that shapes as a result of China's increasing presence in the region and U. S. fears, which are causing security concerns that in the long run will affect Argentina because it is in a vulnerable international position.

The triangular logic between a rising power and defending power forces a vulnerable country like Argentina to actively think about its positioning in the face of explicit or indirect pressures that may happen. The room to be neutral became much smaller. The policy that began at the end of 2015, known as "Intelligent Engagement" with the world, now should be recalibrated based on the need to create autonomy in an interdependent world. Autonomy involves much more than just increasing its maneuver in a complex world. This concept involves ensuring that the pursuit of the national interest by building power and well-being in a world of multiple grids of connection, which involves extensive levels of interpenetration, where dissimilar actors can generate blockades that are difficult to anticipate.

Policies of coercion, attraction, and blockade are realities that empowered countries and are used to achieve certain ends, as can be seen in Latin American political reality. Venezuela is a tragic reminder of how quickly the most vulnerable countries in the international system can be exposed and suffer the designs of the great powers and their competition.

Technologically, we are in a stage of the competition for access. In the second half of the 21st century, we will live under the mistakes and successes we make in this first half. Access not only involves natural resources. Access means freeing the "invisible" power existing in the transformation of matter, the creation of life and the leap to one possible, expected and exponential future, which was challenging to achieve as a consequence of not having the right tools until now. In terms of technology, we are converging to our next evolutionary leap as Yuval Noah Harari points out in his book Homo Deus.

However, one of the troubles that new technologies generate over the distribution of power of countries that there is a growing willingness from big powers and part of the business community to limit such access. Firstly, to actors who can make harmful use of them, and secondly by states who want to steal developments that may have implications in the field of military or citizen security, which generates ongoing tensions between technology developers, users, governments and companies. In political terms, strategic considerations have begun to displace economic considerations, and such displacement acts as a brake on the technological potentials offered today.

If technology ensures access to different spaces and promotes a particular type of globalization, it can also allow policies to build capabilities to prevent and eventually deny unwanted, unauthorized access from a potential competitor. The North American liberal globalization project enabled for the American preferential access, eventually that "access granted" was eroded as time goes by, as a result of the rising national counter-projects which use globalization means for national ends. They did not share the liberal spirit, but they bear the same ambition to maximize so much that they could offer the world, as well as reap the benefits of their new competitive skills and efficiency as demonstrated by Fareed Zakaria in his book "The Post-American World".

We can appreciate that tensions characterize this period as a consequence of the passage from an order focused on a universal or global consensus among various state participants, which allowed to advance a certain shared rules to which subjected to all who feels part of the so-called international community. The liberal order, on which the Obama administration tried to add China as a "responsible shareholder", was slowly finding several limits, which came from American mistakes, the successes of competing powers, and increasing dispersion of power among various states and the loss of legitimacy of the action. The erosion of American power, together with the consolidation of the rising with other and different political parameters than Western ones, is resulting in a more limited order. While there is a discussion about "the international disorder," the current situation is significantly closer to the definition that Randall Schwellen provides when talking about an increasingly entropic international system, and therefore neither order nor disorder has preponderance, we rather live in a perpetual state of "volatility".

The sense of "clash of civilizations", strategic competence and pre-eminence of rival identities highlight the difficulties in securing the future that all powers have at this time designed international initiatives, such as the One Belt One Road Initiative and the different reactions it generates from Western powers. Misunderstanding and mistrust in Asia are on the rise because states have raised their concern between each other, and technology is playing a part in this new environment. We are not only hacking systems or computers, and also are trying to hack minds.

We can reduce the strategic competition to one sentence: Securing the future. Today we find great powers in a race to secure geopolitical (including outer space), geo-economic and cyberspace access. All these fields involve different and divergent dynamics in which tensions are increasing.

(1) Militarily the dynamics that exist in Southeast Asia are established by some unstable balance between China and the US, which translates into military power projection strategies such as the so-called Air-Sea Battle (ASB) or Anti-Access and Area Denial (A2/AD). This allows us to conclude that both decode their reality in terms of zero-sum games.

(2) Geo-economic competition is also open, as there are obvious interdependencies and dependencies with different actors and where the

possibilities and areas of cooperation are also shortened, increasing the view of zero-sum game. The United States and China accuse each other of exploiting the vulnerabilities of the weaker states with which they associate. This growing economic penetration also raises intra-regional tensions over the presence of economic actors that generate some resistance in local communities, as the Economist magazine pointed out in its article "The New Colonialists". This situation affects two main Chinese arguments of interaction with the international system because they questioned seriously. One is the perception of peaceful rise, and the other is about the "harmonious world" of cooperative coordination. However, limitation to those critics also appears because China, especially in the field of technology, for a significant number of countries, remains as the leading partner in its development aspirations.

(3) For both, today, cyberspace is a source of instability where there is already a clear perception of the zero-sum game too. Mutual accusations of espionage, industrial theft, patent fights and major future markets positioning, China and the United States perceives that there is no room for cooperation, fears rise and models of control and use of cyberspace differ actively. Add to that the "platform economy" that is subtle but intrusive, as author Shoshana Zuboff points out. The fact that it is not yet clear which of the two actors will benefit most from the contest, even though the forecasts place China in a better position so that in a relatively short period, maybe in about 2030 to dominate broad spectrums of the international sphere.

Securing the future involves understanding how the competitive rivalry produced by these three material races will be solved, and that will define the structural position of both actors because in addition to being interrelated they create the strategic military and economic advantages. During 2007 it was noted that we had entered the race for "what was left" about state competitions for the Arctic or Antarctica in the words of Michael Klare; we are now in a race of greater complexity which we could identify as a career for "what follows".

"What follows/what is the next disruption" is to think in terms of the next evolutionary step, as—if the parallel applies—a new "race to the moon", or a revolution in strategic perspective or strategy 2. 0, as a result of the fourth industrial revolution. The technologies involved are robotics, space, communications, artificial intelligence, and digital biology. Like other races, we are facing a short-stroke, long-range race, where the first sprint is essential. That is where the Trump administration complains mainly about China's behavior with patents and uses it to clash with the Chinese under the current trade war. Their argument is while the United States considers that they do Research & Development its Chinese counterpart performs Research + Development + Thievery according to Graham Allison in its already classic book Destined for War.

Securing the future means choosing the best strategic option. The United States and China have their options open, yet more and more limitations are appearing on the American side. Both countries have their versions of "being great again", which, however, reflect different positions and considerations about their role in the international system. Both know that order is constructed but also know that order expires. China, however, smartly raises its relationship with the world differently. The Chinese narrative goes through that of the future, especially presenting a "brilliant" future for all. The American narrative puts things in terms of security and risk, which creates limits in cooperation and sense of urgency. They offer security, but not future. This is especially counterproductive to South Americans, who are mindful of the U. S. role in the region, their levels of interference and divisive behavior throughout the 20th century, especially in the latter half. China is unknown and "distant" geographically, but close because migration that increasingly interacts with local communities, showing a friendly profile and communications opportunities.

If we consider that the American Grand Strategy has gone from off-shore balancing logic to another known as accommodation strategy (which may contain appeasement options) to the present strategy which is considered a strategy of smaller international involvement. The U. S. National Security Strategy considers that the main objective of the 21st century is that of competition with Russia and China, particularly to maintain a degree of technological supremacy, on sensitive issues such as detection, directed energy weapons, autonomous weapons, quantum detection, nuclear defenses and the modernization of nuclear arsenals, in the face of growing capabilities by Russia and China. An example of this is the creation of the various space forces and the decision to eventually install offensive weapons in it.

President Trump's logic has allowed previous administrations to close policies regarding the aggressive positioning of the United States, considering them as distractions from "real" competition. Bush and Obama began wars of various kinds and intensity, leading to nearly twenty years of open intervention, continuing only with the operations inherited from the administrations that preceded it and which currently highlights the maintenance of the war in Afghanistan. The path of selective engagement seems to be the only one left for the United States to sustain its position in the international system, and this high-strategy discussion is one that Democrats also begin to take on for an eventual electoral contest. The liberal supremacy strategy, as Stephen Walt calls them, has proven costly, reckless, and ineffective.

Measures taken to decoupling the value chains previously created in the technological field are some of the steps in the construction of a more rigid and less fluid world. That is why American universities, technology companies, and all those at the core of American national security are rethinking their relationship with China. While this situation makes it easier for China to seek partnerships with other countries, the United States simultaneously lets the potential partners know that a close relationship with the Asian giant is detrimental to a sustained relationship with Washington. It is not clear for everyone which side any country is going to take.

The option to use military power in a crisis appears unlikely, according to Rand's U. S. -China Military Scorecard. That report notes that there is parity in six of nine areas of conventional military capability (attacks on bases areas, attacks on surface units, achieving superiority to prevent an opponent from launching space-based weapons) and that in the next 15 years China will be able to prevent American military superiority. The United States retains an advantage in cyber warfare and also in nuclear stability issues. U. S. military spending is about $605 billion, if it has no more significant upside-in margin without moving negatively on the overall U. S. budget, while China's is $150 billion with enough room to continue growing. The United States is concerned not only about relative changes in power but also about the intentions they involve.

Both China and the United States are trying to recreate a world of dependencies in a system characterized by interdependence. That is why in a sense trade war allows them to carry out a degree of decoupling, and to the extent that they advance in that decoupling, they will mark many limitations for the secondary actors of international politics. As time passes, the divergences between the leading countries will accentuate the structural limitation of actors of less relative power. The third world countries will have less autonomy in the second half of the 21st century.

Where this situation leaves us, in 2011, a foreign policy decision linked us to China's military space complex—changing the traditional policy of keeping Argentina relatively neutral from power competition in the 21st century. Likewise, China has a growing weight not only in Argentina but also in Latin America. Smart insertion has involved two crucial issues, (1) getting along with all those in the national interest of the country; (2) reflecting values but realizing that in a multipolar world, the universality of them is limited.

The dynamics of rising new powers and change in the structure of international politics condition affects the maneuver capabilities of the countries. They should have to identify the convergence agendas in the region and link them and try to understand the adverse consequences that some issues will have in their bilateral relationship. Decision taken to deal with divergent interest will be a central element in building intelligent autonomy. Argentina needs both countries, and our future is related to find a way to deal with the great power competition that is already ongoing.

Session II
New Adjustments in the Regional Security Order

New Adjustment in the Regional Security Order

Tran Dac Loi

Vice President of Vietnam Peace & Development Foundation,
Former Deputy Head of the Commission for External
Relations of the Central Committee of the
Communist Party of Vietnam

East Asia has enjoyed nearly two decades of peace and stability since the end of the Cold War. The United States has reduced its military presence in the region by withdrawing the 7th Fleet from the area and abandoning its military bases in the Philippines. Peace was restored in Cambodia as Indochina turned from the battlefield to the marketplace, and ASEAN gradually expanded its membership from five to 10 nations and moved toward a single community. China pursued the "peaceful rise" policy, improved its relations with countries in the region, signed and implemented the TAC and DOC with ASEAN. The South China Sea has been relatively peaceful and stable despite existing differences in territorial claims among the parties concerned. There is no doubt that despite many territorial disputes during this period, including the Asian financial crisis, peace and cooperation have been a prevailing trend, dominating the world and, especially, the region. Globalisation and international integration have accelerated. Trade and investment have expanded, and multilateralism has been strengthened. And there is no doubt that all nations in this region has benefited from this trend that has made East Asia the most dynamic and leading locomotive for economic development of the world.

This relatively short *belle epoch* of regional stability started to take shape since the end of the first decade of the 21st Century. Clashes and growing militarisation in the South China Sea and rising tensions also on the Korean Peninsula caused serious tension and strategic distrust in the region and raised deep concerns among the international community. The United States was "pivoting" back to the region by implementing the "re-balancing" and then the Indo-Pacific strategy while China has taken new moves in the South China Sea as well as new strategic approach towards the region. Major powers increased their military presence in the area. Military spending increased significantly in many countries. International laws and multilateralism has been undermined in many cases by unilateral actions of major powers. Terrorism, cyber-crime, climate change and growing extreme nationalism, among others, is posing increasing threats to the stability of the region.

What happened recently between the United States and China shows that there is not only a trade conflict between the two biggest world economies, similar to the case of the United States and Japan in the 80s, but much beyond that. It moves from cooperation and competition toward the direction of strategic containment and geopolitical confrontation with many components of the Cold War, which poses a very serious challenge to the future of the region and the whole world.

The East Asian region's security and stability today are facing three levels of major challenges. First and foremost is strategic competition and confrontation between major powers in the region, especially between the United States and China. Second is the impact of global threats to regional peace, stability and development. And last but not least is intra-regional issues rising from strategic mistrust and conflict of core interests among the countries in the region, especially concerning the territorial disputes in the South China Sea.

The region is at a crossroads, facing a choice of moving in the direction of peace and stability or conflict and instability, cooperation or confrontation, multilateralism and international laws or unilateral actions and isolation. History and reality show clearly that confrontation will benefit no one and will only lead to common losses. Particularly, what's happened in the Middle East once again proves that external interference, intervention and imposition will bring about only chaos and disaster to the countries and people in the region and the world over.

In today's globalised world all nations are connected by trade, investments, communication and people exchanges and we have become much more interdependent on each other. No nation can develop in isolation. Security becomes indivisible for all. Facing the global threats of terrorism, climate change, epidemic diseases, cyber and transnational crimes, etc. , requires joint cooperation of the whole international community. This era requires more political wisdom than muscle. And I think our choice should be only the road of peace and stability, cooperation and development for all.

The core principles of the international law such as respect for all nations' independence and sovereignty, non-interference into internal affairs, peaceful resolution of all disputes and conflicts, no use of force or threat to use force, etc. , should be strictly observed. Development and prosperity of one nation should not undermine development and prosperity of any other nation. This largely depends on the conduct of the major powers as well as collective efforts of all countries in the region.

The great powers such as China and the United States have the greatest role and, therefore, a prime responsibility in this process since their bilateral relations and conduct will affect the whole world-but primarily the region. I think that greatness of any nation is measured by what it can contribute to the peace, development and prosperity of humanity and not by showing its muscle and hegemony. We all live in one region and one world which should not and cannot be divided. Therefore, it's necessary to work together and to avoid any kind of second Cold War or "clash of civilizations". The great powers are expected to be a leading example of adherence to international laws and multilateral cooperation and to refrain from unilateral actions harming the interests of any other nation or the common security and prosperity.

Preservation of peace, security and stability in the region requires the setting and observance of sufficient rules and norms of conduct, as well as an effective collective mechanism for conflict prevention. We can remember that Europe was the center of confrontation between the two camps during the Cold War with the highest level of concentration of armaments. The Helsinki process led to the signing of the Helsinki Accord and the formation of the Organisation of Security and Cooperation in Europe (OSCE) which helped to prevent conflict and maintain peace in this region.

Unfortunately, that is not the case for Asia-Pacific today. In fact, we are still lacking such rules and mechanism while the region is facing very serious and growing security challenges. Therefore, I think that we need to work together to fill this crucial gap. We can work out collective agreements regulating armaments, military deployment and exercises, ensuring freedom and safety of navigation and aviation, fighting terrorism, cyber and transnational crimes, while protecting the environment and addressing climate change as well as all the other threats to regional security and stability. We can jointly create an collective security mechanisms for maintaining peace and prevention of conflicts in the region. I am sure that by doing so, we will strengthen mutual strategic trust among us and we can ensure preservation of long-term peace, security and stability in the region.

Fortunately, we can promote this process not with empty hands. There are number of important and useful agreements already achieved such as ASEAN's Treaty of Amity and Cooperation (TAC) in Southeast Asia, the Declaration on Zone of Peace, Freedom and Neutrality (ZOPFAN), the Treaty on the Southeast Asian Nuclear Weapon-Free Zone (SEANWFZ), and the Declaration of Conduct (DOC) in the South China Sea between ASEAN and China, among others. Also a number of mechanisms exist which can be strengthened and developed further for ensuring security in the region such as ASEAN Regional Forum (ARF), ADMM+ and particularly the East Asian Summit (EAS). Unlike the case of the European mechanism of collective security created by the two opposing blocks, our mechanism should be created by all parties concerned. In this process the central role of ASEAN would be very useful and important. In today's interdependent world, such a mechanism should be open to all interested parties.

Last but not least, the issue of the South China Sea is very crucial for peace, security and stability of the region. The South China Sea is a traditional living space for all coastal nations there and one of the most important international maritime roads. Maritime territorial sovereignty is a core interest of all coastal nations while peace, stability, freedom and safety of navigation in the South China Sea is an essential interest of the whole international community. The conduct of parties in the South China Sea and particularly their handling of existing disputes has a decisive impact on the building of strategic trust among all parties concerned as well as on the political-security picture of the whole region. That's why the settling of the issue of the South China Sea is critical in the process of building regional peace and security.

I am sure that peace, stability, cooperation and development is our common interest. Experience of the past and in various parts of the world shows that disputes do not necessarily lead to confrontation or conflict and can be resolved peacefully. And I am sure that if we all have enough good will and political wisdom, we can work jointly to turn the South China Sea into the zone of peace, friendship and cooperation which will benefit all of us.

Historical Experience for and Realistic Challenges to Build Security Order in the Asia-Pacific Region

Yang Mingjie

CPAPD Executive Council Member,
Director and Research Fellow, Institute of Taiwan Studies,
Chinese Academy of Social Sciences

Compared with the rest of the world, the Asia-Pacific region has maintained a relatively stable and prosperous overall posture in the past three decades. Despite the ups and downs of hot security issues exist in the region, they have been basically under reasonable crisis management and control. In the region, the mechanism of security dialogue and cooperation from bilateral to multilateral has also yielded fruitful results. The shaping and maintenance of this security situation benefits from the economic pursuit of freedom and openness as well as common prosperity; the pursuit of comprehensive measures and win-win cooperation on security; and the strategic pursuit of increasing trust, dispelling doubts, seeking common ground while reserving differences by the relevant countries in the region. However, this promising security situation is facing severe challenges, and the building of security order in the Asia-Pacific region has reached a new historical turning point.

I. From the perspective of historical experience, the relatively prosperous and stabile Asia-Pacific region benefited from the positive interactions among the region's strategy, development and security. The concept of common, comprehensive, cooperative and sustainable security is being practiced steadily.

First, giving importance to and seeking pursuit of economic and social development by regional countries have become an important cornerstone of regional security. To a large extent and on a considerable scale, it has become the consensus of regional countries to seek security through development and promote security through development. Particularly, the economic development of the Asian region has been in the forefront of the world economy in recent decades, and the regional economic growth accounts for more than 60% of the world economic growth. Economic prosperity is not only conducive to the internal stability and social governance of various countries, but also radiating externally, boosting the positive momentum of regional economic cooperation. Under the guidance of the concept of seeking common development and sharing prosperity, the economic and trade cooperation mechanisms at various levels in a sense have also become the "ballast stone" of regional security relations. Economic cooperation frameworks at regional and sub-regional levels continuously transmit positive energy to the field of security.

Second, mutual trust measures and institution building in the field of security are highly valued and begin expanding to the field of economic and social development. Although the Asia-Pacific region is facing many security differences and difficulties, in the past quite a long time, the regional major countries highly treasure the overall interests of various countries and the region, and actively build multi-level security dialogue channels and mutual trust mechanisms through different channels and in different forms. These channels and mechanisms have effectively dispelled the strategic doubts and differences on specific issues of relevant countries, and have achieved relatively effective crisis management and control of some sensitive hot and difficult issues. The new inter-regional security cooperation mechanism has not only yielded tangible results in non-traditional security fields such as anti-terrorism and transnational crime, but some mechanisms also begin to incorporate economic and social development cooperation. The combination of development and security has played an energy multiplier role in promoting regional stability.

Third, it is true that major countries have strategic differences to different degree, but dialogue and cooperation are generally taken as the main strategic option. Structural and non-structural contradictions among major countries in the region exist for a long time, even get intensified in a certain time and space. However, the relevant countries basically insist on not rashly touching each other's bottom line and red line, and still base themselves on strategic management and control even in the process of crisis. This tacit understanding of strategic choices among major countries has made positive contributions to regional security and stability posture.

II. Currently, the relatively stable security posture in the Asia-Pacific region is encountering deep-seated strategic threats and challenges. The positive interaction among strategy & security and development may be reversed.

First, against the background of weak global economic recovery and de-globalization process, individual countries have rampantly challenged the order of regional economic cooperation based on freedom and openness out of unilateral consideration. The prospect of Asia-Pacific cooperation, which is undergoing a new process of regional economic integration, is greatly shadowed. Unilateralism, trade protectionism and bullying in the economic and trade fields do not only spill over into the security field, but also have a great negative impact on the cultural exchanges in the Asia-Pacific region. The concept of economy and security based on the common pursuit of the people of this region is challenged.

Second, the extremist perception and behavior of the security cooperation structure seriously impacts the current stable posture. On the one hand, an individual country has pieced together new networks of allies and partnerships aimed at third countries, which have unjustifiably increased regional tensions. On the other hand, new demands on the existing traditional military alliances increase the difficulties of strategic choice of regional allies, and even create new security issues.

Third, the return of an individual country's security strategies to the traditional confrontation between major powers intensifies regional tensions and brings the strategic choice of dialogue and cooperation as the mainstream back to confrontation and suppression.

Faced with new threats and challenges, we must earnestly sum up our historical experience, in combination with development of the current security situation, constantly strengthen the regional economic and security dialogue and cooperation, jointly resist unilateral bullying, oppose risky and extreme acts of strategic choices of some major powers, and reshape a new pattern of benign interaction of regional security.

New Adjustments in the Regional Security Order in Asia

Aizaz Ahmad Chaudhry

Former Foreign Secretary of Pakistan,
Director General of the Institute of Strategic Studies, Islamabad

The world order shaped since the end of Second World War is rapidly collapsing. With the rise of China as an economic giant, and several other states asserting their economic and military power, a multipolar world is emerging. And with that a quest for a new balance of power, particularly in the Asia-Pacific region. Sino-U. S. relations are going through a competition-prone transformation, as the United States now regards China as a "strategic competitor", even rival. A new Cold War seems to be germinating.

Unfortunately, however, multilaterism is increasingly getting marginalized in the wake of U. S. pursuit of its "America First" policy. Narrow nationalism, laced with populism, is raising its head in many other countries as well. As Francis Fukuyama argues in his book 'Identity', nation, religion, sect, race, ethnicity, gender are the categories of identity that have overtaken broader, more inclusive ideas of who we are. Nowadays walls are going up instead of bridges.

Yet, globalism is not dead. There are major attempts to keep the world inclusive and inter-dependent. One such area is the deepening economic cooperation between China and Eurasian nations through the Belt and Road Initiative (BRI) and Asian Infrastructure Investment Bank (AIIB). The BRI seeks to connect over sixty countries through mutually beneficial economic and commercial opportunities. Many in the United States blame China for practicing "debt-trap diplomacy" to expand its presence in Asia, and allege that Beijing's goal is to dominate Asia, though they have not yet provided much evidence for that. Regardless, the Chinese leaders seem convinced that globalism and connectivity would eventually benefit all and help build what they call a "community of shared future". Many nations are responding positively to the Chinese call for connectivity and operability. The Shanghai Cooperation

Organization (SCO) is also emerging as an important platform for the countries of the region to address common challenges.

I. Are China and the United States heading for a war?

A summary of U. S. National Defense Strategy released in January 2018 charges that China is pursuing a military modernization program that, "seeks Indo-Pacific regional hegemony in the near-term and displacement of the United States to achieve global preeminence in the future ".[1] Responding to U. S. statements, China's Foreign Ministry urged the United States, "to stop deliberately distorting China's strategic intentions, and abandon such outdated concepts as the Cold War mentality and the zero-sum game". [2]

A growing trade war has become the center-stage of U. S. -China relations with direct national security implications for both countries. Leaders of both nations have stated that "economic security is national security". U. S. -China negotiations on trade have stalled and nationalistic rhetoric has increased.

Washington is also blaming China for forced technology transfer, intellectually property theft, cyber espionage, and other unfair trade practices. In recent months, the Huawei case has added a new layer of complexity. The United States and other Western nations are resisting new technologies of Huawei in information systems on the grounds that it could give Beijing a backdoor into most sensitive Western defense and security systems. Meanwhile, Beijing regards these moves as less about security concerns and more about containing the development of China.

U. S. leaders are now talking about re-orienting U. S. military from fighting regional conflicts in Middle East and Afghanistan to prepare for great power competition. In the recently revealed details of the Indo-Pacific Strategy Report at Shangri La dialogue in Singapore in June 2019, the United States alleges that China was seeking to reorder the region to its advantage by leveraging military modernization, influence operations, and predatory economics to coerce other nations. This, coupled with ongoing U. S. -China trade disputes, could deepen the mistrust between these two leading world powers.

Several studies have emerged speculating that misunderstandings about each other's intentions could lead them into a dangerous Thucydides trap, so they should take necessary and bold decisions not to let their conflicts reach beyond the tipping point where war becomes inevitable.[3] This demands mature leadership and prudent handling of the multiple bilateral crises that both nations are now embroiled in.

II. Asia−Pacific — the focus of global geo−political games

Seen in the backdrop of the complex geo-politics in Asia-Pacific, it is clear that the region is likely to remain, for the near future, a venue for global and regional geo-strategic and geo-economic competition between the major powers. There is no shaped regional security order that could prevent conflict in the Asia-Pacific. There are multiple power centers/heavy weights within the regional settings which are more receptive to external influences, such as that of the United States, etc.

Some broader trends common to the Asia-Pacific region are quite discernible. First is the advent of U. S. -China strategic rivalry referred sometimes as the forthcoming "New Cold War". Within this context, Chinese neighborhood in South, Central and East Asia is being re-organized by the United States to build a containment arc against China. China, on its part, is making its own counter moves in the form of economic outreach in Asia-Pacific (BRI policy) and strengthening its strategic power. Meanwhile, China is also open to dialogue and cooperation with the United States on select issues in Asia-Pacific, e. g. North Korea and anti-terrorism policy. Second, the United States seems to be trying to draw a wedge between China and Russia in order to prevent a joint China-Russia block against the United States. Recognizing its strategic relevance, Russia is leveraging both the United States and China to increase its regional influence, particularly in Central Asia and Middle East. Third, trend in the Asia-Pacific region is a convergence between the United States, China and Russia on the issue of fighting transnational terrorism, especially the Islamic extremism.

There are significant trends of transformations, continuity and adjustments in various sub-regions of Asian continent: South Asia, Central Asia, East Asia and the Middle East (West Asia). Following region wise adjustments are worth noting:

South China Sea : Chinese are deeply concerned about the US's freedom of navigation operations (FONO) in South China Sea (SCS) and Western Pacific. Earlier this year, the quadrilateral network among the United States, Japan, the Philippines and India conducted FONO exercises in the SCS.[4] Around $ 5 trillion worth of global trades passes through the SCS, there is no doubt of its importance. The United States is now encouraging a more active role for Southeast Asian countries like the Philippines, Brunei, Malaysia and Vietnam to fight for a free and open SCS, and is also enthusiastic about greater Indian naval engagement on the South China Sea front.

South Asia: The United States is clearly building up India as a regional counter-weight to China. In this context, both the United States and India aim to neutralize Pakistan as an obstacle to Indian rise by using a mix of lawfare, economic coercion and sub-conventional warfare strategies. Pakistan, on its part, is trying to balance the U. S. and Chinese interests, without getting into anti-China camp. For the United States and India, both China and Pakistan represent a challenge to their designs for the regional order in the Asia-Pacific. The United States is using Pakistan's cooperation to cool down the Afghan theatre, which has become the longest war for the United States. Other countries in South Asia, i. e. Bangladesh, Nepal and Bhutan have largely adjusted their regional policies along the lines of Indian interests.

The major source of tensions in South Asia is the gross mistrust between India and Pakistan. As nuclear states, both have a shared responsibility to maintain strategic stability in South Asia. Unfortunately, time and again India has tested the limits of nuclear deterrence, is feverishly arming itself, adopting aggressive war fighting doctrines like Cold Start, preemptive counterforce first strike, and appears to be shifting from its already vague No First Use (NFU) position. Of late, India has embarked upon a dangerous practice of threatening neighboring Pakistan with surgical strikes, like the one it carried out on 26th February this year. Indo-US nuclear deal has further emboldened India, which now has access to international nuclear market through 2008 NSG waiver, and nuclear agreements with UK, France, Japan and the United States. India and the United States have signed agreements like Logistic Exchange Memorandum of Agreement (LEMOA) and Communications Compatibility and Security Agreement (COMCASA) which gives both countries access to designated military facilities, and which further enhance the logistical and communication capabilities of the Indian forces.[5] India is also embarking on nuclearization of Indian Ocean by acquiring nuclear powered submarines, which gives it a second-strike capability. India is acquiring Ballistic Missile Defense (BMD) technologies, and has recently carried out an anti-satellite test (ASAT).[6]

The above facts clearly indicate that India is pushing ahead with its regional and global ambitions, with little or no regard for strategic stability in South Asia. Pakistan, on the other hand, is strictly adhering to credible minimum deterrence and would not like to indulge in any arms race. Pakistan believes that the two contiguous nuclear powers should behave in a responsible manner. For its part, nuclear Pakistan has focused on achieving highest standards of nuclear safety, nuclear security, strict export controls, and robust command and control. If Pakistan is pursuing its nuclear program with restraint and responsibility, then why is it that India feels the need to pursue such an ambitious nuclear and conventional program? Is it the desire to become a regional hegemon, or status-seeking global power, or is it simply an irresponsible conduct of a nuclear power? Or perhaps all three.

Part of the answer became evident in the post-Pulwama actions taken by India. While remaining below the nuclear threshold, India is increasingly instigating conventional confrontation with Pakistan. On 26th February 2019, Indian aircraft intruded in Pakistani airspace and dropped a payload in an empty plot in Pakistan. On 27th February, two Indian planes violated Pakistan airspace, which were downed by Pakistan air force and a pilot captured. What if Pakistan had responded in kind? Did India think of the consequences? In sharp contrast to this irresponsible bravado, which violated international law and norms, Pakistan acted maturely, and released the Indian pilot as a peace gesture and to de-escalate the dangerous situation. Further, Indian leadership continued to hurl threats against Pakistan during the election campaign.

The larger question is, should a nuclear state conduct itself in such an irresponsible manner? India wants the international community to believe that it was a like-minded responsible state. Is what India did post-Pulwama by violating Pakistan's sovereignty and territorial integrity, the conduct of a responsible nuclear state or an irresponsible nuclear state? The United States and other world powers need to weigh in on India to act more responsibly and work towards peace and stability in South Asia.

Central Asia: Central Asia is a natural resource-rich region, with its strategic location as a Heart of Asia. Traditionally considered as Russian backyard, Central Asia today is reflecting the signs of U. S. and Chinese ingress. China has lately been investing heavily in the region, as a part of its Belt and Road Initiative (BRI), by linking these states with economies of Chinese provinces. Russia is cooperative to the Chinese strategic outreach in the region. It has not been easy for the United States to break the region away from Russian influence (Russia reversed "color revolutions" of 2004-2005). Russians are working with the existing regimes in Central Asia via anti-terrorism cooperation and energy sector reform policies to extend its influence.

Central Asian states are keen to diversify their energy markets southwards towards India (via TAPI) and eastward towards China. The United States supports these diversifications, possibly to reduce Russian influence in the region.

A major hotspot in this sub-region is Afghanistan, which remains in turmoil. Currently, a peace process is underway between the United States and the Taliban. The breakthrough came when the United States agreed in principle to withdraw its forces from Afghanistan according to a timetable yet to be firmed up. The Taliban announced their commitment not to allow their territory to be used for terrorism against any other country. This is an important step forward. However, the road to peace is still fraught with several serious challenges. First, all Afghan factions must agree to work towards a peace agreement. To that end, an intra-Afghan dialogue is essential. Second, Afghanistan needs a ceasefire that holds. Not only that, all parties must commit to a ceasefire, and there must be an enforcement mechanism. Third, there should be a regional consensus whereby the neighbors of Afghanistan and others commit to give peace a chance in Afghanistan. For too long, Afghanistan has witnessed proxy wars by outside powers. Notably, the progress in the peace process being led by the United States at this time is significant. It appears that the United States, Russia, China, Pakistan and other countries are all supportive of the peace process. Though there are still some roadblocks, it is in the interest of the entire region that peace returns to Afghanistan. For its part, Pakistan, which has suffered the most from instability in Afghanistan, is facilitating the peace process as it regards a peaceful, stable and prosperous Afghanistan to be in its own interest.

South East Asia, East Asia, and Pacific: It is this sub-region where the pull of U. S. -China strategic rivalry is felt the most. There are multiple hotspots in the region, chief among them are: South China Sea, Korean Peninsula, and Taiwan. China's main thrust of response is also seen in this region. All three hotspots have lately seen heightened military activities that have the potential to blow into a larger conflict. In addition to this, South East Asia hosts Malacca Straits, through which the oil and gas are transported to China, Japan and other countries.

The region is economically vibrant and has witnessed high growth rates. Whereas the overall global economic growth has slowed down, South East Asia has become a low cost manufacturing hub due to which the ASEAN countries are assuming a bigger say in regional affairs.

To the East Asia, the United States is trying to cool the North Korean front, with limited success thus far. On Taiwan, China has demonstrated its firm commitment to defend its "One China Policy". The United States often tests the limits of Chinese patience, but has not yet crossed the Chinese redline.

Middle East: The Middle East remains turbulent. The Palestinian crisis is unresolved. Terrorism continues to afflict various countries. Iraq, Syria, and Libya are suffering political instability and violence. Yemen has become a venue for proxy wars. Tensions between Iran and Saudi Arabia are a matter of concern for the countries of the region. The recent standoff between Iran and the United States has also kept the region on the edge. The U. S. pullout of Joint Comprehensive Program of Action (JCPOA) has been a setback to international diplomacy. The continuing U. S. sanctions on Iran have constrained Iran's economic and commercial interactions with the region and the world at large.

Russian influence in the region has increased, especially in the wake of the Syrian crisis. Though the Middle East is not geographically linked to China, the latter is heavily dependent upon the energy supplies from the Gulf region. This is the region where Chinese influence is minimum, and China looks keen to deepen its economic ties with the Gulf region. The United States and Europe continue to enjoy significant influence in the region.

III. Three possible prospects for the Asia-Pacific security situation

From a conceptual lens, there are three determinants of regional security order. The first is the relationships between major global powers or those major powers who matter in a specific region. The second is the response of regional major powers to the power politics. The third is the ability of major powers to impact the decision making of regional powers. On all three counts, we see that new circumstances borne out of growing Sino-U. S. competition would continue to pose serious challenges for the nations living in Asia. In the absence of a regional security architecture, all nations bear the responsibility to stay positively engaged and work towards regional stability in this important Continent.

In the context of the above discussion, there are three scenarios that can be envisioned for regional security in the Asia-Pacific. The first is an inadvertent limited conflict between the United States and China. The most likely venue for this limited conflict is the South China Sea and the Taiwan Strait as U. S. and Chinese vessels have come dangerously close to standoff in recent months. Moreover, since tensions are increasing in these areas, the U. S. -led naval exercises can become a precursor to a limited conflict. China's focus would be diverted from development to conflict. The second scenario can be called as " Cold Peace " which would mean "neither war, nor peace " state. This may resemble the current state of affairs where U. S. -China tensions are manageable at the strategic plan. This would, however, mean that new forms of covert warfare would ensue in sub-regions of Asia-Pacific. The regional powers in

Asia-Pacific will be further pressed to choose sides in this new form of conflict. India has had a head-start in this game as it escalates its covert war and terrorism as part of its campaign against Pakistan. The third scenario can be termed, in Trumpian phrase 'a new deal of the Century', where strategic circumstances force the United States and China to back down from current positions and negotiate their new role/share in the global balance of power. China has periodically signaled that it wants to work together with the United States on global issues. While the mutual trust between China and the United States is on the decline, the Sino-U. S. cooperation requires a major change in U. S. domestic politics, or Chinese economy, or any other unexpected development could force this change.

There are other possibilities that can also be imagined. But the real crisis the world at large or the Asia-Pacific region faces today is the lack of an alternate narrative to thriving populist nationalism at the world stage. Till that emerges, we should be ready to embrace an unstable regional security environment.

Footnotes:

1. US Department of Defense. "Summary of the National Defense Strategy of United States 2018. " Accessed June 14, 2019. https://dod. defense. gov/Portals/1/Documents/pubs/2018-National-Defense-Strategy-Summary. pdf.

2. Xiang Bo, "China Urges US to Abandon Cold War Mentality," *Xiahuanet*, December 19, 2017. http://www. xinhuanet. com//english/2017-12/19/c_136838057. htm.

3. Graham Allison, "The Thucydides Trap: Are the U. S. and China Headed for War?," *The Atlantic*, September 24, 2015. https://www. theatlantic. com/international/archive/2015/09/united-states-china-war-thucydides-trap/406756/.

4. Special Correspondent, "Navy Joins Exercises in South China Sea," *The Hindu*, May 09, 2019. https://www. thehindu. com/news/national/navy-joins-exercises-in-south-china-sea/article27084481. ece#.

5. Ankit Panda, "What the Recently Concluded US-India COMCASA Means," *The Diplomat*, September 09, 2018. https://thediplomat. com/2018/09/what-the-recently-concluded-us-india-comcasa-means/.

6. Anjana Pasricha, "India Claims Successful Anti-Satellite Weapon Test," *Voice of America*, March 27, 2019. https://www. voanews. com/south-central-asia/india-claims-successful-anti-satellite-weapon-test.

New Adjustments in the Regional Security Order: Thailand Perspectives

Gen. Surasit Thanadtang (Ret.)

Director, Thai-Chinese Strategic Research Center (TCSC),
National Research Council of Thailand (NRCT)

The current Asia-Pacific order is undergoing a profound change. The Asia-Pacific strategy of the Trump administration has been redirected. Under the guidance of the statecraft "America First", the United States raised the banner of unilateralism and trade protectionism, accentuating the preponderance of its military forces and the deterrent effect, and attempting to break the international multilateral trade system and rules and to launch a trade war with China. It brings greater and more uncertainty not only to its Asia-Pacific allies, but also to the security situation of the regional security order. The United States and other important actors of the region, such as India, Japan and Australia, have participated in and initiated various regional security and development agendas including the development and evolution of "Indo-Pacific" based on their respective abilities and interests, which is shifting the geopolitical pattern and situation of the region.

In Southeast Asia, due to the differences in national conditions and endowments, there is a tension of competition and cooperation between domestic and foreign policies in each country. Contrary to the uncertainty of the evolution of the Asia-Pacific order, China-Thailand relationship shows strong mutual trust and resilience, facing new opportunities and challenges. With the belief that "China and Thailand are kith and kin", we understand and promote the Belt and Road Initiative (BRI) cooperation comprehensively. Since then, Thailand and China enhance communication and mutual support in the international and regional multilateral mechanisms, reinforce risks control and crisis management in the people-to-people exchanges, strengthen the IR studies on China-Thailand relations, so as to make their relationship go steady and far for the stability and prosperity of the region.

Looking at the comprehensive changes on Asia's security, one can look at 4 main phenomenon as a result from the relationship of the "balance of power" between the United States and China, which can be an emerging influences in Asia as New Regional Security Spectrum, namely 1) "Washington consensus 2. 0" that makes the United States play a big role on world's geo-politics, 2) "China-India Axis" as the United States fails on containing the rise of China, 3) "Multipolar balance of power" as the United States still controls and acts as the world's hegemony, and 4) "New bipolarity" as China gains major influence but there will be many challenges and problems ahead.

Since ASEAN is not monolistic and self-contained, many regional "Security Think Tanks" have addressed their perspectives on new regional security spectrums and implied that two superpowers, the United States and China, have been competing with each other for disseminating their influence through FOIP and BRI in order to gain a competitive advantage in each region around the world. Consequently, impacts, from Indo-Pacific and BRI, consist of advantages from a balance of power between the United States and China, as well as benefits from the proposal which both the United States and China offer to ASEAN for exchanging support to their strategy and initiative. Conversely, most ASEAN member states have expressed and awarded of disadvantages from inequality and lack of transparency from both Indo-Pacific and BRI, as well as concept and action of ASEAN member countries that might affect the unity of ASEAN. As a small country, Thailand has to manage well the relationship and effective negotiations with Indo-Pacific and BRI, and gained mutual benefits for all sides, which are not causing any conflicts among ASEAN and other countries outside the region.

The New Adjustments in the Regional Security Order can be focusing on the new aims and ways of co-operative context of social development for humanity rather than "power competition".

Since the joint efforts to build the BRI reflect humanity's common aspiration for a bright future, some international and regional communities have still not identified the idea of building a "global community" of shared future advocated by the BRI; while some ask whether it is "Chinese community". The idea is in fact in harmony with the need for world economic development and the direction of the progress of world civilization.

In ASEAN states, the Initiative is becoming an important platform for building regional connectivity. The BRI upholds its non-competitive and non-exclusive nature to the fully extent, and reflects the international community's demand for a global governance system that is fair, egalitarian, open and inclusive, it is an important public product oriented toward today's world. As UN SG Antonio Guterres has pointed out, the BRI and the UN's Millennium Development Goals share the same goals, and both are pubic goods offered to the world. The BRI not only promotes international trade and people-to-people exchanges, but also enhances understanding between countries and reduces cultural barriers, and ultimately, achieves peace, harmony and prosperity

"Wisdom competition" based on national principle of ethical thinking and peaceful acting will be the key ways and means for the sharing regional security and future peaceful world. "Harmony without Uniformity" from Confucius can be seen as the "beauty of diversity" and this is the reality of mankind and the nature. The art of living is how people can live together peacefully under multi-culture, which is a challenge but a possible way in many parts of the world. The relationship between China and Thailand is an example. "Oriental Wisdom" emphasizes thinking well, speaking well, and doing well, all of which means Do not do onto others what you would not have done onto you.

Looking into the future, the adjustment of regional security order should pay more attention to following aspects:

1. Legal System Construction

Legal is the moral principle and the law red line that we should never cross in the regional security cooperation. We should develop legal cooperation on the basis of relevant international conventions and bilateral treaties of the United Nations, provide institutional safeguards for both sides of economic cooperation at the national level, and effectively create a positive and friendly international investment and business environment.

2. Expanding Communicating Channels

Since the world is more and more connected, mutual understanding is more crucial. Economic emerging, disrupting society, non-traditional challenges can boot and create more and more unfavorable conditions for humanity. Communicating links both horizontal and vertical linkage within the regional and at the national level should be established or restored, which will help facilitate not only the economic growth and social development but also the regional security as a whole.

3. Promoting the People-to-People Ties

The continuous development of closer people-to-people ties has deepened the understanding of the peoples of various countries in all regions, particularly along the line of BRI. All countries in the region should be willing to establish a multi-ticred mechanism for cultural and people-to-people exchanges, and shall cooperate more in protecting historical and cultural heritage, providing foreign and cultural relics protection and promoting joint archeological activities. Finally yet importantly, we should enhance exchanges between political parties, NGOs, women and youth to promote inclusive regional security.

Evolution of Security Concepts and Global Security Governance in the North-East Asia

Yury V. Kulintsev

Research Fellow at North-East Asian Strategic Issues
and SCO Center, Institute of Far Eastern Studies,
Russian Academy of Sciences, Moscow, Russia

The term North-East Asia is a term to refer to a sub-region of Asia: the northeastern landmass and islands, bordering the Pacific Ocean. It includes the core countries of East Asia and their neighbors, which are linked together historically, geographically, economically, politically, and even culturally which possess several similar socioeconomic parameters. In this sense, the core countries constituting North-East Asia are People's Republic of China (PRC), Japan, Mongolia, Democratic People's Republic of Korea (DPRK) and Republic of Korea (ROK)[1]. In most cases, given the regions' common problems and their inter-penetration, the North-East Asia's direct ties with the United States and Russian Far East are singled out, which expand the contents of the North-East Asia and have a special impact on shaping and developing strategic approaches by the region's countries.

For the purposes of creating a global security system, it would be advisable to distinguish several levels in understanding the region, namely, the macro-regional and the sub-regional. The macro-regional level constitutes the totality of the Mongolian Plateau, the Manchurian Plain, the Korean Peninsula and the mountainous regions of the Russian Far East, stretching from Lena River in the west to the Pacific Ocean in the east, plus United State north-western coast. At the sub-regional level, we should cover the area within the boards of Japan islands, Korean peninsula and Chinese Northeast region (Dongbei). Historically and geographically, this sub-region includes China, North Korea, South Korea

---

[1] Gilbet Rozman (2004), *Northeast asia's stunted regionalism: bilateral distrust in the shadow of globalization*. Cambridge University Press, pp. 3-4.

and Japan. Distinguishing between the macro-regional and the sub-regional countries will allow for a more precise definition of the possible interaction between the sub-region's countries and their neighbors, which also play the roles of power centers in Asia-Pacific region.

I. Introduction

The transformation processes in Asia that started in 2011-2012 have seriously undermined the already fragile political power balance in the countries of Asia-Pacific region. Nonetheless, despite the existing and constantly emerging new threats and the high level of dependence on external factors and players, these processes highlight new opportunities for shaping a more stable system of regional relations.

The threat of Weapons of Mass Destruction (WMD) proliferation, permanent conflicts, international terrorism and statehood crises are the primary challenges faced by the states in various parts of Asia. The low level of confidence between the principal regional actors and the permanent presence of major foreign actors in these regions remain a key problem. At present, these factors have not yet resulted in the formation of effective regional institutions capable of resolving development issues in the countries of North-East Asia. Of particular significance is the lack of intraregional institutional foundations for maintaining and enhancing security. Unsolved border issues and nuclear program of the DPRK are the principal factors exacerbating the instability. Overcoming this situation will require a comprehensive concept for building and enhancing mutual confidence, primarily between the DPRK and its neighbors, which would have to take the interests of all Asian states into account. It is therefore necessary to make every effort to create and develop a global security governance system.

Despite the positive message this initiative contains, creating such a system of relations will cause much controversy. This is largely due to significant differences in the ways that countries involved (China, Russia and U. S. satellite states) in the region's affairs and views of the paths to and methods of building and developing security systems. The existing system of ties between the regional actor states will have a great influence on the process; the chosen priorities of these states at the times of crisis will be decisive. However, the threats and challenges faced by the world today, and by North-East Asian countries in particular, make the entire complexity of connections in the region undergo certain changes.

II. Problems involved in security governance in North-East Asia

All main actors face the same security threats in North East Asia and the most critical of them is the nuclear issue of Korean Peninsula. The next challenge is that the North East Asian states need adaptation to the growth of Chinese economy and its influence. The situation is worsening by the trade war between China and United States, and by the sanction of Western countries against Russia, which lead to the lowest ever level of cooperation between Moscow and Washington. Nevertheless, these countries have the differences in the approaches to the security concepts and global governance system; there are still substantial common interests, and cooperation within the areas of these interests could be beneficial to each of the country and to the region.

Many experts believe that within the next decade the Asia-Pacific Region will become one of the most important economic and political centers of the world. With this regard the long-term stability and peace in the region cannot be taken for granted because of many security challenges which could undermine the stability.

The main and critical-hotspot in the region is the nuclear issue on the Korean peninsula. The possibility of the foreign military involvement in the issue (which has been announced as a possible option by U. S. leader) is unacceptable and has too high costs with grave consequences. There are several reasons for that. First of all, military actions are not sanctioned by the UN Security Council and it would just undermine the current international order guaranteed by the UN. Secondly, it would cause enormous humanitarian and economic losses to the participating and neighboring countries. And finally, it is an obviously more dangerous approach. If we look at it from the security concept prospective, it would be the end of peace period in the region which has lasted for more than 50 years; it also could be the trigger for other states to consider the employment of military force as a possible option in future. It means that successful military operation, even if it causes no immediate full scale military conflict, could be the begging of the more dramatic war in future.

In the meantime the DPRK successfully uses the opportunity window which opened after Winter Olympic Games 2018 in PyeongChang. At the end of April 2018 there took place the high level meeting between the leaders of two Koreas[1], which was followed by the historical DPRK-U. S. summits in

---

[1] North and South Korean Leaders Held Historic Summit: Highlights // CNN. 27. 04. 2018. URL: https://edition. cnn. com/asia/live-news/north-korea-south-korea-summit-intl/index. html.

Singapore. The activization of the DPRK's foreign policy confirmed by the series of meeting with ROK President Moon Jae-in and with Chinese President Xi Jinping, second summit with President D. Trump in Hanoi and high level negotiations with President V. Putin in Vladivostok give the hope to the international society that the global war is unlikely. But it is still unclear whether those events are the breakthrough in the international security governance and the signs of the long-term stability on the peninsula or are the indicators of a just temporary normalization .

The next issue of security governance concern for North East Asian countries is the rise of China and its growing economic, political and military power. Japan and the United States consider it as a challenge for the global order. The possible long term consequences of the changing global order and growing responsibility of Asian countries are to be taken into account while discussing the security concepts. Some experts[1] believe that if Beijing decides to challenge the U. S. -dominated world order, the security balance in the region will be shifted.

Regional relations in North-East Asia are characterized by weak institutional basis. Breaches in the system of international institutions and regulations limit the opportunities for cooperation and have a destructive influence on the confidence between the countries in North-East Asia, as well as on the balance of power and the co-existence of states. The region's problem is manifested in the existence of long-lasting and "irresolvable" conflicts. There is also destructive competition between regional actors. Given the absence of a clear leader in the region, competition between claimants to leadership has a negative impact on general security.

We have to also admit the weakness of global governance institutions (primarily the UN) in resolving problems in North-East Asia. Frequently, the UN not only fails to demonstrate a unified approach to solving regional crises, but it also does not possess effective instruments to monitor the situation and implement decisions that have already been adopted. Given the absence of an auxiliary regional structure, actions taken by the UN run into constantly emerging obstacles, which makes moving forward impossible. The objective lack of resources, the diversity of regimes and differences in the national development goals in the region should be also mentioned.

---

[1] V. Nelidov. Regional security in the North East Asia and Russian – US – Japan triangular // Analytic materials. RIAC. May, 2018, p. 7.

Thus, the issues of strategic balance and security governance have the critical importance for the North-East Asian region. Discrepancy between Russia and United Stares reinforced after Ukrainian crisis in 2014 and especially after the accusations against Russia's interruption into U. S. president elections in 2016, these issues do not advantage the security situation and confidence building in the region.

III. Conditions and opportunities for shaping global security governance in North–East Asia

Today, changes are taking place both inside and outside the region that could give a different kind of impetus to the negotiations on creating a global security system in the macro-region of North-East Asia. Setting up provisional working groups comprised of regional leaders (or using similar formats) appears to be the most adequate solution; strategically, the most appropriate option would be to create a comprehensive security system. Productive activity within this framework of such a mechanism would largely be tied to developing integration projects in the North-East Asia. Inter-country projects related to economy and infrastructure will be of key importance.

The countries take a positive stance towards the strengthening of the current regional multilateral cooperation formats, towards the assessment of its mechanisms and promote international dialogue and the prevention of politicizing specific features.

When tackling the issue of security governance in North-East Asia, the following goals should be addressed as a priority: scaling down the "security dilemma" and restoring confidence between countries; promoting peace and stability in the macro-region; and promoting effective political transition in the macro-region's unstable countries.

The following can be listed as the priority tasks for the global security governance:

a) creating conditions for confidence-building measures between the countries that shape the global security system;

b) enhancing the nuclear non-proliferation regime and creating a nuclear-weapons-free zone;

c) ensuring interaction between the states themselves and between the new regional system and the UN in ensuring comprehensive security;

d) monitoring the situation "on the ground";

e) ensuring post-conflict demilitarization of the population and arms control, including weapons of mass destruction.

The previously noted lack of confidence between North-East Asian countries is a serious obstacle for the development of intra-regional and inter-regional ties. The decision to create a global security system in North-East Asia could be directly tied to intensified interaction within the existing regional structures: The Conference on Interaction and Confidence-Building Measures in Asia (CICA), the Shanghai Cooperation Organization (SCO) and the Asia Cooperation Dialogue (ACD). All these platforms could be employed to initiate a working discussion of the prospects of enhancing the global security governance for North-East Asia.

China and Russia support the preservation of, and adherence to, the principle of the sovereign equality of states and is in favor of enhancing the role of the UN and multilateral institutions in promulgating the principle of universal participation in multilateral international cooperation. Additionally, experts call for the prevention of illegal international intervention in the affairs of other states and to make it impossible to export nuclear technologies to potential terrorist organizations, and to other states of the Asian region.

Russian national interests in the North-East Asia are stipulated by the need to develop its Far Eastern region. According to Russian President V. Putin, the region's development is the country's national priority for the XXI century[1]. It means that peaceful and friendly relations with the key regional players, such as China, the POK and Japan, are the prerequisite for economic development of Russian Far East. The main program documents on foreign policy-National Security Strategy (2015) and Russian Foreign Policy Concept (2016)-confirm that Korean peninsula is one of the seats of tension in the world. Meantime Moscow's position is opposite to Tokyo's and Washington's one, who blame the DPRK as the only party in fault for tensions. Russia constantly states for the nuclear-free status of the Korean peninsula and will promote its denuclearization in every way possible. It is also declared that Russian will make an effort to decrease the level of confrontation, slacken tensions on Korean peninsula and approach the peace regime and cooperation between two Koreas by development of political dialogue as the only possible mean.

Neither any statement of Russian political leaders, nor any program

---

[1] V. Putin. Russia's Role in Securing Asia's Prosperity // Bloomberg. 08.11.2017. URL: https://www.bloomberg.com/view/articles/2017-11-08/vladimir-putin-russia-s-role-in-securing-asia-s-prosperity.

documents contain the ideas that Moscow has any worries about the rise of China. On the contrary, one of the Russian priorities is promoting the cooperation with China in all spheres. Moscow and Beijing have the same opinion that multi-polar world is more preferable compared to unidirectional under the U. S. authority.

The mutual relations between Russian and Japan in the field of security governance experience some difficulties. On one hand, Japan has followed the Western countries' example and imposed sanctions against Russia in 2014. On the other hand, according to the experts' opinion, those sanctions were symbolic and had almost no effects on bilateral economic relations[1]. Moreover, Japanese prime-minister S. Abe's official visit to Russia and Russian President V. Putin's official visit to Japan in 2016 accompanied by multiple meetings within the frame work of different international events show the evidence of the positive tendency in the bilateral ties. Resumption of the "2 + 2 meeting" format (Ministers of Defense and Ministers of Foreign Affairs) in 2017 confirms that both countries consider the security governance discussion and cooperation in military field as important goals[2]. Russia-Japanese relations have been intensified during the previous several years. But there are still the problems of peace treaty and the settlement of the territorial disputes, which are far away from being solved.

One approach to the security governance on the Korean peninsula supports dialogue and mutual cessation of aggressive actions. The best example of the strategy is the joint Russian and Chinese plan of "double freeze". The other approach to the security governance on the Korean peninsula belongs to United States. Washington wants to establish nuclear free zone in North Korea in order to minimize the threat and physical possibility of nuclear attack on its territory. The U. S. strategy could combine the tendency for dialogue and the readiness to increase the pressure on DPRK. D. Trump has been criticized for the unconsidered rhetoric and actions which could fraught with serious consequences[3], but he clearly gives to understand that topple of regime in the

---

[1] A. Panov. Japan has made a choice in favor of Russia // Arguments and facts. 29. 10. 201. URL: http://www. aif. ru/politics/world/aleksandr_panov_yaponiya_sdelala_svoy_vybor_v_polzu_rossii.

[2] Japan, Russia hold first 'two – plus – two'talks since Crimea annexation // The Japan Times. 20. 03. 2017. URL: https://www. japantimes. co. jp/news/2017/03/20/national/politics – diplomacy/japan–russia–resume–ministerial–security–talks–tokyo–looks–progress–isle–row/#. WqPTB–jFKUk.

[3] In confronting North Korea, Trump risks disaster // The Washington Post. 01. 02. 2018. URL: https://www. washingtonpost. com/news/worldviews/wp/2018/02/01/in–confronting–north–korea–trump–risks–disaster/? utm_term=. 2db89eb9061b.

DPRK is not his goal[1]. It means that the current American president doesn't want to follow the way that has involved the previous administrations into protracted and expensive conflicts in the Middle East, he doesn' t want to cause worsening of cooperation with any actor on scenario of Ukrainian crisis as it happened to Russian-U. S. relations. It means that Moscow's and Washington's approaches to solve Korean problem differ more tactically, than strategically.

Any integration initiative should be based on the principle of the territorial integrity and equality of states, at the same time presupposing possibilities for intra-regional and inter-regional interaction. It is important to create the necessary conditions for carrying out political transition in united Korea by implementing diplomatic initiatives to reconcile the position of DPRK leaders with ROK's administration while continuing to support the nuclear free negotiation effort.

The multiplicity of crises in Asia enhances their cumulative nature. Resolving these problems is impossible without a comprehensive collective approach. Such a "multi-component" security challenge in the indicated region could create the perquisites for laying the foundations for joint actions intended to overcome the crisis phenomena through adequate employment of security concepts.

Global security governance would advance the entire process of strengthening both regional and global peace and stability, and form conditions for solving the development tasks faced by the region's states. Despite the worsening crisis of confidence and mounting security problems in North-East Asian countries, creating a comprehensive security governance system appears to be the most effective mechanism for stabilizing the situation in the region.

---

〔1〕 Donald Trump: "We will stop racing to topple foreign regimes"// The Guardian. 07. 12. 2016. URL: https://www. theguardian. com/us-news/2016/dec/07/donald-trump-we-will-stop-racing-to-topple-foreign-regimes.

The American Indo-Pacific Strategy and Asian Security Order

Han Hua

CPAPD Council Member,
Associate Professor, School of International Relations, Peking University

In November 2017, President Trump clearly put forward the outline and conception of the U. S. Indo-Pacific strategy for the first time in his speech at the APEC Summit held in Vietnam, which marks the adoption of the Trump Administration's Asia policy, and also ensures the "Indo-Pacific" concept brewing in the policy circle for 10 years formally reflected in the U. S. government's official policy. In June 2019, the U. S. Department of Defense issued the U. S. Indo-Pacific Strategy report, which comprehensively and systematically elaborated the U. S. Indo-Pacific strategy. So far, the Indo-Pacific strategy officially replaced the "Asia-Pacific rebalancing" strategy of the Obama Administration as the U. S. Asia Strategy of the Trump Administration. The United States, as a world hegemonic country that regards the Indo-Pacific region as its strategic focus, has formulated and adjusted its strategy for the region, which is bound to have an important impact on the political, economic and security fields in the region, and the security order in Asia will change accordingly.

I. Trump's Indo-Pacific Strategy

Since 2007, the concept of Indo-Pacific often appears in think tank reports or scholars' articles in India, Australia and other countries. However, apart from Japanese Prime Minister Abe's upgrading the concept of Indo-Pacific Ocean to Japan's official strategy of Indian and Pacific Oceans and promoting this strategy to India during his visit to India in 2007, the Indo-Pacific concept has not become the official strategy of relevant countries. During the Obama Administration, although the United States showed interest in the concept of Indo-Pacific, the official documents still refer to the region as the Asia-Pacific and the Indian Ocean.

After Trump took office, he became very interested in the concept and incorporated it into his Asia strategy. In his speech at the APEC Vietnam Summit 2017, "Indo-Pacific" concept became the keynote of his speech. If it can be said that Trump's speech at the Vietnam Summit explained more about the U. S. Indo-Pacific concept from the perspective of economy and trade, then the U. S. Indo-Pacific Strategy report issued by the U. S. Department of Defense explains the U. S. Indo-Pacific strategy from the perspective of security. Trump's speech and the Indo-Pacific Strategy report constitute the basic contents of the U. S. Indo-Pacific strategy, mainly including as follows:

1. Based on the close ties between the United States and the Indo-Pacific region and the strong political, economic and military presence of the United States in the region, emphasizing that the region is the most important region in the future for the United States, and declaring the U. S. interests in the region and its determination to safeguard these interests, meantime, putting forward the principles advocated by the United States, i. e. , the international order based on rules and principles, and emphasis on fairness and interaction economically, and openness and freedom in terms of security.

2. On the basis of listing various security challenges in the region, highlighting geopolitical challenges and threats, and defining China, Russia and D. P. R. Korea as challengers to Indo-Pacific security, among them, emphasizing that China tries to exercise power over other countries through its military modernization, strategic action and economic leverage, with an attempt to change regional order. In response to these geopolitical challenges, the United States vows to maintain regional order by strengthening competition, deterrence and winning war.

3. While reiterating the importance of U. S. allies and strategic partners in the region and the security commitments to them, and strengthening the cooperation with each other, meanwhile requesting these countries to share the costs corresponding to the security commitments they have obtained.

4. On the basis of reassessment of security threats, reallocating military capabilities, human and material resources, formulating new warfare, putting forward various initiatives, and strengthening relationship with countries the United States considers important.

From the above-mentioned, Trump's Indo-Pacific strategy has the following main characteristics. Firstly, Trump's Indo-Pacific strategy is a compromise product of the debate of "active intervention " or "rational contraction" in the U. S. strategic community in the context of the relative decline of the U. S. overall strength. Trump's "America First" and his repeated emphasis on U. S. allies bearing responsibilities for their own security reflect a certain posture of strategic contraction, but his emphasis on the era of major powers competition also requires the United States to play an active role in the center of world geopolitics. Therefore, the posture shaped by the Indo-Pacific strategy seems between maintaining the strong presence of the United States in Indo-Pacific and properly sharing the security responsibilities of its allies in the region. The "QUAD" mechanism set up by the Trump Administration in the framework of the Indo-Pacific strategic framework is to some extent the arrangement for sharing security responsibilities. Among them, Japan and Australia can provide strategic assistance to the United States in the Asia-Pacific region, and by pulling India into the Indo-Pacific strategy, the United States also expects India to play a "net provider" role in the Indian Ocean security. Secondly, competition among major powers is the main goal and interests of Trump's Indo-Pacific strategy, counter-terrorism and other non-structural security issues are no longer the main factors dominating U. S. Asia policy. Among them, China and Russia are regarded as the main rivals of Indo-Pacific region, and the antagonism between China and the United States, between Russia and the United States has increased significantly. In the past 20 years, the elements of "engagement" and "double edging" in the U. S. China policy become weakened and containment tendency gets obviously intensified. Thirdly, geographically, Indo-Pacific is the expansion of the Asia-Pacific and the expansion of Obama's "Asia rebalancing". The United States will form a containment (if not encirclement) of China between the Indian Ocean and the Pacific Ocean—a larger space than the Asia-Pacific region. If it can be said Obama's "Asia rebalancing" strategy is centered on the South China Sea and its adjacent areas, the focus of Trump's strategy is the Pacific and Indian Oceans as well as areas along the Belt and Road Initiative of China. Fourthly, the Trump Indo-Pacific strategy will be implemented more through the establishment of a "network" of cooperation between the United States and its allies & strategic partners in the region. That is to say, while strengthening cooperation and coordination with its Asian allies and partners, the United States emphasizes strengthening cooperation and coordination between allies and partners, so as to build a "vast escape-proof network" of Indio-Pacific security.

II. The existing Asian security order

In the eyes of many people, Asia lacks regional security mechanisms, because some are extremely puzzled by the fact that there has been no war in Asia since the end of the Cold War, and still some people believe that peace and stability in Asia are full of uncertainties. However, Asia does have its own security order, although it is significantly different from that of Europe.

In the 30 years since the end of the Cold War, the Asian security architecture consists of two coexisting systems. One is the "axle-spoke" security system established by the United States with the United States as the center and the bilateral security alliance between the United States and its Asian allies as the main formation. Among them, the U. S. -Japan alliance is regarded as the cornerstone of the U. S. Asian security strategy, plus bilateral alliances and partnerships with South Korea, Australia and the Philippines. In this system of bilateral alliances, the United States, supported by its own military strength, provides security, including nuclear security, for its allies. This arrangement makes the United States play a dominant role in Asian security affairs, and also becomes the main basis for Americans to regard it as the guardian of Asian security. In the past 30 years, Asian countries have put forward regional security initiatives, but they are inadequate to shake the "axle-spoke" security system of the United States.

In addition to the U. S. -led security system, there is also an ASEAN-led security system in Asia, which is significantly different from that in Europe. Different from NATO as the main mechanism and the arrangement of the security obligations of the member states provided by the formal alliance treaty, the security mechanism in Asia emphasizes more on cooperative security. Cooperative security has no treaty-binding obligations of member states, has no specific adversaries in mind, and takes "declarative" diplomacy as the main form of coordination. This system strengthens the coordination and communication of security issues in the form of Asia-Pacific Economic Cooperation, ASEAN Regional Forum and ASEAN 10 +, and has also gained the support or acceptance of China, the United States and other major countries. Although some people have doubts about the effectiveness of this security architecture, it is in existence and has developed for a long time since the end of the Cold War and has become a cooperative security practice led by the alliance of small states and coordinated by major powers.

III. The impact of Trump's Indo-Pacific strategy on the existing Asian security order

As mentioned above, the Trump Administration's Indo-Pacific strategy presents new contents and features, which are not only the adjustment of the previous U. S. Administration's Asia policy based on the Trump Administration's assessment of the new reality of today's international relations, but also mean the profound impact of the new strategy on the existing Asian security order, shown in the following two aspects:

1. **The Indo-Pacific strategy has an impact on the U. S. existing Asian order of "axle-spoke".** As the United States has a new interpretation of the source of the security challenges in Asia, China, Russia and D. P. R. Korea (more in Asia is China) have become adversaries of different levels in the geopolitics of the United States. Some people in the United States policy circle believe that the original alliance system dominated by the bilateral alliance of the United States can no longer meet new security challenges, so it is necessary to reconstruct the alliance system. The reconstruction is reflected in the attempt of the United States to trilateralize the alliance between the United States and Japan and between the United States and South Korea during the Obama Administration, although this effort was unsuccessful. Now, the Trump Administration has a new orientation for the reconstruction of the Asian alliance system. Firstly, the United States proposed to restart and build a " four nation security dialogue " (QUAD) mechanism between the United States, Japan, Australia and India. Although there have been twists and turns in this attempt, the success of its efforts has been questioned, the recent efforts of the United States to promote the development of the mechanism are strengthened. Recently, the foreign ministers of the four countries met during their participation in the United Nations General Assembly, raising the mechanism targeted at China, which has long been maintained at the bureau level, to the ministerial level for the first time. Secondly, the United States encourages the strengthening of coordination and communication between its allies and strategic partners, so as to build a network of security partners dominated by the United States, with which to balance the continuous rising of China.

2. **As Trump's Indo-Pacific strategy is put forward in response to the "major power competition", the geopolitical competition between major powers has become the "main melody" of the Indo-Pacific region,** which objectively affects the original significant role of small countries represented by ASEAN on the regional arena, thus weakening the regional security system "led by ASEAN

and coordinated by major powers". Not only that, as the relative strength between China and the United States approaches gradually, the speech of "power transfer between China and the United States" is becoming more and more popular in the American policy circle, and the antagonism in China-U. S. relations is becoming increasingly obvious. As a result, small countries find themselves increasingly forced to choose between China and the United States. The room for maneuver between China and the United States is shrinking, and the efforts of small countries to maintain the original balanced diplomatic space are becoming more and more difficult, resulting in dependence of small countries on China economically, and on the United States for security, which indirectly challenges the original "cooperative security" architecture in Asia.

To sum up, since Trump came to power, Obama's Asia-Pacific rebalancing strategy is largely adjusted, and the tendency of "major power competition" shown in the rebalancing strategy is further strengthened. China and Russia are more clearly defined as "revisionist" countries and seen as competitors that challenge the U. S. -dominated Asian order. On this basis, Trump puts forward a series of countermeasures and policies to respond to the "challenges", including the reconstruction of the original alliance system and the expansion of the region for dealing with the challenges from the traditional Asia-Pacific region to the Indian Ocean. These new developments have had an impact on the existing security order in Asia and a negative impact on peace and stability in the region.

FOIP 2.0: The Evolution of Japan's Free and Open Indo-Pacific Strategy[1]

Yuichi Hosoya

Senior Researcher at the Nakasone Yasuhiro Peace Institute,
Professor at the Faculty Of Laws, Keio University

I. Introduction

Since Japanese Prime Minister Shinzo Abe launched a new foreign policy doctrine at the opening session of the Sixth Tokyo International Conference on African Development (TICAD VI) on August 27, 2016, Japan's "Free and Open Indo-Pacific" strategy, or FOIP, has stimulated a broader debate on the future Indo-Pacific regional order.[2]

No Japanese prime minister has ever presented such a globally discussed foreign policy vision before. One of the reasons for this would be the fact that Shinzo Abe is now becoming the longest-serving prime minister in Japanese history. If he can remain in power until November 20, 2019, Abe will surpass Katsura Taro as the longest-serving prime minister in the history of Japan's constitutional government.[3] Based on a stable majority in Japan's National Diet, Abe has been able to pursue a long-term foreign policy vision, such as the FOIP.

Abe's role in today's international politics is significant. He now becomes the second longest-serving leader at the G7 summit meeting next only to German

---

[1] This paper is originally written for *Asia-Pacific Review*, Volume 26, Issue 1, 2019.

[2] Address by Prime Minister Shinzo Abe at the Opening Session of the Sixth Tokyo International Conference on African Development (TICAD VI), August 27, 2016, Nairobi, Kenya. https://www. mofa. go. jp/afr/af2/page4e_000496. html. This FOIP is now generally regarded as a "vision", rather than a "strategy". See Shinichi Kitaoka's "Vision for a Free and Open Indo-Pacific" in this issue. However, I will use the term "strategy", as Japan's government had also used repeatedly until recently.

[3] Japan Data, "Abe Shinzo on Track to Become Japan's Longest-Serving Prime Minister," October 3, 2018, *Nippon. com.* https://www. nippon. com/en/features/h00296/abe-shinzo-on-track-to-become-japan%E2%80%99s-longest-serving-prime-minister. html.

Chancellor Angela Merkel. In addition, Abe has been playing a key role in defending the rules-based international order. Soon after Donald Trump became President of the United States, John Ikenberry, professor at Princeton University, wrote in his article to *Foreign Affairs* that the future of the liberal international order "will rest on the shoulders of Prime Minister Shinzo Abe of Japan and Chancellor Angela Merkel of Germany, the only two leaders of consequence left standing who support it."[1] Likewise, Jeffrey Hornung, a security expert at RAND Corporation, wrote that, "Under the current prime minister, Shinzo Abe, Japan's role in supporting the international order has been particularly notable."[2] Hornung also noted that "It was part of his broader Free and Open Indo-Pacific strategy, which the Trump Administration later endorsed, and which places more of the burden on Japan for protecting freedom, the rule of law, and market economies in the region."[3]

On the other hand, Japan's Free and Open Indo-Pacific strategy has also invited criticism from several quarters. Michael Swaine, a China expert at the Carnegie Endowment for International Peace, warned that, while the "FOIP would aim to defend against the ways a rising China ostensibly threatens the rules-based international order, universal liberal values, and free access to the maritime global commons," in reality, the "FOIP is likely to have the opposite effect, provoking Beijing, alarming other Asian nations, and driving the region toward a highly tense, zero-sum competition."[4]

The FOIP is an amorphous concept. Ash Rossiter, a professor at Khalifa University at Abu Dhabi, correctly argued that "there is little consensus as to what the FOIP actually entails, let alone the ways by which it may influence future Japanese foreign policy."[5] In this article, while admitting Rossiter's argument that the FOIP is indeed an amorphous concept, it will be argued that the current

---

[1]　John Ikenberry, "The Plot Against American Foreign Policy", *Foreign Affairs*, May/June 2017, p. 3.

[2]　Jeffrey W. Hornung, "The Fate of the World Order Rests on Tokyo's Shoulder", *Foreign Policy*, October 30, 2018. https://foreignpolicy. com/2018/10/30/the – fate – of – the – world – order – rests – on – tokyos–shoulders/.

[3]　Ibid.

[4]　Michael D. Swaine, "A Counterproductive Cold War With China: Washington's 'Free and Open Indo-Pacific' Strategy Will Make Asia Less Open and Less Free", *Foreign Affairs*, March 2, 2018. https://www. foreignaffairs. com/articles/china/2018–03–02/counterproductive–cold–war–china.

[5]　Ash Rossiter, "The 'Free and Open Indo-Pacific' Strategy and Japan's Emerging Security Posture", *Rising Powers Quarterly*, Volume 3, Issue 2, 2018, p. 114.

Japan's FOIP strategy is different from what Shinzo Abe once proposed in his article to *Project Syndicate*, namely, "Asia's Democratic Security Diamond."[1] As the current version of Japan's FOIP is less confrontational, less divisive, and more cooperative toward China, it should be called "FOIP 2.0."

II. Origins of the FOIP 1.0 in the era of China's rise

The Japanese government had not officially used the term the "Free and Open Indo-Pacific" before its first launch in August 2016. However, after Shinzo Abe became prime minister in his first administration in September 2006, the Japanese government often implied that cooperation among democracies in the Indo-Pacific region should become the core of the regional order.

The FOIP 1.0 originated in Prime Minister Abe's policy speech at the Parliament of India on August 22, 2007. Abe argued that, "by Japan and India coming together in this way, this ' broader Asia' will evolve into an immense network spanning the entirety of the Pacific Ocean, incorporating the United States of America and Australia. Open and transparent, this network will allow people, goods, capital, and knowledge to flow freely."[2] In this speech, Abe mentioned key components of the FOIP, such as openness, freedom, broader Asia, and the cooperation among the United States of America, Australia, India, and Japan. Then, Abe presented his vision of a new regional order in his speech by combining the two Seas. He stated that, "now, as this new ' broader Asia' takes shape at the confluence of the two seas of the Indian and Pacific Oceans, I feel that it is imperative that the democratic nations located at opposite edges of these seas deepen the friendship among their citizens at every possible level."[3]

At this moment, Abe's administration had simultaneously promoted a long-term grand strategy named the "Arc of Freedom and Prosperity."[4] This strategy was based on the values-oriented diplomacy that aimed at promoting democracy, freedom, human rights, and the rule of law "along the Eurasian

---

[1] Shinzo Abe, " Asia's Democratic Security Diamond", *Project Syndicate*, December 27, 2012. https://www. project-syndicate. org/commentary/a-strategic-alliance-for-japan-and-india-by-shinzo-abe.

[2] Speech by Prime Minister Shinzo Abe at the Parliament of the Republic of India, "Confluence of the Two Seas", August 22, 2007. https://www. mofa. go. jp/region/asia-paci/pmv0708/speech-2. html.

[3] Ibid.

[4] On the " Arc of Freedom and Prosperity", see Yuichi Hosoya, " The Rise and Fall of Japan's Grand Strategy: The 'Arc of Freedom and Prosperity' and the Future Asian Order", *Asia-Pacific Review*, 18 (1), pp. 13-24.

continent to form a rich and stable region based on universal values."[1] This largely overlaps geopolitically with the region that is indicated in the FOIP.

We can notice that there exist some links in the personnel level. National Security Advisor to Prime Minister Shotaro Yachi, who is also Head of Japan's National Security Secretariat (NSS), was Vice Minister for Foreign Affairs in Abe's first administration from 2006 to 2007, and Nobukatsu Kanehara, who is currently the Deputy Head of the NSS, was then the Director at the Policy Coordination Division in the Ministry of Foreign Affairs (MOFA). Those who drafted the "Arc of Freedom and Prosperity" in October 2006 are main designers of the FOIP in Abe's second administration.

These Japanese initiatives can be regarded as a response to rapidly rising China.[2] Japanese policymakers were trying to shape a regional order, rather than to be shaped by China. They believed that the United States, India, and Australia, together with Japan, should be the main players in this regional architecture, as they shared core values such as democracy, freedom, and the rule of law. Therefore, the Japanese government began to promote security cooperation with Australia and India during this period. In May 2007, the first Quadrilateral strategic dialogue, or the "Quad," began with the initiative of Prime Minister Abe and the then American Vice-President Dick Cheney.

This "Quad" faced several difficulties. First, the Chinese government began to consider that this security cooperation was aimed at encircling China. Therefore, China endeavored to criticize this initiative by enhancing bilateral cooperation with Japan and with Australia. Lavina Lee of Macquarie University appropriately summarized that "Japan's first attempt to engender deeper strategic cooperation between Japan, Australia, India and the United States—the Quadrilateral Dialogue (QD) of 2007—was a short-lived experiment that ultimately failed to gain traction in the face of strong Chinese opposition and the loss of office by its major proponents in Australia, Japan and the United States."[3] Lee also pointed out that " Prime Minister Abe was widely acknowledged as the main protagonist behind the QD, with firm support from the

---

[1] Speech by Foreign Minister Taro Aso, "Thee Arc of Freedom and Prosperity: Japan's Expanding Diplomatic Horizons", 30 November 2006. https://www. mofa. go. jp/announce/fm/aso/speech0611. html.

[2] Mie Oba, "Nihon no 'indo-taiheiyo' koso", *Kokusai Anzenhosho*, vol. 46, no. 3, 2018, p. 15; Rossiter, "The 'Free and Open Indo-Pacific' Strategy and Japan's Emerging Security Posture", p. 114.

[3] Lavina Lee, "Abe's Democratic Security Diamond and New Quadrilateral Initiative: an Australian Perspective", *The Journal of East Asian Affairs*, Vol. 30, No. 2, Fall/Winter 2016, p. 3.

Bush Administration, particularly U. S. Vice President Dick Cheney."[1] Soon after Abe stepped down from office, Japan's new administration began to enhance its cooperation with China, leaving the "Quad" aside. Both Japan's new Prime Minister Yasuo Fukuda and Australia's new Prime Minister Kevin Rudd prioritized their friendly relationships with their Chinese counterparts to the advancement of the "Quad".

Second, some ASEAN countries presented serious concern over the development of the "Quad," as this would seemingly depart from the basic principle of ASEAN centrality. Until that time, Asian regional cooperation had been based on ASEAN centrality. ASEAN countries did not like to see the move towards great powers-led situation in the region.

Third, the U.S. government under its new president, Barak Obama, started to prioritize the bilateral relationship between the United States and China to the "Quad". There existed an optimistic view within the U.S. administration that the United States could enjoy developing its friendly bilateral partnership with then the second largest economy in the world, namely China. This move coincided with the difficult bilateral relationship between the United States and Japan due partly to Prime Minister Yukio Hatoyama's mishandling of the Futenma U.S. bases reallocation issue.

Since 2008, China had begun to become more assertive particularly in the South China Sea and the East China Sea. A Chinese trawler collision incident in the Senkaku Islands in September 2010 marked an important turning point for Japanese officials and public opinion, and the Japanese government started to become more vigilant toward China's activities in the surrounding areas.[2] While the Obama administration noticed the difficulty of creating a cooperative relationship with China, Tokyo became aware of the necessity of using a different approach for responding to the rise of China.

Around this period, several experts began to write on the new regional

---

[1] Ibid.

[2] RoyoseiKokubun, Yoshihide Soeya, Akio Takahara and Shin Kawashima, *Japan-China Relations in the Modern Era*, translated by Keith Krulak (London: Routledge, 2017) p. 180.

concept of the Indo-Pacific.[1] For example, Michael Auslin wrote in a report for American Enterprise Institute that " The Indo-Pacific's economic strength, military power, and political dynamism will make it the world's most important region in the coming decades, and its significance will be felt throughout the globe."[2] Auslin encouraged the United States and its allies to have an Indo-Pacific regional strategy. In 2011, Rory Medcalf and Raoul Heinrichs, both of the Lowy Institute, also highlighted the importance of a regional concept of Indo-Pacific in their report.[3] Likewise, David Scott wrote in his article for *Asia−Pacific Review* in 2012 that "Political practices in the Indo-Pacific involve institutional frameworks and inter-state operations that mesh the two oceans together."[4]

In Japan, security experts such as Matake Kamiya, professor at the National Defense Academy, began to focus on the importance of the Indo-Pacific region for the foreign policy of Abe's second administration.[5] Kamiya noted the importance of Prime Minister Abe's usage of the regional concept of the "Indo-Pacific" in his speech in Washington, DC on February 22, 2013.[6] Shinzo Abe can be regarded as the first political leader who identified the significance of the new regional concept of the "Indo-Pacific".

When he returned to Prime Minister's Office in December 2012, Shinzo Abe revived the old idea of the "Quad" in his article to *Project Syndicate*, entitled

[1] On the development in the regional concept of " Indo−Pacific" , see Yoshinobu Yamamoto, "Indo− taiheiyogainen wo megutte " , in Japan Institute of International Affairs (ed.), *Ajia* (*tokuniminamishinakai−indoyo*) *niokeruanzenhoshochitsujo* (Tokyo: JIIA, 2015) pp. 5−23; Kazutoshi Tamari, "'Indotaiheiyo' gainen no fukyukatei" , *Kokusai Anzenhosho*, Vol. 43, No. 1, 2015, pp. 68−86; TeruakiAizawa, " The Philosophy and Practice of the 'Free and Open Indo−Pacific Strategy (FOIP) ' decoded from the Ministry of Foreign Affairs Website" , Ocean Policy Research Institute, The Sasakawa Peace Foundation, July 30, 2018; and Oba, Nihon no ' indo−taiheiyo' koso".
[2] Michael Auslin, "Security in the Indo−Pacific Commons: Toward a Regional Strategy" , A Report of the American Enterprise Institute, December 2010, p. 5.
[3] Rory Medcalf and Raoul Heinrichs with Justin Jones, "Crisis and Confidence: Major Powers and Maritime Security in Indo−Pacific Asia" , Lowy Institute for International Policy, June 2011.
[4] David Scott, "The 'Indo-Pacific'—New Regional Formulations and New Maritime Frameworks for US−India Strategic Convergence" , *Asia−Pacific Review*, Vol. 19, No. 2, 2012, p. 87.
[5] Matake Kamiya, "Nihon to 'Indo−taiheiy' —kitai to mondaiten" , Japan Institute of International Affairs (ed.), *Ajia* (*tokuniminamishinakai−indoyo*) *niokeruanzenhoshochitsujo* (Tokyo: JIIA, 2015) pp. 25−45.
[6] Speech by Prime Minister Shinzo Abe, " Japan is Back" , at the Center for Strategic and International Studies (CSIS), February 22, 2013. https://japan. kantei. go. jp/96 _ abe/statement/ 201302/22speech_e. html.

"Asia's Democratic Security Diamond".[1] Recalling his own speech to the Indian Parliament five years previously, Abe wrote in this article that "Peace, stability, and freedom of navigation in the Pacific Ocean are inseparable from peace, stability, and freedom of navigation in the Indian Ocean."[2] He "spoke in India of the need of the Indian and Japanese governments to join together to shoulder more responsibility as guardians of navigational freedom across the Pacific and Indian Oceans".[3]

Abe's two important messages, namely the "Confluence of the Two Seas" and "Asia's Democratic Security Diamond," created the core of the FOIP 1.0. The basic feature of the FOIP 1.0 was a competitive strategy towards China. Professor Ken Jimbo of Keio University argues that Japan's Indo-Pacific vision clearly has both the dimension of "competitive strategy" and the dimension of "cooperative strategy."[4] As the FOIP 1.0 has a much stronger character of "competitive strategy" in it, it would be natural that Japan's initiative invited criticism from several Asian capitals, as it seemed that it would create division and confrontation in the Indo-Pacific region. Remembering these criticisms, Prime Minister Abe has refrained from using the concept "Asia's Democratic Security Diamond" since then.[5]

III. From FOIP 1.0 to FOIP 2.0

The FOIP 1.0 has a clear dilemma, that it now becomes clearer that not so many Asian countries would welcome an increasing division between China and America and its alliances. If Japan's initiative is seen as an attempt to isolate China in a broader regional framework of the Indo-Pacific, a majority of Asian countries would hesitate to participate in that initiative, as China is their largest trading partner.

At this moment, China and the United States were intensifying their rivalry particularly in the South China Sea. Richard Javad Heydarian, a Manila-based foreign affairs analyst, wrote on Japan's initiative that, "If implemented, Abe's policies will inject Japan into the intensifying struggle between Beijing and

---

[1] Abe, "Asia's Democratic Security Diamond," *Project Syndicate*, December 27, 2012.

[2] Ibid.

[3] Ibid.

[4] Ken Jimbo, "'Indo taiheiyo' koso no shatei to kadai", *Kokusai Anzenhosho*, vol. 46, no. 3, 2018, pp. 4–5.

[5] Oba, "Nihon no 'indo−taiheiyo' koso", p. 18.

Washington for Pacific maritime dominance and stir new concerns, especially in China, over a possible re-emergence of Japan's militaristic past."[1]

It would be important to understand that a Japan-China bilateral relationship has been recovered since the first summit meeting between Prime Minister Abe and President Xi Jinping on November 10, 2014. Abe showed his desire to rebuild the relationship on the concept of a Mutually Beneficial Relationship based on Common Strategic Interests.[2] Since then, Japan under Prime Minister Abe has developed a stable bilateral relationship with China, leaving the territorial issue aside.

When Abe launched his "Free and Open Indo-Pacific" strategy at the TICAD VI meeting in Nairobi, Japan needed to maintain Japan's cooperative relationship with China. In his speech, Abe underlined the importance of combining two oceans, as well as combining two continents. Abe stated that "What will give stability and prosperity to the world is none other than the enormous liveliness brought forth through the union of two free and open oceans and two continents."[3] He implied the importance of the "union of two free and open oceans", namely the Indo-Pacific region.

A factsheet published by Japan's MOFA in April 2017 stated that "Japan will promote strategic and effective development cooperation to advance its foreign policy, including the 'Free and Open Indo-Pacific Strategy'."[4] It also said that "a key for stability and prosperity of the international community is dynamism that is created by combining 'Two Continents' and 'Two Oceans'."[5] In Africa, this factsheet explains that "Japan will provide nation-building support in the area of development as well as politics and governance, in a way that respects the sovereignty of African countries."[6]

In Japan's Diplomatic Bluebook of 2017, there is a special section on the FOIP. It explains that "Japan considers the key to the stability and prosperity of

---

[1] Richard JavadHeydarian, "Japan's 'democratic security diamond'", *East Asia Forum*, 15 February, 2013. https://www. eastasiaforum. org/2013/02/15/japans-democratic-security-diamond/.

[2] Kokubun*et al*, *Japan-China Relations in the Modern Era*, pp. 192-4.

[3] Address by Prime Minister Shinzo Abe at the Opening Session of the Sixth Tokyo International Conference on African Development (TICAD VI), August 27, 2016, Nairobi, Kenya.

[4] International Cooperation Bureau (MOFA), "Priority Policy for Development Cooperation FY2017", April 2017, Tokyo, Ministry of Foreign Affairs. https://www. mofa. go. jp/files/000259285. pdf.

[5] Ibid.

[6] Ibid.

the international community to be the dynamism created by the synergy between the ' two continents' —Asia, which is recording remarkable growth, and Africa, which is full of potential—and two free and open seas—the Pacific Ocean and the Indian Ocean. By regarding these continents and seas as an integrated region, Japan intends to open up a new frontier of Japanese diplomacy."[1] It can be understood that the FOIP is aiming at enlarging Japan's economic interests as well as at contributing to peace and stability in the Indo-Pacific region. As this diplomatic initiative tends to be a more cooperative strategy than a competitive strategy toward China, this should be regarded as the FOIP 2.0.

On June 5, 2017, Prime Minister Abe clearly showed his willingness to support China's One Belt and One Road Initiative in his speech for the first time. Abe stated that "I would expect that the "One Belt and One Road" initiative will fully incorporate such a common frame of thinking, and come into harmony with the free and fair Trans-Pacific economic zone, and contribute to the peace and prosperity of the region and the world."[2] It was reported in the editorial of *The Japan Times* that reversing his position, Prime Minister Shinzo Abe has indicated that Japan is ready to cooperate with China's "One Belt and One Road" (OBOR) Initiative for cross-continental infrastructure development under certain conditions.[3]

Then, at the Japan-China Summit meeting on July 8, 2017, Prime Minister Shinzo Abe and President Xi Jinping shared the following view that "Japan and China will discuss how to contribute to the stability and prosperity of the region and the world, including the One Belt and One Road Initiative."[4] Around this time, the Japanese government seemingly endeavored to coordinate two diplomatic initiatives, namely China's BRI and Japan's FOIP. Although there existed several hurdles to clear, the two governments began to refrain from criticism towards the respective diplomatic visions. This signifies that the FOIP 2. 0 is different from the FOIP 1.0 which was regarded as a competitive strategy to deny China's diplomatic initiatives.

---

[1] Ministry of Foreign Affairs, Japan, *Diplomatic Bluebook* 2017: *Japanese Diplomacy and International Situation in* 2016 (Tokyo: Ministry of Foreign Affairs, Japan, 2017) p. 26.

[2] Speech by Prime Minister Shinzo Abe, "Asia's Dream: Linking the Pacific and Eurasia", the Banquet of the 23rd International Conference on The Future of Asia, June 5, 2017. https://japan. kantei. go. jp/97_abe/statement/201706/1222768_11579. html.

[3] "The Editorial: Japan and 'One Belt, One Road'", *The Japan Times*, June 24, 2017.

[4] Ministry of Foreign Affairs, Japan, "Japan–China Summit Meeting", July 8, 2017. https:// www. mofa. go. jp/a_o/c_m1/cn/page4e_000636. html.

Therefore, Akihiko Tanaka, former President of Japan International Cooperation Agency (JICA), criticizes that "The media often explain that a free and open Indo-Pacific strategy is Japan's diplomacy to counter China's One Belt and One Road Initiative."[1] Tanaka wrote that "it is short-sighted to conceive of a strategy toward such broad and promising region as the Indo-Pacific only to counter activities of other countries," and "the emergence of the Indo-Pacific as a regional concept combining the Indian and Pacific Oceans reflects the long-term development of the global economy."[2]

David Brewster correctly argued that "Japan's vision involves developing new economic and transportation corridors from the Pacific across the Indian Ocean to Africa. As the name implies, its stated focus is on building an open and not exclusive system of infrastructure."[3]

In his speech to the National Diet on January 22, 2018, Prime Minister Shinzo Abe clearly proclaimed the "Free and Open Indo-Pacific Strategy". He stated: "A vast expanse of sea stretches from the Pacific Ocean to the Indian Ocean. Since ancient times the people of this region have enjoyed affluence and prosperity from this large and free body of water. Freedom of navigation and the rule of law form their bedrock. We must ensure that these waters are a public good that brings peace and prosperity to all people without discrimination into the future. To this end we will promote the Free and Open Indo-Pacific Strategy."[4] He showed no intention to divide the Indo-Pacific region into two blocs, and underlined the importance of including "all people" who can benefit from it. China can also naturally enjoy such peace and prosperity within the free and open Indo-Pacific.

IV. Conclusion

One of the most significant problems for Japan's FOIP is that this diplomatic initiative is often confused with the American Indo-Pacific strategy, which is

[1]　Akihiko Tanaka, "The Range of a Free and Open Indo-Pacific Strategy", *Discuss Japan-Japan Foreign Policy Forum*, No. 44, March 8, 2018. https://www. japanpolicyforum. jp/archives/diplomacy/pt20180308182133. html.

[2]　Ibid.

[3]　David Brewster, "A 'Free and Open Indo-Pacific' and what it means for Australia", Lowy Institute for International Policy, 7 March 2018. https://www. lowyinstitute. org/the-interpreter/free-and-open-indo-pacific-and-what-it-means-australia.

[4]　Speech by Prime Minister Shinzo Abe to the 196th Session of the Diet, January 22, 2018. https://japan. kantei. go. jp/98_abe/statement/201801/_00002. html.

centered at the more military-oriented "Quad". Particularly, in American *National Security Strategy* (*NSS*) of 2017, it is stated that "A geopolitical competition between free and repressive visions of world order is taking place in the Indo-Pacific region."[1] Those who read this document would naturally have an impression that the Indo-Pacific region was divided into two camps, namely the U.S.-Japan alliance's FOIP and China's BRI. However, Japan's approach to the free and open Indo-Pacific is more comprehensive, more inclusive, and more cooperative than what is written in *NSS* of the United States.

In China, as well as in several ASEAN countries, some experts previously presented their concern over the future division of the Indo-Pacific region, and then the FOIP was denounced by them as a tool to divide the region. However, as this article already described, Japan's FOIP 2.0 has been carefully avoiding the impression that Japan and the United States are intending to contain China. The period when Japan has been promoting this diplomatic initiative largely overlaps the time of Japan-China rapprochement. As Donald Trump's administration intensifies its confrontational stance towards China, the Chinese government approaches to Tokyo have become more conciliatory than before.

Abe's more cooperative approach to China is basically welcomed not just by China, but more broadly as well. Andreea Brinza wrote in *The Japan Times* that "the steps that Abe has taken may bring peace into the region and may enable Japan to strengthen its presence in the Asia-Pacific region."[2] In this way, Japan's FOIP would be acceptable to ASEAN countries, as well as to India and Australia, which are less confrontational to China than the United States is. Thus, Japan's move from FOIP 1.0 to FOIP 2.0 is a necessary evolution to respond to the voices of Asian countries.

---

[1] The White House, *National Security Strategy of the United States of America*, Washington, D. C., December 2017, p. 45.

[2] Andreea Brinza, "Abe Strikes a 'Belt and Road' Balancing Act", *The Japan Times*, November 13, 2018.

New Adjustments of Regional Security Order from the Japanese Perspective (Main Points)

Satoru MORI

Professor, Hosei University, Japan,
Senior Fellow, the Nakasone Yasuhiro Peace Institute

One of the main changing features of the strategic landscape in the Indo-Pacific region has become the shift in the U. S. approach toward China from engagement to competition. [1] According to the U. S. *National Security Strategy* published in December 2017 (NSS2017) the question of whether China could potentially become a "responsible stakeholder" was apparently settled in the negative, and that China was now a "revisionist power". [2] NSS2017 declared that "great power competition returned" and the summary of the *National Defense Strategy* stated that "the central challenge to U. S. prosperity and security is the reemergence of long-term, strategic competition. " [3]

Under these circumstances, there appears to be two kinds of U. S. -China competition that have regional implications. First, there is the bilateral competition over the construction of next-generation military, industrial and information power. China's rise has coincided with what has been called the Fourth Industrial Revolution where many highly advanced technologies ranging from artificial intelligence to synthetic biology have achieved near simultaneous breakthroughs. Advanced states such as the United States and China are now trying to exploit these technologies for industrial purposes to advance economic growth and enhance international economic competitiveness. China's *Made in China* 2025 initiative is a case in point. Furthermore, defense authorities and military organizations are also seeking to exploit the same cutting-edge technologies for military purposes in order to strive for military overmatch. The U. S. Department of Defense is pursuing defense innovation in which artificial intelligence is among the primary technologies selected for military application. China makes a national effort to create synergy between military and commercial technological innovation through its military-civilian fusion strategy. The United States and China are engaged in a straightforward bilateral competition over national power. The bilateral competition is essentially about who will lead in the application of cutting-edge technology for military, industrial and information purposes.

Export control of emerging and foundational technologies, and Chinese 5G equipment adoption policy appear to be focal points where regional states will have to make decisions. U. S. allies like Japan are likely to take steps to coordinate with the United States. Japan has decided to institute cyber security measures to protect Japanese networks and critical infrastructure from malicious cyber attacks and manipulation.

Second, a geo-strategic contest over influence in third countries is unfolding in at least three forms: maritime competition, infrastructure financing competition, and digital network competition. The digital network competition is both an economic contest over patent and intellectual property associated with the next-generation information technology and a strategic contest over global digital data dominance. China's so-called "information silk road" or Digital Silk Road (DSR) seems to loosely encompass China's effort to export telecommunication equipment and infrastructure, fiber optic submarine cables, mobile networks, cloud computing systems, electronic commerce, and smart cities. [4] On the other hand, the United States largely follows the market principle to allow private companies to freely compete in various markets around the globe. Under the rubric of its Indo-Pacific strategy, the countries concerned are pursuing a regional line of effort devoted to digital connectivity and cyber security partnership. [5] There appears to be a debate over how the effort to keep out Huawei equipment from certain countries will affect 5G infrastructure cost and roll out, but it remains to be seen whether other 5G equipment suppliers such as Nokia, Ericsson, and Samsung will be able to pick up the slack. [6]

The U. S. -China geo-political competition is unfolding in the Indo-Pacific region and beyond. The regional states worry about the economic consequences of the so-called U. S. -China tariff war, but U. S. security initiatives are generally welcomed in the Indo-Pacific region. Japan, Australia and India are pursuing multi-faceted engagement initiatives in the region with the aim of forging an inclusive rules-based order. Intra-regional security cooperation pursued by Japan provides options for regional states that are ambivalent about becoming overly dependent on either China or the United States.

Footnotes:

1. David M. Edelstein, "The Persistence of Great Power Politics", *Texas National Security Review*, Vol. 2, No. 2 (February 2018), pp. 117-120; Kurt M. Campbell and Ely Ratner, "The China Reckoning: How Beijing Defied American Expectations", *Foreign Affairs*, Vol. 97, No. 2 (March/April 2018), pp. 60-70; Aaron L. Friedberg, "Competing with China", *Survival*, Vol. 60, No. 3 (June/July 2018), pp. 7-64; Peter Mattis, "From Engagement to Rivalry: Tools to Compete with China", *Texas National Security Review*, Vol. 1, No. 4 (August 2018), pp. 81-94; Robert Sutter, "Pushback: America's New China Strategy", *The Diplomat*, November 2, 2018, https://thediplomat. com/2018/11/pushback - americas-new-china-strategy/.

2. The White House, *National Security Strategy of the United States*, December 2017, p. 25.

3. U. S. Department of Defense, *Summary of the National Defense Strategy of the United States*, February 2018, p. 2.

4. John Chipman, "China's long and winding Digital Silk Road", IISS Analysis, the International Institute for Strategic Studies, January 25, 2019, https://www. iiss. org/blogs/analysis/2019/01/china-digital-silk-road; Brian Harding, "China's Digital Silk Road and Southeast Asia", CSIS Commentary, the Center for Strategic and International Studies, February 15, 2019, https://www. csis. org/analysis/chinas-digital-silk-road-and-southeast-asia.

5. See Secretary of State Mike Pompeo's speech on the free and open Indo-Pacific strategy. U. S. Department of State, "America's Indo-Pacific Economic Vision", July 30, 2018, https://www. state. gov/secretary/remarks/2018/07/284722. htm.

6. Arjun Kharpal, "Huawei ban won't make the US fall behind in 5G technology, experts say", CNBC Online, March 5, 2019, https://www. cnbc. com/2019/03/06/huawei-ban-wont-make-the-us-fall-behind-in-5g-experts. html.

ASEAN Centrality and Regional Security

Rear Admiral Roberto Q. Estioko

AFP (Ret), PhD, MNSA,

President, National Defense College of the Philippines

The regional security environment of the Asia-Pacific region is evolving. Changing power dynamics, and new security challenges are looming over the strategic horizon. Cooperation among all nations, regardless of their size, is necessary to ensure a more prosperous and secure future for the region.

In this session on the "Evolution of Security Concepts and Global Security Governance," please allow me to discuss a specific security concept: ASEAN Centrality, in particular, the role of this security concept in the regional security architecture and the prospects.

I. Understanding ASEAN Centrality

ASEAN or the Association of Southeast Asian Nations is arguably one of the most diverse regional organizations in the world. ASEAN has ten members: Brunei, Cambodia, Indonesia, Lao PDR, Malaysia, Myanmar, the Philippines, Singapore, Thailand, and Viet Nam. Collectively, these countries characterized by its vast diversity of domestic political traditions, and varying levels of economic development.

ASEAN was founded on 8 August 1967 through the signing of the Bangkok Declaration. A key objective of ASEAN, as outlined in the Bangkok Declaration, is "to promote regional peace and stability through abiding respect for justice and the rule of law in the relationship among countries of the region and adherence to the principles of the United Nations Charter".[1]

To meet its objectives, ASEAN operates largely through the principles of consultation and consensus. These principles of regional cooperation have been

---

[1] ASEAN Bangkok Declaration, Paragraph 2.

enshrined in various treaties, particularly the Treaty of Amity and Cooperation (TAC), and the ASEAN Charter. The TAC provides:

"*In their relations with one another, the High Contracting Parties shall be guided by the following fundamental principles: a) Mutual respect for the independence, sovereignty, equality, territorial integrity and national identity of all nations; b) The right of every State to lead its national existence free from external interference, subversion or coercion; c) Non-interference in the internal affairs of one another; d) Settlement of differences or disputes by peaceful means; e) Renunciation of the threat or use of force; f) Effective cooperation among themselves.* "[1]

The ASEAN Charter also outlines various principles of regional cooperation:

"*(a) respect for the independence, sovereignty, equality, territorial integrity and national identity of all ASEAN Member States;*

(b) shared commitment and collective responsibility in enhancing regional peace, security and prosperity;

(c) renunciation of aggression and of the threat or use of force or other actions in any manner inconsistent with international law;

(d) reliance on peaceful settlement of disputes;

(e) non-interference in the internal affairs of ASEAN Member States;

(f) respect for the right of every Member State to lead its national existence free from external interference, subversion and coercion;

(g) enhanced consultations on matters seriously affecting the common interest of ASEAN;

(h) adherence to the rule of law, good governance, the principles of democracy and constitutional government;

(i) respect for fundamental freedoms, the promotion and protection of human rights, and the promotion of social justice;

(j) upholding the United Nations Charter and international law, including international humanitarian law, subscribed to by ASEAN Member States;

(k) abstention from participation in any policy or activity, including the use of its territory, pursued by any ASEAN Member State or non-ASEAN State or any non-State actor, which threatens the sovereignty, territorial integrity or political and economic stability of ASEAN Member States;

(l) respect for the different cultures, languages and religions of the peoples of ASEAN, while emphasizing their common values in the spirit of unity in diversity;

---

[1] Treaty of Amity and Cooperation, Article 2.

(*m*) *the centrality of ASEAN in external political, economic, social and cultural relations while remaining actively engaged, outward-looking, inclusive and non-discriminatory; and*

(*n*) *adherence to multilateral trade rules and ASEAN's rules-based regimes for effective implementation of economic commitments and progressive reduction towards elimination of all barriers to regional economic integration, in a market-driven economy.* " [1]

By placing premium on the principles of non-interference in the internal affairs of each other, as well as by decision-making through consultation and consensus, ASEAN partly made itself one of the key players in the multilateral affairs of the region. Indeed, coupled by the member-states' diversity, these various principles of cooperation gave credence to ASEAN's credibility as an inclusive international organization upon which other platforms of regional cooperation are anchored.

II. ASEAN in the Regional Security Architecture

In the post-Cold War era, ASEAN has increasingly played the role as an "honest broker" in promoting multilateralism in the Asia-Pacific region, particularly in providing platforms for dialogue and cooperation in addressing non-traditional security issues.

ASEAN's role in global security governance can be seen in two fronts. First, in terms of membership, ASEAN-led platforms have a broad membership. While such platforms are not global in terms of membership, the membership nonetheless covers the major global players, particularly the United States (U. S.), China, the European Union (EU), Russia, among others. Second, ASEAN plays a role in terms of setting the agenda, particularly in terms of non-traditional security cooperation.

ASEAN is at the center of various platforms for regional security dialogue and cooperation, particularly the ASEAN Regional Forum (ARF), ASEAN Defense Ministers' Meeting Plus (ADMM-Plus), and East Asia Summit (EAS).

ARF is arguably the most inclusive ASEAN-led platform in the Indo-Asia-Pacific region. The objective of the ARF is " to foster constructive dialogue and consultation on political and security issues of common interest and concern," and "to make significant contributions to efforts towards confidence-building and preventive diplomacy in the Asia-Pacific region. "

---

[1]　ASEAN Charter, Article 2.

Founded in 1994, ARF has the following countries as members: Australia, Bangladesh, Brunei Darussalam, Cambodia, Canada, China, Democratic People's Republic of Korea (DPRK), India, Indonesia, Japan, Lao People's Democratic Republic (PDR), Malaysia, Mongolia, Myanmar, New Zealand, Pakistan, Papua New Guinea, the Philippines, Republic of Korea, Russia, Singapore, Sri Lanka, Thailand, Timor-Leste, the United States, Viet Nam, and EU. The membership of the ARF alone suggests the extent of inclusivity which ASEAN seeks to promote. The two Koreas are members of ARF, as well as China, India, and Pakistan—all of which have a history of armed conflict with each other. Indeed, ASEAN promotes an open regionalism.

Founded in 2010, the ADMM-Plus is another platform for security cooperation in the region. While ARF is led by the foreign ministers, the ADMM-Plus, as its name suggests, is led by the defense establishments of the ASEAN Member-States (AMS) and of the following dialogue partners: Australia, China, India, Japan, New Zealand, ROK, Russian Federation and the United States. The objectives of the ADMM-Plus are as follows: 1) to benefit ASEAN member countries in building capacity to address shared security challenges, while cognizant of the differing capacities of various ASEAN countries; 2) to promote mutual trust and confidence between defense establishments through greater dialogue and transparency; 3) to enhance regional peace and stability through cooperation in defense and security, in view of the transnational security challenges the region faces; 4) to contribute to the realization of an ASEAN Security Community which, as stipulated in the Bali Concord II, embodies ASEAN's aspiration to achieve peace, stability, democracy and prosperity in the region where ASEAN member countries live at peace with one another and with the world at large; 5) to facilitate the implementation of the Vientiane Action Program, which calls for ASEAN to build a peaceful, secure and prosperous ASEAN, and to adopt greater outward-looking external relation strategies with our friends and Dialogue Partners. To operationalize these objectives, the ADMM-Plus has a total of seven Expert Working Groups (EWGs) for the following issues: humanitarian assistance and disaster relief (HADR), maritime security, military medicine, counter-terrorism, peacekeeping operations, humanitarian mine action, and cyber security.

Founded in 2005, the EAS has the AMS, and the following members: Australia, China, Japan, India, New Zealand, the Republic of Korea, Russia and the United States. Hosted by Malaysia, the first EAS Summit also issued the Kuala Lumpur Declaration on the EAS, which outlines the priority of the

ASEAN-led body:

"[a] *Fostering strategic dialogue and promoting cooperation in political and security issues to ensure that our countries can live at peace with one another and with the world at large in a just, democratic and harmonious environment;*

[b] *Promoting development, financial stability, energy security, economic integration and growth, eradicating poverty and narrowing the development gap in East Asia, through technology transfer and infrastructure development, capacity building, good governance and humanitarian assistance and promoting financial links, trade and investment expansion and liberalization; and*

[c] *Promoting deeper cultural understanding, people-to-people contact and enhanced cooperation in uplifting the lives and well-being of our peoples in order to foster mutual trust and solidarity as well as promoting fields such as environmental protection, prevention of infectious diseases and natural disaster mitigation.* "[1]

The Chairmanship of the ARF, EAS, and ADMM-Plus all coincide with the AMS that holds the ASEAN Chairmanship.

III. Prospects for Multilateralism

In the Indo-Asia-Pacific region, there are indeed undeniable shifts in the dynamics of major power relations.

ASEAN provides some measure of stability amidst the uncertainties of regional power shifts through the efforts in institutionalizing the three pillars of ASEAN Community-Building (Political-Security Community, Economic Community, Socio-Cultural Community) and the ASEAN Way of diplomatic interaction, as enshrined in the ASEAN Charter. The Charter marks a crucial milestone in ASEAN's forward march towards a more cohesive community where platforms for diplomacy across a wide spectrum of government and non-governmental sectors are strengthened and regularized. ASEAN community-building involves not just the executive organs and official channels of diplomacy, but also parliamentarians, economic and business groups, think tanks, and non-governmental organizations, among many others. ASEAN now has a pervasive presence in many aspects of governance in Southeast Asia. With community-building taking a firm foothold in the most important sectors in Southeast Asia, the organizational cohesion envisioned by the Charter is gradually achieved, thereby contributing to a more solid and amplified ASEAN voice in the wider Indo-Asia-Pacific. ASEAN's organizational integrity and internal

---

[1]　Kuala Lumpur Declaration on the East Asia Summit, Paragraph 4.

cohesion provide the necessary diplomatic gravitas in exercising solid leadership and significant credence to ASEAN's organizational neutrality in dealing with major global powers and championing the cause of international peace and stability. Naturally, power shifts will entail some strains, or even occasional tensions, among regional stakeholders. However, if ASEAN remains to be seen as united and firm in managing conflict and preserving avenues for diplomacy, even (and especially) during the most difficult political climate, the organization can exercise solid leadership to diplomatically pull regional actors away from the brink of disaster and violence. It is therefore in the interest of global players to support ongoing efforts in ASEAN for community-building. A cohesive and consultative regional organization is more likely to be able to exercise effective, impartial, and non-confrontational leadership in regional multilateral diplomacy.

ASEAN's promotion of open regionalism complements efforts in building an inclusive Indo-Asia-Pacific region. Indeed, ASEAN and ASEAN-led platforms can be seen as a church open to all faiths. Perhaps as a consequence of the organization's internal diversity in terms of political traditions and levels of economic development, ASEAN has traditionally been inclusive, consultative, and open to engaging a wide array of non-ASEAN stakeholders, including global powers. On numerous occasions, ASEAN has vowed to promote mutual respect and non-interference in internal affairs, thereby posturing itself as an organization that does not discriminate on the basis of domestic political systems and economic status. This openness creates a diplomatic environment conducive to dialogue and adjustments, matters that sometimes need to stay away from the glare of media cameras and myopic commentaries.

New Adjustments of the Regional Security Order: A Look at the Southern African Development Community (SADC)

Danisa Khumalo
Former Director, Denis Hurley Peace Institute of South Africa

Introduction

The national and regional security concerns have become priority areas for most countries around the globe. In the last decades, countries have prioritized issues of security. There has been a rise internationally of security concerns because of the terrorist threats from all over the world, the different coup d' état, political instability, civil wars and civil unrest. Without exception, the Southern African region has been pre-occupied with the issues of security in so far as responding to the emergence of threats is concerned. This paper's focus is on the Southern African region which is grouped together under the Southern African Development Community (SADC). SADC members are Angola, Botswana, Comoros, Democratic Republic of Congo, Lesotho, Madagascar, Malawi, Mauritius, Mozambique, Namibia, Seychelles, South Africa, Swaziland, United Republic of Tanzania, Zambia and Zimbabwe.

There is no consensus on how to tackle security issues in the SADC region in most cases. The security sectors (defense, intelligence, police, navy and air force) are well funded in most of the SADC countries. For instance, Botswana (Defense and Security Sector) 14. 4% of the total budget; Namibia (Defense and Safety and Security) 17. 2%; Zambia (Defense and Public Order and Safety) 9. 1%; Lesotho (Police and public safety, Defense and National security) 12%; Mauritius (Public Order and Safety) 10%. This information is based on the 2018-2019 budgets.

Currently, the threat from outside is minimal in the SADC region but the greatest threat is from within (issues like HIV and AIDS, immigration, the proliferation of small arms, corruption, Ebola). To discuss security only in terms of relations in SADC between states, intra-and inter-state security concerns would ignore the most salient threats facing SADC countries such as HIV and AIDS, Ebola, immigration and others. The police forces in countries such as Zimbabwe, Zambia and South Africa are known for corrupt practices that compromise the security of the citizens. SADC as a regional body is weak by the failure of the leaders to challenge each other. This governance deficit is a source of instability in the region. Although most SADC countries have been relatively peaceful, the region still faces challenges of "armed insurgency, the crisis of governance and lack of socio-economic development and SADC are ill-prepared to manage such issues effectively" (Aeby 2018:3). The lack of development in some African states poses a major long-term risk to peace and security of the region. Some (2015:45) describe the peace and security climate in Africa as dominated by "*failed and failing states, its institutional weaknesses and attendant ungoverned spaces combined with the increasing gaps between the 'haves' and the 'have−nots', conflict in Africa has increasingly become endemic and the African environment today is a dynamic one, characterized by a volatile mix of conflict, instability and state weakness*".

National/regional security can never be disentangled from the state of the economy. In this respect, Africa has fostered the creation of several regional bodies that can address issues that pertain to the different regions that states belong to, for example, Arab Maghreb Union (AMU), Common Market for Eastern and Southern Africa (COMESA), Community of Sahel-Saharan States Community of Sahel-Saharan States (CEN-SAD), Economic Community of West African States (ECOWAS), Economic Community of East Africa (EAC), Economic Community of Central African States (ECCAS), Intergovernmental Authority on Development (IGAD), Southern African Development Community (SADC).

The SADC region still faces security threats that manifest itself in active armed military activities such as the Democratic Republic of Congo (DRC). The DRC is currently hosting the largest United Nations-sponsored Peacekeeping Force. Besides DRC, the past few years have proved that countries such as Lesotho, Zimbabwe, Swaziland and Malawi have relatively fragile political institutions within the broader SADC region.

I. SADC Security Concerns

The SADC Treaty was signed in Windhoek in August 1992. Its aim was "forging of links to create a genuine and equitable regional integration" (SADC Declaration and Treaty 1992:1). The focus was that of economic integration and increasing cooperation in addressing developmental problems in the region. SADC agreed on seven areas of cooperation and the last of these being, "politics, diplomacy, international relations, peace and security" (SADC Declaration and Treaty 1992:2). Although security was not on top of the agenda of SADC when it was established, security has increased, the region has to respond to the security challenges that its members face. SADC is a regional body that was formed out of the Southern African Development Coordination Conference in 1992. SADC was founded soon after the end of the cold war and gaining independence for Namibia. Laurie Nathan (2006), points out that SADC failed to establish a common security regime and also failed to play a significant peacekeeping role in the SADC region. The cause for SADC's failure is attributed to three problems faced by SADC at that period: these are the absence of common values among member states, which inhibits the development of trust, common policies, institutional cohesion and unified response to crises; secondly the reluctance of states to surrender sovereignty to a security regime that encompasses binding rules and decision-making; and thirdly the economic and administrative weakness of states" (Nathan 2006:605). However, SADC played a peacekeeping role such as the need for the Democratic Republic of Congo in 1998, and the Lesotho army rebellion also in 1998 of which Botswana and South Africa intervened.

Map of SADC States

(https://doi. org/10. 3390/su11061532)

It is imperative to point out SADC has the economic, social, political, cultural and security commitment principles within the region. For security commitments, the SADC Organ on Politics, Defense and Security was established in 1996 but there "was no clarity on how the security organ's Chairman (who at the time of establishment was President Robert Mugabe) would fit into the SADC leadership structure" (Hammerstad 2005:77). The functions of the organ included the prevention of conflicts within a country or between countries and the resolution of these conflicts. The security organ initially lacked the legal instrument "setting out its tasks and responsibilities and delineating the scope of its powers (Hammerstad 2005:79). South Africa is credited for pushing for regional diplomacy especially towards "the need for 'good governance' and 'democracy' alongside a discourse associated with 'growth' and (to a lesser extent) development" (Taylor 2011:1236).

II. Protocol on Politics, Defense and Security Cooperation (2001)

The Protocol on Politics, Defense and Security Cooperation that was accepted and endorsed by the member states is aimed at protecting people of the region against instability that arises from conflicts as the SADC region had witnessed many conflicts in its territories such as the unrest in Lesotho, the DRC civil war. From a historical point of view, the Angolan civil war between the government and UNITA rebels which ended in 2002 had destabilizing effects on SADC. Remarkably, the SADC leaders realized that the civilian population is the one that suffers worse in these conflicts. The objectives of the protocols were to "promote regional coordination and cooperation in defense and security, conflict prevention, management and resolution, implementation in response to external military threats, cooperation between law enforcement agencies and state security services among member states." (SADC Protocol 2001). This protocol envisaged that SADC would be able to act as a unit in confronting threats to its member states instead of acting individually as the countries had done before. The leaders of SADC also wanted this protocol to increase their capacity especially when they acted as a unit to prevent any coup d'état or any subversion of an elected constitutional government. This was also an opportunity for SADC states to eliminate the threat of terrorism.

SADC came up with the Defense Pact in 2003 and it focused on issues of "conflict resolution, military preparedness, collective self-defense and self-action, destabilizing factors and settlement of disputes" (SADC Mutual Defense Pact Document, 2003: 1). One of the clear challenges facing Southern African region was that development in many spheres was lagging, so there was a need to create an environment that enhanced the "peace, stability and concomitant towards democracy" (SADC 2003:2). The Organ on Politics, Defense and Security were viewed as a vehicle that would bring the Southern African region into the environment of peace, security and stability. The region also needed to strengthen its solidarity with one another.

III. A critical appraisal of SADC's efforts on Security Issues in the region

I have presented the efforts of the SADC leaders in building pillars that were meant to promote the security of the Southern African region. SADC as a regional body cannot still challenge some member states whose political behavior has the potential to destabilize the region.

SADC member states can exert different types of pressure on the regional structure. South Africa, for example, is the largest economy in the SADC region. It is also technologically more advanced and has a big influence on the setting of the SADC agenda. The SADC Secretariat is viewed as weak and its budget (40% plus) is mainly funded by donors. Most programs except for peace and security efforts are also mostly donor-funded. This dependency often leads to a lack of ownership and a buy-in by member states. SADC Secretariat is mainly an administrative body that carries out decisions taken by the leaders of member states at their summit.

Finally, SADC is administratively hindered by the fact that most members belong to other regional blocks. There are examples such as the Democratic Republic of Congo and Angola, which also belong to the Economic Community of Central African States. Tanzania is part of SADC but also belongs to the East African Community. Such countries end up lacking the capacity to devote to their role in one or two economic communities. Moreover, such affiliations imply that member states may uphold different principles depending on the regional block they belong to which makes consensual obligations rather difficult.

IV. Possible security threats in SADC

It would not be fair to discuss the regional security order without pointing at other threats that are found among the citizens of Southern Africa. The threat of HIV and AIDS is a serious security concern in the SADC region. According the United Nations AIDS (UNAIDS), "Eastern and Southern Africa remains the region most affected by the HIV epidemic, accounting for 45% of the world's HIV infections and 53% of people living with HIV globally". This is a serious security threat that needs more attention especially to be paid by the SADC countries. The challenge of Ebola in the Democratic Republic of Congo and Uganda poses a serious security threat in Southern and Eastern Africa. With porous borders and disease control mechanism, more needs to be done in this area. Immigration is a human phenomenon but the challenge of forced migration is a security threat in some receiving countries in Southern Africa. Currently, South Africa is a major receiver of many forced migrants from Southern Africa and many other countries beyond SADC. According to Statistics South Africa, during the census of 2011, there were 2. 2 million immigrants in the country. The current numbers are at best, estimates or calculated guesswork. The porous borders in Southern Africa make it easier for people to cross these boundaries and at times, they put a strain on the resources of the receiving country.

V. The Role of South Africa in Conflict Management in the SADC region

It is important to pay attention to the role played by South Africa in SADC especially when issues of peace and security are under consideration. South Africa is the most developed economy and has the most advanced security sector in the region. It is a member of Brazil, Russia, India, China and South Africa (BRICS) countries and is the only African country to be included, which is in itself an acknowledgement of its power and strength in the African continent. South Africa has not used its economic, political and security muscle to intervene in the conflicts that have plagued the SADC region or Africa as a whole. South Africa has been pushing for "quiet diplomacy" approach to dealing with some conflicts such as in Zimbabwe from 2000 onwards. This approach was used especially when South Africa had to deal with the Zimbabwean conflict from 2000 onwards. South Africa especially through its former president, Thabo Mbeki used quiet diplomacy to negotiate with the Zimbabwean leaders without imposing its will or ready-made solutions.

It has also pushed for "African Solutions to African Problems" approach that is also being promoted by the African Union. Lastly, South Africa has allowed the regional bodies such as the SADC and the African Union to lead the way in conflict management and resolution and it has co-operated in this framework. The South African strategy has respected the sovereignty of other nations, no matter their size or military strength, and also prevented it from being viewed as "the big brother" to intervene in conflicts in the region.

The African solutions for African problems mantra resonates especially in the peace and security sector of the SADC and the African Union. "The concept of 'African solutions' is meant to evoke a sense of self-reliance, responsibility, pride and ownership amongst all Africans" (Lobakeng 2017:2), meaning to promote African initiatives to conflict management. It also tries to curb the non-African global players who usually have other interests in the African conflicts.

There are adjustments needed for the SADC regional security order, and there is a need to strengthen the peer review mechanism scheme. Such peer mechanisms would entrench practices that promote security within the region.

References

Cheeseman N. & Klaas B. , 2018. How to Rig an Election. New Haven: Yale University Press.

Dashwood H. , 2002. Mugabe, Zimbabwe, and Southern Africa: The Struggle for Leadership. International Journal, Vol. 57, No. 1, pp. 78-100.

Forere M. , 2012. Is Discussion of the "United States of Africa" Premature? Analysis of ECOWAS and SADC Integration Efforts. Journal of African Law. Vol. 56, No. 1, pp. 29-54.

Hammerstad A. , 2005. Domestic Threats. Regional Solutions? The Challenge of Security Integration in Southern Africa. Review of International Studies, Vol. 31, No. 1, pp. 69-87.

Hentz J, J. 2009. The Southern African Security Order: Regional Economic Integration and Security among Developing States. Review of International Studies, Vol. 35, pp. 189-213.

Nathan L. , 2006. SADC's Uncommon Approach to Common Security, 1992-2003. Journal of African Studies, Vol. 3, pp. 605-622.

Saurombe A. , 2010. The role of South Africa in SADC Regional Integration: The Making or Braking of the Organisation. Journal of International Commercial Law & Technology. Vol. 5 Issue 3. Pp. 124-131.

Solomon H. , 2015.

Tavares R. , 2011. The Participation of SADC and ECOWAS in Military Operations: The Weight of National Interest of Decision Making. African Studies Review, Vol. 54, No. 2, pp. 145-176.

Taylor I. , 2011. South African "Imperialism" in a Region Lacking Regionalism: a Critique. Third World Quarterly. Vol. 32. No. 7 pp. 1233-1253.

Session III
New and Emerging Technologies and Global Security

New Technologies and Global Security from the Perspective of Global Security Governance

Dr. John Borrie [1]

Researcher with the United Nations Institute for
Disarmament Research (UNIDIR),
Head of WMD and other Strategic Weapons Programme/
Research Coordinator in Geneva

The technologies discussed are anti-ballistic missile defenses, hypersonic and other advanced long-range weapons, anti-satellite weapons, un-crewed weapon systems, cyber, artificial intelligence and machine learning. Machine learning, although not a new technology *per se*—yet, is a more "usable" weapon. Individually or in combination with each of these developments has implications for the nuclear balance or will have actual effects in crisis situations that may be hard to predict, or both.

Taken together, these technologies are one of four sources of growing strategic unpredictability—making the world a more dangerous place. The other sources are more nuclear-armed states uncertanties; tenser relations between some of these states; and, lastly, the deterioration of the fabric of international institutions and norms that contribute to stability. In this regard, the weakening of the "arms control enterprise" can be seen in stalled bilateral nuclear reductions between the United States and Russia. [2] At the multilateral level, the Conference on Disarmament (CD) is still deadlocked after more than two decades and the Nuclear Non-Proliferation Treaty (NPT) regime is struggling to contain political divisions exacerbated by lack of progress on nuclear disarmament.

As bleak as the current outlook is, arms control approaches on new strategic technologies could contribute to stability as in the past, greater strategic dialogue, clarifications of nuclear use doctrines and crisis communication improvements could help strengthen nuclear weapon risk reduction measures, and in turn could contribute to the trust necessary for states to agree to resume progress toward a nuclear-weapon-free world.

Several main technological developments are relevant to thinking about two problems in global security. The first issue concerns their implications for the nuclear balance, which makes these technologies both products of—and fodder for—strategic modernization and arms racing among major strategic competitors like the United States, Russia, China, and India. The second is that although several of these technologies are ostensibly intended to strengthen deterrence, in crisis escalation situations their actual effects may be difficult to predict and contribute to greater crisis and instability instead. These are important reasons why intensified efforts toward strategic arms control agreements are needed in the two major triadic nuclear relationships: U. S. -Russia-China, and China-India-Pakistan. In addition, without strengthening the multilateral disarmament, arms control and non-proliferation in these strategic relationships, it is difficult to prevent powers' conflict and nuclear war.

I. New technology and nuclear instability

After the United States detonated atomic bombs in Japan in 1945, nuclear weapons were recognized as something qualitatively different from all previous strategic technologies. No means existed to effectively counter them, and nuclear strategy proceeded from this dreadful and inescapable fact. Although "Mutually Assured Destruction" was never official U. S. policy, yet it captured the sentiment of nuclear deterrence due to the absolute certainty of catastrophically damaging nuclear reprisal. The 1972 Anti-Ballistic Missile (ABM) Treaty between the United States and the Soviet Union in effect acknowledged this. While it was held, the ABM Treaty removed the risk that one side would lose its retaliatory nuclear capability to the other due to missile defense developments. It thus served to open the way for strategic nuclear reductions.

Today, nuclear war planners are less certain than they were about that "strategic stability". The possibility of new technology leading to nuclear vulnerability that forms the basis for nuclear deterrence is a vexing issue for them. Nuclear planning is based on worst-case contingencies. Certain contingencies that would have major ramifications cannot be excluded (say, a "bolt-from-the-blue" or "decapitated" attack in which national nuclear command-and-control systems were to be destroyed, nullifying one's nuclear deterrent), then steps have to be taken to forestall them. This is one reason why so much nuclear "modernization" has an element of qualitative improvement to it. It also helps to explain why arms racing dynamics can take hold among states. And it also means some strategic technologies developed to enhance the credibility of one's nuclear deterrent capability can, in crisis situations, potentially be destabilizing.

II. Which technologies are of strategic concern?

a. Anti-ballistic missile defences

Since it left the ABM Treaty in 2002, the United States has developed more advanced missile defense systems to intercept missiles on ballistic flight paths. Progression developing reliable homeland missile defense has so far remained limited. However, missile defense at the tactical and theatre levels focused on missions to protect military assets and troops have become capabilities of importance to more countries as the technology has improved. The United States, Russia, India, France, Israel and China have all developed missile defense systems, and the United States has made systems available to its allies including Saudi Arabia in the Middle East, and Japan and South Korea in Asia.

As ballistic missile defense systems advance, they are becoming more integrated "systems-of-systems". It means previous distinctions between systems intended to intercept non-nuclear missiles and nuclear-armed missiles may be blurring. Russians say it is concerned that missile defense capabilities deployed in Eastern Europe could undermine its second strike nuclear retaliatory capability. In March 2018, Russian President Vladimir Putin cited a new generation of Russian strategic nuclear systems as stemming from U. S. withdrawal from the ABM Treaty. [3]China may conceivably share this concern in Asia due to its relatively small number of deployed nuclear missiles.

b. Hypersonic and other advanced, longer-range weapons [4]

Hypersonic weapons travel through the atmosphere at more than five times the local speed of sound. Several states are actively pursuing novel long-range manoeuvrable weapons, most significantly hypersonic boost-glide systems equipped with hypersonic glide vehicles (HGVs). HGVs are unpowered after separation and do not follow a ballistic flight path after the boost phase. They may have an enhanced ability to overcome missile defenses due to both this manoeuvrability as well as their depressed trajectories relative to standard ballistic missiles. Today, the United States, Russia, China, and most recently France have active HGV acquisition programs. Other states are reportedly interested in the technology. The U. S. intends to use boost-glide technology with conventional or kinetic (non-explosive) warheads; it is unclear whether Russia and China's systems will be nuclear-armed.

Although the military utility of HGVs remains unclear, an arms race dynamic is unfolding in pursuit of this technology. Possible ambiguity about the nature of an HGV's warhead (nuclear or conventional), together with uncertainty about its intended target, means the potential for strategic misunderstanding is considerable. Missiles launched carrying HGVs could be interpreted as signaling an imminent nuclear attack. Even if HGVs are subsequently shown on impact to be conventional, it could also prompt "use it or lose it" dilemmas for nuclear-armed states at risk of being targeted if they believe these weapons have been directed against their nuclear early warning, command and control infrastructure. In view of these ambiguities it is conceivable that the advent of HGVs will prompt some nuclear-armed states to amend their doctrines to expand the conditions necessary for the use of nuclear weapons in response to HGV deployments, or/and by placing their nuclear forces on higher alert.

Other developments in advanced, longer-range missiles may also put pressure on nuclear doctrines and war plans. Russia and China have long asserted that conventional cruise missiles could upset the strategic balance.[5] In recent years, the United States has produced and exported to some allies the air-to-ground missiles, a low-observable air-launched conventional cruise missile it first used in Syria in April 2018. A new version of this missile with an extended range of around 1,000km is entering service.[6] Launched from bombers outside an adversary's most heavily-defended airspace, such cruise missiles could evade air defences due to their stealthy characteristics to strike strategic targets such as nuclear command and control systems and mobile nuclear launchers. A related issue, as in HGVs, is that strikes with conventional cruise missile systems may be misidentified as air-launched nuclear-tipped cruise missiles by the targeted state.[7]

c. Anti-satellite weapons [8]

States have long appreciated the importance of outer space for many military functions ranging from communications to surveillance to early warning of nuclear attack, and many military operations rely on satellite access today. The 1967 Outer Space Treaty prohibits the stationing of nuclear weapons in space, although a proposal by China and Russia for a treaty to prevent placement of other weapons there has not achieved widespread attraction.[9] Western countries claim it would not be verifiable, and that in any case it is not necessary to put weapons in space to pose a danger to other space objects. Indeed, three countries to date (the United States, China and, in April 2019, India) have tested ground-launched anti-satellite (ASAT) interceptor capabilities.[10] However, it is not only such missile interceptors, but also a variety of "non-kinetic" cyber and electronic counter-space capabilities that can disrupt or destroy satellites. [11] And any space object is at risk from collision. This makes the increasing ubiquity of co-orbital drone technology the significant international concern, especially as it is difficult to identify the intentions of proximity manoeuvres until collision is imminent.

Why are anti-satellite weapons of strategic concern? The most obvious reason is that various countries are increasingly reliant on space high-tech for civil and military purposes. Even if states have not placed objects in space that are unambiguously weapons and have not deliberately collided with or blown up each other assets yet, non-kinetic offensive space operations have been going on for some time. [12] The formation of national "space forces" of the United States and India reflects concerns as to their vulnerability of space-based infrastructure, but may also contribute to more overt competition and arms racing dynamics. If space-based systems to detect missile launches and flight paths are deployed, it will in turn increase the desire for ASAT capabilities. However, debris created by the destruction of space objects using direct-ascent ASATs would likely cause major disruption and could render space effectively unusable for some time, with major consequences for daily life on earth for billions of people. [13]

d. Un-crewed weapon systems

In 2013, the United Nations Human Rights Council's Special Rapporteur presented two important reports. One concerned armed unmanned aerial vehicles (UAVs, or armed drones), [14] and the other focused on so-called " lethal autonomous robotics"[15] (LARs). These brief papers were influential in prompting international concern on these topics. First, there is international disquiet over the role of remotely-piloted UAVs in clandestine operations outside conventional battlefields in which it is not always clear which legal rules apply. Yet these concerns have not yet crystalized into focused discussions in an international forum. [16] In contrast, these topics were mentioned in discussions of the UN Convention on Certain Conventional Weapons, and these discussions continue. Questions raised there include what the implications are of machines selecting targets and attacking human beings. Whether such systems can be sufficiently predictable or reliable, and whether autonomous weapons are ethical. [17]

Although considered separately to date, both armed drones and autonomous weapon systems have yet produced significant impact, but could create similar issues in situations of strategic escalation or crisis. From an operator's perspective both kinds could be more attractive for some military roles as they are more expendable than crewed platforms (for instance, able to be sent into contested airspace or waters to gather intelligence even if likely to be intercepted and destroyed). However, there is evidence to suggest persistent differences between how users and those on the receiving end would view the use of un-crewed systems in this manner. [18] These differences could result in misunderstanding and further escalation. [19] After one incident involving a Chinese drone in 2013, Japan stated it had new rules of engagement to shoot down any further drones incurring on its airspace. China stated that any attack on its drones would be an "act of war" and that China would "strike back" if that happened. [20] And despite the best efforts of designers and operators, un-crewed aerial systems have higher rates of acting unpredictably and of crashing. These can add additional variables in tense situations or crises.

e. Cyber

Modern life, including modern military systems, depends on digital data created, kept, managed and moved around on cyber networks. The exploitation of code for hacking, spoofing, phishing, stealing, disrupting and even altering or destroying data has moved in from the margins to become a major security focus over the last decade. Now, despite the difficulty of attributing hacks, it is a poorly kept secret that several of the major military powers undertake offensive cyber operations against each other, as well as others. [21] Cyber offensive operations are increasingly ubiquitous and persistent. The lines are blurry between state versus-state offensive operations, espionage and other activities, including theft and extortion, in which civilian infrastructure and bystanders are victims.

Cyber offensive capabilities rise to the level of strategic concern in two kinds of scenario. The first is hacking or other cyber interference with nuclear early warning, command and control or decision support systems—or creating fear in a target country. The target country claims that it is under cyber threat, which could lead to nuclear escalation;*in extremis*, nuclear "use it or lose it" scenarios are even conceivable. The second kind of scenario concerns those in which an aggressor uses cyber offensive means to disable the critical societal infrastructure an adversary's population relies on. [22] In June 2019 it was reported that both the United States and Russia were penetrating deeply into each other's electric utilities, planting malware potentially capable of disrupting their national power grids. [23] It is significant then, that in its 2018 Nuclear Posture Review, the United States pointedly refused to rule out a nuclear response to "non-nuclear strategic attacks" like a major cyber-attack. [24] Thus, cyber threats already appear to be impacting the nuclear use doctrines of various states.

f. AI and machine learning [25]

Dramatic advances in artificial intelligence (AI) are having wide-ranging societal impacts. Algorithm-based machine systems are becoming vastly better at self-optimizing their performance based on various techniques, many of them related to pattern recognition and matching of data. This will improve the ability of machine systems to perform various critical military functions with a greater level of autonomy ranging from communications and logistics, to network defense, fire control, intelligence analysis support and even the selection of targets and launching of attacks. Concerns are being expressed about the emergence of an "AI arms race" between the United States and China or an "AI cold war that threatens all" in particular. [26]

Concerns that AI will exclude humans from decision making in conflict are probably overblown, at least for now. As one recent study found, there are greater risks from machine learning-powered AI applications and autonomous systems being too brittle in their design: "They may fail spectacularly when confronted with tasks or environments that differ slightly to those they were trained for. Their behavior is also unpredictable as they use algorithms that are opaque. It is difficult for humans to explain how they work and whether they include bias that could lead to problematic—if not dangerous—behaviors. They could also be defeated by an intelligent adversary through a cyber-attack or even a simple sensor spoofing trick. An immature adoption of the latest developments of AI in the context of nuclear weapons systems could have dramatic consequences. " [27]

At the same time, systems of various kinds based on algorithms are increasingly indispensable to militaries. Two reasons in particular need to be strengthened over increasing reliance of military command chains on automation for early warning and detection of nuclear or other strategic attack. First, with such techniques advance in the nuclear context, prospective capabilities in machine learning and other AI-related techniques could affect assured nuclear retaliatory capability and thus current strategic balances. [28] Second, the uptake of AI will be a continuous process with heterogeneous impacts on human decision-making processes in nuclear early warning, command and control systems, even if the final decision to launch nuclear weapons always lies with humans. Yet a lesson from crises in the Cold War is that such human contextual awareness was crucial in averting nuclear use on several occasions. [29] Will human decision makers be able to make the right call when they depend on AI?

g. More "usable" nuclear weapons

While not strictly speaking a new technology, more usable nuclear weapons are mentioned here because they are becoming part of the mix of strategic technologies. [30] To this end, there are discussions within some nuclear-armed states about deploying "more usable" nuclear weapons. It seems intended that these weapons could be tactically useful and might even scare an adversary. [31]

Deploying nuclear weapons in these ways would in fact most certainly be very destabilizing. At present, nuclear-armed states try to be very careful in terms of the roles they accord to nuclear weapons—emphasizing deterrence and nuclear weapon use only in extreme cases of existential self-defense. This has contributed to a nuclear non-use norm. More usable nuclear weapons promise to undermine the non-proliferation norms like those embodied in the NPT. In peacetime it requires changes in doctrines of nuclear use, and such changes to doctrine could add ambiguity to crisis situations, and in effect lower the threshold to nuclear use.

III. Why new technology demands arms control

Each of the developments outlined above has implications for the nuclear balance or will have actual effects in crisis that may be very difficult to predict, or both. In all cases this has implications for global security, since there are few things more "global" than a nuclear crisis or use of nuclear weapons.

Of course, it is hard for scholars or decision-makers to foresee the precise ways in which these technologies and other factors will interact. Of course, it is impossible to know whether any will offer any of the world's major strategic rivals a significant or lasting comparative advantage over others. In the absence of strategic trust, this uncertainty tends to contribute to arms race and further instability. How can the world's major strategic competitors find a way out of this mess?

One fundamental process at work is the increasing speed of modern warfare, driven by the computer microprocessor and the relevant technologies, and which often serve to compress human decision-making time. There is a pressing need to ensure that, where the use of nuclear weapons is concerned, human decision-makers are not simply swept along with the tide in a crisis. Dialogue is needed between policy makers from different governments developing—or thinking of developing—the technologies discussed in this paper to ensure that they understand the implications and can account for differences in how others see these.

This kind of exchange could be part of strategic dialogue oriented toward nuclear weapon risk reduction pathways and measures. Risk reduction frameworks, elements and pathways are already something that research institutes like UNIDIR focus on,[32] and nuclear risk reduction has recently attracted broad support in discussions contexts like the NPT. As part of this, attention should be paid to the implications of new technologies discussed here for nuclear doctrine, strategy, operations, and transparency that goes much further than the periodic exchanges seen among the five NPT nuclear-weapon states although these are welcome.[33] There are a range of ideas for practical measures that could help reduce nuclear risk, including better means of crisis communication not only bilaterally, but in the context of the U. S. -Russia-China and China-India-Pakistan strategic triads.

Nuclear risk reduction measures can help to pave the way toward the development of specific arms control measures, which could capture aspects of the new technologies discussed in this paper and contribute to greater strategic trust. The goal must be to resume progress toward a nuclear-weapon-free world, which the United Nations Secretary-General recently called for in his May 2018 *Agenda for Disarmament*.[34] While this might seem utopian to some, it is more utopian to believe that nuclear deterrence can operate indefinitely without an accident, miscalculation or other situation leading to nuclear use, especially in today's more complex and changing strategic landscape. And it is sometimes forgotten that arms control was born in the 1950s during a nuclear arms race in which new technologies—the hydrogen bomb, inter-continental ballistic missiles, satellites—were being introduced and trust between the two superpowers of the time was low. Arms control has always been a matter of enlightened self-interest, whether for the purposes of "stability" or more durable security conditions: today, as the strategic balance has shifted it also requires initiative and leadership beyond Washington and Moscow. China has an important, constructive role to play.

Footnotes:

1. Dr. John Borrie is Head of Weapons of Mass Destruction and Other Strategic Weapons Programme. The views expressed here are the author's own, and do not necessarily reflect those of UNIDIR, its research funders, or the United Nations. The author thanks Dr. Pavel Podvig, Dr, Ryan Snyder and Daniel Porras and for their critical feedback on a draft of this paper.

2. Lewis A. Dunn, *Reversing the Slide*: *Intensified Great Power Competition*

and the Breakdown of the Arms Control Endeavour, Geneva, UNIDIR, February 2019: <http://unidir. org/files/publications/pdfs/reversing-the-slide-en-755. pdf>.

3. Vladimir Putin, "Presidential Address to the Federal Assembly", 1 March 2018: <http://en. kremlin. ru/events/president/news/56957>.

4. Some of this section is drawn from John Borrie, Amy Dowler and Pavel Podvig, *Hypersonic Weapons: A Challenge and Opportunity for Strategic Arms Control* (A Study Prepared on the Recommendation of the Secretary-General's Advisory Board for Disarmament Matters), New York, United Nations, February 2019: http://unidir. org/files/publications/pdfs/hypersonic - weapons - a - challenge - and-opportunity-for-strategic-arms-control-en-744. pdf.

5. Nikolai N. Sokov, "Modernization of nuclear weapons: How it influences strategic stability", Moscow, PIR Center, 13 December 2018: < https://www. pircenter. org/en/articles/2184-7054883>.

6. Oriana Pawlyk, "U. S. May Ramp Up Buy of the Missile That Just Made Combat Debut in Syria ", *Defense News*, 17 April 2018: < https:// www. military. com/defensetech/2018/04/17/us - may - ramp - buy - missile - just - made-combat-debut-syria. html.

7. As of 2017, the U. S. , France and Russia reported stocks of nuclear-armed cruise missiles. See Christine Parthemore, "The unique risks of nuclear-armed cruise missiles", Chapter 4 in John Borrie, Tim Caughley and Wilfred Wan (eds.), *Understanding Nuclear Weapon Risks*, Geneva, UNIDIR, 2017, p. 45. See also Sokov, *op cit* (2018).

8. Daniel Porras, *Briefing paper for the United Nations Disarmament Commission—Shared risks: An examination of universal space security challenges*, Geneva, UNIDIR, February 2019: < http://unidir. org/files/publications/pdfs/ shared-risks-an-examination-of-universal-space-security-challenges-en-775. pdf>.

9. Treaty on the Prevention of the Placement of Weapons in Outer Space, the Threat or Use of Force against Outer Space Objects (PPWT).

10. Russia has not tested a direct-ascent ASAT but is generally believed to have at least a limited capability. See Brian Weeden and Victoria Samson (eds.), *Global Counterspace Capabilities: An Open Source Assessment*, Washington D. C. , Secure World Foundation, April 2019, p. 2-21.

11. Rajeswari Pillai Rajagopalan,*Electronic and Cyber Warfare in Outer Space* (Space Dossier 3), Geneva, UNDIR, 2019: <http://unidir. org/files/publications/ pdfs/electronic-and-cyber-warfare-in-outer-space-en-784. pdf>.

12. See Weeden and Samson, *op cit* (2019).

13. Daniel Porras,*Towards ASAT Test Guidelines (Space Dossier 2)*, Geneva,

UNIDIR, 2018: http://unidir. org/files/publications/pdfs/-en-703. pdf.

14. Christof Heyns, *Report of the Special Rapporteur on extrajudicial*, *summary or arbitrary executions*, United Nations Document A/68/382, 13 September 2013: < http://justsecurity. org/wp - content/uploads/2013/10/UN - Special-RapporteurExtrajudicial-Christof-Heyns-Report-Drones. pdf>.

15. Christof Heyns, *Report of the Special Rapporteur on extrajudicial*, *summary or arbitrary executions*, United Nations DocumentA/HRC/23/47, 9 April 2013: < https://www. ohchr. org/Documents/HRBodies/HRCouncil/RegularSession/ Session23/A-HRC-23-47_en. pdf>.

16. John Borrie, Elena Finckh and Kerstin Vignard,*Increasing Transparency*, *Oversight and Accountability of Armed Unmanned Aerial Vehicles*, Geneva, UNIDIR, October 2017: < http://unidir. org/files/publications/pdfs/increasing - transparency-oversight-and-accountability-of-armed-unmanned-aerial-vehicles- en-692. pdf>.

17. See UNIDIR's series of briefing papers on these and other questions related to the autonomization of weapon systems: <http://unidir. org/programmes/ security - and - technology/the - weaponization - of - increasingly - autonomous - technologies-phase-iii>.

18. J. Schaus and K. Johnson, *Unmanned Aerial Systems' Influences on Conflict Escalation Dynamics* (CSIS Briefs), 2 August 2018, < https:// www. csis. org/analysis/unmanned-aerial-systems-influences-conflict-escalation- dynamics>.

19. George Woodhams and John Borrie,*Armed UAVs in conflict escalation and inter-State crisis*, Geneva, UNIDIR, 2018,pp. 7-8: <http://unidir. org/files/ publications/pdfs/armed- uav - in - conflict - escalation - and - inter-state - crisis - en - 747. pdf>.

20. Paul Scharre,*Army of None*: *Autonomous Weapons and the Future of War*, New York & London, W. W. Norton, 2018, p. 208.

21. China, Iran, Israel, North Korea, Russia, the UK and U. S. all have active cyber offensive operations capabilities. See David Sanger, *The Perfect Weapon*: *War*, *Sabotage and Fear in the Cyber Age*, Melbourne & London, Scribe, 2018.

22. Gordon Correra, "NHS cyber-attack was ' launched from North Korea' ", *BBC World News*, 16 June 2017: < https://www. bbc. com/news/technology - 40297493>.

23. David E. Sanger and Nicole Pertroth, "U. S. Escalates Online Attacks on Russia's Power Grid",*New York Times*, 15 June 2019: https://www. nytimes. com/

2019/06/15/us/politics/trump-cyber-russia-grid. html.

24. "The United States would only consider the employment of nuclear weapons in extreme circumstances to defend the vital interests of the United States, its allies, and partners. Extreme circumstances could include significant non-nuclear strategic attacks. Significantnon-nuclear strategic attacks include, but are not limited to, attacks on the U. S. , allied, or partner civilian population or infrastructure, and attacks on U. S. or allied nuclear forces, their command and control, or warning and attack assessment capabilities. " See U. S. Department of Defense, 2018 *Nuclear Posture Review*, p. 21: <https://media. defense. gov/2018/ Feb/02/2001872886/-1/-1/1/2018 - NUCLEAR - POSTURE - REVIEW - FINAL - REPORT. PDF>.

25. This section is based on John Borrie, "Cold war lessons for automation in nuclear command and control systems" in Vincent Boulanin (ed.), *The Impact of Artificial Intelligence on Strategic Stability and Nuclear Risk Volume I Euro-Atlantic Perspectives*, Stockholm, SIPRI, May 2019,pp. 41-52: <https://www. sipri. org/sites/ default/files/2019-05/sipri1905-ai-strategic-stability-nuclear-risk. pdf>.

26. Remco Zwetsloot, Helen Toner and Jeffrey Ding, "Beyond the AI arms race: America, China, and the dangers of zero-sum thinking", *Foreign Affairs*, 16 November 2018; and Nick Thompson and Ian Bremmer, "The AI cold war that threatens us all", *Wired*, 23 October 2018.

27. Boulanin, *op cit*, p. xi.

28. Geist and Lohn (note 3).

29. Patricia Lewis et al, *Too Close for Comfort: Cases of Near Nuclear Use and Options for Policy*, London, Chatham House, 2014: <https://www. chathamhouse. org/sites/default/files/field/field _ document/20140428TooCloseforComfortNuclear UseLewisWilliamsPelopidasAghlani. pdf>.

30. Julien Borger, "Nuclear weapons: experts alarmed by new Pentagon 'war-fighting' doctrine", *The Guardian*, 19 June 2019: <https://www. theguardian. com/world/2019/jun/19/nuclear-weapons-pentagon-us-military-doctrine>.

31. Nikolai N. Sokov, "Why Russia calls a limited nuclear strike "de - escalation", *Bulletin of the Atomic Scientists*, 13 March 2014: <https://thebulletin. org/ 2014/03/why-russia-calls-a-limited-nuclear-strike-de-escalation>.

32. See Wilfred Wan, *Nuclear Risk Reduction: The State of Ideas*, Geneva, UNIDIR, April 2019: < http://unidir. org/files/publications/pdfs/nuclear - risk - reduction-the - state - of - ideas - en -767. pdf>; and John Borrie, Tim Caughley and Wilfred Wan (eds.), *Understanding Nuclear Weapon Risks*, Geneva, UNIDIR, 2019: <http://unidir. org/files/publications/pdfs/understanding - nuclear - weapon - risks - en -

676. pdf>.

33. China, France, Russia, the United Kingdom and United States.

34. https://www. un. org/disarmament/sg-agenda/en/.

High-tech Progress and its Impact on Global Strategic Stability

Wu Jun

CPAPD Executive Council Member,
Deputy Director and Research Fellow with the Center of
Strategic Studies, Chinese Academy of Engineering Physics

Currently, the rapid progress of high and new technology represented by artificial intelligence (AI) will have an impact on future war decision-making and warfare. The usage of some technologies and equipments can replace some functions of nuclear weapons in some aspects, and will affect global strategic stability. But in terms of destructive power, it is still the nuclear weapons that can destroy mankind. If AI weapons, cyber weapons and nuclear weapon systems are linked together (disrupting nuclear command systems, attacking nuclear facilities and striking nuclear weapon launching systems, etc.), they will have disastrous consequences for the whole world. Therefore, rules of conduct for cyber weapons and AI weapons must be adopted as soon as possible. Starting with development of AI and cyber weapons, this paper discusses their military applications and their impact on global strategic stability. It is proposed that if AI weapons and cyber weapons are willfully developed for attacking nuclear facilities, it will cause disastrous consequences for the whole world. In order to ensure that nuclear weapons are not used, the nuclear-weapon states should adopt the policy of no-first-use of nuclear weapons as soon as possible to reduce the alert level of nuclear weapons.

I. Current Development of Emerging Science and Technology

With social progress, global integration, especially cooperation of scientists in the field of science and technology, the emerging science and technologies have developed rapidly, brought about many conveniences to human life and created tremendous value, particularly the development of artificial intelligence, cyber network and outer space technology makes our life incomparably convenient.

Meanwhile, their enormous military values have also attracted the attention of various countries in the world. The military application of these new technologies may undermine the global strategic stability, and bring about disastrous consequences to mankind, and should be prevented in advance.

(1) Development of high and new technology represented by AI technology

After the "Deep Blue" chess master in 1997, Master-the 2017 "Alfa Go" upgraded version-defeated many top chess players such as Ke Jie and so on, showing that AI has made significant progress in rapidly processing big data and acquiring useful information. The way of autonomous learning and the application of big data in learning process make the future application of AI technology change subversively. Considering the future development, the storage capacity of computer processors can be almost unlimited. Machines are getting themselves constantly improved through self-learning. Meantime, robots are tireless and respond to the outside world much faster than human. Therefore, in many areas of human life, AI robots to replace human activities will become a trend.

In the field of military security, the use of robots may radically change the future warfare. In the Afghan battlefield, the BigDog robots used by American soldiers help war-fighters implement accompanying support and subvert the battlefield logistics support mode. Unmanned aerial vehicles (UAVs) equipped with artificial intelligence can avoid radar and missile attacks automatically and can attack the key targets and change the warfare through image recognition system.

Battlefield perception means integration with information processing capabilities of the artificial intelligence have great advantages in their use on battlefield. With the help of artificial intelligence, the human reaction time in battlefield is greatly shortened, and more accurate judgment and action can be made, thus gaining the battlefield advantage. It is proved that pilots assisted by artificial intelligence have an overwhelming advantage over pilots without assistance of artificial intelligence in air combat drills.

Self-learning AI can command information comprehensively and can make accurate computing on advantages and disadvantages as well as gains and losses through analysis of the previous battles, can play an important role in battlefield decision-making in the future, and can create subversive changes especially in military planning, logistic support-organizing, battlefield real-time information acquisition, analysis, target image analysis, etc.

The lethal autonomous weapon system is the product of the cross-integration of information system, artificial intelligence, robots, unmanned system and traditional weapon platform technology, and can independently find, locate, identify and strike targets with high intelligence. Currently, with the rapid development of autonomous technology, lethal autonomous weapons and intelligent weapon systems are developing rapidly.

Nowadays, the AI application in military affairs and lethal autonomous weapons are still in the stage of development and evolution, without clear physical form and capability characteristics; different countries have different levels of development and application capabilities, and there are still some deviations in understanding among various countries since they have different development level and application capacity. Therefore, up to now, the international community has not yet reached a clear definition and unanimous understanding of AI weapons and lethal autonomous weapon systems.

(2) The trend of cyberspace becoming battlefield and weaponized accelerates, and the means of cyber attack is used in actual combat

The extensive application of cyberspace brings about infinite convenience to human life and creates tremendous value. Cyberspace is increasingly closely related to national security and strategic interests. According to public data, more than 100 countries have issued cyberspace security-related strategies and policies. More than 40 countries have issued cyberspace-related military plans or established corresponding institutions and military forces, nearly 20 of which have explicitly developed offensive cyber-warfare forces. In June 2016, NATO formally defined cyberspace as a field of operations parallel to land, sea, air and space, and stressed that cyberspace defense should be integrated into the operational planning and operational tasks of the alliance. The battlefield-incubating of cyberspace is becoming increasingly prominent.

In order to safeguard its interests in cyberspace, the United States would ensure its dominant position in cyberspace. Since January 2017, the United States has issued a series of strategic documents on cyber security, highlighting the importance of cyber security in American national security, and the U. S. determination to safeguard its position and absolute advantage in cyberspace.

The U. S. Department of Defense (DoD) in 2016 planned to spend $ 34. 7 billion in five years to enhance cyberspace security, among which $ 14. 3 billion is spent on cyberspace activities, supporting the offensive cyberspace operations and defensive military operations in cyberspace. On February 25, 2016, the U. S. DoD submitted its 2017 budget proposal to the House of Representatives, planning to increase $ 900 million on upgrading the combat capability of cyberspace and achieving the goal of deterring the "most powerful opponent". On March 16, 2017, President Trump released the "America First" federal budget plan for fiscal year

2018, and the defense budget grew by 10% over the previous year, reaching $ 639. 0 billion. The budget significantly increased the portion for responding to the threat of cyber attacks.

The U. S. Cyber Command is upgraded to an independent united Command. The Cyber Task Force has achieved full operational capability, and the cyber space force building and institutional setting are further improved. On May 4, 2018, the U. S. Cyber Command was formally upgraded to an independent joint command at the same level as the Indo-Pacific Command and the European Command, and can report directly to the Secretary of Defense in performing its tasks. On May 17, 2018, officials from the U. S. DoD Cyber Command said that all the 133 cyber task force under the U. S. Cyber Command had full operational capability. The United States frequently organizes various exercises related to cyberspace security, aiming at enhancing the offensive and defensive capabilities of cyber security staff, improving inter - agency collaboration and emergency response capabilities, and training cyber security personnel.

Currently, the cyber network has become a field of intense confrontation among various sides. Cyber attacks occur now and then, especially some cyber attacks against civilian infrastructure, such as virus attack on the Iranian Stuxnet, and it is reported that Russian state grid is planted with virus. All these indicate that the current cyber attack has reached the stage of actual combat employment.

II. The Progress of Emerging Technologies may Shake the Existing Strategic Stability

Artificial intelligence and cyber network technology bring convenience to human life and improve the quality of human livelihood, but its military application is inevitable, which will have an impact on international security. With continuous development of the technology, the deception and destruction of AI systems are difficult to predict and understand, which will bring huge risks to national security and key infrastructure. But from the destruction perspective, AI weapons and cyber weapons are unable to replace nuclear weapons.

Presently, the world is in a period of peace, and opposing war has become the consensus of all countries in the world. With development of artificial intelligence, the rapid progress of artificial intelligence and the application of new materials will greatly reduce the cost of war; meanwhile, the role of human in the battlefield will decline, and the human casualties will also decline. When considering gains and losses, policymakers have less worries, so people's understanding of the warfare will change, which may lower the threshold of war, make violence return and make the world more turbulent.

Nowadays, it is generally believed that human intervention is very important in AI decision-making process, but with the continuous progress of learning AI, the probability of error is very small in most cases. The consequence is that human beings depend more and more on AI, habitually rely on AI for decision-making and voluntarily withdraw from participating in the control of AI robots. This can have serious consequences.

The threshold of AI application is not high, any non-governmental organization or individual may use AI to carry out destructive activities. With the AI progress, these destructive results may be serious.

Artificial intelligence may destroy the existing strategic stability. For example, it is always believed that the mobile missile launcher can improve the survivability of missiles, but artificial intelligence plays a key role in intelligence, monitoring, reconnaissance and analysis systems, making mobile missile launchers vulnerable to pre-emptive strike. The Ballistic Missile Defense Review report of the United States proposes to develop laser-loaded UAVs and strike missiles before launch. This is also a reflection of AI undermining strategic stability.

People can't separate from the cyber network in their daily life. The damages to the national economy caused by cyber attacks may be no less than a large-scale war. The destructive effect of cyber attacks on national economy has been verified. Some media reported that the United States implanted viruses in Russia's power grid, trying to control Russia's power grid at a critical moment. If implemented, serious consequences may arise. Especially if the cyber attacks against a nuclear command system affects command and decision-making system, the consequences will be unthinkable.

III. Making AI and Cyberspace Code of Conduct is currently the Important Work

In May 2016, the G-7 summit released the G-7 Principles and Actions on Cyber, which advocates strengthening cyber security cooperation among member states, jointly protects key-infrastructure, encourages more countries to join the *Budapest Convention on Cybercrime*, collectively cracks down on cyber crime, supports the application of existing international law to cyberspace, and formulates stable strategic framework for international cyberspace.

Cyberspace arms control has begun becoming an important means for major countries in the world to maintain their own security and promote their security and diplomatic strategies. International exchange platforms have begun to address many related issues. Governments, experts and scholars of various countries have made more and more in-depth research on the issue of cyberspace arms control, and have begun to formulate more specific cyberspace-related arms control measures. It is very important to formulate AI code of conduct. The international community should make joint efforts to guide AI developing in the direction of benefiting human beings. Nuclear-weapon states should keep AI far away from any area related to nuclear war.

From a technical point of view, no weapon can replace nuclear weapons at present. Nuclear weapons remain an important force in maintaining global strategic stability. The rapid development of AI technology and cyberspace technology make the existing nuclear weapon systems vulnerable, and may upset the existing strategic balance, thus resulting in serious consequences. In order to prevent AI from playing a destructive role, nuclear-weapon states should minimize the role of nuclear weapons, pursue the policy of no-first-use of nuclear weapons, and ensure that there will be no nuclear war in the future.

In short, the development of newly emerging technology brings convenience to human life, but also many uncertainties to the world. Just as President Xi Jinping points out, "the new generation of AI is booming all over the world, injecting new energy into the economic and social development, and is changing people's way of life. Commanding well this development opportunity and dealing well with the new issues raised by AI from the perspectives of law, security, employment, ethics and government governance require deepening cooperation and joint discussion among various countries". This is also a major problem facing the newly emerging technologies represented by artificial intelligence, so various countries in the world should cooperate closely to collectively create a community with a shared future for mankind conducive to human happiness and welfare.

New Technologies and Global Security

Ulf Sandmark

Economist, President of Schiller Institute in Sweden

Presently, the existing world order is disintegrating, and international law is being increasingly disrespected. The sovereignty principle that the U. N. Charter establishes should be the basic principle for the contemporary international relations, and sovereignty of its member states should be respected no matter how big or small it is. In fact, the principle stipulates not only a "passive" peace of non-interference in each other's internal affairs, but also an "active" peace policy of promoting "the benefit of the others". This active concept of promoting peace can be found in the Chinese policy of promoting a New Paradigm of "win-win" cooperation.

In today's world, we see many negative examples. The so-called war on terror has become an excuse for transcending any border with drones, special forces, intelligence agencies and military interventions. Instead of promoting the benefit of peace to others, today the pseudo-science of geopolitics has been re-launched to actively promote destabilizations of other nations. Sorry to say that, supporting this form of "armed struggle" for the purpose of regime change in Syria with humanitarian aid, the Swedish government, as other Western governments, refuses to acknowledge that its proxy war is lost and refuse to normalize relations with Syria, thus prolonging the war with its disastrous humanitarian consequences. The geopolitical doctrine and its promoters in the United Kingdom and United States are based on control of the Eurasian HEARTLAND by isolating it from the surrounding Eurasian RIMLAND, which is in contact with the seas. The Western policy of disregarding the basic rules of international law has led to a breakdown of the international order, has also triggered trade wars, extreme tensions and war danger between the great powers. As President Putin warned that the U. S. -Russian relations were "deteriorating by the hour".

While the great powers-led outdated security concept is unable to respond to the new security situation, it is indispensible to readjust their security concept, or the security will be in disorder. To establish a New Paradigm of understanding and cooperation among nations, we need to address the urgent problems of mankind from a higher standpoint, for example the threats like poverty, food, health service, education, housing, water and electricity or nuclear extinction. With this perspective, it is possible to bring in the New and Emerging Technologies to find an efficient way forward towards global security.

Actually, mankind is not only hostage to the threat of extinction with nuclear weapons, but is also exposed to dangers from space in the form of asteroids or various forms of comets, solar flares, cosmic radiation, galactic weather, etc. The Department of Celestial Mechanics at St. Petersburg State University recently reported that the 370 meter wide asteroid Apophis will make several near-Earth passes, in 2029, 2036, and 2068, with the 2029 pass to be only 1/10th the distance from the Earth to the Moon! There are serious discussions of a cooperation mission to attempt diversion of the pass of asteroid Apophis between Russia and the United States.

Space science is very important. To certain extent, the elevation into space has also an elevating effect of the minds of people absorbing the minds into science, which transcends all cultural barriers uniting mankind. The space exploration is not simply an end in itself, but the incorporation of man into the Universe would be a concrete expression of his creative potential, as well as a new means to radically accelerate creative growth. The space partnership established between China and Pakistan is an exemplary way to use emerging technologies to forge long term cooperation in a new paradigm of relations among mankind. The participation in the Chinese Change 4 landing on the backside of the moon by German and Swedish scientists bear witness of the role of science to transcend political conflict and pave the way for human communication when brought to the highest conceptual level of science and creativity, and is viewed as a new symbolic cooperation between Europe and China.

In a vision of the future, we can accomplish a world with energy and raw materials security for all of humanity. The successful exploration of Helium-3 will make production of nuclear fusion energy possible. Nuclear fusion power will also give mankind the better conditions for space science, precision medicines, and celestial body research with constant acceleration. This emerging technology will radically change the availability of raw materials. Nuclear fusion energy is almost limitless energy source, and will make it possible to mine any rock in the world for minerals or even the salt of the sea water. It will for good refute the theory of the zero-sum game of geopolitics. The economic productivity per square kilometer of existing territories will see dramatic increases, making conquests and war even more "unprofitable". China is taking real actions to explore and employ nuclear fusion energy.

The development of world connectivity with the Belt & Road Initiative (BRI), launched by President Xi Jinping in 2013, is also an advanced concept. The concept of the BRI is committed to developing a worldwide network of different kinds of infrastructure, is creating a new productive economic platform and is not the primitive policy of geopolitics which divides the world into isolated economic enclaves. The more advanced economic platform of the BRI makes it possible for the world economy to reach a higher level of productivity, which makes investments generally more profitable and secure. The Belt & Road Initiative is beneficial to promote internationalized application of the new emerging technology, to establish a more secure economic and financial system, to advance the building of a community with a shared future for mankind and to build a better future for humankind.

Militarization of Artificial Intelligence and Its Security, Ethics and Legal Challenges

Zhu Qichao

Director and Professor, Center for National Security and Strategic Studies,
College of Advanced Interdisciplinary Studies,
National University of Defense Technology,
Research Fellow with the Think Tank for Defense
Technology and Strategic Studies

In recent years, with the rapid growth of big data, the remarkable improvement of computing power and the progress of deep learning algorithm, artificial intelligence (AI) has built the third wave of development after two ups and downs, which is deeply impacting the political, economic, military, social, cultural and other fields of various countries. Various countries in the world, especially the major military powers, are accelerating the military application of artificial intelligence. Thus, the nature and form of war are undergoing profound changes. As a new subversive technology, what kind of prospect will AI bring to the future war? How will a new round of military change be promoted? What challenges and worries will the AI military application bring? This paper tries to make a preliminary exploration on these issues.

I. The Historic Evolution of Warfare Driven by Artificial Intelligence

War is a special activity of human society. It refers to the organized and planned use of force to carry out intense military confrontation for certain political and economic purposes. It is the highest form of struggle to solve contradictions and conflicts among classes, nationalities, political groups and countries. It is the continuation of politics through violent means. Carl Clausewitz pointed out that war is the continuation of political interaction through another means. The form of War refers to manifestation of the external form of war or external manifestation of the inevitable connection of its internal essence. It is determined by the economic situation, political nature and military development level of the period. The change of technological form influences the change of military form and promotes the transformation of war form. In other words, the breakthrough and application of the symbolic (subversive) technology of an era promotes the fundamental change of the structure and function of military system, i. e. qualitative change in the main carrier of operation, tools of operation, space of operation, mode of operation, establishment of military system, military theory, etc. Only in this way can the qualitative leap of military system be promoted and the form of war be transformed accordingly. In this way, the basic elements of the form of war include the main body of war, the tools of war (weapons and equipment), the space of war (battlefield), the style of war (war fighting), the theory of war, the configuration of armed forces and other specific aspects. The transformation of the form of war means that some or all of these elements have undergone significant changes, which promotes the war to jump to another form.

Throughout history, major technological breakthroughs and applications have often brought revolutionary changes to war. Since ancient times, there are roughly four major military revolutions in human society. The first military revolution is a metallized military revolution in which metal weapons such as bronze and iron replaced the stone aged weapons such as stone, sticks weapons; the second military revolution is a gunpowder military revolution in which hot weapons replaced cold weapons; the third military revolution is a mechanized military revolution brought about by the emergence and popularization of mechanized equipments; and the fourth military revolution is a informationized military revolution in which information technology innovation led the advancement of information-based weapons and equipments into the battlefield. Between the third and fourth revolutions, there is also a military revolution marked by nuclear weapons. It is easy to see that the triggering of these four military revolutions is inseparable from the emergence and development of disruptive technology in that era. From smelting technology to propellant technology, mechanization technology, atomic energy technology and information technology, the four military revolutions are affected by the core role of technological revolution. In line with the four military revolutions, human society has gone through four major forms of warfare: cold weapon warfare, hot weapon warfare, mechanized warfare and informationized warfare. From the appearance of the formal war of mankind to the beginning of the 19th century, it belonged to the era of cold weapons war. During this period, the dominant weapons and equipments were cold weapons such as knives, axes, rods, spears, bows, crossbows and others. The main way of releasing energy from weapons and equipment was to transform physical energy into mechanical energy, which mainly tested the physical ability of combatants. In the era of thermal weapons war, the dominant weapon equipments are gun and artillery based on gunpowder. The main way of weapon destruction is to convert thermal energy into chemical energy, which mainly tests the skills of combatants. The era of mechanized warfare is roughly from the beginning of the 20th century to the middle of the 20th century. During this period, aircraft, tanks and other mechanized weapons and equipment platforms began to mount the stage of warfare. The main way of energy release is the conversion of chemical energy into mechanical energy. Since the middle of the 20th century, informationized weapons such as precision-guided weapons have stepped onto the stage of history, and human society has gradually entered the stage of information warfare.

Currently, mankind is still in the era of information warfare. Meantime, with the rapid development of AI technology, and the emergence of concepts and weapons related to military AI, countries are actively adjusting the existing military theory and institutional configuration, and the trend of the transformation of warfare to military AI is becoming more and more obvious. The main carrier of war will change from the original military organization, state and national alliance composed of humans to the military organization, non-military organization, non-state organization and robotic force composed of humans; the form of military revolution will change from metallization, gunpowder, mechanization to informationization, intelligence and unmannedness; the dominant factors of war game will transform from the original material and energy to information and intelligence; warfare style will change from cold weapon killing to robotic warfare, cyber-centric warfare, algorithm warfare, cognitive warfare, etc., with the characteristics of hybrid warfare becoming richer; confrontation mode will change from weapon confrontation and platform confrontation to system confrontation and man-machine combined confrontation; battlefield space will further expand from physical space such as land, sea and air to space, cyber, electromagnetism, biology, cognition and other fields, with cross-domain operations becoming normal. The branches of traditional forces will continuously be reinforced by the new branches such as cyber forces, space forces and robotic forces.

II. Artificial Intelligence Promotes a New Round of Military Reform

It is generally believed that when new military technologies, weapons and equipments, operational concepts and organizational configurations interact to significantly enhance military operational capabilities, new military changes will be promoted. AI is more and more widely used in the military field, is becoming important pusher of military reform, has promoted the emergence of new war patterns and changed the internal mechanism of victory in war. On the one hand, the AI employment will probably shape subversive military capabilities, which will lead to a doubling or a substantial leap of combat effectiveness. On the other hand, it will also bring new challenges to the innovation of military theory and the practice of military capabilities.

(1) Impact on the traditional concept of war

The history of human warfare has gone through the cold, hot, mechanized and information age. AI has accelerated the arrival of the era of intelligence. For military capacity building, if mechanization is the foundation and informationization is the nerve and blood, intelligence embodies the ultimate confrontation between human intelligence. Can intelligence be divided into high-tier intelligence and low-tier intelligence? Does the army with high-level intelligence have an overwhelming advantage over the army with low-level intelligence? If combat effectiveness is the man, weapon and combination of man and weapon, then, how to define the relationship between man, robot and intelligent information system in the era of intelligent warfare? If the "mechanization" of human beings and the "humanization" of machines are two inevitable trends of development, would it be contrary to the traditional war ethics that thinkable robots replace human beings to fight? AI makes the battlefield perception and information processing capabilities unprecedentedly improved. Does the "dense fog" of war still exist in the high-tech battlefield? Understanding these issues requires a brainstorming concept renewal in the military field.

(2) Making weapons and equipments and command decision-making intelligent

On the one hand, AI as an enabling technology will be embedded in the traditional weapon system to enhance its intelligence and combat effectiveness. On the other hand, AI will also give birth to new weapons and equipments, such as highly autonomous unmanned aerial vehicles, unmanned vehicles, unmanned submarines and other new unmanned combat platforms, and " unmanned bee colony" and bionic robots. In the field of intelligent command and control, military forces of various countries develop diversified military information systems in order to build a powerful grid of cyber information system and improve the ability of intelligent evaluation and auxiliary decision-making. In recent years, the U. S. military has established and upgraded the Cyber Command, and vigorously strengthened the building of cyber attack and defense capabilities, focus on intelligent diagnostic information system for cyber intrusion based on the research and development of cloud computing, big data analysis and other technologies, which can automatically diagnose the source of cyber intrusion, the degree of attacker's cyber damage and data recovery capability. In addition, the U. S. military is promoting the employment of AI in defense intelligence analysis, assisting the Department of Defense and other military levels in war decision making, and improving the scientific, effective and reliable nature of intelligence analysis and decision-making. On April 26, 2017, Robert Walker, deputy Secretary of Defense, signed the memorandum and authorized the establishment of the "algorithm war cross functional group", aiming to "rapidly transform the massive data of the DoD into usable information, effectively promoting the application of AI, big data, machine learning and other technologies in the field of military intelligence". It is not difficult to predict that AI will gradually enter the key fields of war design, strategic policy and operational command, etc. The human-robot integration mode will become the basic form of command and decision-making in the future.

(3) Promoting the innovation of military theory

The constant updating of the material and technological basis of war and the continuous evolution of the form and style of war naturally open up a new space for the innovation of strategic theory and concept of war. For example, with the vigorous development of information technology, its role of its catalyst, adhesives and efficiency multiplier has become increasingly prominent, which has led to the continuous emergence of new disruptive technologies in the field of AI. On the other hand, it has also made it possible for those who are in the technological advantage to provide "strategic guidance" and "technical deception" to imitate followers; the combined application of precision ammunition, unmanned equipments and cyber information system has led to the emergence of new intelligent warfare theories such as "distributed killing", "mother ship theory", "battle cloud" and "bee colony tactics". Depending on the information superiority and decision-making superiority of one's own, how to cut off and delay the opponent's information and decision-making loop in the decentralized battlefield network has become the core problem to be solved in order to win an intelligent war. It can be predicted that "unmanned cluster warfare" and "man-machine cooperation warfare" may become the mainstream warfare mode in the future. The distributed operational unmanned trunking system has the capability of "observation and combat integration", such as reconnaissance and surveillance and autonomous attack, has high cost performance and can be recovered. It has great advantages in saturation attacking on the enemy. The U. S. military is stepping up the research of "unmanned bee colony" represented by "elves" and other projects to verify and evaluate the feasibility of low-cost unmanned systems clustering technology. In addition, man-machine cooperation operations are increasingly favored by various countries' armed forces, and the "warrior" explosive ordnance robot which cooperates with soldiers has demonstrated its strength in the battlefields of Afghanistan and Iraq.

(4) Renewing the means of military education and training

The AI wide application in the military field will lead to new changes in the military education and training. Weapons, equipments and systems that win in battlefields are becoming more and more intelligent, and are more and more closely connected with scientists, advanced technology laboratories and battle laboratories. So the situation that scientists design war, military strategists command war, and AI wins war will come. Traditional education and training subjects will be further compressed. Intelligent training platform in the forms of game-play, experiential virtual reality and augmented reality technology will provide new means for military training. Knowledge exploring and data exploring process supported by super-large-scale computing, cloud computing and big data technology are themselves important parts of ability building. The development of AI technology will also provide new means for the evaluation of military personnel's physical skills, physiological functions, psychological effects and other levels of education and training. On June 18, 2018, the National Defense Authorization Act for fiscal year 2019, which was formally passed by the U. S. Congress, specially set up a section entitled "bringing advanced technology into vocational military education", which stressed the need to strengthen the application of advanced technologies such as AI in vocational military education, and requested the Secretary of Defense to report to Congress before December 1, 2018 the feasible plan of embedding AI technology into vocational military education projects, concretely including the establishment of appropriate vocational military educational institutions, and expansion of enrollment by vocational military education institutions in private sectors.

III. Security, Ethics and Legal Concerns of AI Militarization

The AI is accelerating its penetration into the military field, which not only brings tremendous opportunities for military change, but also contains many risks, generally speaking, in the following aspects.

(1) Security Concerns

An AI arms race and strategic instability. "Strategic stability" means that when potential opponents realize that conflict with each other is difficult to gain, the two sides will not act rashly, resulting in strategic stability. According to the theory of Offensive-Defensive balance, the strategic stability will be strengthened when the defensive is dominant, while the strategic stability will be weakened when the offensive is dominant. The emergence and employment of lethal AI weapons will have a great negative impact on strategic stability and threaten regional and international security. Specifically, AI weapons may enhance the dominance of offensive side and have a series of serious consequences, including preemptive strike to be the best means to gain strategic advantages, the best defensive strategy being to launch preemptive strike, which will lower the threshold of the use of force among countries and increase the possibility of an arms race. In addition, the use of AI weapons will pose a huge problem to the accountability of users, which will easily lead to strategic misjudgment and destroy strategic stability. Furthermore, the asymmetric nature of armed conflicts between countries will be magnified by the AI weapons going to the battlefield. The gap between countries with advanced technology and the ability to develop, procure and deploy AI weapons and those without these capabilities is likely to continue to magnify the asymmetric nature of armed conflicts in the future. Besides, the strategic stability of major powers is largely based on the nuclear deterrence of "mutually assured destruction", i. e. both sides have the capability to deter the counterpart's pre-emptive second nuclear strike. However, the rapid development of sensor technology at present may make the retaliatory weapons such as submarines and mobile missile systems easier to be detected, located and destroyed, and increase the vulnerability of the secondary strike ability, thus eroding foundation of the nuclear deterrence system. According to reports, the US DoD is funding a mobile missile launch platform aimed at using AI to help identify and predict the launch of nuclear missiles, as well as tracking and targeting the DPRK and other countries. If true, it will undoubtedly greatly undermine strategic stability. According to a report by RAND Corporation, AI may trigger a large nuclear war before 2040.

The risks of proliferation and malicious use of AI weapons and equipments. AI is a neutral technology, but users are not neutral, so there is a risk of malicious use. This wave of AI mostly appears in the private sector. AI technology itself has obvious dual-use and proliferation, and AI software can be replicated and disseminated at almost zero cost, which also reduces the threshold and difficulty for users to acquire such technology. As long as one has enough funds, it can effectively improve the cyber attack ability without requiring too high technical capability. The advantages of AI technology, weapons and equipments have great attraction for non-state actors such as terrorist organizations and transnational criminal groups, can multiply the strength of force, effectively reduce the cost of attack, save their own combatants and make them more capable of launching terrorist attacks. For example, there are already technologies for developing unmanned aerial vehicles to transport explosives. Once such technologies fall into the hands of terrorists, they will provide new means and methods for the lone wolf terrorist attacks, making it more difficult to prevent and trace accountability. Therefore, the development of AI weapons may aggravate the threat of terrorism and worsen global or regional instability. In addition, research shows that AI technology can be used not only to collect and analyze data, but also to produce false information including automatically generated images, videos and texts. It is not difficult to predict that the AI capacity to produce false information such as "false news" and "false intelligence" will be used maliciously, which will surely cast another layer of "dense fog" on the war, and make it more difficult to distinguish the true and false information in the future battlefield.

AI limitations. Although AI technology has many advantages, it also has many limitations, which can be divided into internal and external limitations. There are three main internal limitations: one is "narrowness". The current AI technology basically belongs to the category of "weak AI" or "narrow AI". Although it can show great superiority over human beings in systems with definite rules and complete information, it still needs human intelligence such as rational analysis ability, flexible response ability and moral identifying ability when solving war problems beyond programming. In this respect, AI is unable to replace and surpass human intelligence. In other words, current AI technologies and systems lack the ability to understand generalized context, lack human knowledge and flexibility, which is also a "Moravec's Paradox". The second is "vulnerability". This means that once the real world environment changes, AI systems may fail or even disrupt, from "super smart" to "super stupid". If such AI systems are used in highly changing military battlefields, once confusion occurs and operators fail to stop it timely, catastrophic consequences may be generated. For example, the launched missiles by the automatic missile early warning system with false warning may lead to accidental injury or even escalation of the crisis. Third, it is difficult to explain and predict. Unlike traditional information technology, AI technology has high complexity, and may easily bring about uncertainty and unpredictability. Concretely, AI has inherent defects of "black-box algorithm". Its mechanism is difficult to be fully understood by human beings who involve in, deploy and operate such machines, and the results are more difficult to be predicted and guaranteed. In addition, when different schemes and configurations of systems or the interaction between systems and codes is too fast, such risks may be aggravated, and system failures caused by system self-interaction are difficult to eliminate. On the other hand, the external limitations mainly come from human-computer interaction errors, cyber network attacks (such as encountering disastrous consequences of enemy hacker attacks, virus data injection, etc.). AI weapons and equipments need to rely on computer software and systems to operate, and software and systems are easily attacked by enemy network hackers, resulting in the risk of losing or even changing side on the battlefield.

(2) Ethical Concerns

In 1942, Asimov, the famous American-Russian writer, in his book "Amazing Science Fiction" first proposed the ethical problem of robots, and set the "three laws for robots" in order to constrain the behavior of machines and make them comply with the mandatory ethics of protecting human beings. Nowadays, the AI rapid development increasingly upgrades the autonomy of robots and gradually moves to battlefield, which also poses a significant challenge to traditional war ethics.

The increasingly autonomous weapons and equipments will impact the traditional man-machine relationship. The relationship between man and technology-supported weapons and equipments constantly evolves in history. For a long time since the emergence of human social warfare, no matter how weapons and equipments get developed, they after all are only tools in the hands of human beings, but only differ in lethality, complexity and precision. In other words, during this period, human beings are always the absolute controllers of weapons and equipments. Weapons and equipments are only the extension and expansion of human physical strength and intelligence, and do not pose a direct challenge to human beings as a whole. Nowadays, the rapid development of AI technology may make weapons equipments more and more autonomous. In the long run, if war robots develop self-consciousness and have the judgment and decision-making ability similar to or even beyond human beings, and changing from technical substitution to decision-making substitution, will pose a subjective threat to the survival of mankind as a whole, seriously impacting the traditional ethics and morality of human beings and human dignity. In the near future, if it is technically feasible, should the "decision-making power of life and death" be transferred to inanimate machines so that they can launch attacks independently on the battlefield to determine human life and death? This problem will pose a serious challenge to the Asimov Law of "no harm to human". Should human ethics be implanted into increasingly intelligent machines? What kind of ethical norms should be implanted and how to implant them? Should the development of lethal autonomous weapons be restrained? These problems will become the difficult matters that AI has to face when it gets to military employment.

Intelligent weaponry challenges traditional war ethics . With the trend of AI weapons moving towards battlefield, the traditional war ethics such as the justice of launching a war, the justice of fighting a war, and the justice of ending a war will be seriously challenged. Concretely, in terms of war justice, more and more non-state actors can also acquire cheap and easy-to-spread AI weapons and equipments. Once they launch an attack on a state actor, the elements of legitimate authority and legitimate reasons will be impacted. In addition, with more and more AI-supported unmanned weapons and equipments going to battlefield, the casualties concerns of the national war options are weakened, and the threshold of war may be significantly lowered, and small-scale wars dominated by unmanned combat platforms are more likely to break out. In terms of warfare justice, it is difficult for the current AI weapons to distinguish between military troops and civilians, military facilities and civilian facilities. Once put into use in a battlefield, it may cause large-scale accidental killings and injuries, resulting in innocent civilian casualties. What's more, if the lethal autonomous weapons without human supervision going to battlefield, because of its high degree of autonomy, lethality and emotionless, they will have no sense of guilt and compassion for killing living beings, which will seriously impact the bottom line of human ethics and morality. In the aspect of ending-war justice, the military application of AI weapons and equipments may cause the predicament to decide the subject of war responsibility. In the past wars, only human beings are the only legitimate subjects and responsibility bearers. But with the increasing autonomy of battlefield robots and intelligent systems, can robots become moral subjects and responsibility subjects and shoulder unjust and illegitimate responsibilities in war operations? This problem will become increasingly highlighted.

(3) Legal Concerns

In addition to security and ethical concerns, the AI militarization has also brought many legal problems.

War accountability. The development and employment of AI weapons and equipments may lead to a "blank accountability" problem, the main reason of which is that the attribution of responsibility will become more and more difficult. For the misconduct caused by an AI weapon systems, especially UAVs operations, the accountability investigation and allocation may involve many levels such as state actors, individuals and weapon systems, covering the whole process of system R&D, producing, arming and employing. Therefore, the event-related operator, manufacturer, programmer, purchaser, arms dealer, military commander, equipment support personnel and even the weapon system itself are to blame, and the difficulty of tracing and distributing responsibility will be greatly enhanced. How to allocate relevant responsibilities? Should we trace the legal liability of robot crime? How can weapon systems feel punished and deterred without life and self-awareness? What is the legal and practical value of tracing its responsibilities? These problems remain unresolved. In the future, the two trends of "mechanized man" and "humanized machinery" will become more and more obvious, by then, the allocation of war responsibilities may face greater difficulties.

The core principles of international humanitarian law will face profound challenges. Under the background that AI is moving towards battlefield increasingly, the core principles of international armed conflict law, such as the principle of necessity, the principle of distinction, the principle of proportionality and the principle of humanity, will be challenged severely, facing the problem of how to apply and adjust them. Concretely, the principle of necessity means that the necessary operational actions taken in order to make the enemy yield are justified, but obviously unnecessary military actions are prohibited. The principle of proportionality means that when attacking military targets, incidental or collateral damage to civilians and civilian objects should be minimized. The collateral damages caused in military operations should not exceed the damages produced in order to achieve the expected direct and specific military advantages. The principle of distinction refers to the distinction between combatants and civilians and the protection of victims in armed conflicts. The principle of humanity means that all human beings involved should be treated humanely. Currently, robots in battlefield are still unable to effectively distinguish between combatants and civilians, and indiscriminate killing of innocents will pose a major challenge to the principles of distinction and humanity once used in battlefield. The collateral damage caused by the use of robots in battlefield will challenge the principles of proportionality and humanity. The overflow of UAVs impact the necessary principles by lowering the threshold of war. Currently international law is undoubtedly human-centered, but can robots become legal subject? Is the existing law of international armed conflict sufficient to regulate the increasingly autonomous AI weapons at present and in the future? Is there a need to amend or enact new international humanitarian law? How to make it? These matters need further study and discussion.

An objective view of the security, ethical and legal challenges that may arise from the AI militarization is the premise for us to understand, develop, manage and control AI. The characteristics of AI itself have brought difficulties and even obstacles to people's understanding of AI. An objective view of the security, ethical and legal challenges that may be generated by the AI militarization is first of all necessary to establish correct conception.

Firstly, upholding a scientific attitude. The security challenges brought by AI may come from immature technology, or from the negligence of human management and control, so it is necessary to conduct a practical and realistic analysis with a scientific attitude. Generally speaking, the security problems caused by AI can be divided into three levels: firstly, the security risks in the management of proper operation rules within an industrial sector, an aspect or a system; secondly, the security challenges at the national security level to the fields of politics, economy, finance, science and technology, national defense; thirdly, challenges caused by the transnational use of AI technology such as the cyber security, space security, nuclear security, counter-terrorism operations and even international security governance. The security challenges brought by AI at different levels have different characteristics and should be responded accordingly, which need to be treated differently rather than put in one basket.

Secondly, adhering to the attitude of development. In overview, the security challenges brought by AI are still in a controllable range. People are worried about the future development of AI mainly because AI as a technology may trigger more security problems. Historically, at the beginning of each industrial revolution or technological revolution, people are panicked to a certain extent because of the relative lack of knowledge and practical experience of the technology. For example, in the early days of the first industrial revolution, workshop workers boycotted and destroyed machines, and in the early days of the second industrial revolution, people panicked about the casualties caused by improper use of electricity. As a product of the evolving human civilization, we need to look at the positive role of AI and its security challenges from the perspective of development, bring the potential of AI into full play for the welfare of mankind, and manage and control the security crisis that AI may cause in advance. The more people can objectively view the security challenges brought by AI, the more they can explore the blue sea of AI security technology and security industrial innovation.

Thirdly, sticking to the attitude of cooperation. AI technology is closely related to the development of information technology, and technological breakthroughs in mobile broadband communication, big data, cloud computing, Internet of logistics and other fields will promote the maturity of AI-related technologies and industries. From the technical perspective, AI technology is similar to information technology, which has the characteristics of low cost, easy diffusion and difficult control, but once this technology matures, the marginal cost of the market will be greatly reduced, even considered as a technology of "zero marginal cost". This makes the security problems that may be caused by AI easy to spread and difficult to control. For example, if there is a failure of supervision, a hacker may use new AI algorithms and intrusion technique to disrupt normal operation of a country's power grid, public transport control network and so on, causing large-scale catastrophic consequences, and even harming innocent people. In theory, the higher the level of information society and intelligence, the more the dependence on the technology system will be. Once the original technology system is impacted, new uncertainties and vulnerabilities will arise. In the rapid development era of information technology and AI technology, the security challenges we are facing are characterized by technical complexity and system vulnerability. Because of this, we must adhere to the attitude of openness and cooperation. Government departments, social sectors and individual citizens should work together to strengthen the technological cognition and practice experience of AI, and jointly respond to the security challenges which AI may bring. Those who would act alone will get more and more delinked with the era.

In short, regarding the wave of AI militarization, we can not just see its benefits to blindly praise it, or hesitate to move forward because of its potential security, ethical and legal challenges. We should objectively understand the development and application of AI. If misunderstanding, misjudgment and misuse of AI-related security matters can be constantly avoided in future practice, human kind can still command its own destiny.

Brazil and the Debate About Technological Issues in International Security: An overview

Monique Sochaczewski Goldfeld and Gabriel Torres [1]

Brazilian Center for International Relations

CEBRI (Brazilian Center for International Relations) is the top think tank in international security issues in Latin America[2] with the research activities related to international system operation and its concerns. The major activity linking CEBRI to international security, though, is the annual organization of the "Forte de Copacabana" International Security Conference, in partnership with the Konrad Adenauer Foundation's Office in Brazil and with support from the Delegation of the European Union to Brazil[3].

I. Brazilian

The popularly known "Forte Conference" has been organized annually since 2004, in the city of Rio de Janeiro, usually during September, and traditionally featuring opening remarks from the Brazilian Minister of Defense. Its main purpose is to debate, envision and disseminate actions and strategies for international security from the standpoint of Europe and South America. The Conference aims to combine analyses from diplomats, militaries, academics, public officials and even politicians on the challenges of global geopolitics, highlighting the specificities, challenges and possibilities for both regions.

The "Forte Conference" also represents an important event for undergraduate

---

[1] Monique Sochaczewski holds a PhD in History, Politics and Cultural Assets from the Getulio Vargas Foundation and is Academic and Project Coordinator at the Brazilian Center for International Relations (CEBRI). Gabriel Torres is a student of the Professional Masters in International Policy Analysis and Management at PUC-Rio and Project Analyst at CEBRI.

[2] See: University of Pennsylvania. 2018 Global Go Think Tanks, p. 110. Pennsylvania, 2019.

[3] The Conference was initially conceived as a partnership between CEBRI, KAS, Sciences Po's Mercosur Chair and the Center for American Studies of the Candido Mendes University. Since 2010, however, it is organized by CEBRI, KAS and the Delegation of the European Union to Brazil.

and graduate students of international relations and correlated fields, which usually comprise most of the audience. The Conference also plays a key role in expanding and consolidating the field of security and defense in Brazil, having evolved in parallel to the creation of several institutions and programs connected to the subject. The Brazilian Association of Defense Studies (ABED), for example, was born in 2005.

The Forte de Copacabana Conference, ABED and the above-mentioned academic programs are part of a recent growing effort towards broadening the debate on security and defense matters beyond the military realm, including as much as possible civil society sectors. It also largely involves representatives of Brazilian media, with an important role in forming public opinion on the themes addressed.

The topics that have guided the first editions of the Forte de Copacabana Conference mainly addressed public policies for international security and possibilities for regional cooperation. Throughout the years, topics discussed ranged from the international security effects of U. S. elections to issues connected to peace-building operations and the role of multilateralism, considerations and specificities of Brazil in these discussions. In recent years, the debate on technological issues in international security has gained momentum.

II. Technological Security Issues

First, it is worth mentioning that the activities of the "Forte Conference" also comprise two preparatory meetings, a closed roundtable and an open seminar, in addition to publications gathering articles by speakers and non-speakers on the topics discussed. The major event occurs in September, but the discussions around the selected topics of each edition are conducted throughout the year. The organizing institutions in February of each year jointly decide the themes.

It is noteworthy that Brazil ranks as the fourth country in the world with the highest number of internet users, according to a 2017 report by the United Nations Conference on Trade and Development (UNCTAD). With around 120 million people with access to internet connection, Brazil only lags behind the United States, India and China. It is also one of the countries with the highest number of social networks users, considering that Brazilians compose the second largest group of Facebook users. However, in 2017, Brazil only ranked 38th in "The Global Cybersecurity Index (GCI)" of the International Telecommunications Union, the UN.

As mentioned above, a significant share of Brazil's existing technical operations for cyber security is headed by the military, such as the Ministry of Defense's Cyber Defense Center (*Centro de DefesaCibernética do Ministério da Defesa*) and the Institutional Security Cabinet of the Presidency (*Gabinete de SegurançaInstitucional da Presidência da República*). In the civilian realm, these topics have also attracted the attention of other think tanks such as the Institute for Technology & Society in Rio de Janeiro (Instituto de Tecnologia e Sociedade do Rio-ITS Rio), the Igarapé Institute and the Institute for International Relations and Foreign Trade (*Instituto de RelaçõesInternacionais e Comércio Exterior*-IRICE) in their events and press notes. [1].

Since 2017, these topics finally became present at the Forte de Copacabana International Security Conference and its preparatory meetings,and during the 14th conference edition, the main topic was "*Security Architecture: An Exchange between South America and Europe*". The Conference's discussions addressed challenges to the concept of "security architecture" within a global order in transition-encompassing challenges associated to cyber security, which gave title to the Conference's first panel: "Security Architecture and Cyber Threats". The panel discussed the progress and limitations of national and regional strategies to manage cyber threats, highlighting the fundamental dilemma between data protection and respect to privacy in this process.

In 2018, the overall theme of the "Forte Conference" was "International Crisis Management", focusing on the management of the current migrant and environmental crises. However, the Conference's first preparatory meeting, which took place in Brasilia, in April 5, focused on technological issues. It gathered representatives from the public and private sectors, academia and civil society. The official title was "Cyber security and national interest during campaign period" and the debate revolved around the influence of *fake news* and *bots* on public opinion during elections, with special attention to the role to be played by government, the press and civil society. Attention was also given to foreign actors' interference and their impact on the credibility of election results, as well as to strategies adopted to prevent, deter and retaliate cyber-attacks.

Such discussions led to the elaboration of a policy paper titled "Cybersecurity and National Interest during Campaign Period", which respected the Chatham House rule of non-attribution and was distributed to participants during the larger

---

[1] The Conference was initially conceived as a partnership between CEBRI, KAS, Sciences Po's Mercosur Chair and the Center for American Studies of the Candido Mendes University. Since 2010, however, it is organized by CEBRI, KAS and the Delegation of the European Union to Brazil.

Conference in September. As indicated by its title, the paper's main goal was to address security issues in the context of national elections—discussing the experience of the 2014 Brazilian presidential elections, when the country received over 200,000 attacks per second, aiming at crashing servers. During this period, concerns started to take shape about the roles that *fake news* and *bots* would eventually play—and indeed played—during Brazilian presidential elections in 2018. It is worth highlighting that, since 2016, the world at large has increasingly engaged with discussions, research, studies and even open accusations concerning this subject, featuring some level of "paranoia". In the specific case of Brazil, cyber threats in the year of 2016 was particularly noteworthy due to the organization of the Olympic Games in Rio de Janeiro. This occasion represented the culmination of a series of mega-events taking place in Brazil, ranging from the 2007 Pan American Games to the 2011 Military World Games and the 2014 FIFA World Cup.

Returning to the subject of the 2016 Olympic Games, according to participants of the first preparatory meeting in 2018, around 40 million cyber-crime alerts occurred during that period (Segurança Cibernética···, 2018). The Rio de Janeiro Olympic Games were, in fact, preceded by intensive coordinated governmental efforts to ensure the protection of sensitive information systems and prevent cyber-attacks during the event in particular, through the creation of an integrated Operations Center (*Centro de Operações do Rio*-COR) 6 years prior to the event itself. Relying on big data analysis COR employed last generation software to monitor every aspect of the Rio de Janeiro Olympic Games from urban transport flows to security breaches and cyber-attacks.

It was in this context, on the eve of the Olympic Games, that the Brazilian Anti-Terrorism Law was approved—which, notably, criminalized preparatory actions to possible terrorist attacks. The first case of enforcement of the Anti-Terrorism Law-Operation Hashtag took place precisely in the weeks leading to the Olympic Games: On this occasion, a group of individuals was arrested due to alleged involvement with the Islamic State in plotting a terrorist attack during the Games, after having their online communications monitored (France, 2018). These arrests, which had their legitimacy questioned for the lack of concrete evidence, ultimately illustrate the role played by social media and online communications not only in organizing and promoting terrorist actions, but also in preventing such security incidents.

Finally, the main theme of 2019 Conference will center on "The Fourth Industrial Revolution: Impacts on International Security and the Reshaping of

Global Order". The first preparatory meeting in Brasilia addressed precisely cybersecurity and artificial intelligence issues, gathering speakers from high-level military academies. The focus of the debate to be broadened during the main Conference in September is the security implications of the Fourth Industrial Revolution, the strategies adopted to manage its correlated cyber security challenges, the impact of the global race for technological leadership on reshaping the global order, and the risks and opportunities posed by autonomous weapons in conflict situations. Experts have highlighted the urgent need of cooperation between academia, the public and private sectors to deepen the debate on technological issues and their impact on security and defense. Key questions include: How to react to the intensification of the competition regarding the technological realm? How to manage issues such as hybrid warfare, cyber war and asymmetric conflict? What defense capacities are more adequate to address these issues?

III. Concluding Remarks

The field of security and defense studies is strengthened in recent years in Brazil with cooperation of the Forte de Copacabana International Security Conference.

The specific subject of the impact of technological issues in international security has gained momentum in Brazil, especially since 2016, due to the mega-event recently hosted by the country: the Rio de Janeiro Olympic Games. The presidential election of 2014 was already an important precursor to such issues, which took center stage in 2018.

From the discussions within the Forte de Copacabana Conference, we observe that legislation is still incipient in Brazil and the most effective means to manage these concerns are primarily studied by military institutions. Academic research is still in initial stages, as well as broader debates in civil society even though the topic is increasingly urgent. It is relevant not only in the geopolitical realm, in which great powers compete for technological supremacy, but also security concerns in Brazil where this is a pressing issue. To what extent, for example, is it worth using drones in cases of urban violence? How to use technology in favor of intelligence for preventing and efficiently investigating national and transnational organized crime networks?

Overall, it is a promising research field, posing more questions than answers at this stage.

References

Colberg, H. **As capacidades europeias contra ameaças cibernéticas** : fortalecendo a segurança de TI na Alemanha. Coleção de PolicyPapers-XIV Conferência do Forte de Copacabana. Rio de Janeiro: Fundação Konrad Adenauer, 2017.

Cooper, Betsy. **The Cybersecurity of Olympic Sports** : New opportunities, new risks. Center for LongTermCybersecurity (CLTC). UC Berkeley. White Paper Series, 2017.

France, Guilherme de Jesus. **As Origens da Lei Antiterrorismo no Brasil.** Belo Horizonte: Letramento, 2018.

Loretta Napoleoni. **A Fênix Islamista** . Rio de Janeiro: Bertrand Brasil, 2015.

Lourdes Puente, M. ; García, S. **As capacidades Sul-Americanas contra ameaças cibernéticas** : das fragilidades atuais a uma resposta comum. Coleção de PolicyPapers-XIV Conferência do Forte de Copacabana. Rio de Janeiro: Fundação Konrad Adenauer, 2017.

Segurança Cibernética e Interesse Nacional durante o Período de Campanha [Coleção de PolicyPapers 1/6]. Rio de Janeiro: Fundação Konrad Adenauer, 2018.

Session IV
Evolution of Security Concepts and Global Security Governance

The Path to Pursue Global Security

Sergey A. Ordzhonikidze

Vice President of the Civic Chamber of the Russian Federation,
Former UN Under-Secretary General

The current stage of international relations development is to a big extent determined by the intensified struggle for opportunity to determine the "rules of the game" within the framework of the emerging multipolar world pattern. Today, one can observe how certain countries are trying to secure an exclusive right for decision making on behalf of the whole world. To achieve this goal, the daunting arsenal of methods of pressure on competitors is used. Generally accepted international legal norms and principles are ignored or selectively applied, and multilateral institutions are deliberately weakened. All these factors bring serious strategic uncertainty in international affairs, which in turn leads to an increase in mutual distrust and narrows the space for constructive interstate cooperation. Against this background, the global security and strategic stability nowadays face numerous challenges.

I. The international disarmament system is seriously impacted

First of all, the aggressive foreign policy of certain states endangers the non-proliferation regime, as only with nuclear weapons some weaker countries feel protected against foreign military interference. Furthermore, we observe with regret the undermining of the existing system of nuclear arms control treaties. Within recent years the issues of nuclear weapons proliferation and collapse of the nuclear arms control system have gained dangerous momentum. Especially it concerns the binding-loss of the treaties between the major nuclear powers, such as the United States and the Russian Federation.

The intensity of discussions on arms control and non-proliferation was sharply reduced by Washington in 2014, along with the U. S. closure of contacts between the two militaries. In his contacts with President V. Putin, President D. Trump has repeatedly spoken in favor of engagement to curb the arms race.

However, instead of establishing a dialogue, the American Administration provoked the final demise of the INF Treaty. The Americans blamed Russia for its alleged violation of the Treaty but never provided any evidence whatsoever to substantiate their accusations, and also refused to discuss our legitimate reciprocal concerns. On February 2, 2019 the U. S. State Department formally notified that the United States suspended their participation in the INF Treaty, and would withdraw from it after six months.

The White House has also not decided on the possibility of extending after 2021 the Treaty on Measures for the Further Reduction and Limitation of Strategic Offensive Arms (the New START). The Russian side has fully complied with the Treaty obligations. At the same time, the figures presented by the United States were achieved only thanks to real arms reductions. On the contrary, the re-equipment of fifty six Trident-II SLBM (submarine-launched ballistic missile) launchers and forty one B-52H heavy bomber aircrafts was designed in such a way that we cannot confirm their conversion to a state unsuitable for use of nuclear weapons.

The openly anti-Russian and anti-Chinese nuclear doctrine of the U. S. (the Nuclear Posture Review, 2018), in which the nuclear conflict is considered a real political option certainly gives rise to very serious concerns. We also find the America's persistent calls on China to join the nuclear arms control negotiations between Russia and the USA utterly unjust and farfetched as such negotiations must engage all the nuclear powers, including the military allies of the United States, i. e. the UK and France.

II. Space militarization activities worth high vigilance

Another issue of very high concern is the destructive plans of the USA to deploy space-based anti-missile weapons in order to ensure the "American dominance" in space. We believe that such steps would be extremely dangerous for global security as it will no longer be possible to stop an arms race in space after the deployment of weapons into Earth orbit by one country like opening a Pandora's box . Therefore, it is absolutely necessary to intensify international efforts in the sphere of arms control in space. A treaty on Prevention of an Arms Race in Outer Space (PAROS) proposed by Russia and China within the UN framework would establish reliable guarantees against the deployment of weapons into Earth orbit.

III. Cyber space international cooperation faces obstacles

The traditional conflicts between the major political and military powers nowadays are intensified against the backdrop of new socio-cultural and political realities as well as unprecedented technological advancement.

The cyber security problems remain a major challenge for the modern world as its dependence on new technologies is growing. Nowadays, the cyber-attacks can target critical infrastructure and defense of any state. Fully aware of the potential threats in the ICT field the Russian Federation has repeatedly brought up the issue of cyber security on the international stage both in bilateral dealings with the governments of other countries and in the framework of the United Nations. Russia has also made serious efforts to elaborate the rules of conduct in the international cyber space in collaboration with the Shanghai Cooperation Organization (SCO) members. Among the SCO achievements is the Agreement among the Governments of the SCO Member States on Cooperation in the Field of Ensuring International Information Security concluded in 2009. In 2015 the SCO submitted to the UN General Assembly (UNGA) the draft on International Code of Conduct on Information Security.

Meanwhile, we can observe how certain states unwilling to bind themselves by any international obligations in the sphere of ICT security hypocritically accuse other countries of aggressive actions in cyberspace. The United States and their allies do not support the Russian initiatives as they probably believe that they can achieve domination in cyberspace. In the last years of the Obama Administration the White House in particular ignored the Russian proposal to conclude the document that could guarantee non-interference in internal affairs of each other by using cyber technologies.

We strongly believe that the risks connected to the ICT security field are often greatly underestimated and urgent international efforts are needed in confronting them. In the fall of 2018 Russia submitted a draft document on cyber security to the UNGA. This document provides for the consideration of three major topics: the standards of responsible behavior for states, the applicability of international law to information space, and assistance to developing countries in ensuring cyber security. These rules are supported by most of the UN member states except for the United States and some of its allies. In December 2018 the UNGA approved the Russian initiative on creation of an Open-Ended Working Group (OEWG) on International Cyber Security which started its work in June 2019, which helps to ensure the negotiations at UN on this area more democratic, inclusive and transparent. Such constructive and peaceful approach to cyber security was introduced by Russia as early as in 1998 but it was repeatedly categorically rejected by Washington.

IV. The Political will to counter terrorism needs to turn into real actions

Following the rise of fundamentalist ideologies, terrorism has become one of the most urgent threats to global security in the 21st century. The support to terrorist organizations by certain states that pursue their political interests through their proxies in other countries is absolutely unacceptable and irresponsible. The international community must unequivocally condemn terrorism and make every effort to jointly respond to its threat. It is indeed a good sign that despite the complicated bilateral relations the Russian Federation and the USA continue their joint counterterrorism efforts. Thus, it was possible to reconstruct the working group on countering terrorism, which had existed in 2002-2014. The first meeting in an updated form was held on December 13, 2018 in Vienna. On March 26, 2019 also in Vienna, a meeting of experts took place. Such meetings demonstrate that when there is political will the cooperation between the two countries is possible.

As a whole, the current dangerous developments in the world are certainly connected to the lack of strategic stability and the challenges of multipolarity. Nevertheless, we must realize that the already existing architecture of global security embodied in the United Nations Organization remains the greatest achievement of the humanity in the 20th century and has yet no alternative to this day. It appears that it would be in the interests of the overwhelming majority of states to streamline international relations on the basis of a return to recognition of the basic principles and norms of international law as uniform "rules of the game" and the inviolability of the UN role as a universal regulator of world politics. It is necessary to respect the cultural, historical and civilizational values and interests of all countries, to rejection of "zero-sum game" logic, double standards and bloc thinking, especially in the matters of maintaining international security, which is in great demand.

Just like in the UN in this room there are no "chosen nations" and we must seek the solutions to global security issues together.

Establishing a Rule-based International Order Is a Difficult and Long Process

Yu Hongjun

Vice President of the CPAPD,

Former Vice Minister of IDCPC

In recent years, the complex and changeable world situation has become particularly prominent, and the trend of international relations, especially the major country relations is uncertain, which is of great concern. The establishment of a new international order based on new rules is becoming the focus and gravity of study of international relations.

The history of human society, in the final analysis, is from irregularity and disorder to rules and order, and to the establishment of new rules and new order, and is a lasting cyclical process. In the 14-13 century BC, the Egyptian empire in North Africa and the Hittite Kingdom that ruled the Syrian region, after fighting for hundred years for hegemony, finally signed a treaty of friendship aimed at creating endurable peace and harmonious coexistence with each other, creating an ancient example of the great powers practicing self-restraints and seeking common security. However, it was impossible for human society to establish universally accepted norms of interrelationship and universally binding norms of conduct. After the advent of the Egyptian-Hittite Peace Treaty, human society still lived under the law of jungle. The path of human development and progress was repeatedly disrupted by the struggle for hegemony among great powers and the inevitable rivalry for hegemony by strong powers.

After entering the stage of capitalist development, the Europeans who experienced thirty years of religious war felt the necessity of delimiting boundaries, establishing rules and maintaining order among different nation states, so the famous Westphalia Peace Treaty came into being in 1648. From then on, an international order took shape basically with the mutual equality of state sovereignty as the important premise, the non-interference in internal affairs as the basic principle, guaranteeing the inviolability of state territory and independence as the common criterion as well as the multilateral conferences as the dispute settlement mechanism.

More than two hundred years later, European and American countries began seriously considering the issues of common security and common development. Their focus was first on the issues of human life and dignity, which are generally concerned by human society, and secondly on the issues of technological progress and management that are of common concern to all countries. In the year 1863, the International Committee of the Red Cross was established. In 1864, 12 countries including Switzerland and France, signed the Geneva Convention on care for the sick and wounded in war. In 1865, the International Telegraph Union was founded. In 1874, more than 20 countries in Europe and the United States established the General Postal Union, which was upgraded to the Universal Postal Union in 1878. In 1889, the Inter-Parliamentary Union came into being in the world. In 1899 and 1907, European and American countries held two international peace conferences in the Hague, Holland. The conference adopted not only the Hague Convention with the main content of the Convention on the peaceful settlement of international disputes, but also set up the first Permanent Court of Arbitration in the world.

Back then, the understanding of international relations and international order by human society was relatively naïve, and in the process of implementing the peace treaty, the parties concerned did as they wished, and sometimes behaved unorthodoxly. The Westphalia Peace Treaty system was still not enough to cope effectively with the new challenges brought about by the changes in international power balance and restructuring relations among major powers. The accumulation of contradictions in the capitalist era, especially the formation of the two major groups of countries in Europe, finally triggered the First World War in 1914.

The First World War brought great destruction and terrible consequences. Thus, under the leadership of the victors such as the United States, Britain and France, the famous Paris Peace Conference was held in 1919, and then the Washington Conference was held. There were the Treaty of Trianon and Versailles system, and there were new multilateral cooperation organizations such as the International Committee on Global Navigation. There were even the Non-War Convention, the League of Nations, the Permanent International Court of Justice, and Interpol, then known as the Interpol Commission. Then, the international community rejoiced over the establishment and operation of these intergovernmental organizations. The major powers like the United States and Europe were proud of their dominated international relations and world order.

However, the United States, then as a strong world power, refused to participate in the League of Nations initiated by itself because its intention to dominate the world was not fully reflected. The Soviet Union was excluded from the League of Nations for many years because its social system and ideology were different from those of the West. The United States, Britain and France kept major reservations to the Non-War Convention in order to maintain the right to overseas military operations. In 1932, the World Conference on Disarmament died short of life due to the withdrawal of Japan and Germany. It was precisely because the United States was absent from the League of Nations and the Soviet Union was excluded from the League of Nations, so the Non-War Convention became a piece of waste paper. The world disarmament conference became a fond dream, and the Versailles system and the League of Nations were rather weak. Facts also fully proved that the Versailles system and the League of Nations did not contain the rise of fascist Germany, Italy and Japan, and failed to restrain the appeasement policy of Britain and France. The Second World War broke out across the board in 1939. The fierce fighting and the painful casualties far exceeded people's imagination and endurance. The international community began to reconsider the issue of formulating new norms of international relations and building broader intergovernmental cooperation organizations. In the autumn of 1944, the Dumbarton Oaks Conference outlined the general blueprint for the United Nations. In February 1945, the Yalta Conference of the leaders of the United States, the Soviet Union and the United Kingdom made a final decision on the post-war world pattern, the distribution of the interests of major powers, the arrangement of international order, especially the establishment of the United Nations, etc.

In October 1945, a United Nations organization, totally different from the old League of Nations, came into being. The Charter of the United Nations, a historic document symbolizing the new international order, was solemnly signed. Since then, a large number of agencies and related organizations of the United Nations system have emerged. Many of them, such as the International Court of Justice, GATT, WHO, the International Monetary Fund, the World Bank, UNESCO and IAEA, etc. have played an undeniable role in establishing and maintaining the post-WWII international political and economic order, promoting the process of peaceful development, addressing major issues and crises, and responding to global challenges.

To adapt to these developments, the international law instruments already in existence before World War II, such as the Geneva Convention and the Hague Convention, become an important part of the new international law system after being amended and supplemented. A series of new international law instruments under the guidance of the Charter of the United Nations, such as the Universal Declaration of Human Rights, Vienna Convention on Diplomatic Relations and the Treaty on the Non-Proliferation of Nuclear Weapons, were born one after another. These new documents, which reflected the characteristics of the times and conformed to the direction of human progress, have been widely recognized, and their coverage is much more extensive than that of the Versailles system and the League of Nations. This is a precious result of the mutual efforts of the international community.

However, in the early post-WWII period, the world was divided into two camps, the East camp and the West camp. Because of its unique comprehensive national strength, the United States had a very prominent position in the United Nations system and other multilateral organizations. The Western values and international political thinking represented by the United States still played a dominant role in international affairs. In the late 1940s, the European Recovery Plan, i. e. the Marshall Plan implemented by the United States, accelerated the division of Europe. The North Atlantic Treaty Organization, the Paris Coordinating Committee and the short-lived Southeast Asian Treaty Organization and the Baghdad Treaty Organization, etc. had blown the Cold War to the entire world. The United States is probably to be blame for all these.

After the Second World War, the Soviet Union, which became the second superpower, acted independently and defiantly as a equal with the United States and created the Warsaw Treaty Organization and the Economic Mutual Aid Committee. The two sides competed strategically not only in the United Nations system, but also across the world. In the late 1980s and early 1990s, the dramatic changes in Eastern Europe, the disintegration of the Soviet Union and the collapse of the Warsaw Treaty Organization led to the breakdown of the Yalta system, which guided the development and changes of international relations in several decades after WWII. Under such circumstances, international relations need to be readjusted, the international legal system needs to be renewed urgently, the international community calls for a new political and economic order, and the world security structure should have new arrangements. The global governance need to be innovated and developed from concept to practice.

Unfortunately, during the great transition period of international strategic pattern from bipolarity to multi-polarity, deepening development of economic globalization, increasing diversity of social system and path options, the phenomenon of "one super power" emerged unexpectedly. Over the past three decades, the Cold War mentality of an individual major power is serious, so power politics and hegemonism have developed further. As a tool of the Cold War, NATO not only refuses to step down from the stage of history with the end of the Cold War but has expanded eastward, and also participated in the U. S. -led Kosovo war. Russia's relations with the United States and Europe have entered another complicated process different from that of the past, and the European security pattern and situation still remain deadlocked. As a result, the turmoil in the Middle East is spilling over, terrorism has become a public enemy of mankind, and the imbalance of development becomes even more prominent. The extreme trends of thought such as isolationism, unilateralism, populism, racism, extreme nationalism and others rise and fall from time to time, like turbid waves surging high.

Currently, human society is at a very important historical juncture. How to adjust the existing norms of international relations, how to improve the international law system mainly based on the Charter of the United Nations, how to build a stable and developing major power relations, and how to build a new world order meet with different opinions, and various regional and global conferences and forums are springing up like grass after rain. The increasingly multiplied and active multilateral mechanisms cover all fields of human activities, and the incomplete Yalta system is repaired to a certain extent.

Since the end of the Cold War, China has always advocated transcending ideological differences and different social systems, and jointly promoting the healthy development of the world's multipolarization and economic globalization, and promoting the establishment of a fair and rational new international political and economic order. President Xi Jinping put forth the new concept of building a community with shared future for mankind and the new idea of establishing a stable, balanced and developing major country relations framework, forming a new concept of the times, a new concept of civilization, a new concept of development, a new concept of cooperation and a new concept of security, which show both Chinese political wisdom and the spirit of the times as well as extensively recognized by the international community. Through vigorously promoting the construction of the Belt and Road, China is leading the world to linked development, to share weal and woe, as well as future and destiny.

It is precisely because of the active participation of China and the developing countries that the reputation and role of the United Nations are markedly strengthened after the Cold War, and the status and influence of the United Nations agencies become more apparent. There is also a new development since the GATT was reorganized into the WTO. The APEC Leaders' Informal Meeting plays an important role in promoting regional cooperation, and the Group-20 becomes the "Economic UN" that the international community has high hopes for. As far as this is concerned, the traditional major powers and the emerging major powers joining hands with the whole international community have made some achievements and contributions in collectively building new international rules and new world order.

Over the past two years, the complex and changeable international situation has become more prominent. The U. S. international strategy and foreign relations are drastically readjusted, and the international community is facing unexpected shocks and challenges in building a new order based on new rules. In view of the special responsibility of major powers for the peaceful development of mankind, mutual respect, inclusiveness, mutually beneficial development, common pursuit for security, carrying forward the cause into the future and weeding through the old to bring forth the new should be the common choice for major powers to build a new system of international relations, i. e. a new order based on new rules. History and practice will eventually prove that this is the only option that countries around the world, especially major countries, can take on the occasion of changing world landscape. In this regard, we should have overall in-depth thinking strategically as well as prepare for a difficult and tortuous long-term game-play.

Jointly Building a New International Order with Better Fairness and Justice

Emmanuel Dupuy,

President of the Institute of European Perspective and Security Studies (IPSE), France

The United States and Russia consecutively announced their withdrawal from the INF treaty, and have strengthened strategic game-play over the Syrian issue and Iranian issue. The Europe-USA differences on military spending and energy supply are difficult to solve, and the Europe-USA relations face more uncertainties. The existing international security order finds it hard to adapt to the new situation, and urgently needs to be reshaped. In recent years, China has shown its growing involvement in operations of UN peacekeeping missions as well as the growing role that Beijing could play in settling the Syrian issue, contributing to climate adaptation and stabilizing regional situations, and has made special contribution to the peaceful and diplomatic settlement of the nuclear crisis with North Korea. France and China should Jointly build a new international order with better fairness and justice.

China and Europe share similarities on upholding multilateralism. Multilateralism is an important feature for the new type of security concept, and adheres to cooperation, common security, and open and inclusive security concept. The reform of the UN Security Council, strengthening the international multilateral institution building represented by the United Nations, the global and regional security order building should follow the multilateral principle, and ensure equal participation in security affairs. Meanwhile, multilateralism should also be concerned with those non-state actors, and helps to reshape international organizations so as to strengthen multilateral international mechanisms.

In the aspects of promoting economic development and maintaining world peace, China has made great contributions. Since 2009, Chinese direct investment in the United States has increased five-fold; its trade with the African continent is now close to $ 220 billion, while the trade balance between France and Africa has increased to 100 billion euros from only "modestly" 54 billion euros, by adding its 26 partners of the EU. Thus, constantly rising of defense budget and active participation in the UN affairs, now make China a top-notch security actor. Under the Belt and Road framework, the Sino-French cooperation has a broad prospect. This new Silk Road launched by the Chinese President, in a speech delivered to students of the Nazarbayev University, Astana, Kazakhstan in September 2013 is of great significance for global economic development in several decades to come. The Belt and Road connects China to Europe and Africa, through Central Asia, the Caucasus, the Balkans and the Middle East. The Road and Belt brings together 60% of the world's population and helps countries along the routes to "compensate" the deficit in infrastructure (roads, bridges, ports, railways, pipelines, airports, etc.). This new Silk Road is a road of win-win cooperation, and demonstrates China's pragmatic attitude. China will, thus, set its major power place in the world.

Certainly, it is difficult for China to exceed the United States currently both in terms of the military budget and the share of Chinese products in world trade, but already, through the $ 100 billion committed since the end of 2014, China has achieved great progress in the Asian infrastructure development. The Asian Infrastructure Investment Bank (AIIB) has admitted various strong powers in the world, and is likely to have the strength to compete sustainably with the United States and the European Union. While in Central Asia and East Asia, a new world order is being decided, in which the concepts of "cooperative" diplomacy, more "people-to-people" development policies are discussed.

However, there are many complementarities between Paris and Beijing. Backed by firm commitments, China has significantly reduced its emissions of greenhouse gas. France and China should also build a community of ecological destiny, and jointly respond to global climate change. France and China should also carry out tripartite cooperation in Africa. Through multi-area cooperation, France-China relations will generate new vitality.

Global Security: Evolution of Security Concepts and Future Global Governance

Arvinder Singh Lamba
President of Institute of Peace and Conflict Studies,
Retired Lieutenant General

I. Evolving Security Concepts after World War II

Global security has witnessed a multitude of tabulations and challenges since World War II. In the post WW II, the world split into two alliances, Warsaw and NATO pact countries with United States and Russia in their leading roles with regional countries, with Japan constrained by a strategic agreement prohibiting its return to military capability.

The end of the WW, also witnessed the Nuclear dimension of war having had made a paradigm transformation from conventional war to a war of assured and complete annihilation of the adversary. But the arms race set off competition in numbers of these nuclear weapons, took the trajectory and scale out of control between the two competing powers, to a state of Mutual Assured Destruction (MAD). The proliferation of nuclear weapons and delivery systems escalated recklessly between the two blocks, with the numbers attaining alarming proportions.

The world compelled the powers to de-escalate the numbers and the threat of such wars. Structures as SALT and START talks attempted to control nuclear arms from becoming weapons of WMD, and their numbers gradually declined into deterrence. The numbers scaled down from the highs to the limitation figures as decided within the treaties. The ABM, and INF set into place some order and control limiting the numbers of weapon systems, ensuring destruction of a class of missiles or completely.

As the geopolitics of those times have changed significantly, treaties as ABM, New START, INF and other treaties are today facing challenges of being violated by signatories.

The only credible global institution and mechanism, the UN and the UNSC despite all the authority to guide the world towards peace and disarmament became unable to impose its guidance on global security and stability.

While USSR went down by dissolution, and WARSAW pact too, the NATO stood firm and expanded making the United States stronger than before. Unipolarity appeared firmly founded with a clarity and perception that the world witnessed for the first time ever. The United States not just emerged as the global driver but a hyper power that appeared to redefine the global map.

Conflict shifted and occurred in multiple regions of the world, primarily the third world. South Asia emerged as the most conflict-prone region with a border war between China and India in 1962, and two wars between India and Pakistan in quick succession in 1965 and 1971. The invasion of Kuwait, Operation Iraqi Freedom I and Operation Iraqi Freedom II set west Asia. Afghanistan emerged as the epicenter of U. S. -Russia Cold War that set a clincher dynamic for return to unipolar world led by the United States .

By the end of the 20th century, China surprised the world with enormously growing military and technological might, nuclear capability and its outreach to position itself as a strategic stake holder in every global issue. The impact of China's rise was significant, primarily economically, followed very closely, by its strategy of increasing assertiveness in its immediate neighborhood over disputed territories, the South China Sea and in other parts of the world. The unprecedented rise of China became the first challenge to unipolarity.

Beginning the 21st century, three major evolutions have marked history: unprecedented rise of China setting a new challenge to the existing world order, a growing direct military contestation if not a confrontation between Washington and Beijing and the rise of terrorism.

The shift from unipolarity to bipolarity and multipolarity is significant as highlighted by speakers in this conference: China on the rise, Russia in resurgence and the United States intending to contain China. As Prof Jaques from Cambridge University pointed out, the conflict is arising out of U. S. over-reach and China's over reaction, with policies adopted by both at conflict and intended to allege the other for the situation.

II. The evolving nature of war

The nature of war has changed with the concepts of Force Centric conventional wars involving physical engagement of forces and big militaries to wars of high technology, information warfare, artificial intelligence, that are beyond visibility, attributability, ownership, that change the way war can be controlled and monitored.

Nuclear weapons have taken central stage this time at regional and sub-regional levels. While here as well, the option may be diminished to that of a credible deterrence, the risk of nuclear war by both non-state or state actors is high in states with their military as a lead player in policy formulation, or those that support terror not just as an option alternate to war, but make terror a part of their integrated war machines. Given the political choices of "rational irrationality" the risk in such regions is extraordinarily high.

III. Terrorism

Terror is the new weapon, that has added an extraordinary dimension to conflict beyond the conventional, delivering power through threats of irrational destruction and killings across the world. The scale of terror has become the formal signature of not just groups or individuals, but states who use terror.

In the post-Cold War, involvement of non-state actors in global affairs represents fundamentally shifting relations of power, integration of national economies and empowering convergence of policies across various issues and domains. Rise in extremism and social unrest will continue due to economic inequality both within and between states through and finally for human development. There needs to be a global position on the scourge of terrorism, on the lines of nuclear disarmament, to prevent threats to security of affected nations as much as the global community.

IV. Global governance for future

The basic tenets of global governance are undergoing a paradigm shift. While the United States remains as the leading power in the current system of global governance, China with its allies or partners is seeking reordering in the current state of global governance. The United States and China will continue as rivals at different levels of political clout and outreach and military systems that are in intense engagement for primacy.

The authority of traditional global institutions as the United Nations, the UN Security Council, the International Court of Justice and other institutions such as the International Monetary Fund, and World Bank must be respected than be challenged for power and political gains. Political divisions and partisan interests within the Security Council, particularly the use of veto power by some of its permanent members, that have impacted international response to the situation in Syria , response to the threat of terrorism and the influx of refugees, must be prevented.

India and EU are likely to be great powers in the near future, and Russia may be the nation of major military consequence once it returns. The rise of India is not just foreseeable but perceived. India's emergence is viewed as the new dynamic and leading game changer.

Sovereignty, territorial integrity and human struggles for power and equity are shaping international relations and governance very diversely. The complete frame work of foreign policy which reflects the paradigm shift in international relations has to be effectively re-addressed by global leaders and the global community. Declining diplomacy, increasing militarisation, receding trust, and threats of nuclear war by smaller third world countries increases the potential for conflict and raises a major challenge to global governance. While bilaterals will be the core strength of relationship between two nations, cross cutting strategic issues as acquisition of weapon systems and integration with military systems of different architecture will continue to add to acrimony at a regional level.

V. **Diplomatic strategy and policy**

Traditionally, diplomatic strategy and policy rationally remained secret, or at least ambiguous to certain extent, however, today, these diplomatic strategy and policy are expounded clearly in the national security policy and strategy or white papers, so leading to irrational understanding and analysis.

Diplomacy today is succumbing to positions adopted by national leaders today on international situations and challenges and their personal aspirations of power in the international arena. Poor diplomacy or strategic leadership, that can be a graver threat than any other irrational behavior out of misjudged political and military situations, will have to be addressed. President Trump's recent diplomatic catastrophe in threatening war on Iran after withdrawal from the nuclear deal added enormous uncertainty to the stability and peace in West Asia.

Strategic partnerships are the new norm for bilateral engagement short of alliances, where these engagements between big powers and regional and small and middle group countries / groupings, are having very complex implications for global stability.

Indo-Pacific Concept no matter how disapproved by powers that be, has changed the dynamics of the region. Security threats and economic pressures are compelling regional groupings and organizations that can remain free from big power involvement. Big powers on the other hand, must discontinue to manipulate their way into these groupings and disrupted for economic reasons. Extra regional groupings are becoming more prominent if not dominant yet.

At the global level, U. S. -China contestations in Asia and China's increasing assertiveness in the South China Sea and the Indian Ocean region is redefining regional and global peace and stability.

India's recognition as a force for good by a huge number of nations is evident. India's diplomacy and diplomatic strengths are visible in India's growing partnerships with every major power and regional forums as the United States, China, Russia, and regional groupings as ASEAN, East Asia, SCO, Central Asia, which are adding to existing contradictions and contestations and events that deter cooperation and better relations.

VI. Conclusion

Power competition has been intensifying, leading to break down in cooperation and dialogue. We are experiencing an age of narratives of negatives that are precipitating conflict and conflict situations. The established role of diplomacy, foreign policy and national leaders alone can realign good global governance.

China has far greater convergence in will and strategy for global good. China is under major reform towards upholding international system, through cooperation and consideration, and is emerging as a contributor to development, space, trade, international cooperation and multi-lateral coordination. China's perception of being supported by the international community for staking a more responsible role, if validated, can contribute enormously to global stability and peace.

The United States, Russia and China supported by the rising powers will need to realign their extra regional outreach and stand on nuclear disarmament, limitation talks and treaty adherence, and terror in the emerging global scenario to enable good governance, regional and global stability.

As an alternative, with the big power contestations, it may be time for the rising and formidable powers in being as India, Japan and the European Union, given their significantly growing and positive global acceptance, to take the lead in creation of new institutions that can assure the world of better global governance.

The paradigm shift from strategic stability to crisis stability with high possibility for escalation to conflict or conflict situation, must be reversed.

Sustainable Security Concept and Global Security Governance

Liu Jiangyong

CPAPD Executive Council Member,
Professor with Institute of International Relations, Tsinghua University

The year 2019 is the 70th anniversary of the founding of new China, and is also the 5th anniversary of the concept of common, comprehensive, cooperative and sustainable security proposed by Chinese President Xi Jinping. Today, it is of great significance to discuss the concept of sustainable security and global security governance.

I. Achievements in the past five years since China-proposed concept of sustainable security

On May 21, 2014, Chinese President Xi Jinping first put forth at the 4th Summit of the Asian Conference on Interaction and Confidence Building Measures in Asia(CICA) held in Shanghai, "We should actively advocate an Asian concept of common, comprehensive, cooperative and sustainable security, innovate the concept of security, build a new framework for regional security cooperation, and work hard to pioneer a path of Asian security with joint contribution, shared benefits and win-win results." This new security concept was written into the Shanghai Declaration issued by the CICA Conference and became an important consensus of the participating countries.

In September 2015, President Xi Jinping reiterates in his speech at the UN General Assembly that the new concept of common, comprehensive, cooperative and sustainable security should be established. Since then, China's concept of sustainable security is not only limited to Asia, but has global significance. More and more countries are beginning to realize that the pursuit of sustainable security is to achieve the sustainability of higher quality security with lower cost of security through common security, cooperative security and comprehensive security. This is a scientific security concept leading global security governance.

In the past five years, the development and changes of the global, regional and national security situations have further proved that the concept of sustainable security is a beacon light guiding global security governance in today's era. This new security concept conforms to the basic laws of contemporary national security and international security, is consistent with the security interests of the peoples of various countries in the world and has important reference value for the correct security decision-making by various countries in the world.

In the past five years, the concept of sustainable security has been actively interacted by the countries around China, is becoming the guiding ideology of security decision-making of various countries, and is gradually implemented in the security policies-making and cooperation, which has rapidly and effectively changed the international security environment around China. From Northeast Asia, Southeast Asia, South Asia to Central Asia, China has reached consensus on sustainable security with almost all neighboring countries, and has initially been benefited by common security.

For the past five years, China has been an advocate and practitioner of the concept of sustainable security. The concept of sustainable security has become an important part of China's governing strategy. The report of the 19th National Congress of the Communist Party of China in 2017 points out, to promote the construction of community with a shared future for mankind, we must keep in mind both our internal and international imperatives, unswervingly stay on the path of peaceful development, continue to pursue a mutually beneficial strategy of opening up. We will uphold justice while pursuing shared interests, and will foster new thinking on common,comprehensive, cooperative and sustainable security. We will pursue open, innovative, inclusive development that benefits every one; boost cross-cultural exchanges characterized by harmony within diversity and inclusiveness, mutual learning and cultivate ecosystems based on respect for nature and green development. China will continue its efforts to safeguard world peace, contribute to global development and uphold international order.

Over the past five years, based on the concept of sustainable security, China has played an important role in changing the situation on the Korean Peninsula, which is in a state of long-term danger and tension, and achieved remarkable results. In 2017, when the Korean Peninsula was in a tense situation, China stressed that the resolution of the Korean Peninsula nuclear issue should take into account the security concerns of all parties concerned, i. e. , common security; while adhering to the general direction of denuclearization of the Korean Peninsula, China supported the DPRK's development of economy and improvement of people's livelihood, i. e. , comprehensive security; China advocated peaceful multilateralism, and encouraged the "dual track" of establishment of a peace mechanism and denuclearization on the Korean Peninsula, i. e. , cooperative security; China held that the two sides on the Korean Peninsula should achieve national reconciliation through dialogue and consultation, and oppose the use of force or threat of use of force, i. e. , focusing on sustainable security. As a result, with the joint efforts of all parties concerned, especially between the two sides on the Peninsula, since 2018, the situation on the Korean Peninsula has undergone unprecedented and gratifying changes in more than 70 years.

Over the past five years, following the concept of sustainable security, China-Russia comprehensive strategic partnership of coordination is significantly strengthened, the Shanghai Cooperation Organization has played an increasingly important role, and the CICA Summit has brought together more synergy for sustainable security. In July 2017, China and Russia announced in a joint statement that the two sides will continue to cooperate in CICA, East Asia Summit, ASEAN Regional Forum, ASEAN Defense Ministers' Meeting, ASEM and other regional organizations, so as to promote the building of an open, comprehensive and transparent security architecture in the Asia Pacific region, adhering to international law, common, comprehensive, cooperative, and sustainable security, and equality based on cooperation, with peaceful settlement of disputes, no use of force or threat of use of force as the principles. As an important legal measure for sustainable security, the leaders of the six countries concerned signed the SCO Convention Against Extremism on June 9, 2017. At the 5th CICA Summit held in Dushanbe, Tajikistan, on June 15, 2019, leaders of the participating countries expressed that they would continue to practice the concept of sustainable security. The declaration of the 5th CICA Summit reaffirmed to seek common, comprehensive, cooperative and sustainable security and promote development and progress. It has been proved in practice wherever the sustainable security concept is recognized and practiced, wherever the bond between security cooperation and mutual trust between countries is stronger.

In the past five years, the concept of sustainable security has become an important concept of ASEAN countries' security cooperation. The theme of the 13th ASEAN Defense Ministers' Meeting held in Bangkok on July 10, 2019 is "sustainable security". This meeting is of special significance for the international community to further popularize the concept of sustainable security and promote the practice of international cooperation on sustainable security. Because this is the first time for the international multilateral security cooperation conference to use the keyword of "sustainable security" as the theme of the conference; the ASEAN 10 defense ministers who participated in the conference signed the "ASEAN Defense Ministers' Joint Declaration on Sustainable Security" on October 11, which is also the first multilateral international joint declaration on sustainable security. The Joint Declaration on sustainable security emphasizes that in order to achieve the sustainable security of ASEAN countries, it is necessary to further strengthen cooperation within ASEAN, between ASEAN and dialogue partners, and jointly respond to non-traditional and cross-border security threats. ASEAN countries are aware that with the rapid change of regional security environment, the continuous enhancement of regional integration, connectivity and technological progress, the region is facing complex and changeable non-traditional security threats and cross-border security threats, and the frequency and severity are increasing. Countries need to strengthen cooperation within ASEAN and between ASEAN and its dialogue partners. ASEAN countries should strengthen cooperation in border management, military medical exchanges, maritime risk prevention, counter-terrorism information exchange and other fields. The meeting proved that the new concept of common, comprehensive, cooperative and sustainable security has become an important security theory for ASEAN countries to guide the practice of security cooperation. In the future, the implementation of ASEAN countries' sustainable security strategy will not only benefit the security governance of ASEAN region, but also radiate the sustainable security effect of ASEAN to a broader scope through cooperation with ASEAN dialogue partners, providing a new example, new experience and new path for global security governance.

II. Challenges faced by global security governance

(1) Threats to global security are increasingly diversified and specialized

Lasting peace is the common ideal of mankind. For most countries in the world, since the 21st century, the security issue in a state of peace has become more prominent. On this point, the Copenhagen School of Thought in Europe has a relatively early awareness. Unfortunately, after the Cold War, NATO members have launched many regional wars or military strikes in the Middle East in the form of violent multilateralism. As a result, Europe has been plagued in recent years by the refugee tides, terrorist attacks, populism and rising centrifugal tendencies. The European integration process, the European multilateral security mechanism and the status of the euro have all been weakened.

Compared with the issue of peace, the security issue has greater coverage, universality, diversity and professionalism. There are not only hot and sensitive issues, but also challenges brought by ethnic and religious conflicts, terrorism, transnational crimes, environmental security, cyber security, energy and resource security, major natural disasters, etc. Traditional security threats and non-traditional security threats are intertwined, and the connotation and extension of security issues are further expanded. Space security, Ocean security and polar security are major issues of global security governance. For the Pacific island countries, climate change directly threatens their living space, and the carbon emissions and vegetation reduction caused by the war may actually far exceed the industrial carbon emissions.

Because of this, President Xi Jinping, having put forth the concept of sustainable security, proposes for the first time on April 15, 2014 the adherence to the overall national security concept, related to many fields such as politics, military affairs, home land, economy, finance, society, culture, science and technology, cyber network, ecology, resources, nuclear energy safety and so on. The comprehensive security in the overall national security concept and the sustainable security concept is overlapping. The overall national security concept mainly refers to China's domestic national security strategy, while the sustainable security concept involves more issues in the areas of international security and global security governance, which are supportive of each other.

(2) Trade protectionism poses a threat to the external environment for the development of various countries in the world

There is nothing wrong with President Trump's ambition to make the United States "great again", but it will be widely questioned if it is achieved increasingly at the expense of the security and development interests of other countries.

The security strategic thinking of American policy makers is still basically the belief of realism of traditional power politics, with little understanding that human society in the 21st century, including the United States, needs common, comprehensive, cooperative and sustainable security. In order to ensure the power of controlling other countries, the United States often does everything. As a result, it is difficult for the United States to become a contributor to global security governance, but often becomes a "troublemaker", which will eventually harm the American people and the U. S. security interests. Since the end of the Second World War, there are many such examples, which occur more and more after the end of the Cold War.

Since the year 2018, the United States has brought the thinking logic of power politics from the military and diplomatic fields to the fields of economy, trade, science and technology, and people-to-people and cultural exchanges, which has directly impacted the Sino-U. S. relations. In the field of economy and trade, unilateralism is carried out, and trade war is launched by levying heavy tariffs; national forces are mobilized to suppress and block China's Huawei's 5G system on the basis of the so-called security risks. These practices have seriously endangered the free trade system and market rules. In this regard, most members of the 2019 Osaka G20 Summit expressed their worries and voiced to safeguard multilateralism and free trade.

(3) Geostrategic game-play and the rising military security risks

This is mainly reflected in three parts: firstly, the deepening of geopolitical strategic contradictions between NATO's eastward expansion and Russia, especially the possible intensification of arms race and security confrontation in Europe after the withdrawal of the United States and Russia from the INF treaty. Secondly, in the Middle East, after the U. S. withdrawal from the Iran nuclear deal, the warring situation in Syria and Yemen continues, and the confrontation between the United States and Israel with Iran is at the daggers drawn. Thirdly, the United States pursues the "Indo-Pacific strategy", regards China as its main strategic competitor, brings multinational naval forces into the South China Sea, and attempts to establish the maritime hegemony led by the United States.

The core goal of the U. S. geopolitical strategy in the Middle East is to take over Iran, control the Persian Gulf, and then control the maritime oil channels for China, Japan and Europe, and further control the energy hinterland of the former Soviet Union such as the Caspian Sea area in the north. These will inevitably bring some uncertainty and potential risks to China's cooperation with the countries along the Belt and Road, and meantime, will lead to the rising cost of security for the United States, and will decline quality of security and is destructive. On the contrary, China's new security concept and the Belt and Road Initiative are constructive. The geopolitical and geo-economic theory of sustainable security pursues the theory of land and sea integration of "extensive consultation, joint contribution and shared benefits", rather than the theory of land and sea hegemony.

III. The way out for global security governance in the 21st century

The concept of sustainable security is as important as the concept of sustainable development, which can be termed a scientific security concept with universal value. In the past five years, the concept of sustainable security has been recognized by more and more countries and has strong vitality. In December 1953, Zhou Enlai first proposed the Five Principles of Peaceful Coexistence when he met with the Indian delegation, which was endorsed by India, Myanmar and other countries, and later became the basic principles of China's diplomacy and handling relations between various countries. The new security concept of common, comprehensive, cooperative and sustainable security confirmed by the CICA Summit is of equal importance. After test in practice, the four-point sustainable security concept can also be the guidelines for global security governance.

First, adhering to the four-principled sustainable security, including China and the United States, establishing a common understanding of common, comprehensive, cooperative and sustainable security among various countries; forming a common document of sustainable security in the process of bilateral security dialogue; reducing the zero-sum game and confrontation brought by the old thinking of traditional power politics and geo-strategy; enhancing the awareness of common security, improving the comprehensive security capacity, and broadening security cooperation areas, reducing the cost of sustainable security, and building a community of shared future for international security.

Second, adhering to the four-principled sustainable security, concerning global hot and difficult security issues or the security field, integrating theory with practice, accumulating successful cases and striving to transform the concept of sustainable security into national sustainable security strategies, policies and specific measures to effectively solve practical security problems.

Third, adhering to the four-principled sustainable security, including sustainable security agendas in multilateral international security organizations, mechanisms and forums headed by the United Nations. It is necessary to introduce the concept of sustainable security into UN peacekeeping operations and disarmament cooperation. The UN Security Council may consider setting up a sustainable security committee to play a role similar to the UN Commission on Sustainable Development, which carry out systematic study and make proposals for effective governance programs for global sustainable security. It is proposed that 0. 1% or even 0. 01% of the national defense expenses of the UN member states be donated to the United Nations for the establishment of the UN Special Fund for sustainable security.

Acting Postscript

A Speech at the Closing Ceremony of the Second Wanshou Dialogue on Global Security (Acting Postscript)

Wang Yajun

Adviser to the Chinese People's Association for Peace and Disarmament,
Vice Minister of the International Department of the CPC Central Committee

The Second Wanshou Dialogue on Global Security is coming to an end. On behalf of the International Department of the CPC Central Committee and the Chinese People's Association for Peace and Disarmament (CPAPD), I would like to take this opportunity to express my heartfelt thanks to all the guests and representatives who have attended this seminar and all the friends who have made important contributions to the success of the seminar!

During the seminar, Ma Biao, Vice Chairman of the National Committee of the CPPCC and President of the CPAPD, delivered a keynote speech, calling on statesmen, security research experts and peace organization representatives from all over the world to bear in mind the original intention of peace, shoulder the mission of the times and make unremitting efforts to maintain world peace and security. Song Tao, Minister of the International Department of the CPC Central Committee, presided over the opening ceremony and pointed out that the world is facing major changes unseen in a century, and the unstable and uncertain factors of the international situation are more prominent. Only by upholding the concept of common, comprehensive, cooperative and sustainable security can various countries build a homeland of peace and security for mankind. Dignitaries and former dignitaries from Russia, the United States and other countries also delivered speeches on maintaining world peace and security.

Chinese and foreign guests and representatives focused on the theme of "Global Security in the Age of Major Changes", had heated discussions on the four topics of "New Changes within Security Relations among Major Countries", "New Adjustments in the Regional Security Order", "New and Emerging Technologies and Global Security" and "Evolution of Security Concepts and

Global Security Governance", and shared their insights on the international and regional security situation, and reached many consensus.

First, the current international security situation has undergone important changes and is continuously undergoing profound and complex changes, with instability, uncertainty and unpredictability becoming highlighted. To reform and improve the rule-based international order, inject more stability and positive energy into today's world, and strive to build a world of lasting peace and universal security has increasingly become the common voice of all sides.

Second, the balance of international strength has changed dramatically, with the sense of insecurity, doubt and anxiety about other countries rising in some countries, and fierce competition between unilateralism and multilateralism, between protectionism and openness & inclusiveness. In the face of multiple and complex security threats, it is still the mainstream voice of the international community to adhere to peaceful settlement of disputes, oppose force and threat of force, adhere to principle of multilateralism, oppose protectionism and power politics, and adhere to the core position of United Nations in maintenance of international peace and security.

Third, new changes have taken place in the security relations among major countries. In the mainstream of cooperation, competition and confrontation are getting to the surface faster than the past, which have an impact on the existing international order and rules, affect global strategic security and stability, influence the development trend of the world, and hold a stake in the future and destiny of mankind. The cooperation of major powers is crucial to international security. Major powers have greater responsibility for world peace and security and should play an important leading role in maintaining peace, security and stability.

Fourth, the world is facing multiple and complex security threats. Traditional security issues such as geopolitics and arms race are still prominent. Non-traditional security threats such as terrorism, cyber security, climate change, and migrants & refugees are increasingly prominent. The two are intertwined, overlapped and resonant, bringing severe challenges to the world. All countries should adhere to the principles of extensive consultation, joint contribution and shared benefits, take the new concept of common, comprehensive, cooperative and sustainable security as the guiding principle of strengthening global security governance, take building a community of shared future for mankind as the strategic goal of global security governance, strengthen multilateral security cooperation, seek peace through dialogue, promote security through cooperation, and jointly advance the process of global security governance.

Fifth, the "double-edged sword" effect of emerging technology is getting more obvious. The progress of science and technology brings not only human well-being, but also severe security challenges. The international community should take into account both the interests and concerns of all parties, pursue the advantages and avoid the disadvantages, and improve the management and control. It should formulate new regulatory rules, establish new dialogue mechanisms, and build a new platform for cooperation in emerging areas such as space, cyber network, big data, and artificial intelligence, etc. so as to respond well to this new common challenge.

Sixth, development is the foundation and prerequisite for peace. To achieve common development and prosperity is the universal pursuit of all peoples, but military conflicts, threats of force, terrorism, protectionism, etc. are still seriously hindering development of the world economy. Countries should follow the trend of development, resolve contradictions and differences, build an open world economy, and assure people all over the world live a happy and beautiful life.

Seventh, adhering to openness and inclusiveness and strengthening mutual learning among civilizations will help maintain world peace and security. The diversity of civilizations is an important manifestation of the richness and diversity of the world and an inexhaustible driving force for human development and prosperity, but should not be the source of conflict and confrontation. All parties should remove the ideological barriers and shackles, promote coexistence and mutual learning of civilizations, and create a favorable atmosphere for promoting international security and stability.

Of course, due to different historical and cultural backgrounds, varying academic fields and perspectives, there are also some differences in views and opinions, but this does not prevent us from speaking our minds, expressing our views, candidly exchanging ideas and seeking consensus. It is precisely in the spirit of mutual respect, mutual understanding and mutual inspiration that all parties participating in this seminar have made it a friendly, practical, efficient and professional international security conference.

On the whole, the schedule of this seminar is compact and orderly, participants showed active participation, and the discussion and interaction are fully in-depth, which has been unanimously affirmed and highly praised by the attendants. The People's Daily, Xinhua News Agency and other mainstream and important new media of China have made all-round and diversified reports on the seminar, showing the determination of all parties to maintain peace and stability to the world, conveying the aspirations for security and tranquility, and expanding the international influence of the seminar.

In the future, the CPAPD will strive to build the Wanshou Dialogue on Global Security into an internationally renowned, pragmatic, efficient and high-end professional dialogue on security research. We also hope to continuously receive active participation and strong support from all sides. We welcome Chinese and foreign experts to come to the Third Wanshou Dialogue on Global Security in 2020 and contribute wisdom and strength to building a more peaceful and secure world!

Epilogue

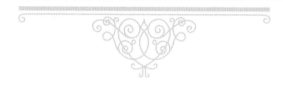

Epilogue

Today's world is in a great change unseen in a century. World multipolarization, economic globalization, informationized society and cultural diversity have developed in-depth. Countries are increasingly connected with each other, and the mega-trend of peaceful development is irreversible. Meantime, the current international security situation is undergoing complex changes, with intensified competition and game-play among major powers, in-depth adjustment of regional security order, interwoven traditional and non-traditional security issues, fierce collision of security concepts, increasingly prominent impact of emerging technology on global security, growing sources of global instability and risky spots, more obvious uncertainty, unpredictability and instability. The international security environment is becoming more and more severe, and strengthening global security governance has become a common concern of the international community.

The 2nd Wanshou Dialogue on Global Security organized by the Chinese People's Association for Peace and Disarmament (CPAPD) was held in Beijing from July 1 to 3, 2019. With the theme of "Global Security in the Age of Major Changes" , the Dialogue had four panels, which are " New Changes within Security Relations among Major Countries", "New Adjustments in the Regional Security Order", " New and Emerging Technologies and Global Security" and "Evolution of Security Concepts and Global Security Governance". Mr. Ma Biao, Vice Chairman of the National Committee of the Chinese People's Political Consultative Conference and President of the CPAPD delivered a keynote speech at the opening ceremony which was moderated by Mr. Song Tao, Minister of the International Department of the CPC Central Committee (IDCPC). Mr. Sergey Ordzhonikidze, Vice President of the Civic Chamber of the Russian Federation, Mr. Somphanh Phengkhammy, Vice President of the National Assembly of Laos, Mr. Douglas Bandow, former Special Assistant to U. S. President Ronald Reagan, and Vladimir Norov, Shanghai Cooperation Organization Secretary

General *as well as* experts on international security and peace organization representatives from over 20 countries including Russia, the United States, the United Kingdom, France, Austria, Sweden, Japan, the ROK, India, Pakistan, Vietnam, Thailand, the Philippines, South Africa, Brazil, Argentina, together with some 50 experts on global security from Chinese Academy of Social Sciences, China Academy of Engineering Physics, China Institute of International Studies, Peking University, Tsinghua University, National Defense University, National University of Defense Technology, China Foreign Affairs University, Beijing Beihang University, University of International Relations and Jinan University, etc. attended the Dialogue.

The Chinese and foreign representatives at the meeting spoke their minds and expressed their opinions candidly on the theme. Both the Chinese and foreign participants generally believed that despite the unstable and uncertain factors in the current international and regional security situation, pursing peace, promoting security and seeking development are still the strategic orientation and interests-pursuing by most countries. Major countries should actively shoulder international responsibilities, strengthen coordination, manage and control diffcrences, build more inclusive and constructive partnerships, and create an international security environment of peace, stability, health, harmony, and win-win cooperation. Regional countries should enhance strategic mutual trust, and strive to build a regional security framework that meets regional realities and needs of all parties. All parties should closely follow the forefront of scientific and technological development, and seek advantages and avoid disadvantages so as to maintain common security and better respond to the security risks brought about by the new round of scientific and technological revolution, and all countries should take a clear-cut stance against the Cold War mentality and zero-sum game, and practice the new concept of common, comprehensive, cooperative and sustainable security.

The 2nd Wanshou Dialogue on Global Security highly conforms to the concerns of global security by the international community, fully reflects the mainstream views of all regions and major countries on the current international security situation, and achieves the purpose of enhancing understanding, seeking common ground while reserving differences and building up consensus. In order to further reflect the results of the Second Wanshou Dialogue on Global Security and expand its social impact, we compiled some experts' speeches and submitted papers into a collection after editing for publication.

CPAPD Secretary General An Yuejun and Deputy-Secretary General Tao

Tao planned and reviewed the draft collection. Chen Xiaohan and Hou Hongyu were responsible for compiling and reading through the contributions. Yang Lei, Song Yiming, Shen Fang, Sun Bowen, Wang Qing, Niu Na and other comrades did some translation and editing work.

This collection of speeches and papers are only for reference to readers, the views of which are those of authors.

Editorial Group
September 2019